White and Earth

A gripping historical novel about the emergence of Islam and the fascinating life of the last Prophet.

Aaron van Altenberg

For questions and suggestions:

WeisserUndErdvater@hotmail.com

Texts: Aaron van Altenberg

Cover design & illustrations: Aaron van Altenberg

Edition: 1st edition 2024

ISBN: 978-3-00-076183-6

Table of Contents

Acknowledgments

My greatest thanks go to my dear wife for her support, patience and prayers at work, as well as to our children.

Preface

More than 1440 years ago, the Arabian Peninsula witnessed the emergence of Islam, a story that is considered one of the most important chapters in human history. This story began in a harsh desert landscape, at a time characterized by human challenges and bitter conflicts between the Roman and Sassanid empires. At the center of this story is the Prophet Muhammad bin Abdullah, the main founder of the Islamic religion. From the Arabian Peninsula, Islam spread to all parts of the world.

It is reported that towards the end of his life, Muhammad recommended: "I am leaving you two things to hold on to, so that you do not go astray after me - one of them is greater than the other: the Book of Allah, a rope that extends from heaven to earth, and my descendants, the people of my house, and they will not separate until they meet me at the pond, so see how you follow me in them." [1] In this testament, Muhammad points out that he will leave two things for people to hold on to so that they do not go astray after him: the Book of Allah, the Quran, and his descendants, his family. He emphasized that these two things will remain inseparable until the Day of Resurrection.

If we want to know the correct biography of Muhammad without additions or omissions, we should take the path he has shown us, namely the path of the Quran and his family. For Muhammad's family knows him better than anyone else, as the saying goes: "The people of Mecca know their alleys best." The Quran is the book that Muhammad brought by revelation from Allah. The Quran says in one of its verses: ﴿ O mankind, there has come to you a conclusive proof from your Lord, and We have sent down to you a clear light. ﴾ [2] This verse has been interpreted as an announcement to the people that Allah has sent them a proof, namely Muhammad, who is endowed with clear proofs and signs, and the light was interpreted as the Quran. Some traditions mention that the light is Muhammad's cousin Ali bin Abi Talib. [3]

Dr. Van Putten's 2022 linguistic study of Quranic manuscripts has confirmed the preservation of the Qu'ran, free from alterations and falsifications. It has been faithfully transmitted letter by letter across generations since the year 650 AD This exciting discovery confirms what Allah has promised in the Quran itself: "Indeed, it is We Who have revealed the Reminder - the Quran - and We will indeed be its guardian, "5 It also validates what Muslims have repeatedly emphasized over the years. This not only demonstrates that the Quran has indeed been preserved, but it also signifies that the Quran will be safe-guarded indefinitely. The era of falsification and alteration in archaeological texts has irreversibly concluded, thanks to printing presses, copyrights, and methods of preserving and handling historical texts. Therefore, the Quran is one of the most important and valuable primary sources for the study of the life of Arab society in the seventh century. However, it is not possible to rely solely on the Quran to write the history of this era in general and the biography of Muhammad in particular, because although the Quran - despite the antiquity and authenticity of its texts [6] - is not a history book or a biography book and its information about the details of Muhammad's life is scanty and insufficient to write his biography, it is therefore necessary to rely on the narrative matter as well. [7]

The narrative sources can be divided into two categories: Islamic sources and non-Islamic or external sources. As for the Islamic sources, the scholars thoroughly examined all the hadiths through the science of hadith and the sci-ence of men (ilm arrijāl)[1] in order to distinguish the correct hadiths and tradi-tions from the fabricated ones. After this sorting of the hadiths, the scholars submitted the hadith to the Quran to check whether the hadiths agreed with the meanings of the Quran or not, because the Quran is the word of Allah, as Muhammad said: and it is protected from falsification, as we have already men-tioned. What agreed with the Quran they accepted, and what did not agree with the Quran 1 They left aside. This gives us a group of correct traditions that we can rely on when researching and writing history.

The study of history is not just the reading of past events, but an attempt to understand and interpret the past. Researching it requires great care and accu-racy. The historian must also have a deep understanding of the historical sources and be able to distinguish fact from myth. To achieve this, the histori-cal researcher must read the historical sources with caution and awareness and search for multiple sources to verify the accuracy of the information they con-tain. He must also think critically about the information and rely on historical evidence and testimonies to confirm or reject the information contained in the

---

1   Hadith science: is a field of study that deals with the traditions of the Prophet
    Muhammad, especially with regard to the transmission, formulation and
    documentation of his sayings. "'ilm arrijāl" or "science of men" is a discipline
    developed by scholars to accurately evaluate the narrators of hadith. This
    evaluation leaves no room for leniency and aims to fully determine the identity
    of the narrator based on scientific principles and established rules.

sources. In addition, the historian must be open to different opinions and be able to evaluate them objectively. He must be honest with himself and with others and try to present an honest picture of history.[8]

Ultimately, the author needs a steadfast criterion for evaluating events and personalities, acting as a benchmark to comprehend and analyze the truth. While scientific research alone falls short in clarifying these matters, the author must continually turn to this standard to verify the accuracy of their work. Thus, the utilization of a reference like the Quran and the family of the house becomes essential in bridging the temporal and spatial gaps between the author and historical events. This reference serves as a trusted witness, allowing the author to confirm the precision of their writings.

In writing this biography, I have considered several aspects, the most important of which are:

Firstly, I have adhered to a simple writing style, without resorting to complex and difficult literary expressions and words, and used the modern Arabic language. In doing so, I have explained the meanings of old and unusual terms in the traditions. [13]

Secondly, I did not limit myself to retelling historical events, but also analyzed them and explained the meaning of some events in a concise manner.

Third: I have relied on correct narrations that are consistent with the Quran and come from the Prophet's family and other reliable sources. Some traditions in the biography books have been ignored due to their inaccuracy according to the research of Sayyid Ja'far al-'Amili[1]. This makes the writing more concise and avoids unnecessary length.

Fourth: I have used some photographic images and drawings to clarify the idea. These drawings are abstract shapes or imaginary three-dimensional drawings created with the help of artificial intelligence. They have no relation to real people or religious symbols, but are only symbolic images to clarify a certain idea in the text. Therefore, I ask the revered reader not to assume or imagine that these drawings or pictures are a real representation of their owners or historical figures.

---

1 See the book 'Al-Sahih Men Sirat Al-Nabi Al-Azam' by Mr. Ja'far Murtada al-Amili.

Fifth: I have standardized the address to the person of Muhammad in the biography to the Prophet Muhammad or the Messenger of Allah, as well as the rest of the historical figures who were known by their titles and epithets. I will also use the word Allah interchangeably with God to ensure consistency and clarity of discourse in the book as it occurs in Islamic historical traditions. In order to respect the Quranic scriptural usage, the Quranic verses have been placed in these brackets: {} and the separator between the verses is is represented by this symbol.

Sixth: In writing the biography of Muhammad, I have taken care to throw light on various aspects of his personality, such as the moral, social, human, leadership and personal aspects, and not only on the military aspect, as many biography books have done. This is to give the reader a more complete picture of Muhammad's biography and personality. In writing this book, I have relied primarily on the Quran and the book 'Al-Sahih Men Sirat Al-Nabi Al-Azam' by 1See the book 'Al-Sahih Men Sirat Al-Nabi Al-Azam' by Mr. Ja'far Murtada al-Amili. [14] Ja'far Murtada al-'Amili, which is characterized by its comprehensive research and analysis of all the traditions of the other Islamic sects and the traditions of the Prophet's family.

The neutrality of reading:

To bridge the vast temporal gap between us and the historical events, traditions, and various customs that prevailed in the society at that time, we must understand that moral constants and human values are the true criterion we must use to understand and evaluate these events. In order to do that, we should also eliminate any prejudices, false beliefs, and false news and have a pure, honest intention to learn and discover the truth for our own benefit and enlightenment. This will make our reading neutral and beneficial.

Final clarification:

The purpose of this book is not to incite sectarian discord or religious disputes. Our societies are confronted with significant crises and immense challenges that impact their present and jeopardize their future, necessitating unity and the rejection of division. I underscore the respect and admiration for all sacred figures, both Muslim and non-Muslim, referenced in the book. My aim was for this book to be a rigorous academic study grounded in precise historical facts, accessible to individuals from all walks of life and diverse cultural backgrounds, enabling them to gain an understanding of Islamic history from its most authentic sources. In conclusion, I wish you a pleasant time and a spiritual atmosphere while reading this remarkable biography. I pray to the Lord for success and guidance for you and that He accepts this simple work and forgives me for what I have overlooked.

21.08.2022 | 22.01.1444

The author

The historical Muhammad

Did Muhammad really exist? Or was Muhammad a real person? This question may seem strange to the Arabic reader and does not come to his mind at all, as he lives in a world that is full of evidences and testimonies in all its aspects pointing to the existence of the Prophet Muhammad, as the saying goes: where there is smoke, there is fire. However, for some Orientalists, this is a subject that requires scientific investigation and evidence. I will not discuss here the reasons for doubting the existence of Muhammad, but I will follow this idea and mention some historical evidence for the existence of Muhammad from non-Islamic sources, starting with this text:

"When I was in Kaiserea[1], I took a boat to Shekamona[2], a town near the sea coast of Haifa, Palestine, and came across people who said that the Byzantine royal guard had been killed. We, as Jews, rejoiced at this news. They also announced that the Prophet had appeared. He had come to the Arabs and announced the appearance of the Messiah. Then I, Abraham, went to an old man who was very familiar with the Holy Scriptures and drew his attention to the matter. I asked him: 'What do you think, master and teacher, about the prophet who appeared to the Arabs? 'He is an impostor,' he replied, groaning loudly. 'Come prophets with swords and chariots. These are truly acts of chaos which started today. I fear that the Christ who once came, whom the Christians worship, has been sent by God. Instead, we will accept Hermolaos[3],' he added. 'For Isaiah[4] said that we Jews have a flawed and hardened heart until the whole earth becomes desolate. But go, Mr. Abraham, and inquire about the prophet who has appeared.' And so I made my inquiries, and those I met told me, 'There is no truth to be found in the so-called prophet, only bloodshed. What the people he met say about his supposed possession of the key to heaven is unbelievable."
[9]

This text is considered one of the oldest traditions narrated by non-Muslims in which Muhammad is mentioned. It is referred to as the teachings of Jacob

---

1 Kaiserea: It is a Palestinian city.
2 Shekamona: A city near the sea coast in Haifa - Palestine.
3 Hermolaos: He was one of the three priests who were killed by Emperor Maximian in 305 AD in Nikomedia (a city in Turkey).
4 Isaiah: One of the prophets of the children of Israel, born in 766 BC, who lived in Jerusalem.

and was written in Africa in 634 AD The text consists of a fictional dialog between the Jewish merchant Jacob and his cousin Justus, who came from Palestine. During a business trip to Carthage, Jacob was forcibly baptized on the orders of Emperor Heraclius, but he quickly convinced himself of the Christian faith. When his cousin Justus arrived from Palestine, they had a discussion about Christianity and Judaism. In the course of the discussion, Justus said that he had received a message from his brother Abraham in Palestine announcing the arrival of a new prophet.

The first thing we notice in the previous text is the presence of a prophet in that region and at that time, and the only person who proclaimed his prophecy was Muhammad. We also notice in the text the joy of the Jews at the redemption from the unjust Byzantine guard and their expectation of the redeeming prophet. We also notice the old man's judgment of the alleged prophet without verifying and confirming his truth. It also appears that this was one of the campaigns carried out by the Muslims that year, which involved fighting against the Romans. What is striking here is that this new prophet proclaimed the coming of the savior after him and claimed that he possessed the keys to paradise.

There is another ancient proof that dates back to 636 AD and was found in a Syrian manuscript from the 6th century containing the Gospels of Matthew and Mark. A few lines about a battle between the Arabs and the Romans were written on the front. The writing is very pale and not all the words are clear:

"In January {the people} of Homs surrendered for their lives (i.e. they promised to submit in exchange for their lives) and many villages were killed by the followers of Muhammad, and many people were killed and {taken captive} from Galilee to Beit. And on the {twenty-sixth} of May, Saki{la}ra departed from the vicinity of Homs and the Romans pursued them {.} On the tenth of {August} the Romans fled from the vicinity of Damascus {and were} killed many {people}, about ten thousand. And at the end of {the year} the Romans came. On the twentieth of August in the year {nine hundred and forty} and seven there gathered {a multitude} of Romans in Jabthah, and many people {of the Romans} were killed, {about} fifty thousand. "[10]

We note the explicit mention of the name Muhammad in the manuscript, and the date mentioned in the text coincides with the date of the Battle of Yarmuk, which is August 20, 636 CE, corresponding to 12 Rajab 15 CE. After examining the text, Nöldeke, and Wright before him, concluded that these notes indicate that their author was a contemporary of the events of that year. [11]

Figure 1: Dirham of Abd al-Malik ibn Abdullah, the governor of Zubair in Bishapur, minted in the year 66 AH / 685-686 CE. This marks the first time that the name "Muhammad" appears in Arabic on a coin.

Finally, I would like to draw attention to the oldest coin bearing the name of Muhammad, on which is written: "In the name of God, Muhammad is the Messenger of God". The Muslims added this phrase to the coin after they conquered the lands of Persia in 685-686 AD [12]

From the previous sources, we realize that the person of Muhammad is a reality and not a fantasy, for his fame reached the distant lands of the Arabian Peninsula, and he was documented by non-Muslims and also by his enemies. This leaves no room for doubt that Muhammad actually existed in this region in the Arabian Peninsula in the seventh century AD and had a leading and prophetic role. I will content myself with this and leave the matter to the researcher to delve into the other historical sources so that the speech does not become too long and the book deviates from its main objective.

Writing the biography of the prophet

An author should be neutral in his writing, precise in his criticism, objective in his presentation. But is there a neutral author? Every author has his own ideas and beliefs, on which he has grown up, which he carries in his head, which will be reflected in his writings and his way of presentation. You will hardly find a hundred percent objective author. You see him using his research and writings to achieve his goals, something the author cannot hide, no matter how hard he tries.

When you read biographies, you'll notice that Muslims take on the role of defending Muhammad and portray him in the positive image they desire. Sunnis tend to lean Muhammad towards the Companions and Abu Bakr and Omar, while Shiites lean Muhammad towards Ali. As for Orientalists, they take the side of denial and try to question everything that has been reported about Muhammad. Many of them go further and write the biography based solely on historical reports that attack Muhammad or portray him in a bad light. All these authors may follow the scientific approach in research and writing, and this approach is binding for the author, but they differ in their analyses, interpretations, and conclusions about events, situations, and characters. So, one author interprets an event in one way, while another interprets it in another way. In this way, they impose their personal beliefs and ideas on the writing of the biography, whether they know it or not. And I, like other authors, have revealed my method of writing the biography in the preface of the book. I do not suggest that this approach to writing is wrong, nor do I believe authors should refrain from expressing their opinions to be fair. No, the author also has the right to express his opinion and present his idea, and it is up to the reader to make the final judgment and choose the approach that suits his taste and belief.

Also, readers are different, depending on their backgrounds and cultures, and they can be selective in their reading and understanding, as a result of their preconceived ideas. The best among them is the one who is aware of this fact, puts aside his feelings and preconceived judgments, and tries to read neutrally, and he sets a scale for himself in understanding the texts, so that he does not treat any text unjustly or be deceived by a text (see Neutrality in Reading on page 11).

My approach to writing will primarily involve presenting the results of Sayyid Ja'far al-'Amili's investigations, supplemented at certain points with my own contributions. When dealing with Sayyid Ja'far's research results, I have refrained from reproducing the intricate details of his Investigations, except for a few brief comments, as mentioned in the preface, to avoid overwhelming the reader with excessive detail. For instance, there are eight different scholarly opinions regarding Khadija's age when she married Muhammad. Sayyid Ja'far's research concluded that she was twenty-eight years old. In this book, I will mention only the outcome of his investigation, specifically, that she was twenty-eight years old, without delving into the reasoning behind it. This approach allows me to maintain the flow of the biography narrative without getting bogged down in the explanation of every detail over several pages. This methodology applies to all the topics covered in this biography. Readers interested in a more detailed investigation can refer to the original sources.

The study of hadith by the Orientalists

As we have mentioned, the sources for writing the biography are the Quran, traditions and narrations. Although some people would prefer to add sources from non-Muslims, it seems that these sources are rare and do not have the required reliability, especially in the early period of Islam. Moreover, these sources may not be neutral. Nevertheless, there were some Orientalists who tried to rely only on external sources, but they were unsuccessful in doing so. [15]

Muslim scholars have endeavored to study the Quran and Hadith for long generations dating back to the first century of the Hijrah. They established sciences that are specialized for this, and institutions that cared for the students in countries like Iraq, Iran, Egypt, and others. They wrote thousands of books and scientific studies about it in different languages.

The Orientalists came late to the approach of studying the prophetic traditions. And perhaps the first significant attempt was made by Goldziher in his book (Muhammadan Studies) in 1890 AD, and since then it became one of the most important sources referred to by researchers. He mentioned that the Islamic traditions were written in the second and third centuries of the Hijrah under the influence of several conflicts, and that they are not suitable as a historical source for the early period of Islam.[16] This opinion was supported by Lammens, who added that the existing biography is based on invented stories derived from some hints in the Quran arranged in a chronological order to give the form of a history.[17] Cron reiterated this claim by saying, "Much of the seemingly historical heritage is in fact derived from Qur'anic interpretation. And what remains is jurisprudential and doctrinal Hadith with no basis."[18] Cron presented in her book (Meccan Trade), published in 1987, her attempt to interpret Surah Quraysh by relying on various exegesis books to show how information is invented by the exegetes. Surah Quraysh reads: {For the accustomed security of the Quraysh - Their accustomed security [in] the caravan of winter and summer - Let them worship the Lord of this House, Who has fed them, [saving them] from hunger and made them safe, [saving them] from fear.}[19] Cron could not understand the meaning of the word "Ilaf" and inserted it without translation. She also could not gain a complete understanding of the surah, the same understanding or lack of understanding that Cook had before her [20] and Cron, after a long and confused search, concluded, "That the true meaning of the verses does not exist, and that the interpretation of the surah which we have is nothing but the conjectures of the exegetes, and it does not represent what was in Muhammad's mind when he recited these verses; and the original meaning of these verses was unknown to them."[21] Not all Orientalists agreed with this extreme approach because their study of Quranic verses lacked accuracy and sufficient knowledge of Arabic language and history, which led to misinterpretation of Quranic texts. Robert Bertram Serjeant said of the book (Meccan Trade), "It is confused, illogical and irrational, in addition to its complexity due to their misunderstanding of the Arabic texts, their lack of understanding of the social structure in the Arabian Peninsula, and their distortion of the apparent meaning of other scriptures, ancient and modern, to fit their claims. " [22]

If we go back to the exegesis books, we will find the scientific approach to all the meanings of the words in the verses, then the deduction of the appropriate overall meaning for the verse according to the context and the various evidences. Sheikh Makarem al-Shirazi says: "Ilaf" is the root of the verb "alafa", and "alafa" means to accustom him, that is, to gather him, in a way that is associated with harmony, intimacy and affection. And some said: "Al-Ilaf" is from reconciliation, which is the covenant and the contract, and this meaning does not fit the content of the surah. In any case, the intention is to create affection between Quraysh and this holy land, which is Mecca and the old house, because they and all the inhabitants of Mecca have chosen residence in this land because of its position and security."[23] And the author of Tafsir al-Mizan adds, "And his word: 'For the habituation of Quraysh' the 'for' in it is for justification and the subject for the verb 'habituate' is Allah and Quraysh is its first object and its second object is omitted, which is indicated by what comes after it. And his word: 'Their habituation to the winter and summer journey' is a by-phrase for the 'habituation of Quraysh' and the subject for 'their habituation' is Allah and its first object is the plural pronoun 'their' and its second object is the journey etc., and the complete sentence is: for the habituation of Allah Quraysh to the winter and summer journey."[24] So the meaning is: That Allah gives Quraysh the grace of peace and safety near the House of Allah. And this allows them to settle in the region and continue in their usual trade journeys in winter and summer. Therefore, Quraysh should worship Allah, the Lord of the Kaaba House, in gratitude for these favors. [25]

18

The skeptical approach of Orientalists in dealing with hadith has made it difficult for them to understand Islamic history as it was understood by Muslim scholars.[26] They did not refer to the scholarly methods used by hadith scholars for hundreds of years, but wanted to reinvent the wheel and study it from scratch to extract a kernel of truth from the heritage through which they could write the biography.[27] Their criterion was if the hadiths and messages portrayed Muhammad in a bad light, then they were accepted.[13] In 1950, Schacht presented what he called the theory of the common link as a solution to the problem of the hadiths. The idea of this theory is to collect different versions of a particular hadith, look at its Isnāds (the chain of transmitters of a hadith) and find out if there is a particular person who appears in all of them (the common link); therefore, it is likely that this person is the originator of the hadith. Schacht established a date for the origin of these hadiths according to his theory.[28] Guillaume adopted Schacht's idea and expanded it after a study of a large number of hadith; he noted that some transmitters of the hadith (the common link) in the Isnad trace Muhammad back through a single transmitter of the hadith, which in turn traces back to a single person and then to a single companion until it reaches Muhammad, and concluded that the hadith and the Isnad tracing back to Muhammad are an invention of this common link.[29]

Although the Orientalists' modest attempts to study the hadiths came late, they are moving in the right direction. They have moved from outright rejection of the Islamic heritage to the conviction that it is necessary to develop ways to study it and to recognize the authentic in it.

The study of Hadith among Muslims

The early hadith scholars recognized the reality of the state of historical texts and began to apply scientific research methods in their studies as early as the seventh century AD Their literary and critical research was groundbreaking in this field and they are considered to be the first to establish this knowledge. Linguists wrote books in which they collected individual words and explained their meanings, as well as books in which they wrote down Arabic rules such as morphology and syntax. Muslims wrote books to collect hadiths, books about hadith narrators and books to criticize hadiths. The first type contains hadiths about beliefs and messages, commands and prohibitions, and various types of transactions attributed to the Infallible (al-maʿṣūmūn)[1]. The second type contains the names of the narrators, where each narrator is mentioned with his name and characteristics. This is referred to as the "science of men, DMG ʿilmu arrijāl". And in the third type, it mentions the general systems and rules for knowing the correct Hadiths from others, this is called the "science of understanding, DMG ʿilmu addarāya". The aim of these three types is the same, namely to confirm the Prophetic Sunnah in a correct manner.[30]

A student in the science of understanding knows that a hadith is the statement that narrates the statement of the Infallible One or his action or his confirmation. A message (alk̲abr) is that which sometimes corresponds to a statement and sometimes that which is narrated from someone other than the Infallible One, such as a companion (aṣṣaḥābī) or a successor (attābʿī) and the like. A trace (alʾathr) is more comprehensive than a message and a hadith. Messages have categories: The multiply transmitted message (alk̲abr almutwātr) is that whose meaning has been derived from several common messages and which in itself confirms the certainty of its truth. The single message (alk̲abr alʾāḥād) is the one that in itself only confirms a suspicion. If its chain is known in its entirety, it is supported, and if one is missing from its beginning upwards, it is pendant (muʿalaq). If it is transmitted by more than three in each stage, it is widespread (mustfīḍ), and if it is transmitted by one in one of them alone, it is strange (ġarīb).[31]

As for the hadith, it has two categories: narrated many times (almutwātr) and individual (alʾāḥād). The hadith that has been transmitted many times is the one that is transmitted by a group so large that it is impossible for them to have agreed on a lie. This type of hadith is evidence that must be acted upon. As for the individual hadith, it is the one that does not reach the extent of continuity, regardless of whether the transmitter is one or more.[32] A sign of fabrication of a hadith among the Shi'ah is that it contradicts the text of the Quran, or what has been established in the Prophetic Sunnah, or reason, or that it is poorly worded and not fluent, or that it is a message about an important matter for which there are many reasons for its transmission, and yet it was transmitted by only one person, or that the transmitter is a supporter of the unjust ruler.

---

1   Al-maʿṣūmūn: In Shiite doctrine, the title "The Infallibles" refers to the fourteen Infallibles, including Muhammad, his daughter Fatima, and the twelve Imams who descend from Ali ibn Abi Talib and Fatima.

The hadith al'āhād is divided into four categories: The authentic (aṣṣaḥīh): When the chain of transmitters consists of two imams who are praised as reliable in each layer. The good one (alhasn): If he is affected by a deviation or without it in whole or in part, with the reliability of the rest. Respectable and strong (mawṭq and qawī): If they are not all or some of them imams, with the reliability of all of them. And everything else is weak (ḍa'īf), but may be acceptable if the action is known according to its content, otherwise it is not acceptable.The narrator of the hadith must fulfill five conditions: religious duty (Takleef) and Islam in general, faith and justice and memorization (aḍḍabṭ). Righteousness is the adjustment of psychic powers and the alignment of their actions so that none of them dominates the other. And aḍḍḍabṭ means that the narrator is a hafiz (one who can memorize), wise, vigilant and wary of falsification and error. And it is not necessary for him to be free or male, but he should know the Arabic language.

And how to know the righteousness of the narrator also has a detail, and in short, the narrator must receive a recommendation or testimony from the scholars or the righteous so that his testimony is accepted. If the narrator is not honest or doubtful in his credibility or the strength of his intellect according to the opinion of the righteous, his testimony is rejected, and in this area there is a great detail and several works under the name of criticism and correction (aljarh wa atta'dīl), but they are not dealt with in this book.

This is the method of the Shi'a Muslims in dealing with the Islamic traditions and narrations in brief, and there are many details in the specialized books on this matter, and the Sunni Muslims also have their method in authenticating the hadith. The scholars of Sunni Muslims have collected the authentic narrations in books and labeled them as the correct one (as-sahīh), such as "Sahīh al-Bukhari" and "Sahīh Muslim", and considered them as authentic as the authenticity of the Quran. But the Shi'a Muslims do not consider anything but the Quran as authentic, and everything else must be tested and verified.

There is no doubt that the researcher must study the authentic hadiths and reports about the life of Muhammad in order to write the biography, and the researcher Ja'far Murtada al-Amili has accomplished this task for over 20 years, and he has prepared a large book on the biography of Muhammad based on nearly 1700 sources, and his method was based on narrating the various traditions in the Meccan and Medinan periods in chronological order of events with great detail, then analyzing them from various aspects, using the criteria of knowledge of the news and hadiths, then relating them to the Quran to distin-guish between the authentic and weak traditions. Although the author some-times tended to analyze the historical data with theological beliefs, he generally tried to present a scientific work based on research methods.[33] His book "Al-Sahih Men Sirat Al-Nabi Al-Azam" attracted the attention of academic circles, scholars and universities, and received the book of the year award from the Is-lamic Republic of Iran.

The sources of this book focused on the book; "Al-Sahih Men Sirat Al-Nabi Al-Azam" by the researcher Ja'far al-Amili, which is the basis for this biogra-phy, because his book is the best that has been written in this regard, but he has lengthened the explanations in it and mentioned many things in it that are not needed, so it was necessary to shorten and refine some topics.

Arabia

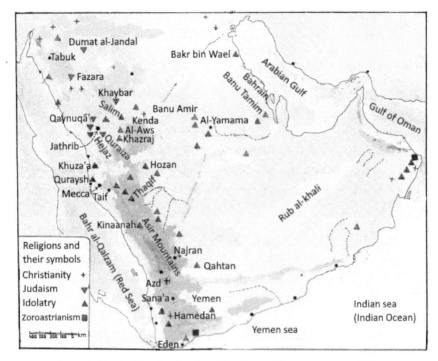

Figure 2: The Arabian Peninsula at the time of the emergence of Islam.

Arabia is a geographical region in southwest Asia, located between Asia and Africa. It is surrounded by the Red Sea to the west, the Arabian Gulf to the northeast, the Indian Ocean to the southeast and land borders to the north.[34] The Arabian Peninsula consisted mostly of barren desert with some mountains, valleys and barren plains unsuitable for agriculture and labor. Rainfall was sporadic in isolated areas and there was not a single river.[35] The inhabitants therefore relied on groundwater and the isolated oases that were present in the region. The prevailing temperature could rise up to 54 degrees Celsius. Since there was little point in settling down and organizing life there, most of the inhabitants of the Arabian Peninsula were nomads who settled in one place and then moved on. There was no dominant state and no responsible government. Although Arabia was surrounded by the Persian Empire to the east and the Roman Empire to the north, the precarious geographical position of the region meant that the Romans and Persians had little ambition to attack or conquer the peninsula.

As a result of these onerous geographical conditions and the lack of human and religious deterrence, people resorted to robbing each other to make a living. This spread fanatical tribal rule, poverty, hunger and misunderstanding. They took pride in their raids and attacks on others because they were victorious for the children of their tribe, whether they were right or wrong. They used to kill their children, especially girls, partly out of fear of raids and slavery and partly out of extreme poverty.[36]

They mistreated women and did with them as they wanted, like their belongings and the animals they owned.[37] On the whole, their cultural level was rather low, with the exception of a few city dwellers who could read and write and who occupied themselves with books in Mecca. They had knowledge of foreign language books and these included "the Hanifs" who knew some foreign languages. They had access to the books of the Jews and Christians as well as other books.[38]

Pre-Islamic occupations included carpentry, blacksmithing, weaving, sewing, goldsmithing, tanning, construction and similar trades, which were mainly practiced by city dwellers. The Bedouin, on the other hand, refused to practice these trades and regarded those who practiced them with contempt and disdain; for in their understanding, these were menial trades, made for slaves, and not appropriate for free people.[39]

They avoided manual labor and agricultural work, and saw pride and self-respect in the exercise of power and control. This lifestyle led them to feel that they had to live freely and without restrictions, to be brave and loyal, and to honor guests in order to survive and coexist with the other tribes in the region.

The period before Islam was referred to as the Age of Ignorance. "Jāhilīya" is a new term that emerged with the advent of Islam. The word "Jāhilīya" means stupidity, ignorance, arrogance, recklessness, anger, non-observance of divine laws and will, and other conditions that Islam condemns.[40] And it is not necessary for this person to be illiterate, meaning that they have no knowledge and cannot read or write.[41] The term "Jāhilīya" was used to designate the period before Islam to distinguish it from the state in which the Arabs lived after the advent of the Message, just as it is customary for us and other nations to use new names for existing eras.[42] The term 'jāhilīya' appears in the Quran in the Medinan suras, not in the Meccan suras, that is, in the suras revealed in Medina and not in Mecca. This indicates that their appearance occurred after the Hijrah of Muhammad to Yathrib, and that their use in this meaning began after the Hijrah and that Muslims have used them since that time and thereafter.[43]

The actions and behaviors of the pre-Islamic Arabs were largely unrestricted and open, which was clearly reflected in their poetry. They sang of wine, hunting, games and love, while on the other hand they boasted of revenge, conflict, theft and capture. Their motives for noble deeds were honor and family feeling, they did not often mention the gods, let alone feel a need for them. A man trusts entirely in himself, he rides alone in the desert, his sword helps him in danger, no god stands by his side, he prays no prayer to protect his soul. His reckless drive might extend to self-sacrifice for family and tribe, but in this heroic act there are no religious motives driving him, only tribalism.[44] Some of them might have a guilty conscience for actions that go against their nature, and they might have religious feelings, especially when they feel weak or when they feel that the storm life is about to end. Then you see them regretting the empty commitment and effort in a mirage. When we look at the verses of the poet Imru' al-Qais, who lived in the time of Jāhilīya, we can understand his view of life and its temptations. We also learn the lessons he learned from his life experiences and the conviction he gained that death is the inevitable end. On this basis, he decided to set noble character traits as his goal. [45]

"We rush towards an unknown goal and forget it while eating and drinking.

We are sparrows, flies and worms, but braver than the puppies of wolves.

My roots reach to the depths of the earth; but this death robs me of my youth,

and of my soul it robs me and of my body, and soon it lays me in the dust.

I have driven my camel through every desert, vast and shimmering with mirage;

and I have ridden in the devouring throng, striving for the honors of greedy dangers,

and I have fought under every sky till I longed for homecoming instead of booty.

But can I, after Al-Harith's[1] death and after the death of Hojr, the noble host,

can I hope for a softer lot from the change of time that does not forget the hard mountains.

I know that I must soon be pierced by its claw and tooth,as happened to my father and my grandfather, not to mention the one who was killed at Al-Kilab[2].
" 492

Mecca

Mecca was one of the most famous cities on the Arabian Peninsula and had been inhabited since the time of the Prophet Abraham [46]. In the book "Geography" by the famous Greek scholar Ptolemy, who lived in the second century AD, a city called "Macoraba" is mentioned.

Researchers are of the opinion that the city mentioned is Mecca. This indicates that it was already known among the Arabs in the second century AD and that it was a holy city visited by people from distant places. Thanks to this sanctity and importance, its name reached the ears of this distant Greek geographer. [47] (See Figure 3).

---

1 Al-Harith ibn Amr: is his grandfather and Hojr ibn Al-Harith ibn Amr is his father and they were kings, the owners of buildings with domes.
2 Al-Kilab: It is a place name where a battle took place. Therefore, one speaks of the first and second day of Al-Kilab, the two well-known days. The "killed one" refers to his uncle Sharhabil ibn Amr.

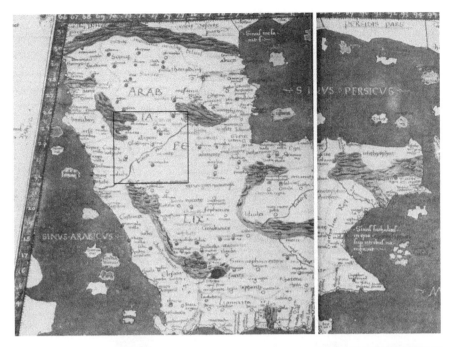

Figure 3: Above is a map of the Arabian Peninsula from the book "Geography" by Ptolemy, who lived in the second century AD. Below is an enlarged representation of the image, showing the names "Macoraba" and "Iathrippa", which denote the cities of Mecca and Yathrib.

In the midst of the Arabs in Mecca, there is the Kaaba[1] where idols were worshipped and to which numerous tribes made pilgrimage to trade and pray. Each tribe and family had its own idol and individual way of worshipping idols. Their motives for worshipping these idols were often emotional, far removed from the methods of rational and logical justification. The Arabs' connection with their idols is due to the fact that they are linked to the history of their fathers or grandfathers.[48] Other nations looked at the Kaaba with envy because the tribes made pilgrimages to it and sanctified it. Out of this envy, they built their own Kaabas in their countries, hoping to redirect the pilgrims to their cities. Examples of this are the Kaaba of Najran, the Kaaba of Yemen, and the Kaaba of Al-Rabe in Taif. [49]

Figure 4: An imaginary depiction of Mecca at the time of the emergence of Islam. Note the idols on and around the Kaaba.

The study of archaeological texts has shown that the religion of pre-Islamic peoples was based on worshipping the heavenly bodies and approaching them through prayers to fulfill the needs of the people. The Arabs before Islam worshipped celestial bodies such as planets, sun and moon, and the sun was called

---

1 The Kaaba: is a cuboid building in the courtyard of the Holy Mosque in Mecca and forms as "House of God".

"God" to honor them.[50] The name of the god "Wadd" was found, a well-known god of the Thamudites mentioned in their scriptures. The Arabs symbolized him by the image of a bull's head, and his worship spread throughout the Arabian Peninsula and persisted until the advent of Islam.

Figure 5 (left): Some statues of gods before Islam, found in Yemen [0].
Figure 6 (right): al-Lāt, the war goddess of the Arabs before Islam, is the figure in the middle of the stone carving, found in Al-Hadhr. The two female figures surrounding her are most likely her daughters al-ʿUzzā and Manat.

The name "al-ʿUzzā" was found in the form "Han-Uzzā" in writings found in the city of Al-Ula in Hejaz. al-ʿUzzā is one of the gods whose worship continued until Islam. The word "Rahmanan", i.e. "the Merciful", was found in a Jewish text dating back to the time before Christ. It reads: "Blessed be the name of the Merciful in heaven, and Israel and their God, the Lord of the Jews, who helped his servant Sharm. "[51] Some researchers have pointed out that the South Arabian Arabs adopted this word and their concept of God from Judaism and that this idea of monotheism only came about through the influence of Judaism, which invaded Yemen. However, there are also researchers who disagree. They argue that the opening of the text with the mention of the Merciful, followed by the reference to the God of the Jews, and the appearance of the word "Rahmanan Baal Saman", i.e. "the Merciful, the Lord of Heaven", in another inscription dated to 459 CE,[52] as well as the appearance of the word "the Merciful" in another text dated to 468 CE, in which the author thanks him for helping to build his house,[53] and the appearance of the worship of the Merciful One in other South Arabian Arabic texts and in texts found in the upper parts of Hejaz, far from the presence of the Jews,[54] all these reasons contradict the opinion of those who say that the doctrine of the Merciful One is a doctrine adopted from the Jews. [55] The people of Mecca were aware of the Merciful One, and there is no doubt that they used the word in the sense of God.[56]

The worship of 'al-Lāt' is found in the South Arabian Arabic inscriptions, but was more prominent in North Arabia and Hejaz and its worship extended to Levant.[57] It is said that a priest named Amr ibn Luhay was the first to bring the idols from Levant and introduce them to Mecca, after which people learned to worship them.[58] There are many archaeological inscriptions that refer to the worship of other gods such as "Ya'uq" and others that I don't want to talk about in this book. Islamic tradition also mentions the god before Islam; there are also references to it in the Quran: ﴿Among His signs are night and day, and the sun and the moon. Do not prostrate to the sun, nor to the moon, but prostrate to Allah who created them, if it is Him that you worship﴾[59] and it is also mentioned: ﴿So have you considered al-Lat and al-'Uzza? And Manat, the third - the other one?﴾ [60], and in another verse: ﴿And they said: 'Do not abandon your gods; do not abandon Wadd, nor Suwāʿ, nor Yaghuth, Yaʿūq and Nasr.'﴾ [61] The Quran addresses those who worship idols and not God, sometimes as disbelievers and sometimes as idolaters or polytheists. This is because they claimed that these idols were gods that brought them closer to God.

There were also individuals who followed the Hanifite religion known as Hanifs. They were a group that mocked the worship of idols and rebelled against them and the prevailing moral norms of the time. They called for far-reaching reforms in life and fought against the many social ills that were prevalent at the time. Their criticism of idol worship and debauchery such as drinking wine, murder and injustice led them to raise their voices, as reformists do in any era calling for reform. This reform movement was met with opposition from the conservatives, the powerful and the followers of idols, as is the case with any reform movement. It is possible that some of them leaned towards Christianity, but they were neither Jews nor Christians, but followers of a monotheistic religion called Hanifism, which dates back to the time of the prophet Abraham.[62]

Some Orientalists have regarded the Hanifs as a sect of Christianity - that is, those bearing a Christian culture - and considered them to be Arab Christians who adapted Christianity a little and added some teachings from other sources.

They based this on the fact that some of them converted to Christianity and on what is found in some pre-Islamic poems, from which they concluded that the people meant were a sect of Christianity. [63] However, the Quran makes it explicitly clear that the Hanifs were neither Jews nor Christians, but followed Abraham in their faith: {They say, 'Be Jews or Christians, and you will be rightly guided.' Say [Prophet], 'Rather, [we follow] the religion of Abraham, a Hanif, and he was not one of the polytheists.} [64]

Most of the Hanifs were travelers who roamed the lands seeking knowledge and fleeing from the pagan reality. They learned to read and write and became scholars and sages. An example of the Hanifs is Quss ibn Sa'idah al-Iyadi, who was one of the wise peers and followers of Hanifism and gave sermons exhorting the people in the market of Okaz in Mecca. [65] Zaid ibn Amr ibn Abd al-'Uzzā was a Qurayshite from the tribe of Uday who disliked the worship of his people. He criticized and mocked them and joined neither Judaism nor Christianity. He abandoned the religion of his people, withdrew from the idols and refused to eat what was sacrificed for the idols and other acts of the pagans. [66]

Among the most famous tribes in Mecca was the Quraysh[1] tribe, including the Banu Hashim. The Hashemites were distinguished by honor and high status because they were the lords of Mecca and the guardians of the Kaaba[67] and were followers of Hanifism[2]. They made pilgrimage to the Holy House and honored it by saying, "It is the house of our Lord. "[68] Among the most important sons of Banu Hashim was Abdul Muttalib, one of the most notable leaders of Mecca, whose lineage goes back to the Prophet Ishmael. He had several children, including al-Abbas, Abu Talib, Hamza and Abdullah (see the figure below).

---

1 The Quraysh (Koreishites) are an Arab tribe that ruled over Mecca at the time of the Islamic Prophet Muhammad.
2 Hanifism: refers to pre-Islamic monotheists on the Arabian Peninsula who were neither Jews nor Christians.

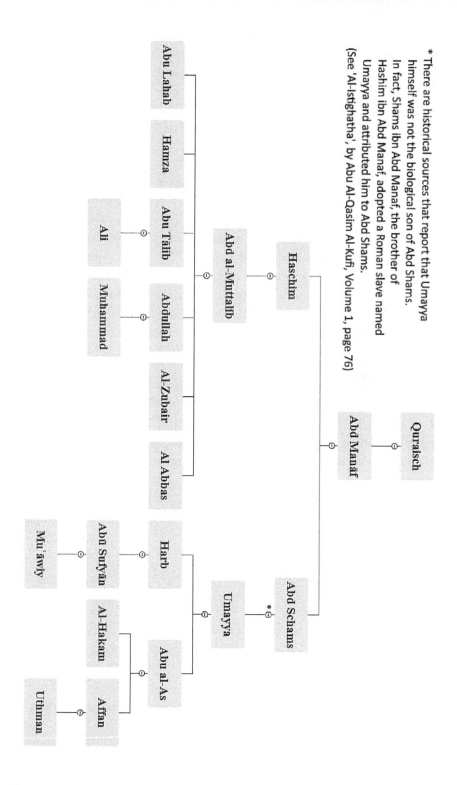

* There are historical sources that report that Umayya himself was not the biological son of Abd Shams. In fact, Shams ibn Abd Manaf, the brother of Hashim ibn Abd Manaf, adopted a Roman slave named Umayya and attributed him to Abd Shams.
(See 'Al-Istighatha', by Abu Al-Qasim Al-Kufi, Volume 1, page 76)

Birth of Muhammad bin Abdullah

In 570-571 AD, Abraha ibn al-Ashram, the ruler of Yemen, led a military campaign against Mecca with an army and a herd of elephants to destroy the Kaaba. His aim was to change the caravan route from Mecca to Yemen and thus stimulate trade in Yemen. However, his campaign failed after God sent birds on his army, which threw stones at them and destroyed them.[69] Inscriptions have been found showing some of Abraha's campaigns, the last of which was in 558 AD.[70] However, his campaign against Mecca is believed to be undated and he died shortly after.[71] Due to the significance of this event, the Arabs dated their events and births from this year and called it the Year of the Elephant. In this year, the Jews awaited the birth of the prophesied prophet and looked for him in the families of the children of Israel, believing that he would come from them and to them and that he would favor them and give them preference over other people both socially and materially and morally.

From the second century AD, Jews gradually settled in the city of Yathrib, Dumat al-Jandal, Khaybar and other neighboring areas, and Some of them were looking for the promised prophet who would come in the Arabian Peninsula region, as indicated by their holy books, and the news that they passed down from generation to generation[72]. Some of them learned the Arabic language and had close ties with the Quraysh. The Arabs respected them, saw them as scholars and sought their advice on questions about history and predictions about the future. The Christians did not penetrate the heart of the Arabian Peninsula, but lived on its fringes in places like Al-Hira and the lands of Levant. Some Arab tribes professed Christianity, but without strongly adhering to their religious rites (see Figure 2).[73]

Most Arabs at that time were illiterate, they studied no books, knew neither the teachings of the prophets nor heaven or hell or the resurrection or the Last Judgment, except a little of what they were told by those who practiced the Hanifite faith or what they heard from the Jews. But this knowledge was not firmly anchored in their hearts, their minds could not fully grasp it, and it had no influence on their daily lives. Among what the Arabs heard from the scholars and what was handed down to them was the prophecy that a prophet would appear in the Arabian Peninsula.[74] When the Jews suffered something they did not like from the Arabs, they said that the time of a prophet now sent was near. They would follow him and cooperate with him to destroy the Arabs as ʿĀd and Iram[1] were killed.[75]

Among those born in the year of the elephant[76] on the seventeenth day of Rabiʿ al-Awwal[77] in the valley of Abi Talib was a child of Abdullah bin Abdul Muttalib, named Muhammad. He was born a half-orphan, as his father Abdullah died before Muhammad saw the light of day.[78] His grandfather Abdul Muttalib then took over the care of Muhammad. After Muhammad's birth, his mother, Āmina bint Wahb, nursed him for several days. It was the custom of the people of Mecca that when the newborn child had completed seven days, they would look for a wet nurse to breastfeed it. When Abd al-Muttalib wanted to find a wet nurse for Muhammad, the women argued about breastfeeding him. Abd al-Muttalib finally chose Halima al-Saʿdia for him.[79]

Figure 7: An imaginary depiction of a family from Mecca celebrating the birth of their new child.

The Jews did not succeed in finding the newborn they were looking for among the families of the children of Israel. They feared that it might have

---

1   The Banu ʿĀd were an extinct Arab tribal people. God sent them a prophet named Hud to guide them on the right path, as they worshipped idols after Noah's flood. However, they denied what he brought them, and so a severe storm punishment from God came upon them, from which no one was saved. And Iram is the name of their tribe or their city.

been born in an Arab family, so they sent someone to look for it in Arab families.

It was customary for the nobles of Mecca to send their sons to the desert, as they believed that their sons would grow up with healthier bodies, eloquent tongues and clearer minds. But the child Muhammad needed none of this, as he belonged to the Banu Hashim, who spoke the most fluent Arabic dialect and had a better foundation of faith than the Banu Saad, Āmina's tribe. It would therefore be better for him to stay with the Banu Hashim. Nevertheless, the child Muhammad was sent with Halima Al-Sa'dia to the village of Banu Sa`d in Taif to live in the desert.[80]

It may seem that Abdul Muttalib sent his grandson to the desert so that he would grow up to be an eloquent person and grow up in a calmer and purer atmosphere, and this is exactly what Abdul Muttalib wanted to convey to the people. The truth, however, is that he sent Muhammad to the desert for security reasons, to protect him from an assassination attempt and to keep him away from Mecca and thus from the eyes of the observers, especially the Jews who had been waiting for the birth of this expected child for a long time. The Jews recognized that the characteristics of the promised prophet did not appear in a child from among the children of Israel, but in an Arab family from the descendants of the prophet Ishmael. They feared that their religion would be endangered by the emergence of a new religion in the region that would compete with them and threaten their existence. Therefore, they planned to kill him.[81] Āmina's separation from her son was not easy, especially after losing her husband Abdullah not too long ago, but the gravity of the situation forced her to agree to Abdul Muttalib's decision to save Muhammad's life.

Muhammad grew up in Banu Saad in the house of Halima al-Sa'dia, and his presence in Banu Saad was a source of blessing and good for her, as the drought and famine were over. Their sheep became fat and she and their children enjoyed a contented and tranquil life after a life of poverty and hardship.[82] Then Muhammad returned to his mother at the age of five, but the joy of meeting his mother and tender breast did not last long as he lost her at the age of six. It was the divine will that Muhammad lost his parents when he was still a small child.78 His grandfather Abdul Muttalib took care of him, where he became like the father he lost. His grandfather taught him values and morals, and took care of him well. He would not eat food unless he was present, and he knew that he was a blessed child and that something great was in store for him.

The signs and indications he saw from Muhammad cemented this belief in Abd al-Muttalib's heart and gave Muhammad a special place with him. [83]

When Muhammad was eight years old, his grandfather Abd al-Muttalib died shortly after choosing his uncle Abu Talib to finance him, look after his affairs and take care of him.[84] When we look at the event of the prayer for rain, we realize how deep the Banu Hashim's faith in the child Muhammad was and how much they believed that he was a blessed child. When the rains of Mecca were withheld and an extreme drought gripped them, they turned to their idols to ask for rain. Some of them said: "Seek help from al-Lāt and al-ʿUzzā," and others said: "Seek help from Manat." Then one of them, who had a wise opinion, said: "Why do you seek help from these idols while among you are still the descendants of Ibrahim and the descendants of Ishmael?" They asked, "Do you mean Abu Talib?" He replied: "Yes. " So they gathered and knocked on his door. Abu Talib came out, accompanied by a little boy named Muhammad, who appeared like a sun on a dark day, uncovered by thick clouds. Around Muhammad were small children. Abu Talib took Muhammad and pressed his back to the Kaaba, and the boy pointed his finger to the sky as if pleading for mercy. There was no cloud in the sky. Then the clouds came from here and there and gathered, and it began to rain heavily in the valley, and the inhabitants of the city and the people of the desert were blessed[1].[85]

Abu Talib was not the eldest son of Abd al-Muttalib, nor was he the richest among them. But he was the one who loved this child the most and cared for him the most. He was also the brother of Abdullah, the father of Muhammad, on both his father's and mother's side. Therefore, after his grandfather, he was the best guardian for him and his greatest supporter in Mecca throughout his life. [86].

---

1   In this context, Abu Talib reminded the Quraysh of his blessing over them in his childhood when they conspired against Muhammad, saying: 'And a white one, whose face brings the clouds to rain...'

Adolescence and adulthood

When Muhammad entered adolescence, he traveled to Syria for the first time with his uncle Abu Talib on a trading trip. When they arrived in the city of Bosra, they met the monk Buhaira. He spoke to Muhammad and asked him questions about his sleep, his appearance and his affairs. Muhammad answered him, and it turned out that Buhaira already knew these qualities that were mentioned about him in the books. The monk realized that he was a blessed child and had characteristics of the last prophets. After Buhaira finished, he turned to Abu Talib and asked, "Who owns this boy?" Abu Talib replied, "He is my son." Buhaira said: "He is not your son, since his father should not be alive." Abu Talib said: "He is my nephew." Buhaira said: "What happened to his father." Abu Talib replied, "His father died when his mother was pregnant with him." Buhaira said: "You have told the truth. Take your nephew back to his country and beware of the Jews. By Allah, if they see him and learn what I know about him, they will do evil to him. Your nephew has a great matter before him. Hurry and take him to his homeland." Abu Talib then brought Muhammad back to Mecca. [87]

When Muhammad reached the age of fifteen to twenty, a war broke out between the tribe of Qais on one side and the tribes of Quraysh and Kinanah on the other. The war between these tribes flared up again and again and then calmed down again.[88] This war lasted almost four years and was called Fijar War[1] because it took place during the holy months when the Arabs forbid fighting so that they could establish their markets for profit and trade. Muhammad witnessed the brutal war, but he did not take part in it and thus did not override the importance of the holy months.[89] Abu Talib prevented anyone from the tribe of Banu Hashim from taking part in this war by preventing Al-Zubair ibn Abd al-Muttalib from doing so. He said about the war: "This is injustice and aggression, a destruction of family ties and a desecration of the holy month. I will not take part in it, and no one from my family will." 82

When the Fijar War was over in 589 AD, Al- Zubair ibn Abd al-Muttalib called for the gathering of the Fudul alliance and organized a meeting in the

---

1 Fijar war means the war of the shameless men.

house of Abdullah ibn Jud'an. They dipped their hands in the water of Zamzam [1] and perfumed themselves. They allied themselves and pledged to support the oppressed, share the food and stop evil, and those who participated in Al-Fudul alliance were Banu Hashim, Banu Abd al-Muttalib, Banu Asad bin Abd al-Uzzi, Banu Zahra bin Kilab and Banu Taym bin Mura.[90] Muhammad bin Abdullah participated in this alliance when he was twenty years old. "I witnessed an alliance in the house of Abdullah bin Jadaan, which I loved more than a herd of red camels[2]. If I were invited again now in the time of Islam, to join it, I would definitely do so." he said. The Al-Fudul alliance is considered the most honorable alliance among the Arabs, which is in accordance with the principles and laws of Islam and is in line with common sense. [91]

Muhammad's marriage to Khadija

Muhammad began working in trade and met Lady Khadija, who was also active in trade and led trade caravans to Syria. Khadija was considered one of the most respected women of Quraysh and was the wealthiest and most beautiful of them all. She was referred to as the "Lady of Quraysh"[92] . Abu Talib encouraged Muhammad ibn Abdullah to trade and do business with her wealth. At the age of twenty-five, he traveled to Syria again to trade.[93] Lady Khadija heard of Muhammad's honesty, dedication to work, and high moral character, so she expressed a desire to marry him. [94]

Abu Talib and a group of the Quraysh then went to her guardian to propose to her. Her guardian was her uncle, as her father had previously been killed in the Fijar War. [95] When they arrived, Abu Talib said: "Praise be to the Lord of this house, who created us from the lineage of Abraham and the descendants of Ishmael and provided us with a secure sanctuary. He has made us rulers over people and blessed us in the land in which we find ourselves. Moreover, my nephew - meaning Muhammad - is superior to any man in Quraysh. He is also morally unsurpassed. Even if he has little money, which is a fleeting shadow anyway, he can provide well for his family. And he has a desire for Khadija, which is why we have come to you to propose to her with her consent. The ad-

---

1   Zamzam Well: is a well in Mecca that opened thousands of years ago when Abraham's son, Ismael, was left in the desert with his mother Hajar.
2   Red Camels: is an old Arab metaphor for valuable things and wealth.

vanced and deferred dowry is on me. And he, by the lord of this house, has great fortune, a widespread religion and a meaningful opinion." [96]

Khadija married at the age of twenty-eight.[97] She was the best example of a free, honorable woman who has no interest in money and fame. Therefore, she refused to marry the great and rich of Quraysh, who frequently requested her betrothal. Khadija offered herself to a poor man who had no money, because for her only the virtuous morals and exemplary qualities, which are incomparable among the young men of Quraysh, were important in that goal.[98] When Muhammad married her, the women of Quraysh became angry with her. They left her and said to her, "The nobles of Quraysh and their great ones betrothed themselves to you, but you did not marry any of them. Now you have married Muhammad, an orphan of Abu Talib who has no money. "[99]

Khadija was not the only one who admired the morals and qualities of Muhammad, rather he was known in Mecca for his honesty, trustworthiness, intellect and wisdom, making him a true role model for the goodness of morality in pre-Islamic society. [100]

Khadija provided her husband with every comfort and Muhammad felt happy and comfortable with her. He had a righteous wife, a home to live in and enough money for both of them. He was a contented man who did not seek the pleasures of the world and had no desire for luxury. However, one event clouded his happiness and affected him and Khadija greatly: the death of their first-born son Al-Qasim and then the death of their other son Abdullah. They were the first two children the Prophet had by Khadija. Given the importance of children in Arab culture, we can imagine the extent of Muhammad and Khadija's grief over these events and their dismay. [101]

After his marriage, Muhammad withdrew to reflect on the creation of the heavens and the earth, on the Creator and on the conditions of his people. This reflection prevailed and urged him to withdraw from people and to distance himself from them outside Mecca in order to devote himself entirely to reflection in this solitude, far from disturbances and harassment. This solitude became very dear to him. So he withdrew to the cave, as his grandfather Abd al-Muttalib had done before him. [102]

Even before his prophecy, Muhammad felt that he had a message and a duty to his people and that he had a different opinion from his people on many matters. The older he grew, the stronger this feeling and his conviction of this message and the need to guide and advise his people became. This feeling drove him to withdraw and isolate himself from the people, to turn away from the worship of idols and not to take part in his people's celebrations of their festivals, as they were associated with paganism. [103]

Birth of Ali bin Abi Talib

On the thirteenth day of Rajab, twenty-three years before the Hijrah, the son of Abu Talib, the uncle of Muhammad bin Abdullah, was born in the hollow of the Kaaba, and he was named Ali. His birth was a strange event, as no one had ever been born in this place of worship before. Muhammad bin Abdullah rejoiced over this child, looked optimistically at this year and regarded it as a year of good and blessing. [104]

After a not too long time, Muhammad said to his uncle Abu Talib, "I want you to give me one of your children to help and support me. I thank you in advance." Abu Talib replied: "Take whoever you want." So Ali ibn Abi Talib was brought to Muhammad as a small child, where he grew up in his house and was looked after by him. Abu Talib's wife Fatima bint Asad looked after Muhammad like a mother and Khadija bint Khuwaylid was also like a mother to Ali. Ali grew up in Muhammad's house and was cared for and educated by him. This gave him an honor that no one else attained. He was inspired by his teacher in the fields of morality, spiritual and intellectual education. [105].

The renovation of the Kaaba

In the eighteenth year before the Hijrah, the Quraysh began the renovation of the Kaaba building, an event of great importance to the people of Mecca. Therefore, all the tribes of Mecca took part in the construction in order to gain the honor of participation and thus boast among the Arabs. When the construction reached the site of the Black Stone[1] , disputes arose. Each tribe wanted the honor of placing it in its place. They had almost come to fighting with each other when the Banu of Abd al-Dar and the Banu Uday came with a They dipped their hands into it, together with the Banu Sahm and the Banu

---

1   Black Stone: a cult stone at the Kaaba in Mecca.

Makhzum, and swore a pact in which they pledged themselves to death. They called this pact "Liqat al-Dam" (The Blood Covenant). Then Abu Umayyah bin Al-Mughirah, one of the nobles of Quraysh, suggested that they resolve the dispute by appointing the first person to come to them through the Gate of Peace as arbitrator. Muhammad was the first to come to them. When they saw him, they said: "This is the honest and trustworthy one, we are satisfied. This is Muhammad." When they told him about the matter, he asked for a piece of clothing and spread it out. He then took the black stone, placed it on top and said: "Each tribe should take one side of the garment and then all of them should lift it together." So they carried the black stone on the cloth together and took it to the Kaaba. When they were near the Kaaba, the Prophet took the black stone with his hands and put it back in its position. Thus the problem was solved and the people were satisfied with this wise solution.

Figure 8: An imaginary depiction of Muhammad, as he contemplates in the desert.

What has been said so far indicates that the people of Mecca were still acting according to tribal logic even in their cooperation in building the Kaaba and placing the sacred stone in its place, which is the holiest of their sanctuaries and the symbol of their honor, glory and dignity. The "blood covenant" pact made when it came to who would lift the stone into place can be seen as the culmination of this issue, which is rejected by common sense. [106]

In his youth, Muhammad was drawn out into the desert, climbing mountains to contemplate creation and ponder the wisdom of existence. He prayed to God and purified his soul in the Hanifite way. Every year, he would retreat for a month to a cave in Mount Hira, about five kilometers from Mecca. There he prayed far away from people, talking to God day and night in this solitude.[107] He thought about the state of his people, their situation, their closeness to the idols, about the universe and life, the fate of man and death and what comes after death. He pondered all these things that revolve the head of a thoughtful person in this life, and directed him to ponder them and to keep him from pondering the pleasures of life that man usually falls in love with at this age. But Muhammad did not give in and did not weaken, but thought more and more about the state of the world the older he got. The accounts of his seclusion in the cave, his seclusion from people and his refusal to spend his time in the company of his peers and spend his time on trivialities and games, as people used to do at that time and in any society where there is leisure, are evidence of this phase that Muhammad went through. It was a phase in which he was confused and thoughtful, trying to reach something that would convince and reassure him, that would solve all these questions and thoughts that had accumulated in his mind and were assailing him. The best way to describe this restless phase of reflection and contemplation that Muhammad went through is the apt and concise description in Surah Ad-Duha: {And he found you astray and guided [you] rightly. } It is a deep restlessness that had gripped the Prophet's heart before the revelation, a restlessness that caused him to lie awake nights, especially towards the end, thinking about these problems and the conditions of his people and their situation. He was not satisfied with these conditions, he saw them as misleading, ignorance and folly and felt that he had to draw his people's attention to them and show them their depravity. But how and by what means? What are the ways to reform and their causes, and what methods are necessary to raise the level of the people from ignorance and misguidance to guidance and the straight path. [108].

608 - 609 AD

The thirteenth year before the Hijrah

The Beginning Of Prophet's Mission

On the twenty-seventh day of the month of Rajab, forty years after the year of the elephant, in the thirteenth year before the Hijrah, while Muhammad was in the cave of Hira in worship, the angel Gabriel appeared to him for the first time and spoke to him. Muhammad had previously heard a voice without seeing the person. Gabriel announced to him the good news that he had been chosen as the prophet of this community and that the first verses of the Noble Quran had been revealed to him by Allah.[109]

Figure 9: An imaginary depiction of Muhammad praying in the cave.

The first verses were: In the name of Allah, the All-Merciful, the Compassionate ❴Read in the Name of your Lord who created; created man from a clinging mass. Read, and your Lord is the most generous, who taught by the pen, taught man what he did not know.❵ [110]

This was the first thing that descended on the heart of Muhammad, and it commanded him to begin by reading the name of Allah and saying "In the name of Allah" at the beginning of his reading of each surah. Read in the name of your Lord, who created creation and provides for its order. He created man as a favor, and the beginning of his creation was from a "Al-Alaqah" (lump of blood)[1] clinging to the wall of the womb. Then it began to develop and complete itself until man came into existence and ascended to become a man. So read, Muhammad, for by the generosity of Allah, who is the Most Generous of the Generous, He has bestowed upon you this gift and made you a reader. This is a great mercy, for it is He who has taught man to write with the pen. With the pen, civilizations, information, ideas and libraries are recorded and through the pen is transmitted what narrators and historians cannot transmit, and human heritage remains protected from destruction and is passed on from generation to generation. Man knows nothing, but Allah has given him hearing, sight and hearts through which he acquires knowledge, and so he became a scholar after his ignorance.

The Prophet Muhammad received the words of his Lord with a calm heart, without terror or fear, knowing that what was revealed to him came from God. The revelation is the word of God that was sent down to Muhammad, and it is the Quran that Muhammad learned from Gabriel. It is therefore the book of God. Likewise, the Jews believe that revelation is the word of Jehovah revealed to his prophets, and their scriptures are the books of Jehovah. [111]

After this experience, Prophet Muhammad returned to his family filled with joy and the certainty that he had seen something great.[112] When he came to Khadija, he said: "Do you remember what I told you. that I saw Gabriel in a dream. Today Gabriel showed himself to me. God sent him to me," he said. Muhammad told her what had been brought to him on God's behalf. He was satisfied with the task that had been entrusted to him, satisfied with what God had honored him with and made him a prophet of this nation.[113] Khadija and Ali ibn Abi Talib believed in his prophethood and became Muslims. Ali was ten or twelve years old at the time. They were the first people to believe in him. [114]

Muhammad was known among his people, his clan and his peers for his morality, straightforwardness and religiosity based on Hanifism. Everyone knew his religious inclinations, which he cultivated and developed through long periods of contemplation in the cave until, after many years of prayer and devotion to his Lord, he was chosen by his Lord to carry his religion, just as he had chosen Moses and Jesus before him to carry the messages of heaven. What Muhammad brought was a great change for mankind, after the revelation had

---

1   "Al-Alaqah" is referred to in embryology as "blastocyst". It is the fertilized egg cell that is surrounded by a shell and has arisen through fertilization with a sperm cell.

been interrupted for more than 500 years, he brought the good news to the people and called them to believe in and submit to their Lord, Allah, in whom a part of them already believed and prayed to him and approached him in their prayers. He also brought a warning to the other part of the people who worshiped gods other than Allah. He called on them all to submit to the new faith, the Islam, and to recognize it. [115]

Figure 10: The Cave of Hira. This is the cave where Muhammad retreated before his call and the revelation of the Quran through the angel Gabriel. The Cave of Hira is located east of Mecca on the mountain of An-Nur, at an altitude of 634 meters. (The image has been digitally edited.)

When the Prophet was called, he was not yet called upon to proclaim the new religion to the general public. Instead, he initially presented this religion only in secret. Gradually, people began to accept Islam. Among the first to embrace Islam were: Zaid ibn Haritha, Khaled ibn Said ibn Al-As, Saad ibn Abi Waqqas, Amr ibn Abasa, Utba ibn Ghazwan, Musab ibn Umair and Al-Arqam ibn Abi Al-Arqam. Ja'far ibn Abi Talib, Bilal, Khabbab ibn Al-Aratt and Al-Zubair bin Al-Awam were also among the first Muslims. [116]

Ali bin Abi Talib was walking through the Sacred Mosque and saw a strange man lying on one side of the Sacred Mosque. He asked him his name. The man told him that he was Abu Dhar of the Ghaffar tribe and Ali then hosted him for three days. Abu Dhar asked him about the Prophet Muhammad, and Ali brought him secretly; there he ordered Abu Dhar to follow him inconspicuously. So it was that he met the Prophet and embraced Islam as his religion. He then went to the sons of his tribe to invite them to Islam, whereupon half of them embraced Islam. [117]

After the increase in the number of Muslims, the people of Mecca became aware of the Prophet Muhammad's call, his message and those who believed in him. Thus, some of the Quraysh began to monitor the Muslims and deliberately harm them, especially when they went out to pray among the mountains and valleys. When the Prophet realized the seriousness of the situation, he feared that there would be clashes with the Quraysh. Therefore, he chose the house of al-Arqam as the center for his Islamic call, which is located on the hill of Al-Saffa, so that his companions could meet with him and keep away from the sight of the Quraysh in their worship and rituals. This method was necessary at that time to preserve the future of the call so that it would not be exposed to armed action that would destroy the Islamic movement in its infancy. It was necessary to find a group of believers, from different tribes, who would carry and defend this doctrine. The said house was henceforth the center of his movement and activities. This phase lasted for three years until the number of Muslims reached forty men. After that, the Prophet began to proclaim his message to all people and a new phase of the mission began. It was the most difficult and dangerous phase in Mecca. [118] .

The beginning of the call

The revelation of the verses to the Prophet continued with further divine revelation, and the Prophet informed those who believed in the words of God to pray with them. Finally, God gave the command to his prophet: {And warn, [O Muhammad], your closest kindred.} [119] to urge him to invite his kin and relatives to Islam. Prophet Muhammad called Ali bin Abi Talib and ordered him to prepare food and invite Banu Abdul Muttalib to talk to them and inform them of this call. Ali prepared a leg of sheep and filled a bowl with yogurt, then invited them. They were forty men that day, among them were the Prophet's uncles: Abu Talib, Hamza, Al-Abbas and Abu Lahab. When they arrived, they began to eat. Ali said: "The people ate until they were full. I couldn't see anything except their hands over their plates. I swear by God, in whose hand is my soul, I saw that each of them was very hungry and yet the food was enough for all of them." Then the Prophet Muhammad said: "Give the guests drinks." Ali brought them a bowl and they drank from it until they were no longer thirsty. When Prophet Muhammad wanted to speak to them, his uncle Abu Lahab said to him, "These are your uncles and cousins, so speak and leave those who have left the religion. and know that your people have no strength against the Arabs. And I have the right to take you. Hold fast to your fathers. And if you stick to what you are, it is easier for them than for the tribes of Quraysh to rise up against you and the Arabs to support them. "[120] Abu Lahab ended his speech with a sharp rebuke to the Prophet, saying, "I have not seen anyone who came to his fathers with worse news than you."

The Prophet remained silent and decided to miss the opportunity for a confrontation with his uncle and did not enter into a discussion with Abu Lahab and did not speak in that gathering, preferring to postpone the conversation until a later time when he himself would speak. On the second day, the Prophet ordered Muhammad Ali bin Abi Talib to do what he had done the first time. After they had eaten and drunk, Prophet Muhammad said to them, "O Banu Abdul Muttalib, I am a warner to you from Allah, and I have brought you something that no one from the Arabs has brought before. If you obey me, you will be rightly guided, prosperous and successful. Allah has commanded me to set this table for you, so I have done so, as Jesus, son of Mary, did for his people. Whoever of you will disbelieve after this, God will chastise him with a severe punishment, who has not punished any of the worlds. Fear God and listen to what I say to you, and know, O sons of Abd Al-Mutalib, that God has not sent a prophet without appointing a brother, a trustee and an heir from his family. He has named me a trustee, as he did for the prophets before me, and he has instructed me to inform you and ask if you are interested in being my trustee. I invite you and reveal it to you so that you will not argue later, since I have appointed someone myself. You are my followers, the purest of my clan. Which of you will be the first to agree to join me in brotherhood with God and support me in this matter and become my brother, trustee and successor among you?"

The participants all held back from it but Ali said: "O Prophet of God, I will be your successor." The Prophet then grabbed Ali by the back of the neck and said: "This is my brother, my successor and my confidant among you. So listen to him and obey him. " The people stood up laughing and said to Abu Talib, "He has ordered you to listen to your son and obey him." Then Abu Lahab said to them, "Your son bewitched you long ago." When Abu Talib saw Abu Lahab's attitude and how he tried to thwart the meeting and end it inconclusively, he turned to him and said: "O shame. I swear by God that we will support him and help him in this." Then he turned to Muhammad and said: "My nephew, if you want to call in the name of God, let us know so that we can help you with weapons.

Although Ali was very young, he was still great in his virtues and abilities, great in spirit and great in his soul and ambitions. The proof of this is that he was the one who responded to the Prophet Muhammad and was the one who wanted to support and help him in this matter. The Prophet came out of this meeting with a successor, Ali Ibn Abi Talib , and additionally with a sure promise of help and support from Sheikh Mecca's Abu Talib. [121]

After the Messenger warned his closest relatives and the news of his prophethood was spread in Mecca, the Quraysh began to realize the seriousness of this problem for them and its dimensions, and began to subject the Prophet to ridicule, harassment and all kinds of accusations. Then Allah revealed to him the Qur'anic verse to command him to announce his call: {So proclaim aloud what you are commanded and turn away from the idolaters. We are sufficient for you (as protection) from the mockers} [122] The Prophet fulfilled the command of God and revealed his call and urged all people to submit to their Lord and become Muslims. One of the converts was Abu Bakr bin Abi Quhafa, one of the important personalities in Mecca. [123]

The Prophet stood on a stone and said: "O Quraysh, O Arabs, I invite you to testify that there is no god but Allah and that I am the Messenger of God. God has commanded you to discard your idols." Their reaction was no different from that of their rulers. They mocked him and said that Muhammad bin Abdullah had gone mad. But they did not challenge him because of Abu Talib's position. [124]

"Then they planned to question him about what he claimed and discuss with him. Utbah ibn Rabi'a, Sheiba ibn Rabi'a, Abu Sufyan bin Harb, Al-Nadr ibn al-Harith, Al-Walid ibn Al-Mughirah and Abu Jahl bin Hisham and other leaders of Quraysh met after sunset at the Kaaba. Then some of them said to each other, 'Send someone to Muhammad, talk to him and argue with him so that you can make an excuse to him so that you will not be held responsible for what happens between you and him.' They then sent to him, 'The nobles of your people have gathered to speak to you, come to them,' they said. The Messenger of Allah came to them quickly because he thought that they had a new opinion about what he had told them. He was very concerned about them and loved their guidance and was sorry that they were so stubborn. When he sat down with them, they said: 'O Muhammad, we have sent to you to speak with you. By Allah, we know of no man among the Arabs who has done to his people what you have done to yours. You have insulted the fathers, despised the religion, insulted the gods, despised the dreams and divided the community. There is no uglier thing than what you have done between us and you. If you seek money with this speech, we will collect you from our money until you have more money than us. And if you seek honor from us with this, we will set you above us. And if you want to be king with it, we will make you king over us. And if what comes to you is an effect of demons, then perhaps it is worth the money we will spend on you to seek a physician for you so that we can cure you of it.'

The Messenger of Allah said to them, 'What you say is not with me. I have not come with what I have brought you to seek your money or to seek honor from you or to be king over you. But Allah has sent me to you as a messenger and revealed to me a Book and appointed me to be a herald of good tidings and a warner to you. I have conveyed to you the messages of my Lord and advised you. If you accept from me what I have brought you, then that is your gain in this world and in the hereafter. And if you reject it, I will wait patiently for Allah's command until Allah judges between me and you.'

They said: 'O Muhammad, If you do not accept anything of what we have offered you, then you know that no one among the people is narrower in land or has less water or is harder in life than we are. So ask your Lord, who sent you with what he sent you, to remove from us these mountains that have constricted us, and to spread out our land and make rivers burst forth in it like the rivers of Sham and Iraq. And send us from those who have gone from our fathers, and let Qusay ibn Kilab be among those whom he sends to us, for he was a true sheikh. So we ask them about what you say, whether it is true or false. If they believe you and you do what we have asked you, we will believe you and recognize your position with Allah that He has sent you as a messenger, as you say.' .

He said to them, 'I was not sent to you for this.' They said: 'Then ask your Lord to send an angel with you to confirm you in what you say and to keep us from you, and ask him to make for you gardens, palaces and treasures of gold and silver that will make you rich from what we see. For you stand in the markets as we stand and seek livelihood as we seek it, until we recognize your merits and your position with your Lord, if you are a Messenger as you claim.' The Messenger of Allah said to them, 'I will not do that, and I am not the one who asks his Lord for it, and I have not been sent to you with it. But Allah has sent me as a herald of good tidings and a warner.

They said: 'Then let the sky fall on us like a roof, as you claim that your Lord will do if He wills. For we will not believe you until you do so. The Messenger of Allah said to them, 'That is up to Allah. If He wants to do this to you, He will do it.' They said: 'O Muhammad, Did not your Lord know that we will sit with you and ask you what we have asked you and demand from you what we have demanded, so he will precede you and tell you what we will discuss with you and tell you what he will do to us with it if we do not accept from you what you have brought to us.' One of them said: 'We will never believe you until you bring us God and the angels.'

When they said this to Prophet Muhammad, he got up and left. Abdullah ibn Abi Umayyah ibn Mughirah, his cousin, also got up and followed him and said: 'O Muhammad, your people offered you what they offered you, but you did not accept it from them. Then they asked you to do something for them so that they could recognize your position with God - as you say - and believe you and follow you. But you didn't do it. Then they asked you to do something for yourself so that they could recognize your merits over them and your position with God. But you did not do it. Then they asked you to bring them some of the things you threatened them with punishment for, but you didn't do it. By God, I will never believe you until you take a ladder to heaven, climb it and I watch you until you get there. And then you bring with you a contract by which four angels testify that you are as you say.'

Then he turned away from Prophet Muhammad, and Prophet Muhammad returned to his family, sad because he had seen what his people had done when they invited him." [125]

They did not believe in what Prophet Muhammad brought because they wanted the miracles they demanded of him in order to believe in him. They also rejected the idea that God had sent them a man like themselves to call them without supernatural powers or accompanying angels. The Prophet could only tell them that he was unable to deliver what they requested and that he was only a messenger delivering the message from heaven. [126]

Uqbah bin Abi Muait, one of the prominent figures in Mecca, did not hesitate to harass the Prophet. When a group of Quraysh observed the Messenger of Allah praying and bowing for a long time, Abu Jahl - a leader of Quraysh said: "Who among you goes to the entrails of a certain animal slaughtered at the bottom of Mecca, brings its filth and throws it on Muhammad." Uqbah bin Abi Muait went and did just that while the Prophet was in prostration. The Prophet got up from his prayer in a pitiable state and told his uncle Abu Talib what had happened. Abu Talib became angry, drew his sword and gathered a group of Banu Hashim. He went to the leaders of Quraysh who were sitting around the Kaaba. When they saw his evil intentions in his eyes, they wanted to leave, but he called out to them threateningly: "By Allah, if a man stands up, I will strike him down with my sword." They remained seated until he approached them. Then he ordered his servant to throw the dirt on their faces in retaliation for what they had done to Muhammad. [127]

Figure 11: An imaginary depiction of the polytheists watching Muhammad while praying.

The Prophet was not safe from the evil of Ibn Abi Muait and his companions even when he was in his house. They threw the filth and entrails of slaughtered animals on his house. The Prophet described them as the worst of neighbors and patiently endured their mistreatment.[128] It was also the custom of Uqbah bin Abi Muait to prepare a meal after a journey and invite the nobles of his people to join him. One day, when he returned from a journey, he went to invite them and came to a group in which the Prophet was. He invited them and him to his meal. The Messenger of Allah said: "I will not get up until you testify that there is no god but Allah and that I am the Messenger of Allah." Uqbah did so, and the Prophet stood up with him. Ubayy ibn Khalaf, one of the leaders of Quraysh and a close friend of Uqba, heard about this and said to him, "Did you say that, Uqbah?" He replied, "No, by Allah, but I was ashamed not to invite him, and if I invite him that he does not eat from my food, so I said something that I did not believe." Ubayy said to him, "I will not speak to you until you reject him and spit in his face." Uqbah went to Muhammad and did just that with all audacity and proclaimed his apostasy from Islam. The Prophet only wiped his face from the saliva, then turned to Uqbah and said: "If I find you outside the mountains of Mecca, I will behead you. "[129] Allah says about him in the Quran that a day will come when this disbeliever will repent the most and regret his deviant position when he was given the opportunity to be on the side of truth. On that day, he will say, "If only I had taken the path of guidance with the Prophet." [130]

Al-Nadr bin Al-Harith, cousin of the Prophet, followed a different method in fighting him because of his hostility towards Islam. He was one of Mecca's successful merchants and earned a lot of money on his travels. He met Jewish and Christian scholars, listened to the stories of the Romans and Persians and learned about religions and historical stories. When the call of the Prophet Muhammad began, he denied it and began to make fun of him. Every time the Messenger preached the message and recited God's words to the people, Al-Nadr sat down afterward and told the story of Rostam and Esfandiyar[1] and the stories and tales of the kings of Iran. When he heard the Prophet reciting the Quran to the people, he said: "We have heard it, if we wanted to, we could say something similar. His narrations are nothing but legends of the ancients, which he copied from their books, just as I have copied them. "[131] He then asked the Prophet, "Are you the one who claims that you will defeat the Quraysh shortly and that God has revealed this to you?" "Yes, and you are one of them," said the Prophet.[132] On this occasion, the Qur'anic verse was revealed to rebuke Al-Nadr and his like, asking, "Have they not looked into the world of the Kingdom, the world of the heavens and the earth, with all its amazing precision and order? They were not created without reason, but for high aims and purposes. Then the verse points out to people that things are not as they imag-

---

1 Esfandiyar was a legendary Iranian hero. Rostam is the most famous legendary hero of Persian mythology from the "Book of Kings" (Shāhnāme).

ine. Their lives are not eternal and opportunities pass like clouds. No one knows whether he will live until tomorrow or not, and if they do not believe in this Quran, with all the clear evidence it contains, then what book do they expect that is better than the Quran to believe in. [133]

When the Prophet stood on Al-Saffa, he called out to the Quraysh. They gathered because of him, and he said to them, "What if I were to tell you that the knights will attack you in the valley of this mountain, would you believe me?" They said: "Yes, you are trustworthy, and we have never heard a lie from you." He said: "I warn you of severe torment. O Banu Abd al-Muttalib, O Banu Abd Manaf..." He went on to enumerate all the tribes of Mecca and their branches, then he said: "God has commanded me to warn you of His punishment and that I have no benefit for you in this world or a share in the Hereafter unless you say, 'there is no god but Allah'" Abu Lahab stood up and shouted at him, "Get lost, that is why you have gathered the people. " This time Allah was not silent about the disrespect to His Prophet on the part of the Prophet's uncle, Abu Lahab, and his wife Umm Jamil, who persecuted the Prophet in the ways and harmed him. Allah promised them loss in this world and fire in the Hereafter.[134] Then the people left him and spoke about him. His people did not believe him, not because of him, but because of the ideas he proclaimed to them, of which they knew nothing. He was regarded like the other prophets who were denied by their people. [135].

611 - 612 AD

The tenth year before the Hijrah

The night journey[1]

In the month of Ramadan, in the tenth year before the migration, after the Prophet prayed at night in the Sacred Mosque,[136] the angels Gabriel, Michael and Israfil brought an animal from Paradise called Al-Buraq to the Messenger of God. Al-Buraq is a horse-like creature that speaks, hears and understands. God created it for his messenger.

Then they told the Messenger of God that God would take him on a journey to show him the kingdom of heaven and earth. Then they put him on Al-Buraq, one held the bridle, the other the stirrup and the last of the three angels put him on.[137] Then Al-Buraq shied away. Gabriel then said to him, "Stay calm, O Buraq, for no one rides you more honorably for God than he. "[138] And it calmed down, finally flew off and lifted him up into the air. With him was Gabriel, who showed him the signs of heaven and earth.

Figure 12: The boundaries of the Al-Aqsa Mosque.

---

1   The night journey (Al-Isra and Al-Mi'raj): "Al-Isra" means the nocturnal journey. "Al-Mi'raj" refers to the elevator or ladder. It idiomatically denotes the journey of Al-Isra and Al-Mi'raj of the Prophet Muhammad.

The Prophet was taken on a nocturnal journey, and Al-Buraq passed a caravan in the darkness of the night. The caravan ran startled by the flapping of Al-Buraq's wings.[139] Then they reached Mount Sinai and Bethlehem, until they subsequently reached Jerusalem. There he entered the mosque and looked at the Prophet's prayer niche[1] and prayed there. Then he ascended to heaven with his spirit and body together with Gabriel, and he saw the angels and the prophets greeting and celebrating him. He ascended until he reached the seventh heaven. Then he entered the Ma'mour House and prayed two rak'ahs in it. He then entered Paradise, ate from its fruits, drank from its rivers and saw its houses, the houses of his family and the Tree of Toba. He continued until he reached the tree of Sidra al-Muntaha, a place that no one can reach. The width of this tree is like a journey of a hundred years and every leaf from this tree can cover the people of the world. [140]

Figure 13: An imaginative depiction of Muhammad during his ascension.

He saw Gabriel there for the second time in his true image, and this vision was one of the great signs of God, for the creation of Gabriel is great. He is one of the spiritual ones whose creation and character can only be understood by God, the Lord of the worlds. [141]

The Messenger of God walked on in this great place, but Gabriel left him and could not go with him. The Messenger of God said: "O Gabriel, in such a place you abandon me.

Gabriel said: "O Muhammad, this is my limit, which God has imposed on me, and I am not able to pass it.[142] Go ahead, O Messenger of God, it is not for

---

1   Prayer niche: also Mihrab, a place where one prays.

me to pass this place, and if I were to go a little closer, I would burn. [143] Go ahead, by God, you have achieved something that no creature before you has achieved. "[144] If the Prophet's soul had not been from this place, he would not have been able to reach it. He was from God, two arc lengths or less away. But Gabriel did not have all of that what the Messenger of God had, because he had neither his knowledge nor his position. Rather, he felt honored to serve him, to benefit from his knowledge and to gain prestige and fame through him.

Then the Messenger of God approached the sacred sheaths of light, he saw the kingdom of heaven and the light of God, there was a barrier between him and God. He saw his Lord with his heart. What he saw was one of the great signs of God.[145] There God said to him: "The Messenger believed in what was revealed to him from his Lord." The Prophet said: "I answer in my name and the name of my nation: and the believers, everyone believes in God, his angels and his books and his messengers. We make no distinction between his messengers, and they said: we have heard and obey." God said: "God does not burden a soul beyond its limits. " Muhammad said: "Our Lord, do not blame us if we forget something or make a mistake." And God replied: "I will not blame you." The Prophet said: "Our Lord, do not burden us as you imposed on those before us." God said: "I will not burden you." He said: "Our Lord, do not burden us with what we cannot bear, forgive us and have mercy on us. You are our Master, so grant us victory over the disbelieving people." [146] Allah replied, "I have made this possible for you and your people. „

Then Allah commanded him to approach al-Saad, a spring that erupts from one of the pillars of the Throne, to perform ablution (wudu), and the Messenger of God prayed two rak'ahs[1] to his Lord.[147] God taught his Messenger verses in prayer, and God's Messenger learns and responds. When he prostrated, he prostrated himself once, and when he raised his head, he remembered the majesty of his Lord and prostrated again. The Messenger of God prostrated again, not because of a command from his Lord, but of his own accord. So it became two prostrations, therefore God made two prostrations (sujud) obligatory.124 After the Prophet spoke with his Lord, he was taken back to the Ma'mour House in the seventh heaven. When the time for prayer came, the prophets and angels were gathered for him, and God commanded Gabriel to announce the call to prayer. The Messenger of God, Muhammad , received the complete legislation of the call to prayer directly from Gabriel, which Gabriel in turn received from Allah. Then the Messenger of God stepped forward while

---

1   A Rak'ah is a unit of Islamic prayer.

the angels and prophets stood in rows behind the Messenger of God.[148] This was one of the signs that God showed Muhammad that he was brought to the Holy House and all the prophets and messengers gathered for him. [149]

Mr. Ja'far Al-Amili says: "The Prophet was indeed elevated in the heavens and reached these levels by what God granted him and qualified him for, by spiritual ascent, by exaltation in the reality of his being, and by deep knowledge of God, the Exalted."

Proximity to God does not mean that the Prophet is physically close to Allah, rather it is a spiritual proximity, as the Prophet reached this position that no creature has ever reached and will ever reach.

Through this journey, God wanted to honor His angels and the inhabitants of His heaven with Muhammad and show His Messenger the wonders of His greatness so that he would recount it after his descent. [150]

When the Messenger of God returned, he said to Gabriel, "O Gabriel, do you need anything?" He said: "Give my regards to Khadija." The Messenger of God gave his regards and she said: "God is peace, and from Him comes peace. Peace be upon him, and peace be upon Gabriel. "[151]

In the morning, the Messenger of God told the Quraysh about his journey and said: "God, His Majesty, brought me to Bait al-Maqdis and showed me prayer niches of the prophets and their houses." One of them said to him, "Do you claim that you traveled fifty days in one night? You are really a liar." Some Muslims who were weak in faith did not believe him when they heard about the journey of the Prophet's Al-Isra and Al-Mi'raj and left Islam because of it.[152] Abu Jahl[1] said: "Muhammad has given you the opportunity, ask him how many pillars and lanterns are in Bait Al-Maqdis." They said: "O Muhammad, here is someone who has entered Bait Al-Maqdis. Describe to us how many pillars, lanterns and niches there are." Gabriel then came and hung a picture of Bait Al-Maqdis in front of him, and the Prophet began to tell them what they wanted. He also told them about the camels that were coming and what they looked like. He also told them that a camel was lost from the caravan. The Prophet also told them that he drank water from the caravan and poured out the rest of the water. They said: "We will wait until the caravan comes and we will ask them about what you said." The Messenger of God said to them, "Proof of this

---

1   Abu Jahl: is Amr bin Hisham bin Al-Mughirah Al-Makhzoumi, he was a master of the Quraysh from the Kenana tribe

59

is that the caravan will appear with the rising of the sun with a red camel at the beginning." When the caravan came in the morning, they observed its arrival and said: "This is the rising of the sun." While they were waiting there, a camel came out at sunrise. At the head of the caravan was a red camel. They asked it what the Messenger of God told them and the caravan confirmed everything: "This camel has strayed to such and such a place towards us, and someone has poured out water." Quraysh still did not believe him, and that only increased their arrogance. [153].

Here Allah swears in Surah An-Najm that Muhammad made no mistake and that there is no deviation in his statements and actions. And that all accusations that accuse him of lying and madness are false. Allah confirms that what Muhammad says comes from Allah Himself and not from him, for what he says is nothing but a revelation revealed to him. He says nothing of his own accord, and the Quran is not the product of his own thinking. Everything he says comes from Allah, and the proof of this claim is in the verses of the Quran itself, and what he has seen are the great signs of Allah.[154]

The incident of Al-Isra and Al-Mi'raj is a great and eternal miracle with which mankind will forever be unable to keep pace and recognize its secrets. The aim of this cosmic view is for the Prophet to experience some manifestations of God's power and gain insight into some of the secrets of His sublime greatness throughout the universe. This fills his soul even more with evidence of the divine greatness and the signs of God in heaven and in the universe. His soul finds in these cosmic signs an additional impetus which it uses to lead man to God. In this way, man can sense the greatness of God, recognize his wonderful work and understand his immense power. This strengthens his self-confidence and his faith and gives him the certainty that his belief in God stands on a firm foundation. He understands that he has turned to a strong support who only wants the best for him, desires all good things, is capable of everything and embraces all beings. [155]

It is likely that the Prophet gradually informed the Muslims about the matter of Al-Isra and Al-Mi'raj according to the interests and requirements of the call to God. For they were not able to carry their meanings and visualize their events. Mentioning all their details and meanings might cause them to fall away from Islam, especially since the belief in this matter is based on their faith. The Messenger of God relied on persuasion based on tangible evidence to facilitate the acceptance of the Night Journey and not relying on faith alone. Therefore, he told them about the Night Journey for the first time, and when they were ready to know about this event, Surah An-Najm was revealed and he told them about ascending to heaven. [156]

After the event of Al-Isra and Al-Mi'raj, the Prophet continued his message in Mecca without finding any acceptance. His people adopted a hostile attitude towards him and his message. While the Messenger of God was in Mecca, he saw Othman bin Talha, the owner of the key to the Kaaba. The Messenger of God came to him and invited him to Islam. Othman replied, "O Muhammad, it is amazing that you are striving for me to follow you, and you have violated the religion of your people, and you have come with a new religion." The Messenger of God wanted to enter the Kaaba with the people. The Kaaba was normally opened to people two days a week. Othman prevented the Messenger of God from doing so, scolded him and insulted him. But the Messenger of God forgave him and did not get angry. Then he said: "O Othman, perhaps one day you will see this key in my hand, and I will put it where I want." Othman said: "The Quraysh would be destroyed and humiliated." The Messenger of God replied, "Rather, the Quraysh will live and be proud on that day. " [157]

Figure 14: A symbolic representation of Abu Talib, the uncle of Muhammad.

When the Quraysh saw the Prophet's unwavering will to spread his religion and belittle their gods, and they saw that his uncle Abu Talib supported him, defended him and stood up for him without handing him over to them, they tried to negotiate with Abu Talib. Men from the nobles of Quraysh went to Abu Talib and said to him, "Your nephew has insulted our gods, denigrated our religion, ridiculed our dreams and misled our children. Either you keep him away from us or you leave us alone with him. Since you are in the same opposition to him as we are, we will take care of him." Abu Talib answered them with gentle words and sent them away kindly. They went away from him. But they came back to Abu Talib again and complained to him. So Abu Talib sent to the Messenger of Allah and when he came, Abu Talib informed him of what they had brought and said to him, "What is the matter with your people that they are complaining against you?" The Messenger of Allah said: "I want them to say a single word by which the Arabs will become loyal to them and the non-Arabs will pay them the Jizya[1]." The Messenger of Allah promised them what their souls desired and aspired to. They said: "A word?!" He said: "Yes, by your father." Abu Talib said: "And what word is that, O son of my brother." He said: "There is no god but Allah." They stood up, shook out their clothes and said: "Does he make the gods one god. This is really something strange!" Then they went away. But they came back after a while when they saw that the Messenger of Allah continued to show his religion and call people to it, until things became difficult between them and him, and until the men became divided and tensions increased, and the Quraysh spoke about the Messenger of Allah more and more frequently. So they went to Abu Talib and said: "You have age and honor and position, and we wanted you to restrain your nephew, but he did not stop. And by Allah, we will not be patient with this insulting of our fathers and ridiculing of our dreams and desecration of our gods until you keep him away from us or we deal with him until one of the two parties perishes."

Then they left. Abu Talib sent to the Messenger of Allah and said to him, "O son of my brother, your people have come to me and told me: Either you keep him away from us or we will deal with him until one of the two parties perishes." Then the Messenger of Allah wept bitterly and said: "O uncle, by God, if they would put the sun in my right hand and the moon in my left hand so that I would desist from this matter, I will not desist from it until God either makes it victorious or I perish in it." [158] Abu Talib promised him victory and comforted his heart, then he began to recite a poem: [159]

"By God, they will not reach you,

Until I am buried in the depths of the earth.

---

1   Jizya: is a tax that is levied in Islamic law by non-Muslim citizens (Dhimmis; the Jews or Christians) in Muslim states. Dhimmis are people who live in an Islamic state and have not converted to Islam.

Proclaim your message, loud and clear,

No injustice will ever defeat you, that is true.

You called me and were my guide,

True and faithful, a true leader.

Your religion was the best of all,

I knew it and was captured by it.

If it were not for the fear of shame,

I would reveal the truth to you."

The Quraysh offered then Abu Talib to take one of them as his son and hand over the Prophet to them to kill him. Abu Talib said: "By God, this is the worst thing you could ever have offered me in exchange. You give me your son to feed him, and I give you my son to kill him, and that, by God, will never happen. " [160]

The truth of what they hid in their hearts and what their souls contained became obvious to Abu Talib and others. Their aim in doing so was to destroy the religion of Allah by all means, which only made Abu Talib more determined to defend that religion and its Prophet. Perhaps the secret behind the arrogance of the idolaters of Mecca and their attempt to destroy this religion is that they exploited these poor, slaves and weak people in Mecca and elsewhere for their interests. In addition, they gained unjust privileges that the Prophet rejected. Thus, they realized that they could not continue their immoral and inhuman practices under this religion. Moreover, they were afraid that the Arabs would reject them and would not be satisfied with them as they would have to give up the idols, which would make them lose their trade and affect their interests.

After the failed negotiations, it seemed to Abu Talib that the situation had become very critical and that he was on the verge of entering into open conflict with the Quraysh. Therefore, caution had to be exercised in this matter. He gathered Banu Hashim and Banu al-Muttalib and invited them to support and defend the messenger of Allah. They responded to him with the exception of Abu Lahab. The Quraysh could not harm him except that they accused him of madness, witchcraft and divination. They said that he was a poet writing the

Quran himself and not from Allah.[161] They also claimed that a Roman boy had heard the stories of the prophets and their messages and was teaching them to Muhammad, and that these verses were his invention which he had dictated to Muhammad. The Quran answers them that this Roman boy does not speak Arabic and that what Muhammad brought is in classical Arabic, so it is impossible that Muhammad learned it from him. They said also that he was suffering from mental and intellectual disorder and that these words and verses were the result of his mental imbalance. They watched him constantly and listened to the verses he delivered. When they saw a verse being abrogated or replaced by another, they said that Muhammad was a liar and a deceiver because he changed the verses at will. The Quran answers them again that Allah knows best which verses are revealed and that they do not understand the wisdom of changing verses.[162]

The Quraysh sensed that attacking the Prophet would cause an armed conflict for which they had not prepared, especially regarding the relations and alliances Banu Hashim had with other tribes and the war might even enable Muhammad to spread his call, the polytheists preferred to stay away from war and adopt a different method. They began to forbid people from meeting the Prophet on the one hand, and on the other hand they followed the method of mockery, contempt and false accusations against him with the aim of influencing Prophet Muhammad. Perhaps he will be psychologically defeated, or perhaps he will give up the whole thing, or those weak in faith will turn away from him and leave him. [163]

Every person in the Quraysh tribes who had converted to Islam and followed the religion of the Prophet was targeted by their own tribe. Their aim was to turn them away from Islam and force them to return to their tribe's religion. The tribes used brutal and inhumane methods, including murder, torture, imprisonment and starvation. Among those tortured were: Jariyah ibn Mu'mal, Khabbab ibn al-Aratt, Umm Shurik, Musab ibn Umair, Bilal the Ethiopian, 'Amir ibn Fuhayrah and others. However, they did not dare to harm the Prophet because he was under the protection of his uncle Abu Talib. [164]

The Muslims were an oppressed minority in Mecca and could not save their comrades. When Prophet Muhammad saw the harm the Quraysh leaders were doing to his companions, he decided to leave Mecca and seek a safe place for them. He said to his companions: "Get away from me. Whoever has strength should stay until the end of the night, and whoever has no strength should leave at the beginning of the night. When you hear from me that I have found a safe place, follow me." The next day, the idolaters arrested Bilal, Khabbab, Ammar and a slave woman from Quraysh named Sumayya, who had converted to Islam.

Under the leadership of Abu Jahl, the idolaters detained them and tortured them in the worst possible way. The polytheists ordered Bilal to renounce his faith, but he refused. They put an iron shield in the sun until it got hot and then put it on him. As soon as they put it on him, he said: "One god, one god." As for Khabbab, they pulled him through the thorns. Abu Jahl stuck four stakes in the ground and fixed the slave woman to them, stretched her and plunged a spear into her heart until he killed her. The Messenger of God passed by them while they were being brutally tortured, and he said: "Be patient, Yasir family, for your meeting place is Paradise. "[165] Under torture, Sumayya, the mother of Ammar ibn Yasir, was killed by Abu Jahl, making her the first female martyr in Islam. Then her husband Yasir, whom they had also detained, was also martyred. The Banu Makhzum tortured her son Ammar until they forced him to say what they wanted to hear about the Prophet, so they left him alone. Then they released Bilal, Khabab and Ammar and they joined the Messenger of God. The three of them told the Prophet what had happened. Ammar was very upset by what he had said and was very sad. He came to the Prophet weeping. When the Prophet saw him, he wiped the tears from his eyes and said to Ammar, "The unbelievers have taken you and immersed you in water." [166] Ammar replied, "They did not let me go, O Messenger of Allah, they forced me until I insulted you and praised their gods." The Prophet asked him, "How do you feel in your heart, Ammar?" He replied, "It is calmed by faith, O Messenger of Allah." The Prophet said: "Do not worry when they return to you, give them what they want. Allah has revealed concerning you: ⟨Except whoever is forced while his heart finds peace in faith.⟩[167] This means that Allah has forgiven him for rejecting Islam and supporting the disbelievers under the torture of the enemies, for it was only a movement of the tongue while his heart remains full of faith.

613 - 614 AD

The eighth year before the Hijrah

The birth of Fatima bint Muhammad

On the twentieth of Jumada al-Thani, in the eighth year before the Hijrah, Fatima was born to Muhammad from his wife Khadija in Mecca. She was also called Al-Zahraa. The Quraysh used to harass the Prophet because he had no offspring. Al-As ibn Wa'il, one of the Quraysh leaders, made fun of Muhammad and said to his people: "Leave him alone, for he is a man without descendants. When he dies, his memory will be wiped out." [168]

Here I wonder in amazement: no matter how low a person sinks in malice, baseness and aggression, it is inconceivable that he sinks so low as to mock others for something that is out of their hands and for which they bear no blame, such as offspring and children.

Joy filled the Prophet's house with this happy birth, and the Messenger of Allah loved his daughter Fatima very much. When she came to him, he would get up from his seat, kiss her on the forehead and put her in his seat. And when he came to her, she would receive him and each of them would kiss the other and would sit together. He said: "Fatima is a part of me, whoever upsets her upsets me." [169]

Migration to Abyssinia[1]

The Quraysh continued to torment those who embraced Islam and who had no clan to protect them. Continuing in this situation was intolerable and would reduce people's desire to convert to Islam as long as this conversion had no consequences other than terror, torture and great misfortune. It was necessary for Muslims to find a place of hope that would help them get rid of the misery and hardship. The Messenger of God decided that Muslims should migrate to Abyssinia. He said: "In Abyssinia is a king who oppresses no one, and it is the land of truth." He referred to the king of Abyssinia as a good neighbor.

---

1 Abyssinia: was a monarchy in East Africa on the territory of today's Ethiopia and Eritrea.

In Abyssinia, there lived a people who adhered to innate disposition (Al-Fi-trah[1]), valuing honesty and purity. The inhabitants of this region were more closely aligned with the remaining teachings of Jesus Christ than others, far removed from the deviations, misconceptions, and doubts prevalent in the lands of the Persians and Romans. This adherence to core principles enabled Muslim immigrants to live there peacefully, free from persecution. In addition, Abyssinia is geographically separated from the Hejaz by the sea, making it impossible for the Quraysh to reach the Muslims and persecute them without ships, which they don't have. The Muslims emigrated to Abyssinia under the leadership of Ja'far bin Abi Talib[2] . They went there secretly in groups, some on horseback and some on foot, until they reached the sea, where they found a ship and boarded it. [170]

The Messenger of God conveyed a letter to the king of Abyssinia in his name and in the name of his followers, saying: "In the name of Allah, the Most Gracious, the Merciful. From Muhammad, the Messenger of God, to Negus[3] Al-Asham, King of Abyssinia: Peace be upon you. I thank God, the King, the Holy One, the Faithful, and I testify that Jesus, son of Mary, is the Spirit of God. I bear witness that Mary, the good and chaste virgin, conceived Jesus through God's words and that God created Him from His Spirit, just as He created Adam with His hand. I invite you to God alone, who has no partner, to be faithful to His obedience, to follow me, to believe in me and in what has been revealed to me, for I am the Messenger of God. I have sent my cousin Ja'far to you and with him a group of Muslims. When they come to you, accept them and do not be prejudiced. I invite you and your soldiers to Allah. I have delivered my message and given advice, so accept it. And peace be upon those who follow the guidance." [171]

It was necessary for the Quraysh to make further attempts to bring back the Muslims in order to remain dominant and decide the fate of this new religion,

---

1 Al-Fitrah: are the original ideas and information that every person knows without the need for a teacher or educator, and it is the intuitive necessary science that every person participates in, because it is part of his humanity, and that Al-Fitrah drives people to perfection and refinement, while the instincts have no direction except securing the specific human need that his body needs.
2 Ja'far bin Abi Talib: He is the cousin of the Prophet and the brother of Ali bin Abi Talib.
3 Negus is in Old Ethiopian the title for a royal ruler. Al-Asham ibn Abjar could possibly have been Armah, who was King of Aksum in the late 6th and early 7th century AD. [493]

which they saw as a threat to their interests and existence. So the Quraysh conferred among themselves and decided to send two men to Abyssinia to bring back the immigrants. They chose Amr ibn al-Aas and 'Amra ibn al-Walid. They brought gifts to the king. They then set off on their journey until they reached the sea, but they could not find any of the Muslims. When they reached Abyssinia, they claimed the following before Negus: "Foolish youths among us have come to your country who have left their religion and have not joined your religion. They have come in the wake of a new religion that they have invented, which neither we nor you know. The nobles of their people, fathers, uncles and clans have sent us to you to bring them back.

The king refused to hand them over until he had questioned them about the truth of what Amr and 'Amra had reported. The Muslims came and the king of Abyssinia asked them about what the messengers of Quraysh had said. Ja'far replied:

Figure 15: An imaginary depiction of Ja'far bin Abi Talib in Abyssinia.

"O king, we were once a people in the time of ignorance (Jāhilīya). We worshipped idols, ate forbidden meat, committed abominable deeds, broke family ties and oppressed the weak. This is how we lived until Allah sent a prophet from among us. We know his lineage, honesty, trustworthiness and chastity. He has called us to worship Allah alone and to renounce what we and our ancestors worshipped besides Him - like stones and idols. He has commanded us to speak the truth, to fulfill the things entrusted to us, to cultivate family relationships, to be good neighbors, to avoid what is forbidden and to refrain from bloodshed. He has warned us against fornication, lying, consuming the wealth of orphans and slandering honorable women. He has commanded us to worship God alone and not to associate anything with Him. He has called us to prayer, almsgiving and fasting."

"Do you have anything with you that has come from God?" asked the Negus. Ja'far replied in the affirmative. Then he recited to the Negus from Surat Maryam from the Quran until he reached: {And mention, [O Muhammad], in the Book [the story of] Mary, when she withdrew from her family to a place toward the east. And she secluded herself from them. Then We sent to her Our Spirit, and he became incarnate for her as a well-proportioned man. She said, "I seek refuge in the Most Merciful from you, [so leave me], if you should be fearing of Allah." He said, "I am only the messenger of your Lord to give you [news of] a pure boy." She said, "How can I have a boy while no man has touched me and I have not been unchaste?" He said, 'So shall it be. Your Lord says, 'It is easy for Me, and We will make him a sign to the people and a mercy from Us. And it is a matter [already] decreed.' "} [172]

Figure 16: An imaginary depiction of Negus Al-Asham, the king of Abyssinia.

When the Negus listened to him, he wept and said: "This one and the one whom Jesus brought are from a single lantern 3. Go, and by God, I will not deliver them to you." When he said these words, he turned to Amr.

The Quraysh envoy did not give up, so Amr ibn al-Aas came the next day to inform the Negus that the Muslims were saying that Jesus, the son of Mary, was a human being. The Negus then called them to inquire about it. Ja'far said to him: "We say about him what our Prophet has proclaimed: He is the servant of God, his messenger, his spirit and his word, which he delivered to the Virgin

Mary. The Negus picked up a small stick from the ground and said: "By God, everything you said about Jesus, the son of Mary, is true, except something like this stick. Go, you are safe. Even if I were given a mountain of gold, I would not harm any of you." He then returned the gifts to the Quraysh, so it was clear that the Quraysh's attempts to recapture the Muslims and bring them back to Mecca had failed. [173] In fact, the migration of the Muslims to Abyssinia was a severe blow to the Quraysh, causing them to lose their minds and destabilizing their existence and unity. After a while, the presence of Muslims in Abyssinia caused some troubles for the Negus, as the people of his country accused him of having deviated from their religion and revolted against him. However, he was able to quell the revolution with his good knowledge and awareness. The Muslims saw what was happening to the Negus because of their presence, and so a group of them decided to return to Mecca in view of the spontaneous relative calm that returned after two or three months. The rest of the Muslims continued to stay with their good neighbor, the Negus. [174]

In 614 AD, news reached the Muslims of the Persian victory over the Romans in the Battle of Antioch. This time in Levante and Jerusalem. This saddened them, as the Romans were a people of the Book. God then revealed the good news in the Quran that the Romans would be victorious in a few years and that the believers would rejoice and that everything was in God's hands.[175].

614 - 615 AD

The seventh year before the Hijrah

Conversion of Hamza to Islam

In the seventh year before the migration, Hamza bin Abdul Muttalib, the uncle of the Prophet Muhammad, embraced Islam. His conversion to Islam was a new development that the Quraysh did not expect and turned their balance upside down. This development increased their fears and made them more restrained. Abu Jahl met the Messenger in al-Saffa. He insulted the Prophet and belittled his religion. The Messenger did not speak to him. When Hamza returned from hunting, he would usually begin by circumambulating the Kaaba, greeting those inside, and then return to his house. This time, when Hamza returned from his hunt, one of the women told him what Abu Jahl had done to the Prophet. Hamza became very angry, entered the holy mosque and saw Abu Jahl sitting with the people. So he approached him and struck him with his bow. The blow caused a significant wound on his forehead. Then he said to Abu Jahl, "How can you insult him while I believe in his religion and I say what he says? Hit me if you dare. "

Figure 17: An imaginary depiction of Hamza bin
Abdul Muttalib, the uncle of Muhammad.

Although Abu Jahl begged him and held his robe, Hamza did not accept it. Then men from Banu Makhzum stood up to help Abu Jahl and they said to

Hamza, "We see that you have converted." Hamza replied, "What is stopping me, I have realized that he is the Messenger of God and he is telling the truth. By God, I will not give up. Stop me if you dare." Abu Jahl said: "Leave Abu Ammarah (Hamza), because by God, I have cursed his nephew with a terrible curse." Then Hamza said to the Prophet: "My nephew, reveal your religion, because by God, I do not like that I have everything that is on earth and I still follow my first religion.

Hamza's conversion to Islam represented pride for the Muslims and happiness for the Messenger. When the Quraysh learned that the Messenger was strengthened by Hamza's conversion to Islam, they refrained from harming him for a while.

During this time, Omar Ibn Al-Khattab, one of the most important personalities in Mecca, also converted to Islam. Before his conversion to Islam, the Muslims suffered the most severe forms of torture and abuse at his hands. He even wanted to assassinate the Prophet. [176]

615 - 616 AD

The Sixth year before the Hijrah

The siege of the mountain pass(Sheib) of Abu Talib[1]

When the Quraysh saw the strength of the Prophet and his followers and the strength of his companions in Abyssinia, and when they saw Islam spreading among the tribes and realized that all their efforts to fight Islam had failed, they tried a new strategy. They imposed an economic and social embargo on the Hashemites and Abu Talib. Either they succumbed to their demands to hand Muhammad over to be killed, or he himself withdrew his call.

The elders of Mecca gathered in the Dar al-Nadwa[2] and wrote an agreement together: that they would not speak to the Banu Hashim, swear allegiance to them, marry them, enter their houses or trade or work with them until they sent Muhammad to them to kill him. They also swore that they would form an alliance against Muhammad to kill him secretly or publicly. [177]

Figure 18: An imaginary depiction of the meeting of
the polytheists of Quraysh in Dar al-Nadwa.

---

1 Tal (Scheib) of Abu Talib: It is an area or a valley in Mecca, which lies between Mount Abu Qubais and Mount Al-Khandama
2 Dar al-Nadwa: It was a place which leader of Mecca, Qusay bin Kilab, founded. He is the great-great-grandfather of the Prophet. The purpose of this house was to be a center for the consultations of the tribal leaders of Mecca in important matters.

They sealed a scroll with forty stamps. Each of the Quraysh chiefs sealed it with his seal and they hung it up in the Kaaba. The Prophet's uncle, Abu Lahab, supported them in what they had agreed upon. This happened in the sixth year before the Hijrah. Abu Talib gathered the Banu Hashim and sought refuge in Sheib (mountain pass) of Abu Talib. He swore to the Quraysh at the house and shrine: "If Muhammad were to be hit by even one thorn, I would take revenge and attack you." He placed guards in the mountain pass and guarded it day and night to protect the Prophet.

The Quraysh imposed a blockade on the Muslims in the mountain pass of Abu Talib so that no one could bring them food. The Muslims spent from the money of Khadija and Abu Talib until it was exhausted. They had no more money and their food had run out, so they were forced to feed themselves on tree leaves. Their children suffered from hunger. The pagans heard the weeping of the children behind the mountain pass. They talked about it among themselves, some were happy about it, while others were saddened by it.

Figure 19: An imaginary representation of the mountain pass of Abu Talib during the siege.

The Muslims did not dare to leave the mountain pass of Abu Talib except during the Umrah[1] season in Rajab and the Hajj season in Dhu al-Hijjah, where they shopped and traded under extremely difficult circumstances. The Quraysh met anyone who arrived in Mecca first and convinced them with exorbitant

---

1   Umrah is a small Islamic pilgrimage to Mecca as opposed to the major pilgrimage (Hajj).

amounts for their goods, provided that they did not sell anything to Muslims. Abu Lahab was their pioneer in this. He advised the merchants to charge horrendous prices so that the Muslims would not get anything from them. He guaranteed to compensate them with money if their trade was affected. The Quraysh threatened even anyone who sold anything to Muslims to plunder their money, and they warned anyone who came to Mecca not to deal with them. This ordeal lasted almost three years. During this time, Ali bin Abi Talib used to secretly bring them food from Mecca whenever possible. If they had caught him doing this, they would have killed him. Abu Talib often feared for the Prophet, especially when he was asleep. He guarded him day and night. When night came, he would stand over him with his sword while the Messenger of Allah slept. When the people went to bed, the Prophet would lie down on his bed so that everyone in the mountain pass of Abu Talib could see it. When the people were asleep, Abu Talib came and woke him up and put his son Ali in his place. Then he put the Prophet in another place so that no one would know where the Prophet was and could murder him in his sleep. One night Ali said to his father: "Father, I am going to be killed. "[178] Abu Talib recited his answer to him as a poem: [179]

Figure 20: An imaginary representation of the mountain pass of Abu Talib during the siege.

"Be patient, my son, for patience is wiser,

And every living person is destined to die.

This is God's fate, a severe test,

For the salvation of the beloved

and the son of the beloved."

Ali replied:"By God, it was not out of fear that I uttered these words,

But that you may see my help, my obedience remains without fear.

For the sake of God and Ahmad, the prophet of justice,

I will strive for victory, my heart always is ready."

In the fifth year before the Hijrah, when the Muslims were confined to the mountain pass of Abu Talib, the miracle of the splitting of the moon took place. This happened when a group of Quraysh asked the Messenger of God to show them a sign or a miracle, and they said: "If you are honest, split the moon in two for us." The Prophet replied, "If I do that, will you believe?" They said yes. He then prayed to God to split the moon and so the moon was split in two. The Messenger of God called them and asked them to witness it. After a while, the moon merged again. They said: "This is a continuous magic." [180]

God told them at that time and at the beginning of the Islamic call that the date of the Day of Resurrection is approaching because the appearance of Prophet Muhammad - who is the last of the prophets - is a sign that the Day of Resurrection is near. God also told them that the splitting of the moon is a sign of the approach of the Day of Resurrection. [181] But the polytheists did not deny it when they saw the splitting of the moon, but simply regarded it as a continuation of the series of magical acts - according to their understanding - which the Prophet presented to them as proof of his prophecy, and they did not see it as a miracle of God. They turned away from it out of stubbornness and intolerance and did not accept it.

618 - 619 AD

The third year before the Hijrah

End of the siege

After almost three years of the siege of the Muslims in the mountain pass of Abu Talib, the Prophet told his uncle Abu Talib that the termites ate everything written in the document of agreement on injustice, and nothing remained in it except the name of God. Abu Talib and the Banu Hashim left the mountain pass and went to the Quraysh. The Quraysh mocked and said: "Hunger drove them out," They said then: "O Abu Talib, it is up to you to reconcile your people." "I have brought you news. Send me your agreement so that there will be peace between you and us," he replied. When they brought the scroll, Abu Talib asked them: "Did you notice anything about it?" They denied any changes. He said: "This is what my nephew told me, and he never told me a lie: God has sent on this scroll the termites that has eaten all the injustice and left behind every name that belongs to God. If he is honest, you will end our oppression, and if he is a liar, we will hand him over to you." The people shouted, "Agreed, we agree with you, Abu Talib." The scroll was opened and taken out, and it was as the Prophet said. The Muslims then shouted, "God is great." The Quraysh were shocked and the color of their faces changed. Abu Talib said: "Now, do you know who the magician and the soothsayer are?" Many Meccans gathered to see this event. On that day, a group of people converted to Islam when they saw this.

The Quraysh leaders showed no mercy or humanity towards Muhammad and his followers. Instead, they declared war on them and cut off all lines of communication and reconciliation with them. Their aim was to wipe out Muhammad and his followers in the most brutal way. After three years of torment, the Prophet resorted to a kind of miracle to get in touch with these people again, in the hope that they would change their minds and accept the obvious truth of the Prophet Muhammad's sincerity. The case of the "termites" represented the hope of making an argument against them or to move the conscience of some of their followers among the people of Mecca to exert pressure on them to rescind this unjust agreement. But the Quraysh were not persuaded and continued to act according to the content of the agreement until a group of them recanted, all of whom were married to followers of Banu Hashem and Al-Muttalib. Abu Jahl wanted to continue to adhere to the agreement, but they did not heed his objection, so the paper was torn up and its effect nullified. The Hashemites then left the mountain pass of Abu Talib. [182]

After the Messenger of Allah left the mountain pass, he continued his efforts to spread his religion and fulfill his mission, while the Quraysh continued to put obstacles in his way. They tried to prevent people from gathering around him and listening to him in every possible way. Nevertheless, the Prophet remained patient and persistent, never tiring nor feeling bored. Despite all the efforts of the Quraysh, they did not succeed in achieving their goals of stopping him.

During this time, the first delegation from outside Mecca came to the Prophet. They were Christians from Abyssinia. The delegation consisted of twenty men, led by Ja'far bin Abi Talib, who came with him when he returned from Abyssinia. They found the Prophet in the Sacred Mosque, and talked to him and asked him questions, while men of the Quraysh listened. After the Messenger invited them to Islam, they embraced Islam. When they stood up, Abu Jahl protested against them and violently attacked them because of their belief in Islam and that they were abandoning their religion. They said: "Peace be upon you. We do not argue with you. We have what we believe in and you have your faith." With these words, they left the Sacred Mosque. This was a severe blow to the Quraysh, their goals and their plans. In particular, the fact that this delegation was led by Ja'far means that the Islamic call began to persuade people living in areas over which the Quraysh had no influence. [183]

Year of Sadness

In the third year before the Hijrah, the Prophet's uncle Abu Talib passed away. With his loss, the Prophet lost a strong, dear and loyal supporter who was his protector and defender of his religion and his message. The Prophet approached Abu Talib who was lying in bed, started wiping his forehead and he said: "O uncle, you have taken care of an orphan, raised a small child and supported an adult. May God reward you for this." The Prophet mourned for him greatly and wept. He ordered his son to wash him and then went to his funeral.

Only three days later, Khadija left this world at the age of fifty-six. She was the best and noblest of the Prophet's wives in terms of her character and behavior towards him. There is no doubt about the great contribution Abu Talib and Khadija made in the spread of this religion, and so the Prophet called the year of their death the year of mourning. The Prophet indicated this when he described the loss of Abu Talib and Khadija as a tragedy for the entire community, saying: "Two calamities have befallen this nation, and I do not know which one grieves me more deeply. "[184]

The Sheikh of Mecca, Abu Talib , was one of the most important pillars on which Islam was built. He knew from his ancestors that the prophecy brought by Muhammad ibn Abdullah was the prophecy of Abraham and Ishmael. It was passed down through the generations by the nobles of the Banu Hashim until it reached him. Thus, from the first hours of the birth of Islam, he became the refuge and support of this message and its leader, the Prophet Muhammad, amidst the heated and aggressive atmosphere of the Quraysh. With his wise policy and unique insight, he established the link between the polytheists of Mecca and the Messenger. He flattered them and pretended not to belong to the religion of the Prophet, although in reality he was a Muslim and supported this religion. He invested all his skills, children and money to support the Messenger of God until the last days of his life. He often confessed his loyalty to the Prophet and said in his poems: [185]

"By God's house, you speak lies when you say that Muhammad should give in while we defend him with sword and force of arms.

We remain faithful and support him, repelling all attacks with sword and shield.

We defend him until no one is left standing, sacrificing children and women until the enemy perishes.

Those who sink into hatred and rage fall at our blows and sink.

We swear by God that we will stand firm, and our swords clash with those who fight us.

We fight for months, year after year, without concession, ever vigilant, ever ready.

And a white man[1], with his face begging the people for rain. He is a refuge for the orphans and a shelter for the widows.

The estranged of the Banu Hashim flee to him and find the support they need in his favor.

By my life, I feel deep affection for Ahmad and his brothers, as is the way of an enduring lover.

For who is like him, who else is so much desired, even when he wrestles with kings, he is not defeated.

Forbearing, wise, just and exalted, he welcomes those who always live by faith.

God will elevate his status, in this world and in the hereafter.

So I have seen it, then and now, just as his grandfather spoke of him in his vision. " .

Journey to Taif

In the same year, Prophet Muhammad saw that the Islamic call was under severe pressure, threatening its spread. Therefore, a new step was needed to give the call a new impetus and make it more vibrant. The attempt was made in the neighboring cities, so the Prophet went to Taif[2] with Ali and Zaid bin Haritha. The people of Taif were economically and socially connected to the people of Mecca and its surroundings because they exported the fruits, which were the main part of their harvest, to Mecca and other surrounding regions. In addition, their idol named al-Lāt was the focus of the Arab caravans' visits due to his religious status.

---

1 Arabs do not mean the skin color when they say; a white man, because for them white stands for the spiritual purity of errors, innocence, and the generosity of morality. If they want to describe the color of white skin, they say red. Here it means; the Prophet Muhammad.
2 Taif: is located in the Hejaz, about 75 km from the city of Mecca, surrounded by mountains on all sides.

When the Messenger of Allah arrived in Taif, he spent several days there and spoke to each of the local dignitaries, but they did not believe him and feared for their children and their interests. They asked him to leave them and incited some people against him. They stood in his way and threw stones at him, while Ali defended him until he suffered a wound to his head. So he left them quickly but was determined to continue his mission and overcome the difficulties. He said to Ali: "God will surely find a way out of what you see and create an exit. God will support his Prophet and spread his religion. "[186]

Abbildung 21: Eine imaginäre Darstellung von zwei Personen aus Taif, die über den Propheten Muhammad sprechen.

The Prophet then went back to Mecca. On the way, he sat in the shade of a tree as he was exhausted due to fatigue and his injuries. He sat there knowing that his enemies in Mecca were preparing to attack him in any way he could not prepare for, as he was unaware of their methods. [187]

At that moment, he prayed to God and said: "O God, I complain to You about my weakness, my lack of strength and the humiliation of people towards me. You are the Most Merciful of the merciful. You are the Lord of the weak, and you are my Lord. To whom have you entrusted me. To a person too far away who has forgotten me or to an enemy who has power over me. If you are not angry with me, I am indifferent to what might happen to me, because your mercy is more generous to me. I seek refuge in the light of your countenance, which illuminates all darkness and in whose light all things in this world and the hereafter are arranged, from your wrath that could befall me. I will continue to satisfy You, if You are pleased. There is neither strength nor power except through you." [188]

The prophet's journey to Taif was not fruitless. This incident left positive effects in the minds of those he met and spoke to, which will later yield the expected outcomes.

619 - 620 AD

The second year before the Hijrah

Famine in Mecca

The Quraysh and the Meccans were struck by a severe famine due to the supplication of the Prophet who prayed against them. They even ate the Al-Ul-huz[1], burned the bones and ate them, they ate dead dogs and dug up the graves. The women ate their children. The people were preoccupied with themselves and their problems, so the prophet had the opportunity to take care of his religion and his message and to continue inviting people to God, even if only for a short time. When the second year before the Hijrah dawned, Abu Sufyan[2] came to the Prophet and said: "O Muhammad, you have come to strengthen the family ties and your people have died of hunger. Pray to God for them." The Prophet then prayed to God on their behalf and God ended the famine. The Prophet responds to Abu Sufyan's request to reveal to him new evidence of the validity of his call and to refute the argument against him and anyone who disagrees with him.

The Messenger of God did not stop calling people to God, , and to the true religion. He took the opportunity during the pilgrimage times and presented Islam to the tribes and invited them to accept and support the Islamic faith. His uncle Abu Lahab followed him where he goes and tried to contradict his words und harass him. He urged the people not to accept him and not to obey him in anything. He also accused him of madness, sorcery, fortune-telling and similar accusations. Most people listened to the Quraysh, either out of fear of their authority and influence or to protect their economic interests in Mecca. When the Messenger of God invited the tribes to Islam, they responded to him with the worst possible answer, retorting, "Your family and clan know you better because they have not followed you."

Once, when the Prophet was presenting his message to the tribes, the Banu Amir ibn Sa'sa'ah came to him. He invited them to accept faith in God and presented his message to them. A man named Buhira ibn Firas from Banu Amir said to him, "By God, if I had taken this young man of the Quraysh, the Arabs

---

1 Al-Ulhuz is dry blood that is ground with camel hair and eaten during famines.
2 Abu Sufyan: was a clan chief and merchant in Mecca. He belonged to the 'Abd-Shams, a clan of the Quraysh tribe.

would have eaten through him." Then he came to the Prophet and asked him, "What if we had sworn allegiance to you at your command. If God gave you power and your religion ruled, would we take power after you?" The Prophet said: "It's up to God. He decides who should take it." He replied, "We expose ourselves to death for you, and if God helps you, others will get the matter. We don't need you!" He refused to follow him.

This shows us that this man is far-sighted. He knows that this message has a future and that anyone who accepts it will gain control over all Arabs. At the same time, however, it is clear that he is an opportunist and an egoist. He does not want to convert to Islam because he loves it, but because he loves leadership, control and wealth. When the people came, Banu Amir went back to their Sheikh and the Sheikh asked them how their Hajj season was. They said: "A young Quraysh man from Banu Abd al-Muttalib came to us and claimed that he was a prophet. He has called us to support him, rise with him and bring him to our land." The Sheikh put his hands on his head and then said: "O Banu Amir, is it possible to rectify this mistake? Is there any way to avoid it? Any chance? I swear, if an Ismaili (descendant of Ishmael) said it, then it is really true. What were you thinking about? Where was your opinion?" The same thing happened to him with the Kinda tribe. [189]

Although the Prophet of Islam was in dire need of help, especially from a large tribe like the Banu Amir who had the means and the numbers to protect and intercede for him, he refused to promise something that he could not fulfill. Even if this promise would bring him great profit. Because the matter belongs to God, he puts it where he wants.

In the same year, while the Prophet was inviting the tribes to Islam and asking them to support him, he met a small group of Khazraj, who are a tribe from Yathrib, on Al-Aqaba, near Mina. So he called them to believe in God and Islam, he recited the Quran to them, and they believed in him. They were six in total, namely: Asad ibn Zurara, Jabir ibn Abdullah ibn Riab, Awf ibn Harith, Rafi ibn Malik, and Uqbah and Qutbah, the sons of Amir. This group asked the Prophet to explain to them what he was calling them to do. He said: "I call you to bear witness that there is no god but Allah and that I am the Messenger of Allah. I call you {not to associate anything with Him, and to be kind to parents; and do not kill your children out of poverty - We provide for you and for them as well - and do not approach the abominations, what is apparent of them and what is hidden; and do not kill the soul that Allah has forbidden (to kill) except for a lawful reason. This He has commanded you, that you may understand. And do not approach the orphan's property except in the best way, until he has reached maturity. And give full measure and weight in justice. We do not impose on any soul more than it is able to bear. And when you speak, be fair, even if [it concerns] a near relative. And keep your covenant with Allah. This is what He enjoins upon you so that you may take admonition.}"[190] After hearing him they believed him and embraced Islam. They then returned to their people in Yathrib, told them about the Messenger of Allah and called them to Islam.

The people of Yathrib had continuously heard news from the Jews regarding the coming of a prophet in the near future, and this mentally prepared them to accept the religion that the Prophet revealed to them.[191] Yathrib is located northeast of Mecca and has been inhabited by the tribes of Al-Aws and Al-Khazraj for decades. But the ongoing wars between the Aws and the Khazraj made life in Yathrib difficult and the situation tragic. The last of these wars was the Battle of Ba'ath, which broke out when the Hashemites and the Prophet were in the Sheib of Abu Talib, in which the tribe of Al-Aws was victorious.

The people of Yathrib did not suffer from the conditions of the people of Mecca who were fighting Islam because they saw it as a threat to their personal interests and unjust privileges. Rather, the people of Yathrib looked forward to getting out of the tragedy of civil war and to their true savior, whom they found in the prophet of Islam, for he brought them the simple and tolerant teachings of Sharia[1]. Since the paganism that the people of Yathrib believed in could not solve their various internal problems or alleviate their severity, and this is exactly the opposite of the polytheists of Mecca who benefited socially and economically from their paganism and possessed many unjust privileges. They were not willing to give up these privileges to serve this religion, even though it called for truth and humanity. Instead, they sacrificed man and truth to their own preferences, deviations and interests. [192]

---

1   Sharia: Sources and traditions of Islamic legal principles, on which obligations and prohibitions for all areas of life are based.

First pledge of allegiance

When those people who had embraced Islam returned to Yathrib, they mentioned the Messenger of God to their people and invited them to Islam until it spread among them. The next year, which was the first year before the Hijrah (migration), twelve men came, two of whom were from Al-Aws and the rest from the Khazraj. They met with the Messenger in Al-Aqaba and gave him their pledge of allegiance, which is known as "the women's pledge of allegiance", that is, a pledge of allegiance that does not include any war obligations. The pledge of allegiance included the following points: "They took an oath not to associate anything with God, not to steal, not to commit adultery, not to kill their children, not to deceive anyone by assigning a child to anyone but its father, and not to disobey the prophet. If they fulfill it, they will enter Paradise, and if they conceal any of it, their fate is with God. If He wills, He will punish them, and if He wills, He will forgive them."

When they returned to Yathrib, the Prophet sent Musab ibn Umair with them to recite the Quran, teach them Islam and give them an understanding of the religion. Musab performed the first Friday prayer in Yathrib, he and those with him who embraced Islam succeeded in calling to God. Saad bin Muadh also embraced Islam, which was the reason for the conversion of his people. After spending some time spreading the message of Islam in Yathrib, Musab returned to Mecca and presented the results of his work to the Prophet. The Prophet of Islam was very pleased.[193]

621 - 622 AD

In the year of the Hijrah

The second oath of allegiance in Al-Aqaba

The following year, a large group from the people of Yathrib, consisting of an estimated five hundred people, came with the intention of making Hajj. Among them were both non-Muslims and Muslims who were hiding out of fear of the Quraysh pilgrims. Some of the Muslims met the Messenger and he promised to meet them in Al-Aqaba at night during the days of al-Tashreeq[1] when the movement calmed down. He ordered them not to wake the sleeping people and not to wait for anyone so that they would not be caught by the Meccans. On this particular night, they slept in their tents until a third of the night had passed. Then, one by one, they began to sneak to the place of the rendezvous so that no one would notice them until they gathered at Al-Aqaba. Among them were about seventy men and two women. They met the Messenger there in the Prophet's house, which is the house of Abd al-Muttalib. They swore allegiance to him on condition that they protect him and his family, just as they protect themselves, their families and their children, and that they shelter, support, listen to and obey him, in war, in peace, in hardship and in relief. They also swore to grant good, to forbid evil, to speak only the truth to God and not to be afraid of anyone in this matter.

One of Al-Khazraj, Ubadah bin Al-Samit, said: "We have sworn allegiance to the Messenger of Allah to be obedient in times of hardship as well as in times of prosperity, in times of enthusiasm and in times of reluctance, and we will not argue with those in power. We will speak the truth wherever we are, and we will not fear anyone for the sake of Allah."

Another from Al-Khazraj, Al-Abbas ibn Abadah, recognized the seriousness of the situation and told them, "O people of Aws and Khazraj, do you know what you are about to do? You are about to enter the war of the Red and Black[2] and the war of the kings of the world. If any misfortune befalls you, you will betray him and leave him. Do not deceive him, for the Messenger of Allah is in honor and power despite the opposition of his people." Abdullah ibn

---

1   Al-Tashreeq: these are the three days after the day of sacrifice, and they are the eleventh, twelfth, and thirteenth day of the month of Dhu al-Hijjah. With this, the pilgrims end their pilgrimage.
2   The Red and the Black: It means Arabs and non-Arabs.

Hazam, Asad ibn Zurara and Abu al-Haytham ibn al-Tayhan said to al-Abbas, "You have nothing to do with speech." Then they addressed their words to the Prophet: "O Messenger of God, we say rather; our blood is sacrificed for your blood, our lives are sacrificed for you. Determine for yourself and your Lord what you wish." Asad ibn Zurara said: "O Messenger of God, every call has a path, either easy or difficult, and you have called the people today to a dicey path that is delicate and difficult for them. You have called us to separate from our neighbors and relatives, near and far. This is a difficult rank and we have accepted it. You called us when we were a community in a house of honor and strength, where no one wants a man who does not belong to us to rule over us, who his people have abandoned him and his uncles have abandoned him. This is a difficult rank, yet we agreed with you and followed you."

After listening to their answers, the Prophet asked them to bring out twelve guarantors for them to represent their tribes.

They appointed nine from the Khazraj and three from the Al-Aws for him, who were the guarantors of their tribe. In the meantime, the Quraysh noticed the meeting. They became agitated and took up arms. When the Messenger learned of the Meccans' attack, he ordered the Muslims to disperse. They said: "O Messenger of God, if you order us to raise our swords against them, we will do so." He said: "I have not been commanded and God has not granted to fight them." They said: "O Messenger of God, will you come with us." He said: "I am waiting for God's command." So the Quraysh came and took up arms. Hamza and Ali bin Abi Talib pulled out their swords.

When they looked at Hamza, they said: "What have you gathered for?" Hamza said prudently to preserve the Prophet , the Muslims and Islam, "We have not gathered, there is no one here. By God, if anyone crosses Al-Aqaba, I will strike him with my sword. Then the group dispersed from Yathrib and the Messenger of God returned to Mecca. The Quraysh went back with obsessive thoughts about the fact that Muhammad was actually making an agreement with the tribes of Yathrib to join his religion and that the Quraysh might lose a strategic ally for them and an important trade route through Yathrib. A group of the Quraysh set out again after sunrise to make sure of the matter, and they went to Abdullah bin 'Ubayy, who was one of the leaders of the Khazraj, and they said to him, "We have been informed that your people have pledged allegiance to Muhammad to support him in the war against us. By Allah, there is nothing worse that we detest more than a war breaking out between us and him through your doing." Abdullah swore to them that they had not done this, that he had known nothing about it, and that they had not informed him of their affair. But the Quraysh then learned the truth. They went out to look for them, and they found Saad ibn Ubadah[1] and Al-Mundhir ibn Umayr. Al-Mundhir managed to escape from them and they arrested Saad and tortured him. He was then rescued by his friends in Mecca. In Mecca, the Quraysh began to harass the Muslims more intensely and persecute them, so that the suffering of the Muslims increased, so that their life there became unbearable. They complained about this to the Messenger of God and asked him to allow them to leave Mecca. He allowed them to emigrate to Yathrib three months after the second oath of allegiance to Al-Aqaba and said to them: "God, the Exalted and Mighty, has made for you brothers and a home where you can be safe." .

Mecca is no longer a safe place for Muslims and no longer suitable for the call, because the Prophet drew the maximum he could from it, and there was no longer any hope of new groups entering the new religion, at least not in the near future. So it became necessary to move to another place so that his call would guarantee himself freedom of movement in speech and deed away from the pressure of the Quraysh. Emigration to Yathrib is a forced solution where there is no choice. This is because migration to Taif would not have been advantageous, nor to Yemen, Persia, Rome, the Levant and others. The regions were subject to the authority of both superpowers, which would pose nothing but serious problems and dangers for the Prophet. As for Abyssinia, it is separated from Mecca due to its geographical location. Since it is not close to Mecca, the Prophet would not have control over it and would not be able to exert political, economic and even military pressure on it. The Prophet wanted to eliminate pagan influence in the region and replace it with Islamic influence. Furthermore, the people of Yathrib themselves demanded this from the Prophet, swearing allegiance to him in Al-Aqaba and promising him victory. The Muslims migrated there secretly as individuals and sacrificed their homes, their relatives and many of them sacrificed their belongings, their social status and everything they owned for their religion and faith. Then God gave his prophet permission to emigrate there as well. [194]

---

1   Saad bin Ubadah: was a leader of the Khazraj in Yathrib.

The Prophet's murder plan

The dignitaries of the Quraysh gathered in Dar al-Nadwa, and none of them were absent. Among them were representatives of: Banu Abd Shams, Nawfal, Abd al-Dar, Jumah, Sahm, Asad, Makhzum and others. They agreed that none from Tihama[1] should enter with them because their inclination was towards Muhammad, just as they insisted that no Hashemites or anyone associated with them should be among them. Iblis (Satan) was present with them disguised as a sheikh from Najd.[195] They consulted among themselves as to what they should do with Muhammad.

Figure 22: An imaginary depiction of the meeting of the leaders of Quraysh in Dar al-Nadwa, to plan the assassination of the Prophet

They considered imprisonment, but they saw that it might be possible for him to contact his supporters who would release him. They also considered exile to some countries, but they saw that this would allow the Messenger to spread his religion further. So they finally agreed on the suggestion of Abu Jahl or Satan that they take a strong young man from each tribe to stand as a candi-

---

1 Tihama: is the strip along the west and south coast from the Hejaz to Yemen.

date and representative for his tribe, give each of them a sharp sword to attack the Prophet with. Then they strike him with a single blow and kill him so that his blood is spread over all the tribes. Banu Abd al-Muttalib would then not be able to fight all the tribes, they would be forced to accept the blood money and Quraysh would give it to them and that is the end of the matter.

Allah informed his Prophet by revelation about this plot and that Allah would foil the devious plan of the disbelievers.[196] The Quraysh chose about fifteen men from their tribes to kill the Prophet with a single blow with their swords. Then they gathered in front of the Prophet's door and watched him while they waited for him to rest for the night.[197] Among them were: Al-Hakam bin Abi Al-Aas, Uqbah bin Abi Muait, Al-Nadr bin Al-Harith, Umayyah bin Khalaf, Abd al-ʿUzzā ibn Abdul Muttalib (Abu Lahab), Amr ibn Hisham (Abu Jahl) and Khaled bin Walid.

Figure 23: Masked men plan to assassinate the Prophet.

Ali in the Prophet's bed

The Prophet learned of the Quraysh's plan to insidiously kill him in his bed or as he was leaving his house. Therefore, he decided to deceive them and make them believe that he was still in his bed while he was actually planning to escape from them. Therefore, he instructed Ali to sleep in his bed after telling him about the Quraysh's plan. Ali replied: "And will you survive, O Prophet of God, if I spend the night there?" Muhammad replied in the affirmative. Ali smiled and fell to the ground thanking God. He then slept in the Prophet's bed and covered himself with the Prophet's blanket. Here begins a story that is one of the most miraculous stories of redemption and sacrifice known, for the brave and heroic are steadfast in battle in the face of their enemies, defending themselves with their weapons and equipment, with their supporters and helpers. They can overcome the battles, stand up to the enemy, but not alone. That a person voluntarily and calmly accepts death without weapons and equipment, as if he is rushing into the arms of a beautiful lover, sleeping on a bed surrounded by dangers and horrors, secluded from everything except his faith, his trust in his Lord, and his endeavor to ensure the safety of the leader, as happened to Ali when his cousin Muhammad suggested that he sleep in his bed so that he himself could emigrate and escape the conspiracy of the Quraysh - this is something that has never happened in the history of bravery, and no one in the history of adventures has ever experienced it, in the name of principle and faith.

Figure 24: An imaginary depiction of Ali sleeping in place of the Prophet to sacrifice himself for him.

Then the Prophet walked in the dark night while the Quraysh guards walked around his house and waited. He came out and recited: {And We have built a barrier wall before them and a barrier wall behind them and covered them so that they cannot see} [198] He had a handful of earth which he scattered over their heads. He passed between them without them noticing and took his way to Mount Thawr.

God, revealed to Gabriel and Michael: "I have created a brotherhood between you two, and I have made the life of one of you longer than that of the other. Which of you prefers his companion to life?" Both of them chose life.

Allah revealed to them: "Do not be like Ali bin Abi Talib. I have made a brotherhood between him and Muhammad." So Ali slept on his bed, redeemed himself and gave him life. "Descend to the earth, protect him from his enemy." So they descended, Gabriel was at his head, Michael was at his feet, and Gabriel said to him, "Congratulations, congratulations." [199]

Allah has revealed that there is a man who sells himself for Allah's pleasure. He wants only what Allah wants, and he is proud of nothing but his Lord. He does not follow his own desires. The existence of a person with these qualities in society is a sign of Allah's mercy towards mankind. If there were no men with these qualities among people and there were corrupt men instead, the pillars of religion would collapse and corruption and falsehood would spread. [200]

The attackers began to throw stones at Ali, assuming that he was Muhammad, while he turned over in bed and wrapped his head in a blanket, which he did not take off until morning. Then they attacked him. When Ali saw them, they drew their swords and approached him, Khaled ibn al-Walid went ahead of them. Ali jumped towards him, surprised him and struck him on his hand so that Khaled was startled. Then Ali took the sword from his hand and attacked them with Khaled's sword. They were frightened by him and left the house like sheep out of fear. When they saw him, they said in astonishment, "You are Ali." He replied, "I am Ali." They said: "We didn't want you. What has your companion done. " He replied, "I don't know." Then they withdrew from him and hurried to their people to tell them what had happened so that they could act before it was too late.[201].

The prophet in the cave

They drove the Prophet out of Mecca. They claimed he was lying and abandoned him, even though they really knew him. They knew his sincerity, his intellect, his loyalty and his good manners. The Quraysh expelled Muhammad, they did not support him, they did not listen to him, and they did not accept what he said: despite the evidence he presented to them. The Prophet fled alone from their treachery. On the way, he met Abu Bakr, who had gone out to hear news. He accompanied him and they traveled together about 5 kilometers south until they reached Mount Thawr and hid in a cave there.

The Quraysh tracked him, searched for him and followed his path and sent an experienced tracker to track them. He informed them that a person had accompanied Muhammad in that area. They followed the trail until they reached the cave, which was covered with tree branches. But God distracted them, because a spider had spun its web at the entrance of the cave and a wild dove had laid its egg there.

Figure 25: The cave of Thawr is located on the north side of the Thawr mountain south of Mecca and about five kilometers south of the Holy Mosque. (The image was digitally edited).

One of them asked those in front: "Why don't you look into the cave?" He replied: "The footprints end here, they have either ascended into the sky or gone underground. I see a dove at the entrance of the cave, so I know that there is no one inside." [202]

From this they concluded that the cave was deserted and no one entered it, otherwise the spider's web would have been torn, the eggs would have been broken and the wild dove would not have settled at its door. The Quraysh made their way to Yathrib in search of him, but in vain, as he remained in the cave for three days.

Ali bin Abi Talib waited until the next night, then he and Hind bin Abi Hala[1] set out under the cover of darkness until they entered the cave of the Messenger of God. The Prophet ordered Hind to buy two camels for him and his companion. Abu Bakr said: "I had prepared two mounts for you and me, O Prophet of God, on which you could travel to Yathrib." He said: "I will not take them, none of them, except for a price." He said: "Then they are yours for a price." He ordered Ali to pay Abu Bakr the price. Then he instructed him to fulfill his obligations and return those entrusted to him. At that time, when the Prophet was in Mecca, the Quraysh and those who came to Mecca from the Arabs during the season used to entrust their money and possessions to the Prophet. The Prophet now wanted to return these deposits and the money to the people, so he ordered Ali to call out loudly in the morning and evening: "Whoever has a deposit with Muhammad should come to get it back." Certainly an arduous, dangerous task in this dire situation, when everyone was looking for Muhammad with their swords and waiting with a great reward for whoever would hand him over or kill him. But for Ali, who had just been lying on the Prophet's bed, this was no problem.

The Prophet then said to Ali, after the polytheists had stopped looking for the Prophet, "They will not be able to do anything to you, Ali, until you reach me; fulfill my deposits in public and I entrust you with my daughter Fatima. I entrust you both to my God, and Allah will protect you both.

---

1 Hind ibn Abi Hala was a nephew and at the same time foster son of Khadija.

Figure 26: The pigeon is at the entrance of the cave.

The Prophet also instructed Ali to buy mounts for him, the women and those from the Banu Hashim tribe who wanted to emigrate with him. After spending three days in the cave, the Messenger of Allah set off for the city of Yathrib. Meanwhile, Ali provided the Prophet with food in the cave and informed him of the news. [203]

It was possible for God to help his Messenger without Muhammad having to resort to the cave or Ali having to sleep on the Prophet's bed by helping him through a brilliant convincing miracle. Allah is capable of all that. He is the one who subjected the spiders' weaving to His messenger, and He grew the trees at the entrance of the cave. Then there were a pigeon with it's eggs and its back-and-forth around its nest, as is the habit of birds in protecting their eggs. But no, the divine plan was for things to happen according to their natural circumstances. However, divine assistance is used in certain matters when the matter is beyond human ability. It happened this way so that this would be an example and an effective lesson for all of us to work diligently on religion and faith, and so that we would not have to wait for a miracle from heaven. For Allah did not save his Prophet by miracles. Moreover, He did not honor him and bestow divine kindness upon him until He saw the willingness, sacrifice and initiative to do so in his Prophet. Allah, helped his Prophet since there was no one with him to help him by sending down Sakīna[1] upon him and supporting him with unseen soldiers. [204]

In these difficult moments, despite the obvious miracles and impressive signs, Abu Bakr lost his confidence in Allah's victory for his Prophet. He was sad and distressed about himself because he saw that the Quraysh soldiers had reached the cave where the Prophet was hiding and that his fate was sealed. Abu Bakr was therefore saddened by his decision to leave the Quraysh and accompany the Prophet on this dangerous adventure. He had lost the Quraysh and his reputation in Mecca, and perhaps he would also lose his life for accompanying the Prophet. The Prophet stopped him and told him that he should not be sad because God is the supporter of his Prophet and that God will also save Abu Bakr by saying, "God is with us." But when Abu Bakr did not respond to the Prophet's request, the Sakīna was taken away from him so that only the Messenger of God received the Sakīna, indicating that Abu Bakr did not deserve this favor and honor from God. [205]

In the cave, the Prophet faced a difficult situation and there was no one to defend him. His companion was not only incapable of defending him, but was also a heavy burden on him due to his sadness and fear. Instead of being a source of relief and support for the Prophet, the Prophet had to comfort and reassure him. Therefore, he had no influence in defending the Messenger or alleviating the difficulties he faced. [206]

On the way to Yathrib

When the Prophet set out from the cave for Yathrib, the Quraysh offered a reward of one hundred camels to the one who brought the Prophet Muhammad. Among those who set out in search of the Prophet was Suraqa ibn Jusham. When Suraqa found the Prophet, he tried to catch up with him. The Messenger of Allah saw him and said: "O God, protect me from Suraqa." Suraqa's camel then fell to the ground and Suraqa said: "O Muhammad, I knew that what hit my camel's legs was from you. Ask God to set my camel free

---

1 Sakīna is a state of soul mentioned in the Koran. There is no exact equivalent in the english language. The terms ataraxia, peace, serenity, peace of mind, (happiness-) bliss, security, and God-consciousness perhaps best reflect the meaning. "Sakīna" is analogous to the Jewish term "Shechinah", which means the presence of God.

again. I swear that if you do not get good from me, you will not get evil from me." So the Messenger of God called out to Allah. God then released his camel. Suraqa, however, returned to his plan to chase after the Prophet. The camel fell again and he asked the Prophet again. The Prophet spoke to God on his behalf until he did it three times. When the legs of his camel were freed for the third time, he said: "O Muhammad, this is my camel in your hands, and my servant for you. I will also send away those who are searching for you." The Prophet said: "I do not need anything from you." The next day, the Quraysh came to Suraqa and asked, "O Suraqa, do you have any knowledge of Muhammad?" He said: "I was informed that he has left you. I have searched this site and I have seen no one, no trace. Return, for I have checked it for you." .

The Prophet walked on until he reached the tent of Umm Ma'bad, descended there and asked Umm Ma'bad for hospitality, and she said: "I have nothing." The Messenger of Allah saw a sheep on the edge that had wandered away from the flock due to its weakness and asked, "Will you allow me to milk it?" She said: "Yes, but there is nothing good about it." He put his hand on the sheep's back, and it became one of the fattest sheep. Then he put his hand on its udders and it gave plenty of milk. They all drank from the sheep's milk until they were full. When Umm Ma'bad saw what had happened to the sheep, she realized that this man was blessed and could help her heal her sick son. She brought him her son, who could neither speak nor stand up, and asked him to help her son. The prophet took a date, chewed it and put it in the child's mouth. The child immediately stood up, walked and spoke. When her husband Abu Ma'bad came back and saw this, he asked his wife what had happened. She said: "A man from Quraysh passed by me, with good looks, shining face, good character, neither tall nor short, he has even features, shining black eyes, long eyelids, hoarse voice, long neck, thick long beard and long eyebrows. When he is silent, he will be dignified, and when he speaks, he will be praised and exalted by splendor. He is the most perfect man, he shines from afar, better and higher up close. His logic is beautiful like falling pearls. His words are balanced, neither little nor much, he has companions who surround him when he speaks, listen to what he says, and when he commands, they hasten to carry out his orders. He is neither grumpy nor playful." Abu Ma'bad knew that he was the Prophet Muhammad. Then the Messenger of God went to Yathrib, and Abu Ma'bad and his family embraced Islam. [207]

The Prophet in Quba

The Messenger of God continued his emigration until he approached Yathrib. He reached Quba first. Quba lies to the southwest about half an hour's walk from Yathrib. He was warmly welcomed there and stayed in the house of one of the companions. Abu Bakr urged him to go to Yathrib, but he refused and preferred to wait in Quba, saying, "I will not go there until my mother's son and my brother come with my daughter (meaning Ali and Fatima)." The Messenger of God stayed in Quba. Abu Bakr became angry, and separated from the Prophet. Then the Messenger of God wrote a letter to Ali asking him to come to him and not to wait. He gave the letter to Abu Waqid al-Laithi. The people were very happy about the Prophet's arrival in Quba. Every day they came in groups to Quba to greet the Messenger.

When the Prophet's letter reached Ali bin Abi Talib, he prepared to go out and emigrate. He informed the oppressed believers who were with him and ordered them to sneak in and go to Dhi-Tawa[1] under the cover of night. He then set off with Fatima, the daughter of the Messenger, his mother, Fatima bin Asad bin Hashim, Fatima bin Al-Zubair bin Abdul Muttalib. Two other men accompanied him, one of whom led the camels hard out of fear. Ali bin Abi Talib said to him: "Calm down, for the Messenger of God said to me: O Ali, from now on they will not harm you." But on the way, masked Quraysh horsemen caught up with him and reached him near Wadi Dhajnan[2]. Then Ali lowered the women and approached the horsemen, brandishing his sword. They ordered him to return. He said: "And if I do not. " They said: "You return willingly or we will return with your head, for you are easy for us to kill." The knights approached the camels to frighten them so that those on them would fall off. Ali went between them. One of them struck him with his sword, Ali evaded him, avoided his attack, struck him on his shoulder and killed him. The knights withdrew from him and said: "Leave us alone, O Ibn Abi Talib." He said threateningly, "I am going to my cousin, the Messenger of God in Yathrib, and whoever likes me to tear his flesh and spill his blood shall follow me or fight me." None of them dared to approach him and they galloped away on

---

1 Dhi-Tawa: A valley that is about five and a half kilometers north of the Kaaba.
2 Wadi Dhajnan: A valley that is 19 kilometers north of Mecca.

their horses. Then Ali turned to his two companions and said to them, "Come on, let's keep moving."

He continued his journey without fear and made his route known until he reached Dajnan. He stopped there and stayed for about a day and a night. A group of fugitive believers joined him, including Umm Ayman, the Messenger's foster mother. So they prayed to Allah that night, standing, sitting and lying down, until he reached the village of Quba. Allah mentioned what they did and how they prayed to Him and supplicated to Him on their journey: (those who remember Allah standing, sitting and (lying) on their sides and reflect on the creation of the heavens and the earth: 'Our Lord, You have not created (all) this in vain. Praise be to You. Save us from the punishment of (Hell) Fire. Our Lord, surely whoever You let enter the Fire, You have disgraced him. And the unjust will have no helpers. Our Lord, surely we heard a caller calling to faith: 'Believe in your Lord. Then we believed. Our Lord, forgive us our sins, blot out our evil deeds and set us apart among the good. Our Lord, and give us what You have promised us through Your messengers, and do not put us to shame on the Day of Resurrection. Surely You will not break what You have promised. Then their Lord answered them: 'I will not let any of your deeds go astray, whether of male or female; some of you are of others. So to those who have migrated and been expelled from their homes, and who have been harmed in My way, and who have fought and been killed, I will surely wipe out their evil deeds and will surely make them enter gardens with streams running through them as a reward from Allah. And Allah - with Him is the best reward. } 208

When the Prophet was informed of their arrival, he said: "Call Ali for me." They said: "O Messenger of Allah, he cannot come." So the Prophet himself came to him, and when he saw him, he embraced him and wept when he saw the wounds and swelling on his feet. He said to Ali, "O Ali, you are the first in this community to have believed in Allah and His Messenger, the first of them to have migrated to Allah and His Messenger, and the last of them to remain with His Messenger. By Him in Whose hand is my soul; only a believer loves you whose heart Allah has tested for faith. And only a hypocrite or unbeliever will hate you. "

In Quba, Ammar bin Yasser suggested building a place for prayer. The Messenger of God approved the idea and ordered the construction of the first mosque in Islam. He ordered Abu Bakr to ride the camel and walk with it to mark the boundaries of the mosque according to its circumference, but the camel did not move. Then the Prophet ordered Omar to do so, but the camel still would not go. Finally Ali was instructed and the camel moved and circled the area. The Prophet said: "Loosen her reins and build on her course, for so it has been commanded. " [209]

Hypocrisy in Mecca

Not all those who had come with the Prophet from Mecca to Yathrib had truly believed in Allah. Some of them had accepted the Islam because they saw in it positive signs that coincided with their dreams and hopes, and what their souls were striving for. Therefore, they supported the message and endured suffering and hardship for Islam.

Figure 27: The hypocrites in Mecca are plotting.

All this was done in the hope that one day they would succeed in achieving their goals and plans that they dream of, getting a position, gaining wealth, great prestige and the like. They did all this even though they may not have believed in this message, and they only did what they saw as necessary to achieve their goals. They accompanied and supported the Islam as long as it did not call for self-sacrifice and death. These people are known as hypocrites. There are verses in the Quran that indicate the presence of hypocrites in Mecca before Medina, including: ❨And among the people there are some who say, 'We believe in Allah.' But when he is afflicted for the sake of Allah, he equates the affliction of people with the punishment of Allah. But when help comes from your Lord, they will surely say, 'We have been with you. Does Allah not know better what is in the hearts of the people of the world? [210].

The hypocrites say, "We believe." in the plural form, they want to include themselves among the believers, in every possible way, that is, we believe like all other people who have believed. When the enemy sometimes attacks them - while they are on the path of Allah and faith - and hurts them, they do not hold on to the pain and difficulty, and they portray the torture of the polytheists and the pain of people as the punishment of Allah that must be guarded against, so they return and leave their faith behind and become disbelievers again for fear of the punishment of people. The interesting thing here is that the Quran refers to Allah's retribution as "punishment" and people's pain as "trial or temptation". This expression indicates that people's pain is not a punishment - in reality - but a test and a path to perfection. Then the verse continues, and when help comes from your Lord in the future, they will surely say, "We are with you," because these hypocrites - weak in faith - see themselves as participating in this victory with the Muslims. Do they think that Allah does not know what is hidden in the depths of their hearts and does not know their true intentions? [211] In the coming chapters, we will uncover the true nature of this hypocritical group and see how they maintained their cover to achieve their material goals. [212]

Arrival of the Prophet in Yathrib

On the twelfth day of the month of Rabi' al-Awwal, fifteen days after his arrival in Quba, the Prophet set out for Yathrib on Friday. He reached the valley of Banu Salim bin Awf[1]. On this Friday, the first Friday prayer led by the Prophet of Allah in Islam took place. He delivered his first sermon there, in which he admonished the Muslims and gave them advice. In his speech, he said: "...Increase the remembrance of Allah and work for what comes after death, for whoever rectifies what is between him and Allah, Allah will suffice him in what is between him and people..." [213] After the Prophet had finished, he mounted his steed and set off for Yathrib, accompanied by Ali, who always accompanied him on his journeys. He reached Yathrib on Friday afternoon.

---

1 At this place, they built a mosque today, which is located in the southwest of the city of Medina and is about 900 meters away from the Quba Mosque.

Hundreds of people in Yathrib were waiting impatiently for his arrival. When he arrived, they rushed to him and gathered around him to welcome him. As the Prophet passed by the families of the Ansar, they confronted him and asked him to stay with them.

The leaders of the Aws and the Khazraj were at the forefront of those welcoming him, among them was Abdullah ibn Abi ibn Salul, who was nominated as the king of Yathrib. Therefore, it was expected that the Prophet would reside in his house because of his position among his people, as it was customary at that time for important personalities to reside in the houses of tribal leaders and nobles. But Allah wanted the true character of Islam to be shown from the first day, so the attitude of the Messenger of Allah came, confirming Allah's will and deciding the matter. When the people of Yathrib insisted on the Prophet to stay in one of their houses, the Prophet did not want to prefer one over another by staying with him, so he came up with a solution that satisfied everyone where he said: "Make way for the camel, it is commanded by God".

Figure 28: The arrival of the Prophet and Ali in Yathrib.

So he set off with it, and the Messenger of Allah let go of the reins so that the camel could run free. He rode the camel on until he arrived near the door of Abu Ayyub al-Ansari the poorest man in the city.

The Messenger of God got down from the camel and the people gathered around him and asked him to stay with them. So Umm Abu Ayyub took the opportunity and rushed to the Prophet of Allah's luggage and took it into their house. When the people became numerous, the Messenger of Allah asked: "Where is the luggage?" They replied, "Umm Abu Ayyub has brought it to their house." Thereupon the Messenger of Allah said : "A man is with his luggage." So the Prophet chose to stay in Abu Ayyub's house where the camel had stopped. This was a revelation from God that this religion is the religion of the oppressed and not the religion of the arrogant. The Prophet stayed with Abu Ayyub for a month, and Ali was with him. The place was also the area where the mosque and the Prophet's house were built.

The Prophet Muhammad changed the name of the city of Yathrib and called it Medina. He also ordered that the Islamic calendar should begin from the day of his emigration. Initially, the Companions dated by months until the middle of the fifth year, after which they began to date by years. [214]

When the news of the Prophet's emigration reached the Muslims in Ethiopia, thirty-three men and eight women returned from there. On their way to Medina, they passed through Mecca, as the route runs along there. The Quraysh captured them and treated them with violence and harshness, regardless of their kinship. They killed two men and captured seven of them. The rest managed to escape and reached the Messenger of Allah in Medina.

The building of the Prophet's mosque

The Prophet bought a piece of land belonging to two orphans from the Khazraj and decided to build a mosque on it. This was the place where the camel had stopped. He announced the construction of the mosque and people began to transport stones from the Al-Hurra[1] area. The women participated in the construction of the mosque, they carried stones to build the mosque at night and the men during the day. The Prophet himself took part in carrying the stones, which made the Companions work hard and diligently. As they worked, they enthusiastically recited rhythmic poems:

---

1 Al-Hurra is a village that is located southeast of Medina. It is a plateau that extends from east to west. It was called Al-Hurra because a large part of its surface is covered with black volcanic stones and rocks that get very hot in the summer.

"When we sit idle and the Prophet works very diligently,

It may seem that we are useless and not ready for action.

But our task is to help and support him,

Because only together can we achieve great results and develop."

Others recited while working:

"O Allah, the reward that matters is that of the Hereafter,

So I ask You to have mercy on Ansar and Muhagirun at the same time."

The Messenger of God built his houses and his companions built their houses around the mosque, and each of them had opened a door to the mosque. The construction of the mosque was the first work that the Prophet began in Medina, and it is a work of great significance and importance. For Muslims have now become two groups: Immigrants (Muhagirun) and Supporters (Ansar)[1].

The Muhajirun are the Muslims who emigrated with the Prophet, while the Ansar are the Muslims from Al-Medina. The circumstances of each of the two groups, their living and psychological conditions and their aspirations were different. The Muhagirun left their homeland and became without money and without a home. As for the Ansar, they were blessed with their homeland and homes, but they were also two competing tribes (Aws and Khazraj), burdened and exhausted by wars. Islam and the Prophet wanted them to deal in this world from a religious point of view and for all to merge in the crucible of Islam so that they become as one body, in their mutual love, mercy, and cooperation. The mosque is the place where all this can be realized. It is not only a place of prayer, but also the most excellent means of intellectual education and of spreading friendship and love among Muslims. It also helps to facilitate relationships within the community and reduce problems in official dealings that point to differences between individuals. In addition, it is a center of leadership, a place to receive guests, a court to settle conflicts, and even a hospital to treat the sick and injured. [215] .

---

1   Muhajirun means emigrants and Ansar means supporters.

622 - 623 AD

The first year after the Hijrah

Aisha bint Abu Bakr in the house of the Prophet

In the first year of the Hijrah, in the month of Shawwal, Aisha moved into the Prophet's house at the age of twenty, after he had married her three years earlier in Mecca. Aisha was one of the Prophet's bravest wives and at the same time the most jealous and envious of them all. She caused problems in the Prophet's life and afterwards. Due to the political situation, the Prophet could not make a final decision about her and had to endure all these difficulties. [216]

Conversion of Rozbeh Khoshfouzdan to Islam

Rozbeh [217] was a monk from Persia who left Zoroastrianism and emigrated to Syria because he was fascinated by Christianity. He then went to Iraq and Turkey and met their scholars. In the first year of emigration, he traveled to the Arabian land in search of the prophesied prophet.[218] He met a group of Banu Kalb and asked them to take him to the Hejaz region, but they broke their promise. They sold him as a slave to a Jew, and then the Jew's cousin bought him from Banu Quraiza until he came to Medina. There he met the Prophet Muhammad. Rozbeh searched for the signs of the prophesied Prophet, which were told to him by one of the monks: that he does not take alms, accepts gifts and has the seal of prophethood between his shoulders. He found that the qualities he was looking for were present in the Prophet Muhammad, so he believed in him and followed him. After his conversion to Islam, the Prophet named him Salman. He became known as Salman the Persian (al-Farsi) and Salman Al-Muhammadi. [219]

The brotherhood

Those among the Muhajirun and Ansar who embraced Islam separated themselves from their own people, their brothers and their tribes in a real and profound way. They faced all kinds of challenges and harm from many, including relatives. Their ties with their kin were severed as if they had no tribe. Some

of them may have felt lonely, without support or tribe. The Islamic brotherhood emerged to fill this void and overcome the feeling of loneliness. A few
months after the Prophet's arrival in Medina, the brotherhood began between
his companions from the Muhajirun and Ansar. At that time, the Muslims who
joined the Brotherhood were ninety men. The Prophet continued the brotherhood depending on who embraced Islam or joined the Muslims in Medina.
Thus a brotherhood was formed between Abu Dhar and Salman al-Farsi, and a
brotherhood between Abu Bakr and Kharija bin Zuhair, and between Omar
and Atban bin Malik, and also between Hamza and Zaid bin Haritha, and so
on, until they reached one hundred and fifty men.

The Messenger of God fraternized the people and left Ali to the last. Ali bin
Abi Talib said: "O Messenger of God, have you made brotherhood among your
companions and excluded me." The Prophet replied, "I have left you to myself.
You are my brother and I am your brother. If anyone asks you, say, 'I am a servant of God and the brother of His Messenger. Only a liar can say that after
you. By the One who sent me with the truth, I have not excluded you except
for myself. You are to me as Aaron was to Moses, except that no prophet
comes after me. You are my brother and the one who receives my inheritance."

The concept of brotherhood is credited with strengthening Islamic society
and reinforcing its bonds. It is a manifestation of social justice and promotes
human and moral values, equality and unity. These values were expressed by
sharing money and accommodation between the Muhajirun and the Ansar and
by overcoming social differences among Muslims. There is no difference between a master and a slave, the rich and the poor, the black and the white.
Brotherhood was not merely an emotional affair or a tribal or personal interest,
but was based on truth and faith in God and His Messenger. [220]

The city constitution

Five months later, the Prophet wrote a document dealing with relations between Muslims and Jews in Medina. It also defines the rights of Jews, their religion and their money, and it was stipulated that they should not help anyone
against him, and if anything happens to them, they must help, just as the Muslims must do so in return.

The document was not limited to regulating Muslims' relations with others, but a large part of it was put forward to define general rules and practical bases for relations between Muslims themselves. This document is a working constitution that contains the basics of relations in the emerging country, whether at home or abroad.

The text of the city constitution reads as follows: In the name of God, the All Gracious, the Merciful. This is a book of Muhammad, the Prophet, between believers and Muslims of Quraysh and Yathrib and those who follow them; he joined them and fought with them, for they are one nation. The Muhajirun of Quraysh decided their affairs and their customs according to the rules of blood money and blood revenge that were common among them. They resolved their conflicts through benevolence and justice among the believers. The Banu Awf, likewise, acted according to their original customs. Each group resolved the captivity of its members through benevolence and justice among the believers, etc.

The document emphasized concepts that were the basis of the Islamic state, including:

1- Diversity of society and the plurality of its spectrum.

2- Presentation of the state as a political state led by the Prophet.

3- The recognition of the freedom of belief and practice of the various religious communities.

4- The fusion of the tribal society in Medina in the crucible of Islam, and Islam is the first reference and the basis for all political, social and economic affairs.

5- Consideration of the Jews as part of the political community in Medina and they participate in war and peace in Medina. [221]

The Jews lived in Medina and the surrounding villages for hundreds of years. They were several tribes, the most important of which were the tribes of Quraiza, Al-Nadir and Al-Qaynuqa. The Jews believe in the superiority of their race and that they are God's chosen people [222] and that they should not allow anyone to share this honor with them, which they see for themselves, and they regard the Arabs with great contempt. Therefore, the behavior of the Jews and their relationship with others was based on mistrust and tendency to isolate themselves,[223] and this contributed to the fact that Judaism was not widespread among the Arabs, except for a few who were influenced by them and adopted their faith.

After the Prophet's arrival in Medina, the Jews of Quraiza, Al-Nadir and Qainuqa to the prophet came and asked for an agreement. He wrote a separate agreement for each tribe but on the condition that they would not help anyone against him, nor would they attack any of his companions with tongue, hand or weapon, secretly or openly, by night or by day. And if they did, the Messenger of God would be free from shedding their blood, taking their offspring and their wives and taking their money.[224]

The Messenger of Allah began the establishment of the first Islamic state under difficult conditions, both at home and abroad. This situation required effective solutions in various fields, be it economic, social, religious or security. In the religious sphere, many regulations were issued, such as: the call to prayer (adhan), prayer, alms tax (zakat), fasting and much more. This legislation began in Mecca and gradually continued in Medina. On a social level, fraternity relations were established between Muslims. Then came the constitution, which legislated a law to regulate the lives of the people in this young state. As external threats continued to jeopardize the existence of this state, it was necessary to be militarily prepared. A strong army had to be built and trained to defend the country and its people. Hence came the concept of jihad[1], which means fighting in the name of Allah in defense of Islam and Muslims. Jihad was not limited to defense, but also played an important role in initiative and attack when necessary. Since to end oppression in the world and establish justice, Islam uses all peaceful means possible. When these are not effective, it resorts to the use of force to achieve these righteous goals. Jihad is therefore a military solution that complies with rational and natural laws as well as Sharia and faith. If Islam had not used the sword, it would not have been the religion of truth and justice, nor the religion of innate nature and reason. It would have been a traitor to society and all mankind throughout history. [225]

---

1 Jihad encompasses all endeavors, whether through action or speech, aimed at advancing Islam, defending Muslims from aggressors, securing the freedom of Muslim nations, or aiding individuals and the Muslim community as a whole. (In this context, it specifically pertains to military operations).

The first campaign

Seven months after his arrival, the Messenger of God began forming saraya groups[1]. The aim of the Saraya was to exert both economic and psychological pressure on the Quraysh. This was to make them realize that the Muslims would not leave them free in the region as long as they expelled them, harmed them, stole their money and killed them.

When the Prophet wanted to send a group, he would call together a saraya and say: "March in the name of God, by God, in the way of God and in the religion of the Messenger of God, and do not go too far, do not mutilate, do not be treacherous, do not kill an old man, a child or a woman, and do not cut down a tree unless you are forced to do so. If a man of the lowest or best Muslims sees a man of the Quraysh, he is safe until he hears the word of God. If he follows you, then he is your brother in religion, and if he refuses, then tell him how he can survive and seek God's help against him." Some of these Saraya had reconnaissance missions in which they observed the movements of the Quraysh in the region and tracked the attackers in the outskirts of the city. The saraya encouraged the Muslims and boosted their self-confidence. As a result of these battles and saraya, there were truces, reconciliations and alliances between the Muslims and many tribes in the region.

More than a year after the Prophet's arrival, the Prophet's first campaign, the so-called "Ghazwa al-Ushayra", took place. This campaign was aimed at a convoy of Quraysh under the leadership of Abu Sufyan. The Prophet Muhammad himself set out with one hundred and fifty fighters. When they came to a place called "Al-Ushayra", they did not find the convoy.

---

1   Saraya refers to a military expedition or campaign in which the Messenger of God does not personally participate. In contrast, Ghazwah is a battle in which the Prophet is personally present.

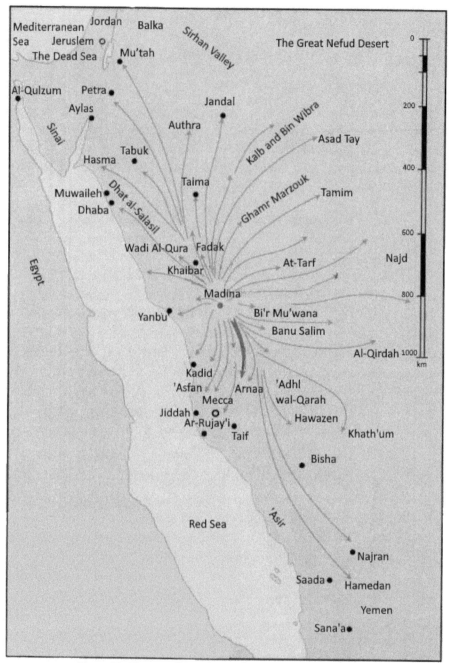

Figure 29: The expeditions (saraya) to the villages and tribes.

The Prophet and his companions stayed for a few days at a place called "Yanbu" to follow the convoy of Abu Sufyan. There they concluded peace agreements with the Banu Madlij and their allies from the Banu Damra. These treaties and agreements between the tribes were important to ensure that they would not attack each other in the future. Ammar bin Yasir and Ali bin Abi Talib went to the Banu Madlij farmers who were working on their water sources and palm trees. They lay down on the ground to rest. When they fell asleep, the Messenger of God came and saw that some dust from the earth was scattered on them. He woke them up and gently said to Ali bin Abi Talib, "Get up, O Abu Turab, Get up, O Abu Turab." Then the Prophet said: "Shall I tell you about the two most unfortunate people?" They replied, "Yes, O Messenger of Allah." He said: "Ahimar of Thamud, the one who slaughtered the camel mare, and the one who will beat you, O Ali, here - and he put his hand on the top of his head - until this gets wet from it." And he took his beard in his hand. [226]

The nickname Abu Turab[1] was the most popular nickname for Ali bin Abi Talib, and it means father of earth.[227] After that they returned to Medina without clashes or fighting. [228]

In one of the reconnaissance campaigns in the second year, the Prophet wrote a letter to the commander of the campaign. He ordered him not to open the letter until it had run for two days. They marched for two days, he opened the letter and found in it after the Basmalah[2]: "Walk with the blessing of God together with your companions who follow you until you reach Batn-Nakchla. Watch over the caravans of the Quraysh and bring us news about them." He told his companions that the Prophet of Allah had commanded him not to force any of those who were with him. They all had the choice of either staying with him or returning. Then they all went with him and stayed there. Then a caravan from Mecca passed by and the Muslims attacked them. They killed one man and captured two others and stole what they had with them. This happened on the first day of the sacred month of Rajab. The sacred months are four: Rajab, Dhu al-Qi'dah, Dhu al-Hijjah, and Muharram. They were named as sacred because the Arabs forbade fighting during them. When they came to the Prophet, he stopped the caravan and the two captives. He refused to take anything from them. Quraysh said: "Muhammad has desecrated the holy month by shedding blood, taking money and kidnapping men in this month." Allegations

---

1 Abu Turab: it means Earth Father in German. This nickname was one of the favorite nicknames of Ali ibn Abi Talib, and he was pleased when he was addressed with it. Then came rulers from the Umayyad dynasty after him, who took a hostile attitude towards him and used this nickname for him derogatorily and cursed him with it on the podiums.
2 Basmalah means, to say: "In the name of the merciful and gracious God".

were made against the Muslims and these were widely disseminated. The situation was further complicated by the involvement of the Jews.[229] As the matter became a topic of widespread discussion, the Qur'an was revealed by Allah to resolve the disputes. He says that although fighting in the sacred months is a great sin, there are exceptions to this rule. It should not be allowed for some corrupt groups to spread injustice and corruption and divert people from Allah's path and deny Allah. In fact, endeavoring to mislead people and turn them away from the way of Allah and His religion and driving the inhabitants out of their homes is worse than murder. [230]

Later, the Quraysh sent the ransom for the two captives and the Prophet released them. The Quraysh realized that they no longer had freedom of movement in the region. They also no longer had full control and could no longer lead their commercial caravans to the Levant easily. They realized that they had to return to reason and wisdom and abandon oppression and arrogance to get peace in return.

After a while, the unbelievers of the Quraysh wrote to Abdullah bin 'Ubayy[1], and those who worshipped idols from the Aws and Khazraj: "You have given refuge to our wanted one, and you are the most numerous people of Yathrib. We swear by God, either you will kill him or drive him out, or we will seek the help of the Arabs against you, or we will march to you until we kill your fighters and take your women as slaves." When this reached Ibn 'Ubayy and those with him among the idolaters, they gathered to discuss this and take action. When this reached the Prophet, he met them in a group and said: "The warnings of the Quraysh have had a great effect on you. They have not conspired against you any more than you would like to conspire against yourselves. You are these people who want to kill your sons and your brothers." When they heard this from the Prophet, they dispersed. The Quraysh disbelievers were informed that their intimidation and threats had failed. [231]

---

1   Abdullah bin 'Ubayy was a leader in Yathrib and the lord of the Khazraj tribe. He was about to become the lord of the city before the Prophet Muhammad arrived. He believed that Islam had robbed him of his power, which led him to fight the Prophet Muhammad secretly and openly.

623 - 624 AD

The second year after the Hijrah

The ransoming of Salman al-Muhammadi

In the first year of the Hijrah, the Messenger of God dictated a contract for the ransoming of Salman Al-Muhammadi, which was written by Ali bin Abi Talib. It stated that "Muhammad bin Abdullah, the Messenger of God, ransomed Salman Al-Farisi from Othman bin al-Ashhal al-Qurazi by planting three hundred palm trees and paying forty ounces of gold. In this way, Muhammad bin Abdullah was freed from the price of Salman Al-Farisi. Salman's loyalty was to Muhammad bin Abdullah and his family, so no one had anything against him."

Figure 30: An imaginary depiction of Salman al-Farsi.

Although the Jewish slave trader demanded an exorbitant amount of money for the release of Salman Al-Farisi, the Messenger of God insisted on ransoming him to free him from the slavery that was exhausting him. The Messenger of God loved this believer and did not accept racial discrimination based on his origin. He once said: "Salman is from us, Ahl al-Bait[1]". [232]

---

1   Ahl al-Bait: is an Arabic expression that literally means "family of the house" and refers to the direct family of the Prophet Muhammad, including his daughter Fatima, his son-in-law Ali, and their descendants, including Hassan and Hussein.

Qibla change

When the Prophet arrived in Medina, he prayed in the direction of Bait al-Maqdis (Jerusalem). But he had a special connection to the Kaaba and was waiting for the order to change the Qibla. Perhaps the reason for this is due to the Prophet's connection with Abraham, in addition to the fact that the Kaaba is the oldest monotheistic base for the Hanifs previously. But the Messenger of Allah did not ask Allah for this matter, but he was fully submissive to the command of Allah, turning his gaze to the sky eagerly, waiting for the revelation to descend with the divine command.

The Jews in Medina began to mock the Messenger because he was praying towards Jerusalem. They said to him, "You follow us, you pray in our direction of prayer, and tomorrow you will convert to our religion." The Messenger of Allah felt very sad and distressed about this, for he feared that the believers might be turned away from their religion and others might refuse to convert to Islam if the insults of the Jews continued because of the direction of prayer.

Then came the revelation with the glad tidings that communicated the words of Allah to Prophet Muhammad: "We see you turning your face to the sky and asking Allah for help. So we will guide you to a direction of prayer that you will love and accept." He then orders him and the Muslims to turn towards the Sacred Mosque (Kaaba). [233]

On the next day and during noon prayer, the prophet with the Muslims in the mosque of Banu Salim finished two rak'āt[1] of the prayer. Gabriel came down, took the arm of the prophet and turned him towards the Kaaba. The rows behind him turned around and they prayed the last two rak'āt to the Kaaba. The Jews said in surprise: "What has turned them away from the direction of prayer they had?". The mosque of Banu Salim, where this change took place, was called the "Mosque of the Two Qiblas". Since then is the direction of prayer to the Kaaba, and this happened in Rajab in the second year of the Hijrah. [234]

---

1 Rak'a: (pl. Rak'āt) is a section in Islamic prayer. Noon prayer consists of four Rak'āt.

Battle of Badr

The Quraysh did not stop using violence and coercion against the Muslims, confiscating their possessions and expelling them in order to force them to change their faith and comply with the Quraysh's demands. Therefore, the Muslims had to defend themselves and not simply surrender to the Quraysh attacks and oppression.

Muslims used to come to the Messenger of Allah in Mecca, sometimes injured and beaten, and complain to him about the suffering they had endured due to the cruelty of Quraysh. The Messenger of Allah said to them: "Be patient, for I have not been commanded to fight. "[235] And after he had migrated to Medina and in the second year of the Hijrah on the seventeenth day of Ramadan, divine permission was given to fight in self-defense: {Permission (to fight) is given to those who are being fought because they have been wronged - and Allah indeed has the power to help them - (to them) who have been unjustly expelled from their homes only because they say: Our Lord is Allah. And if Allah had not repelled some people by means of others, monasteries, churches, synagogues, and mosques in which Allah's name is frequently mentioned would indeed have been destroyed. - And Allah will certainly help those who help Him. Allah is indeed Powerful and Almighty. }[236]

Through the reconnaissance missions, the Messenger of Allah learned of the return of the caravan of Abu Sufyan, which traveled from Syria to Mecca and contained seventy horsemen. The caravan also carried most of Quraysh's wealth, which was estimated at fifty thousand dinars. The Islamic army planned to move out and confront the convoy in order to strike fear into the hearts of Quraysh and put pressure on them. The aim was to make Quraysh change their policy towards Muslims and allow the Prophet and Muslims to practice their religious rites in peace without persecution or harm. Even if it comes to the point where the Muslims take over the trade caravan, it would be as compensation for what Quraysh took from them in an unfair manner. The threat to a convoy of this size on the main transportation route from Mecca, which is considered the economic lifeline of Quraysh, would have serious implications for Quraysh's interests, and Quraysh would not ignore this matter under any circumstances. [237]

The Messenger of God told the Muslims to prepare to go to the caravan. However, many of his companions hesitated and did not want to go with him for fear of an attack by Quraysh, as Quraysh would retaliate against this attack.
238

Abu Sufyan knew through his scouts that the Muslims were coming towards him. He directly changed the route of the caravan and traveled to Mecca via the sea coast (See Figure 31). He also sent an envoy to Mecca to inform them of the matter and ask for help. The envoy of Abu Sufyan shouted in Mecca while he was standing on his camel and tore his robe. He said: "O people of Quraysh. The caravan, the caravan. Your wealth at Abu Sufyan, was attacked by Muhammad and his companions. I do not see that you will reach it. Oh help, oh help." Quraysh then announced general mobilization. Every significant Quraysh leader raised money to equip the army, and they said: "Whoever does not go with us, we will destroy his house." No man stayed behind, and whoever stayed sent someone in his place.

Umayyah ibn Khalaf hesitated to go out because Saad bin Muadh[1] had already come to Mecca as a pilgrim and had stayed with Umayyah because of their friendship. Saad set out to complete the pilgrimage and Umayyah accompanied him. Abu Jahl met them and said to Saad, "I see that you are walking around safely in Mecca, even though you are protecting those who have rebelled against their religion. If you were not with Abu Safwan (Umayyah), you would not return to your family unharmed." Saad said to him aloud, "If you try to prevent me, I will prevent you from something that will be more difficult for you." Then he continued, "Your way to Medina." Umayyah did not agree with him because he addressed the leader of Mecca with a high tone and scolded him. Saad said to Umayyah, "Leave it, because by God, I heard the Messenger of God say: you are dead. You will be killed." Umayyah said in shock: "In Mecca? "Saad said: "I don't know." Umayyah said anxiously, "By God, Muhammad never lied." He then decided not to come out. On the day of Badr, Abu Jahl insisted that he should come out and sent Uqbah bin Abi Muait to Umayyah with a censer that had incense in it and said: "burn some incense since you are one of the women." Then Umayyah became angry and wanted to go out, but his wife stopped him and said: "By God, Muhammad does not lie." But he insisted on going out. The actions and attitudes of Umayyah ibn Khalaf were not based on reason and conscience. Although he believed in the sincerity

---

1 Saad bin Muadh: was a leader of the Banu Aws in Yathrib and a companion of the Prophet Muhammad.

of Muhammad, he did not want to oppose him only out of fear for himself, and when he changed his mind, he took part in the war only out of enthusiasm and pre-Islamic courage. This attitude and mindset led to his loss, as we shall see. [239].

When Quraysh arrived in Al-Juhfa, the Banu Zahra returned and did not take part in the war. This was because their ally Ubay ibn Sharik al-Thaqafi convinced them to return and advised them not to waste their wealth and not to listen to the words of Abu Jahl. [240]

Abu Sufyan saved the caravan by changing their route and approaching Mecca. He then sent a message to the Quraysh asking them to return to Mecca. Abu Jahl, however, insisted on going to battle, chasing the Muslims and staying there for three days to let the Arabs know of their march and gathering and to frighten them. [241]

When the Prophet arrived near Badr, a problem arose. All three parties did not know where the other parties were at that moment due to the acceleration of events, the distances between them and the slow speed of the reconnaissance messengers. The Messenger of Allah did not know that Abu Sufyan had changed the path of the caravan and had taken the coastal route (in Tihama), nor did he know that Quraysh were coming. Abu Sufyan did not know that the Quraysh had come to his aid, and he did not know where the Messenger of God was. Then the Messenger of God sent a reconnaissance patrol to Badr. They found three of the Quraysh slaves trying to bring water from the wells of Badr for the Quraysh. The Muslims arrested them and brought them to the Prophet while he was standing and praying. They said: "We are the water carriers of the Quraysh, they sent us to bring them water." At that time, the Muslims were not aware of the arrival of the Quraysh army, and they did not want to hear such news.

The people became angry at their response and they hoped that they were slaves of Abu Sufyan and the caravan owners. That is why the Muslims beat them. When the Messenger of God finished his prayer, he said: "If they are honest with you, you would beat them, and if they lie to you, you would leave them." His companions said: "O Messenger of God, they say that the Quraysh have come." He said: "They have told you the truth, the Quraysh have gone out to protect their caravan." The Prophet approached the slaves and said: "Where are the Quraysh? They replied, "Behind that mountain you see." He said: "How many are they?" They said: "Many." He said: "How many are they." They said:

"We don't know." He said: "How many camels did they slaughter?" They replied, "Ten one day and nine the next." He said to the people, "Between one thousand and nine hundred." Then he asked the slaves, "How many men from Mecca went with you?" They replied, "There was no one left behind who was able to fight." [242]

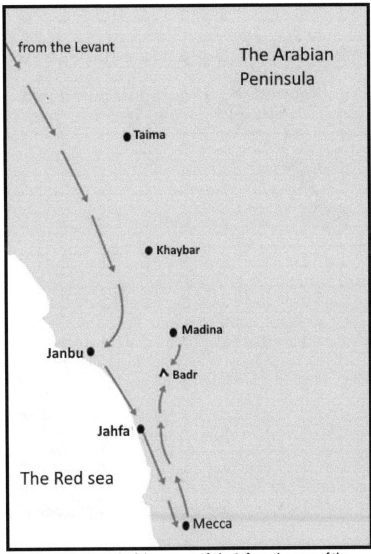

Figure 31: The path of the caravan of Abu Sufyan, the army of the polytheists and the army of the Muslims.

After the Messenger of Allah learned that the Quraysh had come from behind the mountain to rescue the caravan, Gabriel appeared to inform the Messenger that war was inevitable and that the caravan had escaped and arrived in Mecca. So the Messenger of God turned to the people and said: "This is Mecca, has sent its sons to you to fight against you. "[243] The Muslims were afraid of this and were dismayed.

The Prophet was aware of the situation of his companions and their division, and that some of them would refuse to fight against Quraysh. He wanted to hear a firm and courageous stance on war from the Muhajirun to reassure the Ansar. He turned to the Muhajirun and said: "Advise me." Abu Bakr stood up and said: "O Messenger of God, they are the Quraysh and their arrogance. They have not believed since their rejection of Islam and have not humiliated themselves since their pride. and they have not come out in the form of war." The Messenger of God said to him, "Sit down." He sat down, and the Messenger of God repeated the question to them. Omar stood up and said the same as Abu Bakr. Then the Prophet ordered him to sit down, and he sat down. Then al-Miqdad stood up and said: "O Messenger of God, they are the Quraysh with their arrogance. And we have believed in you and we have testified that what you have brought is right from God. And by God, if you commanded us to go through the embers of Ghada[1] and the thorns of Huras[2], we would go through it with you. And we do not tell you what the sons of Israel said to Moses: {They said: 'O Mūsā, surely we will never enter it while they are in it. Why don't you and your master go and fight? We will remain sitting here.'}[244] But we say: Go, you and your Lord. Fight, and We will be there. By God, we will fight on your right and on your left and in front of you, and if you go through a sea, we would go with you, and if you go to Barak Al-Ghamd[3] we would follow you." The Prophet's face lit up at al-Miqdad's words, and he rejoiced and prayed for him.

Then the Prophet turned to the Ansar and said: "Advise me." The Ansar believed that it was their duty to support the Prophet in their house when he got into trouble and to protect him from whatever threatened them. But if he himself was the attacker, or if the war was not in their land, then they would have no duty to support him. This was the obvious agreement made in the allegiance of Al-Aqaba. Therefore, the Prophet feared that the Ansar might not see that it was their duty to support him in this war. Saad bin Muadh stood up and said:

---

1   Ghada: A kind of hard tree whose embers burn for a long time.
2   Huras: A kind of thistle desert plant.
3   Barak Al-Ghamd is now called (Al-Barak) and is a city on the pilgrimage route, 560 km from Mecca.

"May my father and mother be sacrificed for you, O Messenger of God, did you want to know our opinion?" The Prophet said: "Yes." He said: "Perhaps you went out because of a matter in which you were ordered to do something else." He said: "Yes." He said: "May my father and mother be sacrificed for you, O Messenger of God. We have believed in you, and we have testified that what you have brought is true from God. Let us do whatever you will. By God, if you had commanded us to go into this sea, we would go in with you, and perhaps God will show you what will delight your eyes. Let us march with the blessing of God." The prophet set out, ordered them to march, and told them that God had promised him one of two things, either victory or booty[1], and God will not break His promise. Then he said: "By God, it's as if I'm witnessing the death of Abu Jahl bin Hisham, Utbah bin Rabi'ah, Shaybah bin Rabi'ah, Al-Walid bin Uqbah, Umayyah bin Khalaf and Uqbah bin Abi Muait." He moved on until he arrived in Badr. Most of the Companions tended to seek the booty, i.e. the convoy of Abu Sufyan, and avoid fighting with the polytheists who came from Mecca. But Allah wanted to consolidate and support the truth and eradicate disbelief and disbelievers. [245]

The Messenger of Allah did not need their opinion or advice, for the order of war had been established and commanded by Allah. It was the right choice if the Muslims wanted to live in dignity and honor. The order of war was inevitable and commanded by Allah. He consulted them only because they were the ones who would bear the burdens of war and suffer its consequences at various levels. Moreover, the Prophet wanted to extract their innermost thoughts and distinguish the hypocrite from the believer, the coward from the brave, and the one who thinks of his own interest from the one who thinks from the point of view of the religious mission. [246]

The Messenger of God set out with 313 men, and they had seventy camels with them, which they rode alternately among them. The Quraysh, on the other hand, set out while drinking alcohol, having women who beat drums and sang poetry. They had 700 camels and 200 horses, all well equipped, and every day they slaughtered camels to feed them. The polytheists of Quraysh learned that the Muslims had captured the water carriers and panicked. They regretted their decision to come to Badr, especially when they knew that the caravans had escaped. Utbah bin Rabia, whose son Abu Hudhayfah was with the Prophet, admitted that their march after the survival of their caravan was a transgression and aggression on their part, so they tried to return, but Abu Jahl refused and

---

1 The booty from the caravan of Abu Sufyan is meant.

said: "No, by al-Lāt and al-ʿUzzā[1], we will continue until we storm them in Yathrib and take them as prisoners and bring them to Mecca, then the Arabs will know about it, and thus no one will hinder our trade anymore." [247]

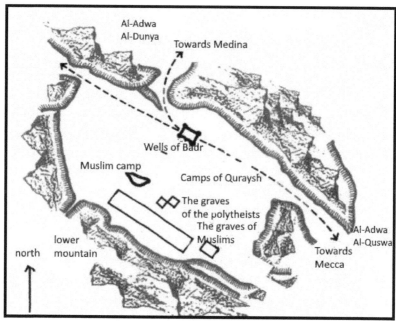

Figure 32: Map of the Battle of Badr.

Quraysh reached Badr first and camped in the farthest position of the valley following Mecca (Al-Adwa Al-Quswa[2]), where there was water, on a stable ground, while the camels of Quraysh were camped behind them. The Muslims were encamped in the lower position of the valley following the Medina (Al-Adwa Al-Dunya), where there was no water and the ground was soft and unstable, and the land consisted of shifting sands on which no foot could find a foothold (see Figure 32). This means that the Muslims' location was inappropriate from a military point of view. But Allah supported his faithful servants. He brought rain on Quraysh during the night, which softened their ground. As for the shifting sand in the Muslims' camp, the rain stabilized it and made it firm. The Muslims collected water in containers, drank, took care of their mounts, washed themselves. [248]

---

1   al-Lāt and al-ʿUzzā: are pre-Islamic goddesses of the Arabs.
2   Al-Adwa: It is the edge of the valley. Al-Dunya: closest to Medina, and Al-Quswa: furthest from Medina and therefore closest to Mecca.

When the Muslims learned of the large number of Quraysh, they were afraid and supplicated to Allah. The Prophet, however, turned to the Kaaba and said: "Allah, fulfill what you have promised me. Allah, if this group is destroyed, you will not be worshipped on earth." Allah answered their prayer and supported them with a thousand angels, not to fight alongside them, but to calm their hearts and strengthen their resolve and encourage them to fight.[249] Allah bestowed upon them sleep and rest, providing them with security and recuperation in preparation for a bloody battle the following day. This was to ensure they would not falter when confronted with the army of enemies.

The next morning, the Messenger of God gathered his companions and gave his banner to Ali ibn Abi Talib. He then began to form the ranks of the fighters. As he was inspecting the ranks and had in his hand a piece of wood with which to align the people, he passed Suwad ibn Ghaziya who was sticking out of the line. He poked him in the stomach with his stick and said: "Stand up straight, O Suwad." Suwad said: "O Messenger of Allah, you have hurt me and Allah has sent you with truth and justice, so allow me to avenge myself." The Messenger of Allah exposed his belly and said: "Avenge yourself." Suwad embraced him and kissed his belly. The Messenger of Allah said: "What made you do this, O Suwad." Suwad said: "O Messenger of Allah, you see what has come, so I wanted my last contact with you to be my skin touching your skin." The Messenger of Allah prayed for him for good and said to him, "Stand up straight, O Suwad."[250]

The Prophet then began to advise the fighters and said to them, "Lower your eyes and do not start fighting, and none of you speak." The Muslims remained silent and lowered their eyes in obedience to their leader's command. This clearly influenced Quraysh to the extent that one of them rode his horse around the Muslims to find out if they had reinforcements or an ambush. He then returned to his companions and said: "They have no ambush or military support. But their fighters endure death. Do you not see that they are like mute and do not speak. They stare like a snake, they have no refuge but their swords. I see that they will not turn away until they are killed, and they will not die until they have killed their equal numbers." Abu Jahl cursed him because he saw how he frightened his companions. Abu Jahl then encourages his companions by pointing out the small number of Muslims: "They are like a small meal, if we sent our slaves to them, they would have overpowered them only with their bare hands." Uqbah bin Abi Muait refused to go out. His companions said to him: "Go out with us. " He said: "This man has already promised me that he would kill me if he found me outside the mountains of Mecca." They said: "You will get a red camel that no one can catch in races, and if a defeat were to occur, you could escape with it." They convinced him and he went with them.

When the two armies met, the Messenger of God tried for the last time to talk to the Quraysh to convince them to adopt a peaceful attitude to avoid war and bloodshed, and to ask them to let him deliver his message in peace. "O people of Quraysh, I hate to start the fight with you. Leave me and the Arabs alone and turn back. If I am telling the truth, you know me well and know that I have always been credible. And if I am a liar, the thieves and deceivers of the Arabs will stop me for you," said the Messenger of God .

Utbah bin Rabia advised the polytheists to accept the Prophet's request. Abu Jahl accused him of cowardice and said: "Utbah is filled with terror when he saw Muhammad and his companions. He fears for his son Abu Hudhayfah, who is with Muhammad." When Utbah bin Rabiah heard Abu Jahl's words, he said: "This coward will see who was afraid: me or him." He was so excited that he put on his armor and came forward with his brother Shaybah and his son Al-Walid to ask for a duel. [251]

The first to fight were Utbah, Shaybah and Al-Walid. Three of the Ansar confronted them. They said to the Ansar, "Go back. We don't want you, we want the most qualified fighters of the Quraysh." The Prophet heard this and brought the Ansar back and stood with his family because he did not want to start with the Ansar. He sent Ubaidah bin Al-Harith[1], Hamza and Ali and said: "Stand up, O Ubaidah, stand up, O uncle, stand up, O Ali, and claim your right that God has ordained for you. For the Quraysh have come with their arrogance and pride to extinguish the light of God. But God does not allow except His light to be completed." The Prophet said that Quraysh wanted to destroy the Prophet and end his religion with this war. But Allah has made it His business to raise the banners of Islam, to elevate its position and to support it, even if the polytheists reject it. Then he said: "O Ubaidah, you must fight Utbah bin Rabi'ah," and to Hamza he said: "You fight Shaybah," and to Ali he said: "You fight Al-Walid."

Then the three of them went into battle. Utbah asked about them and the opponents stepped forward. Shaybah asked about Hamza and he replied, "I am

---

1   Ubaidah bin al-Harith bin al-Muttalib bin Abd Manaf bin Qusay was the cousin of the Prophet Muhammad's father, and one of the early converts to Islam. He was ten years older than the Prophet.

Hamza bin Abdul Muttalib, the Lion of God and the Lion of His Messenger." Shaybah said: "You have met the Lion of the Allies. See how you fight, O Lion of God."

Abbildung 33: Die Aufstellung der Muslime für den Kampf gegen die Polytheisten in Badr.

Ali killed Al-Walid, and when he came to Hamza, who was embracing Shaybah, and their swords were wedged together, Ali said : "O uncle, lower your head," and Hamza was tall. He put his head on Shaybah's chest. Ali struck with his sword so that he cut off half of Shaybah's head. Utbah had cut off Ubaidah's leg, and Ubaidah had struck him on the head. Ali went to him and finished off Utbah as well. Thus Ali ibn Abi Talib was involved in the killing of the three men. Then Hamza and Ali carried Ubaidah bin Al-Harith and took him to the Messenger of God . He was sad for Ubaidah.

Ubaidah said: "O Messenger of God, am I not a martyr?" He said: "Yes, you are the first martyr of my family." Ubaidah said: "If your uncle was still alive, he would have known that I have more right to what he says." He asked, "Which uncle do you mean? " He replied, "Abu Talib, where he says:

By God's house, you are lying,

when you say that Muhammad should give up,

While we swing the bow and spear for his sake.

We defend him until all around him have fallen,

And we sacrifice our children and wives for him."

The Prophet replied: "Do you not see that his son stands like a raging lion before God and His Messenger and his other son fights in jihad for Allah in the land of Abyssinia?" Ubaidah asked: "O Messenger of God, are you angry because of what I said?" The Prophet replied, "I am not angry with you, but you mentioned my uncle and that bothered me." [252]

Ubaidah died of his wounds after the battle when the Islamic army reached Al-Safra.[253] Praise and appreciation came from Allah for Ali, Hamza and Ubaidah. Allah said that they had kept the promise they had made to their Lord and had not changed it as the hypocrites did, and that they were steadfast and patient in the path of truth. Some of them were killed in battle, like Ubaidah, and some await their fate, like Ali and Hamza. [254]

When Abu Jahl saw the killing of Utbah, Shaybah and al-Walid, he tried to save the situation. He said: "Do not be hasty like the sons of Rabi'ah. You should slaughter the people of Yathrib, then you should turn to the Quraysh and capture them until we bring them to Mecca. Then we will show them their madness." [255]

The two armies clashed and the Muslims fought with what modest troops and limited equipment they had. The Prophet said to Ali, "Give me a handful of pebbles," and Ali gave him a handful. He threw them in the faces of the people, and this action had a marvelous effect, for no polytheist remained whose eyes, mouth and nose were not full of pebbles. Then the believers pursued them, killed them or captured them. There is no doubt that it appears that the Prophet and his companions played this role in the Battle of Badr, but the Quran says, "You did not do this yourselves and you did not throw yourself" because the spiritual and physical abilities that are the basis for these results, are all gifts of Allah, and you have been set in motion by the power of Allah and for Allah. Therefore, the real doer is Allah, even though it was done by your free will.[256]

God defeated the Quraysh with a devastating defeat. When one of the polytheists, Taliha bin Khuwaylid, saw the defeat of his companions, he said: "What has defeated you?" One of them replied, "There is no man among us who would not prefer his companion to die before him. And we have come to a people who are prepared to die for their companions." Abu Jahl was killed by one of the weakest fighters among the Muslims, just as the Messenger of God had predicted. In fact, the Prophet had predicted everything about what would happen in the Battle of Badr even before it happened.[257]

Figure 34: The fall of one of the idolaters in Badr.

Abu Lahab did not go to the Battle of Badr himself because he was sick. In his place, he sent Al-'As ibn Hisham Al-Makhzumi, the brother of Abu Jahl, who was also killed in the Battle of Badr. When Abu Lahab heard of the Battle of Badr and the victory of the Muslims, he became angry and died seven days later from his illness. [494]

The onslaught of the two armies in the battle was obvious and interesting, full of enthusiasm and strength. This was due to God's planning. God mentioned that He had shown the army of unbelievers in the dream to the Prophet as a small group so that they would be successful and not quarrel due to their hesitation and fear of confronting the enemy. When the battle began and the two armies faced each other, God revealed to the Muslims the inside and the truth of the Quraysh army, so that they saw the enemy army as small and weak, without the strength to confront. The enemy, on the other hand, did not know the morals of the Muslims and only saw their outward appearance, which they perceived as few. Abu Jahl saw the Muslims like a small meal and believed that he would finish the battle with them in a single day. These two factors had a great influence on the outbreak of the war and the victory of the Muslims. [258]

While the angels defended the Muslims, the demons defended the unbelievers. The devil brightened up their deeds and promised to do everything in his power to defend them in battle, just as a neighbor defends his neighbor in Arab culture. But when the two armies clashed, the devil retreated in fear of the divine assistance he saw in the Muslims, saying, "I fear God, I see what you do not see." The devil spoke to them in the form of an elder of the tribe of Bani Kinanah named Suraqa ibn Malik, although Suraqa had not actually gone to war with them. So the devil deceived them and left them alone to suffer a crushing defeat.[259]

Seventy of Quraysh were killed in Badr, half of them at the hands of Ali bin Abi Talib, because of his bravery in battle called him the Quraysh the "red death". Another seventy were captured. From the Muslims, only ten were martyred and none of them were captured. They captured one hundred and fifty camels, ten horses, goods and many weapons from the Quraysh. [260] The Messenger of Allah ordered that the bodies of the polytheists be collected and thrown into a well. Then he called them one by one and asked, "Have you found what your god promised you? I have found what my Lord truly promised me. You were bad people for your prophet. You denied me and people believed me. You drove me out and the people welcomed me. You fought against me and the people helped me." Omar Ibn Al-Khattab said: "O Messenger of God, do you call those who have already died!" The Prophet replied, "You listen to what I say no better than they do, but they are unable to answer me." Then the Prophet distributed the booty among the Muslims on the way to Medina without taking al-Khums (the fifth) 2 in order to give the warriors a larger share and encourage them. [261]

Badr captives

The Messenger of God made his way to Medina. When he reached Al-Safra, he ordered Ali to execute two prisoners: 'Uqbah ibn Abi Muait, who was known in Mecca for his bad deeds towards Muslims and the Prophet, and al-Nazir ibn al-Harith, who had tortured Muslims in Mecca and had been cruel to the Prophet. Al-Nazir said: "O Muhammad, I ask you to treat me like a man from the Quraysh because of our kinship. If you kill them, you will kill me, and if you release them, then release me." The Messenger of God replied: "There is no kinship between you and me, God has cut the ties of kinship with Islam." Then he turned to Ali and said: "Take him to the front, O Ali, and cut off his head." And so Ali did.

Uqbah said: "O Muhammad, I ask you by God and because of our kinship." The Prophet replied: "Are you one of the Quraysh? Are you only a disbeliever from the people of Saffuriyya[1]. Ali, take him to the front and cut off his head." Uqbah said: "O Muhammad, who is for my children." The Prophet Muhammad said: "Hell (the fire)." Uqbah bin Abi Muait belongs to the group that fought against the Prophet with all their might. Despite all these acts that Ibn Abi Muait committed, which required even the most severe punishment, he was executed for his apostasy from Islam and for inciting individuals and armies to fight and destroy the Islamic call. Therefore, the Messenger of God promised him before emigration that he would cut off his head if he would meet him outside the mountains of Mecca, and so it happened. The Prophet's statement about the sons of 'Uqbah is a revelation about the future that God has revealed to him. For God knew that none of these sons deserved honor and mercy and that their fate will be in Hell because of the injustice and oppression that they will exercise against the people and whose rights they will rob. [262]

When the Ansar saw what happened to al-Nazir and Uqbah, they feared that the Prophet would kill all the captives. "O Messenger of God, we have already killed seventy, and they are your people and your family. Would you finish them all. Leave them to us, O Messenger of God, Take the ransom from them and free them," they said. They said among themselves, "We should send Abu Bakr to the Prophet to talk to him, for he is the kindest of the Quraysh to our clan, and we know of no one who has a higher rank with Muhammad than he." Abu Bakr replied: "Yes, if it is God's will, everything will be fine." He returned to the Messenger of Allah to appease and reassure him and said: "O Messenger of Allah, may my father and mother be sacrificed for you. Among your people there are fathers and sons, relatives, brothers and nephews, and even the most distant of them are close to you. Please be merciful to them. Allah will reward you with favor. Or save them from the Fire by letting Allah redeem them. Take from them what you need to strengthen the Muslims. Perhaps Allah will open their hearts to you." Then Abu Bakr stood up and then returned to him to ask again, saying, "Do not be the first to kill them. May Allah guide them better than if you were to destroy them." Prophet Muhammad then remained silent.

The Prophet did not want to take a ransom and instead wanted to carry out the punishment for all warring captives. Saad bin Muadh noticed what the Prophet wanted and said: "O Messenger of God, this is the first war in which we have encountered the Quraysh, and we prefer that we kill men instead of holding them." Omar said: "O Messenger of God, they have denied you and

---

1   Saffuriyya is a city near Jordan, which is near Tiberias.

driven you out. Bring them forward and strike them on the neck. Let Ali cut off Aqeel's head. Authorize me also to kill one of them and authorize Hamza to kill al-Abbas, for these are the leaders of disbelief." But most of the Muslims wanted to take a ransom and release the prisoners. Gabriel came to the Prophet and said: "God is not satisfied with what your companions have decided to take the ransom. He commands you to give them a choice: Either you shall cut off their heads or take ransom on the condition that they will kill their number from you." When the Prophet saw that they insisted on taking the ransom, he explained to them that taking the ransom would result in the number of Muslims killed being equal to the number of unbelievers captured. They replied: "O Messenger of God, it is about our clans and our brothers. We take the ransom to gain strength against our enemy. And a number equal to theirs will perish from our side."

The Quranic verses came in accordance with the Prophet's opinion and as a warning to Muslims. They emphasize that no Prophet has the right to capture members of the enemy unless he has fixed his foot on the ground, asserted his control and dealt blows to the enemies. Allah rebuked those who disobeyed the Prophet's command because they wanted the ransom.[263] But despite their disagreement with their Prophet, Allah honored them with His favor and forgave them. He allowed them to take the ransom in order to strengthen their hearts, despite the grave consequences this would have. [264]

The Prophet sent someone to Medina to inform the Muslims of the victory. Some did not believe it at first, but then they were sure that it was true after they saw the army returns. The believers rejoiced and greeted the Messenger. The rest of the captives arrived in Medina one day after their arrival. The Prophet distributed them among the Muslims and said: "Be kind to them" until the people of Mecca ransomed them. He set the ransom for each captive from one thousand to four thousand dirhams if he had money, and whoever had no money had to teach ten Muslims to read and write. The Quraysh began to send the ransom money one by one. The Prophet gave each of his companions the prisoner he had captured, and each of them negotiated with the Quraysh himself to ransom his captive. [265]

Among the captives was a son of Umair bin Wahb. He wanted to come to Medina to ransom his son, so he met with Safwan bin Umayyah, who was one of the polytheists. Umair secretly agreed with Safwan ibn Umayyah that he would enter the city and kill the Prophet Muhammad in an assassination attempt in exchange for Safwan paying Umair's debt. They kept the plan a secret. Umair sharpened his sword and prepared to enter the city. The Prophet allowed him to enter, but Omar ibn al-Khattab was afraid of him and arrested him and then took him to the Messenger of God. When the Prophet saw him, he said to Omar ibn al-Khattab, "Bring him in, Omar." Then he asked him why he had come here. He said: "I have come for this prisoner who is in your hands. Treat him well." The Prophet then asked him about the sword, and Umair replied, "Damn this sword, it has done us no good at all." Then the Prophet told him what had happened between him and Safwan in secret. Umair was astonished at the Prophet's knowledge of this secret affair between him and Safwan, and so he converted to Islam. The Prophet then said: "Advise your brother in his religion, read the Quran to him and free his captive." Umair then joined Mecca. Safwan swore not to speak to him or help him in any way. [266]

Another prisoner, Abu Azza al-Jumahi, was a man from Quraysh who had five daughters. He asked the Prophet to have mercy on him and release him for his five daughters. The Messenger of God did so, provided that he did not return to war against the Muslims and that he did not support anyone against him. Abu Azza promised the Prophet that he would not do so. [267]

Al-Abbas bin Abdul Muttalib, the Prophet's uncle, and Aqeel bin Abi Talib, the Prophet's cousin, were also among the prisoners. Both were chained together with the other prisoners. When night fell, the Prophet could not sleep and stayed awake all night. Some of his companions asked him, "What keeps you awake, O Prophet of Allah?" He replied, "The wailing of Al-Abbas." One of the companions then went to the prisoners and untied Al-Abbas. When the Prophet no longer heard the moaning, he asked why, and it was explained to him that al-Abbas had been freed from his handcuffs. The Prophet ordered them to free all the prisoners from their shackles. Then men from the Ansar came to the Messenger of Allah and said: "O Messenger of Allah, allow us to leave the ransom for the son of our sister Al-Abbas." This shows decency and a good choice of words towards the Prophet, because the paternal grandmother of Al-Abbas ibn Abd al-Muttalib was from the tribe of Bani Najjar of the Khazraj, who belonged to the Ansar. Al-Abbas himself was the Prophet's uncle, so the Messenger of Allah was more closely related to Al-Abbas than the Ansar. But they did not say to the Prophet, "Allow us to leave the ransom for your uncle" so that they would have no obligation to the Messenger of Allah. Instead, they wanted the Messenger of Allah to be obligated to them. The Prophet could have given them permission, as this ransom would go to the

Muslims' treasury and they had asked for it. But the Messenger of Allah did not agree and said: "By Allah, you should not leave a dirham of it." This means that if ransom is a general Islamic law, then there should be no difference between a relative or a stranger, and there should be no difference between the Prophet's uncle and any other captive.[268] The Prophet then asked Al-Abbas to ransom himself and his two nephews Aqeel and Nawfal. Al-Abbas said that he had no money, but the Prophet pointed out to him that he had left money to his wife Umm Al-Fadl and told him that Gabriel had revealed this to him. "I swear, no one knows about this except me and my wife, I bear witness that you are the Messenger of God," Al-Abbas said. The Muslims captured 20 or 40 ounces of gold from Al-Abbas and each ounce had 40 mithqal. The Prophet said to him, "What you have brought to support them against us, we will not leave to you. O Al-Abbas, you have fought against God and God has defeated you." [269]

Allah spoke to his Prophet and informed him that he should call the captives to encourage them to believe in Allah and improve themselves. If there is acceptance of Islam in their hearts, Allah would give them something better than what was taken from them, namely material and spiritual rewards and forgiveness from Allah. However, if any of the captives tried to fake Islam to harm the religion, betray the Prophet and take revenge on the Muslims, then they had already betrayed Allah before and were punished with disgrace and loss and Allah is able to do this again. They should learn from this lesson. After this, all the captives returned to their faith except Al-Abbas, Aqil and Nawfal who converted to Islam. [270]

The Muslims who had suffered at the hands of the Quraysh are now defeating their enemy. Those who had tortured them yesterday, driven them from their homes, robbed their money and severed their kinship ties were now placed in their hands and at their mercy. But contrary to all expectations, they did not use the opportunity to take revenge. Instead, they were ordered by the leader to be kind to the prisoners. They obeyed this order and shared their money with them. Even one of them favored his prisoner with his food. [271]

The Quraysh warriors returned to Mecca in a furious state. Abu Sufyan forbade them to mourn their dead and prevented poets from mourning the dead so that their animosity towards the Muslims would not be diminished. Abu Sufyan renounced perfume and women until he could assault Muhammad. [272]

The king of Abyssinia, Negus, was delighted with the victory of the Messenger of God in Badr. But the Quraysh polytheists were determined to take revenge. They decided to ask the king of Abyssinia to send them his followers so that they could take revenge and kill the Muslims. They sent Amr bin Al-Aas and Abdullah bin Abi Rabi'ah to him with gifts and antiquities. The Messenger of God learned of this matter and sent a letter to Negus advising him to protect the Muslims. Negus refused Amr ibn al-Aas's request, so Amr returned from his mission disappointed. [273]

After the Battle of Badr, the Muslims' souls were strengthened and their self-confidence returned in a significant way. The captured goods also helped them to overcome their urgent economic problems. The Arabs realized that the Prophet, who had come to Medina yesterday as a powerless fugitive, had become a force to be reckoned with. They began to think carefully before taking any action against him in the region. The Quraysh realized that their lives were in real danger with the Muslims. Therefore, in their subsequent campaigns, they planned with more precision and concentration to eliminate this movement, which they saw as a threat to their interests and privileges in the region. Some tribes planned conspiracies and raids against the Muslims and even considered going to war with the Prophet. Abu Sufyan was determined to revenge for the defeat at Badr and contacted the Jews of Banu al-Nadir in Medina to attack the Muslims. The Prophet carried out raids and campaigns to thwart these plots and turn their attacks against them. These defeats constituted a psychological war for the polytheists in the region in general and the Quraysh in particular. [274]

Umm Salama in the house of the Prophet

In the month of Shawwal in the second year of Hijrah, the Messenger of Allah married Hind bint Abi Umayyah al-Makhzumi, known as Umm Salama. She was one of the believing women who was known for her beauty, sound mind and correct opinion. After the death of her husband Abu Salama, Umm Salama had no one from her family in Medina except small children and she was not even twenty-five years old. The Muslims mourned her loss greatly. After her waiting period (al'idda[1]) had expired following the death of Abu Salama, Abu Bakr proposed marriage to her, which she refused. Then Omar ibn al-Khattab proposed to her, which she also refused. Then the Messenger of Allah proposed to her. She said: "Welcome, Messenger of Allah," and mentioned that she was jealous and that she had small children. The Messenger of Allah said to her, "Allah will take care of your children. As for your jealousy, I will ask Allah to remove it." [275] Umm Salama was a good wife for the Messenger of Allah. She remained faithful and obedient to him and kept to her home as Allah had commanded her.[276]

As for the Prophet's marriages; after the death of Khadija, his first wife, with whom Prophet Muhammad had spent twenty-five years of his life, Prophet Muhammad entered into a marriage with an elderly widow in Medina. This happened when he was already over fifty years old. Over the next ten years, the Prophet took several wives in marriage, including both widows and virgins from different tribes. These marriages, which were both an honor and a distinction for these women, were for various reasons - legal, social and political. They served to lead a community, to protect Islam and Muslims or to clarify a legal rule.

---

1   Al'idda: in Islam refers to the waiting period that a woman must observe after divorce or the death of her husband before she can remarry. This period serves to ensure that the woman is not pregnant, and varies depending on circumstances, but is usually three menstrual cycles or about three months.

The victory of the Romans over the Persians

In the second year of the Hijrah, which corresponds to the year 624 AD, the Romans under the leadership of Heraclius defeated Persia under the leadership of Khosrau II. This happened after repeated defeats of the Romans in a war that lasted more than twenty years. Allah mentioned this in the Quran when the Muslims were still in Mecca, about eight years earlier. This fulfilled the prophecy of the Prophet Muhammad. The Muslims rejoiced at this victory of the Romans because the Romans were people of the Book, while the Persians were magicians and had no Book. This important victory of the Romans was the beginning of a series of victories that were crowned with the attack of the Romans on the Persians in their homeland in 627 AD [277]

The war against Banu al-Qainuqa

From the beginning of the Hijrah and before the Battle of Badr, the Jews tried to break the agreements they had made with the Messenger of God and to cause unrest among the Muslims. After the Battle of Badr and its astonishing result, the fears of the Jews, Quraysh and hypocrites were intensified, so they continued their acts of sabotage and ignored the constitution of Medina and the agreements they had made with the Messenger of God.

At first, the Prophet followed the method of clear and just warning and punishment of those who break agreements and cause trouble. He passed the death sentence on the ringleaders and saboteurs who agitated against the Messenger of God in Medina and Mecca, collaborated with his enemies, stirred up unrest in the Islamic community, insulted Muslim women and the Prophet's wives, and spread rumors. Some Jews then came to the Prophet and complained that the execution of a Jew was treason. The Prophet explained to them that the Jew had broken the covenant and verbally attacked the Muslims. He then told them that they had to renew the broken covenant and make a new one. He sent them to Ali to make a new covenant. [278]

The Banu Qainuqa were the bravest, most famous and richest Jews in Medina. They worked as goldsmiths and were allies of Abdullah bin 'Ubayy and Ubadah bin Al-Samit. One day, a Muslim woman came to their market and sat with one of their jewelers because of her jewelry. They demanded that she show her face, but the woman refused. The jeweler or another man tied the hem of her dress to her back without her realizing it. When she stood up, her bottom was exposed. She screamed, and a Muslim attacked the man who had done this and killed him. The Jews then attacked the Muslim and killed him. The Muslims were furious and the family of the Muslim who had been killed sought revenge against the Jews. Then the news reached the Prophet, who felt pain and said: "We did not agree with them on such a matter." Ubadah bin al-Samit declared that he had renounced the covenant with the unbelievers and emphasized that he would remain faithful to the covenant with God and His Messenger. As for Abdullah bin 'Ubayy, he refused to renounce his covenant with the Jews, and apologized that he feared problems, and claimed that he might need the Jews one day. The Quran responds here to those hypocrites with sick souls who refuse to abandon their alliance with the foreigners and justify themselves by saying that Jews and Christians might one day seize power and authority. The Quran informed them that they should also consider that Allah might support the Muslims and power might fall into their hands. Then these people would regret what they were hiding in their hearts.[279]

Tensions between Muslims and Jews increased in Medina, threatening security and peace. At the Battle of Badr, Banu Qainuqa showed hostility and rejected the covenant with the Prophet, which stated that they should neither fight against him nor support his enemy. To resolve this turmoil, the Prophet gathered the Jews in their market and said to them, "O Jews, fear Allah lest the same fate befall you as befell Quraysh in the form of calamity, and convert to Islam. For you know that I am a sent prophet, you will find that in your Book and in the covenant of Allah for you." They replied: "O Muhammad, you see what your people are like. Do not be deceived. You have come across people who are ignorant of war and you have found an opportunity with them. By Allah, if we were to fight you, you would know that we are the people."

This hostile reaction of the Jews to the Prophet did not pass without consequences. Allah revealed to his Prophet that he should tell them that they would be defeated and that their fate in this world and in the Hereafter would only be defeat, humiliation and painful punishment. Then Allah mentioned that there is a lesson for the people in the two groups that met, namely the army of the

Muslims and the army of the disbelievers in the Battle of Badr. Allah supported the Muslims and helped them to victory. People of understanding should learn from this lesson.[280] The message came to the Prophet from God to clarify the strict approach that the Prophet should take towards them so that they can be a lesson to others. God gave his Messenger the authority to break the covenant with the Jews if he feels a treachery from them or breaking their covenants, and that is after the presence of reasons and corroborating evidence of their determination about breaking their covenant or making new agreement with the enemy against the Muslims.[281]

The Prophet's patience towards the Jews and his instruction to the Muslims to endure as much as possible made the Jews believe that this was due to weakness and fear, so they continued their harassment. The Prophet did not want to give them any further freedom of action so that they would not take advantage of the situation and gather around them those who shared their opinion, such as the hypocrites and the Bedouins.

After the dissolution of the treaty with the Jews of Banu Qaynuqa and the disclosure of their hostility towards the Prophet, it became necessary for the Prophet to rid Medina of their evil. In the month of Shawwal in the second year of the Hijrah, the Prophet marched to Banu al-Qainuqa. He appointed one of his companions as his representative for Medina and Ali ibn Abi Talib as the Banner bearer, who carried a black flag. When the Jews learned that the Muslims had come to them, they fortified themselves in their strongholds. They were four hundred infantrymen, and three hundred of them carried shields. The Prophet besieged them for fifteen nights. God cast terror into their hearts, and they asked the Messenger of God to release them and evacuate them from Medina, and that they take their wives and offspring with them, and that he get their money and weapons. The Prophet accepted and expelled them from Medina to a city in the Levant called Adhra'. The booty without battle in this case are called Fay'a[1], and they are exclusively for the Messenger of God. But he decided to divide it among the Muslims after taking the al-Khums out of it to help them and sympathize with them.[282] Through this action, the Prophet Muhammad was able to eliminate an internal enemy that was no less dangerous than the external enemy. The external enemy was the Quraysh. The Quraysh would not calm down until they had avenged their dignity and that of their slain nobles. They prohibited crying over their dead in Mecca because they feared that

---

1 Fay'a: refers to the booty that was obtained without a fight and is specifically intended for the Prophet.

the flames of grief would be extinguished by crying and that their crying would bring joy into the hearts of the Muslims. But they later retracted this decision and allowed women to weep because it arouses emotions and reminds men of the shame inflicted on them. [283]

The marriage of Ali and Fatima

In the month of Dhu al-Hijjah in the second year after the Hijrah, Ali ibn Abi Talib married Fatima, the Prophet's daughter. He didn't have much money so he sold his shield and gave her the value of his shield as bride price.[284] The most respected personalities of Quraysh, including Abu Bakr, Omar and Abd Al-Rahman bin Awf, had asked for her hand in marriage but were rejected by the Prophet.[285] When the rejected suitors asked the Prophet for his decision to marry Fatima to Ali, he said: "By God, I did not reject you and give her to him, but God rejected you and gave her to him." [286]

Their wedding was characterized by simplicity, as was their trousseau. It consisted of a sheepskin bed, a hand mill, a jug and a few other simple objects.[287] On the fourth day after the wedding, the Prophet asked his daughter, "How are you, my daughter, and what do you think of your husband?" She replied, "O father, he is the best husband. However, women from Quraysh came to me and said: 'The Prophet has married you to a poor man who has no money. The Prophet replied, 'My daughter, neither your father nor your husband is poor. Are you not satisfied that I have married you to the first of my community who has converted to Islam, who has the most knowledge and is the most intelligent of them?" She replied: "Yes, I am satisfied, O Prophet of Allah." [288]

624 - 625 AD

The third year after the Hijrah

Battle of Banu Al-Nadir

The Jews of Medina had a hostile attitude towards the Islamic call and the Prophet Muhammad. When the Prophet asked them to convert to Islam, they were angered and began to argue with the Messenger of God. They saw that Islamic law was not compatible with their goals, interests and traditions. They hoped that this faith would be wiped out by its own people, the Quraysh. They invented excuses and demanded of the Prophet - not out of faith but to annoy him - that he should send down to them a book from heaven that was written, just as Moses brought the children of Israel the Torah written by Allah on the tablets. Although the Quran, which Allah sent down, is clear proof of his prophethood. Allah rebuked them and said: "O Muhammad, do not be troubled by their demand of you, for they asked Moses even greater things than they asked to see Allah directly. Out of their ignorance of Allah, their insolence towards Him and their self-deception, if you had given them the Book they asked for, they would have disobeyed Allah's command, just as they did after they were revived from their death by lightning. They worshipped the calf as a god instead of Allah." [289]

After Banu Al-Nadir saw how Islam united the people of Medina - the Aws and the Khazraj, who had previously been enemies - and the victory of the Muslims over the Quraysh and control of the trade routes, they felt a threat to their existence and decided to fight the spread of Islam with all their might. They tried to incite the common people and the uneducated people against Islam and to conspire with the polytheists of Mecca and the Arab tribes against Islam. To this end, they used the method of economic pressure on the Muslims and stirred up strife among them, especially between the Aws and the Khazraj and between the Muslims and the Quraysh. They spread lies and plotted against the Prophet's life and incited the people against him.

The Prophet endured their grave offenses with patience in order to avoid a brutal civil war in his new homeland. The Muslims knew that the Jews were taking advantage of the Muslims' circumstances and problems, especially since this insidious enemy lived in the heart of Islamic society. [290]

Six months after the Battle of Badr, the Banu Al-Nadir sent one of their poets, Ka'ab ibn al-Ashraf, along with forty Jewish horsemen to Mecca to plot with the Quraysh against the Muslims. They allied themselves with Abu Sufyan and agreed to take joint action against Muhammad. Ka'ab incited the Quraysh against the Muslims and praised them, then he and his companions returned to Medina. The Messenger of Islam was aware of their actions and had to endure their breach of treaty several times to prevent any excuse for it and to make it clear to everyone what they were hiding from deception and deceit. Therefore, he did not hasten their punishment immediately.

Once, when the Prophet asked them to fulfill their financial obligations according to the treaty that stipulated cooperation in matters of blood money, Ka'ab ibn al-Ashraf plotted to betray and kill the Prophet. He conspired with a group of his followers to do so. When the Prophet came to them to demand payment of the blood money, he and his followers were sitting with the Banu Al-Nadir. The Jews talked among themselves, "You will not get this man in this condition, and now he is sitting near your wall. One of you should go up to the roof and throw a large stone at him and rid us of him." One of them stood up and agreed to carry out the order. He went up to the roof to carry out his criminal act. Before they did it, the Prophet learned of their plan through a revelation and left them immediately, returning to Medina without exchanging a word with his followers. His followers thought that the Prophet would return, and when they later learned that the Prophet was in Medina, they also returned there. It became clear to the Muslims that they had to deal with this enemy with firmness and justice instead of leniency and tolerance. The Prophet considered their conspiracy against the Islamic leadership and their attempt to assassinate him as a final breach of the covenant. He decided to confront them with a firm stance. The fate of every traitor is war and killing, and that is the just punishment, especially if he plots and conspires and then works to implement his plans by striking Islam at its core, namely the Prophet . The Prophet ordered to retaliate against Ka'ab ibn al-Ashraf and later expel the Banu Al-Nadir from Medina. It was the wise and correct decision to make. The Prophet said: "Call Muhammad bin Maslama for me." When he came, he sent him to them to warn them that they must leave their homes. When Muhammad bin Maslama Al-Awsi came to them with the news, they were astonished at it because they had a covenant with Al-Aws. They said: "O Muhammad, we did not think that a man from the Aws would be sent to us." Muhammad bin Maslama replied: "Hearts have changed and Islam has dissolved the covenants. " When Ibn Maslama warned them and ordered them to leave while they were troubled by the death of Ka'ab, they said: "O Muhammad, one disaster after another. Let us weep for a while, then do as you wish. "[291]

Allah had already informed his Prophet about the Jewish conspiracy and mentioned that he would expel them from their homes at the first confrontation of the Muslims with the Jews. They were blinded by their strong fortresses and their material capabilities and believed that they were invincible and that these fortresses would protect them from Allah. But Allah would strike them from where they did not expect it, and He would send an army against them from among them that would bring terror upon them. This terror would cause them to destroy their homes with their own hands and the hands of their Muslim enemies. Such was the fate of the Banu Al-Nadir, from which the thinkers and those of understanding should learn a lesson.[292]

In the meantime, Abdullah bin 'Ubayy sent a message to Banu Al-Nadir: "Do not leave your homes, for I have with me two thousand men from the Arabs who will enter with you, and the Banu Quraiza will also enter with you." Banu Al-Nadir were deceived by these promises. Huyay bin Akhtab, the leader of Banu al-Nadir, sent a message to the Messenger of God: "We will not leave our homes, do as you wish." The message reached Ka'ab ibn Asad, the leader of Banu Quraiza, and he said: "No man from Banu Quraiza will break the covenant as long as I live." One of the Jewish scholars, Salam ibn Mishkam, advised Huyay bin Akhtab and said to him, "You are mistaken, Huyay, by Allah. The words of Ibn 'Ubayy are worthless. He only wants to drive you to destruction so that you will fight Muhammad. Then he will sit in his house and abandon you. He asked Ka'ab ibn Asad for support, but Ka'ab refused." Huyay replied, "My soul is eager to fight Muhammad." . Salam said: "Then, by Allah, it is the expulsion from our land and the loss of our wealth." [293]

When the Messenger of Allah learned of the Banu Al-Nadir's violation of the treaty, he exclaimed, "Allahu Akbar[1]. We are fighting the Jews." and the Muslims shouted takbir. The Messenger of God said to Ali: "Go to Banu Al-Nadir." Ali took the flag and went ahead. The Messenger of Allah came and the Muslims surrounded their fortress for six nights. Their fortress was located east of Medina in the direction of Syria and was surrounded by palm trees. One of the Jews shot at the Prophet's tent with an arrow and the Muslims moved his position. When night fell, they lost Ali. The people said: "O Messenger of God,

---

1 Allahu Akbar (Takbir): is an Arabic phrase that means "God is the greatest" or "God is greater" in english.

we do not see Ali." He said: "I see some things that are good for you." Soon after, Ali brought the head of the Jew who had shot arrows and threw it into the hands of the Prophet. The Prophet asked him, "How did you do this?" Ali replied: "I saw this wicked, brazen man and attacked him. I thought maybe he would dare to come out at night and attack us secretly. Then he approached with nine other Jews, his sword in his hand, and I struck him down and killed him, so his companions fled, but they didn't go far. Send a party with me and I hope to find them." Ali was not known to ask anyone for help when he was fighting, but he wanted to involve the Muslims in the battle. The Messenger of God sent ten men with him, including Abu Dujana and Sahl bin Hanif. They stopped the Jews before they entered the fort and killed them. This striking effect had a great impact on the morale of the Banu Al-Nadir and caused terror among them, especially after their allies abandoned them. Since when a single Muslim fights ten of them and then all ten were killed, this shows that the Muslims are capable of wiping them out and removing their roots with ease and grace.

The Banu Al-Nadir saw themselves as strong and invincible against the Muslims and believed they could meet the challenge if they had the ability to prolong the confrontation. Especially if the people of Khaybar moved to support them, and perhaps Quraysh and their allied tribes could move as well. Therefore, the Prophet saw that there would be no benefit in continuing the siege as long as they were able to entrench themselves in their fortresses and defend them for a long time. Therefore, the Prophet ordered the palms of the Banu Al-Nadir to be cut down and burned in order to create better conditions for fighting and to influence the Banu Al-Nadir so that they would be forced to come down from their castles and fight the Muslims outside the fortress. Thus their last hopes were dashed. And they should practically understand that if they hope to stay in their land, they must accept it as a burnt land. And for them to then see that there is no benefit in continuing in defiance and challenge except to suffer more losses and experience many setbacks. [294]

"O Muhammad, you have forbidden sabotage, so why cut down the palm trees and let them burn?" the Jews shouted. A group of Muhajirun also protested against the Prophet's decision about the palm trees, saying that it was a booty for the Muslims. This objection group of Muhajirun was an independent bloc with their aspirations and outstanding thinking, especially in terms of politics, governance and planning. They felt sympathy for their people in Mecca and for the Jews in Medina. They opposed the prophetic decisions that were not in their interest and aspirations. [295] Allah revealed that this action was not of Muhammad's accord, but by divine command as an exceptional case and within a limited framework for military reasons. [296]

When the Banu al-Nadir realized that things were not going in their favor and that they had made a grave mistake, they realized that no one could prevent the Muslims from inflicting a just punishment on them. Therefore, in order to protect their lives and escape punishment for their treachery, they placed their wealth and land at the disposal of the Messenger of God. The Prophet agreed to the offer. Banu al-Nadir did not want to admit their loss of wealth, so they left their fortress with brilliance and pride, accompanied by female singers beating tambourines and playing flutes.

When a group of Muhajirun saw this, they were shocked and saddened. Hassan bin Thabit said when he saw them: "By God, you have always given alms to the poor, sheltered guests and given water to the thirsty and forgiven those who have offended you and provided help when you were asked for help." Ad-Dahhak bin Khalifah said: "O my misfortune. My soul is your ransom. O people of humility and splendor, help and generosity." Na'im bin Masoud Al-Ashja'i said: "A ransom for these faces that look like lights. They are leaving Yathrib. Who will take care of the poor. Who will give water to the thirsty. Who will serve the fat over the meat. We have no business here in Yathrib behind you." Abu Al-Abbas bin Jabr, hearing his words, said: "Yes, follow them so that you may go to hell with them." Na'im turned to the Aws and said: "Is this your reward for them. You asked for their help against the Khazraj and they helped you. And you asked for help from all the Arabs, but they refused to help you." Abu Al-Abbas said: "Islam has broken the covenants." Although the Banu al-Nadir had betrayed the Muslims and the Muslims had seen their injustice and oppression, the Muslims still sympathized with them, which shows that their Islam was neither deep nor rooted in their souls.

Due to the agreement that led to the opening of the castle, the booty seized from the Muslims was classified as fay'a, meaning that it was reserved exclusively for the Messenger of God. The Prophet nevertheless gave the booty to the Muslims. The Ansar thus had the choice of either sharing what God had granted them and the Muhajirun, or giving all the booty to the Muhajirun so that they could be independent of the Ansar, in which case they would return their lands to the Ansar. Saad bin Muadh and Saad bin Ubadah decided instead to divide the booty among the Muhajirun and house them in their homes as it was before. They called the Ansar and declared that they were satisfied with this decision. The Messenger of God prayed for the mercy of God for the Ansar and their descendants. God sent down praise and recognition for this high spirit of the Ansar. [297] The Prophet divided it among the Muhajirun and ordered them to return what belonged to the Ansar. [298]

Hafsa bint Omar bin Al-Khattab in the Prophet's house

In the month of Sha'ban in the third year of the Hijrah, the Prophet married Hafsa, the daughter of Omar ibn al-Khattab, after her waiting period had expired. Her husband had died in the Battle of Badr. Hafsa was one of the Prophet's wives who, together with Aisha, had conspired against him, causing many problems in his life. This led to some disturbances in his family life. Nevertheless, the Prophet of God showed patience and endured the difficulties in order to preserve his message, which had been entrusted to him by Allah.

Zainab bint Khuzaymah in the Prophet's house

In the month of Ramadan of the third year, the Prophet Muhammad married Zainab bint Khuzaymah, but she died two or three months later. She was the first of his wives to die after Khadija. The Messenger of God had houses (rooms) built for his wives around the Prophet's mosque, whereupon the Companions soon built houses for them around the mosque. Each house had two doors: one door that opened towards the mosque to facilitate their access to the mosque during prayer times, and a second door on the other side.[299]

Juwaybir's story

Some poor companions of the Prophet, especially among the Muhajirun, who had migrated to Medina and had neither wives nor houses, lived in the Prophet's mosque. The Prophet regularly provided them with food and clothing and took care of their affairs. Among them was a young man named Juwaybir. Juwaybir was a small, poor and unattractive man. He was from the people of al-Yamamah and came to the Messenger of God to seek Islam. He embraced Islam and became a good Muslim.

As Juwaybir had no relatives in Medina and no money, the Messenger of God ordered him to stay in the mosque and sleep there at night. "O Juwaybir," said the Prophet, "if you marry a woman, you will be chaste and she will help you both in this world and in the Hereafter." Juwaybir replied, "O Messenger of God, may my father and mother be sacrificed for you, but who will marry me? I have no lineage, no money and no beauty." Thereupon the Messenger of God said: "O Juwaybir, God has humbled those who were honorable during the Jāhilīya[1] with Islam, and He has honored those who were humiliated during the Jāhilīya. With Islam, he removes the pride of the Jāhilīya and the boasting of clan and lineage. All people today, white and black, Quraysh, Arab and non-Arab, are descended from Adam, and God created Adam from clay. The most beloved of God on the Day of Resurrection is the most obedient and pious of them. O Juwaybir, I do not know any Muslim today who is better than you, except those who are more pious and obedient to God than you."

Then he said to him, "Go to Ziyad bin Labid, for he is one of the most honorable men of Banu Bayadah - a tribe of Ansar - and tell him, 'I am the Messenger of the Messenger of God to you, and he tells you to let Juwaybir marry your daughter Al-Dhalfa.'" Juwaybir set off with the message of the Messenger of God to Ziyad bin Labid. He met Ziyad in his house when he was in the company of some of his people. He asked to enter and was admitted. After Juwaybir greeted him, he said: "O Ziyad bin Labid, I am a messenger of the Messenger of God and I have a request. Should I say it now or should I speak to you later in private?" Ziyad said to Juwaybir, "Tell me what you have to say, for it is an honor and a pleasure for me." Juwaybir replied: "The Messenger of God commands you to marry me to your daughter Al-Dhalfa." Ziyad asked him: "Has the Messenger of God sent you to me?" Juwaybir replied, "Yes, I would not lie to the Messenger of God." Ziyad then said: "We only marry our girls to our equals from the Ansar." Ziyad then asked Juwaybir to leave and wait until he had met the Messenger of God and told him about his apology. But Juwaybir objected and said: "By God, the Quran was not revealed with such behavior, nor was Muhammad's prophethood sent with it."

Al-Dhalfa heard what her father and Juwaybir said when she was in her bed. She called her father and asked what was going on. Her father told her that

---

1 Jāhilīya: is an Arabic term that refers to the time of pre-Islamic paganism.

the Messenger of God had sent Juwaybir to him to ask for her hand in marriage. Al-Dhalfa then demanded that Juwaybir be brought back, as he would not lie to the Messenger of God. Ziyad sent someone to bring Juwaybir back. When he returned, Ziyad told him to stay until he comes back. Ziyad told the Messenger of God about the situation, and he said: "A believing man is sufficient for a believing woman, and a Muslim is sufficient for a Muslim woman." Ziyad returned to his house and told Al-Dhalfa about the words of the Messenger of God. She warned him not to be disobedient.

Eventually, Ziyad married Juwaybir and the Messenger and provided a dowry. Ziyad prepared his daughter Al-Dhulfa and dressed her, then they sent to Juwaybir and asked him, "Do you have a house so that we can bring her to you?" He replied, "I swear by Allah, I have no house." So they prepared a house for Juwaybir and furnished it with a bed and furniture and dressed him in two robes. Then Al-Dhulfa was taken to her house and Juwaybir was brought to her. When he saw her and saw what God had given him in favor, he stood up in a corner of the house and prayed to God and read the Quran until morning came. When he heard the call to prayer, he went out and his wife went to pray. She was asked, "Did he touch you?" and she replied, "He was reading the Quran and praying all the time until he heard the call to prayer, he went out." And so it was on the second and third nights. When the father of Al-Dhulfa heard about the incident on this third day, he went to the Prophet Muhammad and told him about what Juwaybir had done.

Then Prophet Muhammad sent someone to look for Juwaybir. When he arrived, Prophet Muhammad asked, "Do you approach women?" Juwaybir replied, "am I not a man? I am interested in women, O Messenger of Allah." Then the Prophet Muhammad said: "I have been told that you are different from what you have described yourself, and that a house, a bed and equipment have been provided for you." Juwaybir replied, "O Messenger of God, I entered a spacious house and saw a bed and belongings, and a beautiful bride came towards me. I then spent the night praying and the day fasting to thank God. I did this for three days and nights. But I will satisfy her tonight." The Messenger of God told Ziyad about Juwaybir's answer. Juwaybir kept his promise and lived happily with his wife until one day he was martyred together with the Prophet in a campaign. [300]

The number of needy strangers in Medina who converted to Islam and stayed in the mosque increased until the mosque became too small. God ordered the Prophet to clean the mosque and ask those who slept in it to leave, and the doors of the Companions were to be closed, except for the door of the house of Ali ibn Abi Talib, which faced the mosque. The Prophet Muhammad ordered that the doors of the Companions be closed and that the Muslims set up a hut for the poor in the back corner of the Prophet's mosque in a place called As-Suffah. The strangers and the needy were brought there and the Prophet took care of them by distributing wheat, dates, barley and raisins. The people of As-Suffah spent their time learning the Quran and accompanied the Prophet on every campaign he undertook.

The decision to close the doors of the Companions caused great resentment among the Muslims, especially because the Prophet had allowed Ali to enter the mosque even when he was junub[1]. Some Muslims were upset that their doors were closed but Ali's door remained open. However, the Prophet explained that he was only following God's orders and was not acting on his own authority. The people said to the Prophet Muhammad: "You have closed our doors and left the door of Ali open." He replied: "I did not lead you out of my own will and leave his door open, but God led you out and left his door open. I am only a servant who obeys what he has been commanded. " Some of the companions nevertheless refused to obey the Prophet's command and close the doors. Finally, the Prophet ascended the pulpit in a state of anger and ordered the Companions to close all the doors except the door of Ali . After disobeying his orders twice, they finally obeyed him on the third attempt. [301]

Birth of Al-Hassan bin Ali

In Ramadan of the third year after the Hijrah, Al-Hassan , the first son of Fatima and Ali, was born. The Messenger of God gave him the name Al-Hassan because Ali did not want to anticipate the Prophet in naming him. Hassan was the first to be given this name. On the seventh day after the birth, his mother, Fatima shaved the newborn's hair and weighed it. The weight was donated in silver as alms. [302]

---

1 Junub refers to the state of ritual impurity due to sexual intercourse or ejaculation. To perform ritual actions or recite the Quran, the major ritual full-body wash called Ghusl is required to end the state of impurity.

Battle of Uhud

Quraysh began to avoid the trade route to the Levant for fear of their caravans, which threatened their existence and future. Therefore, they considered their war with the Prophet and the Muslims as crucial, and their battle with him as a matter of life or death. This was not hidden from the Prophet, who was always ready for any eventuality and followed every move of the enemy with utmost precision. After the existence of the Islamic State had become a real threat to the interests of the Quraysh, they decided to fight it again. Safwan ibn Umayyah, one of the leaders of the Quraysh, said to Quraysh: "Muhammad and his followers have ruined our trade. We do not know what to do with his followers.

They do not leave the coast, and the people on the coast have made treaties with them, and most of them have joined him. We don't know which way to go. If we stay in our land, we will use up our capital and there will be nothing left for us. Our trade goes to the Levant in the summer and to Ethiopia in the winter." [303].

In the month of Shawwal in the third year of the Hijrah, Quraysh began to prepare for battle against the Prophet Muhammad. They mobilized the people and prepared their forces to take revenge and erase the shame. The Jews were fearing for their political, economic and cultural position in the region, incited Quraysh to take revenge against those who had humiliated them and openly proclaimed their hatred and broke the alliance. Quraysh began to send messengers to the tribes to ask for their support, and they mobilized those tribes of Kinanah and the people of Tihama who obeyed them.

The poet Abu Azza al-Jumahi took part in inciting the tribes against the Muslims, although he was in Badr as a prisoner with the Muslims and the Prophet had released him on the condition that he would not incite against the Prophet and the Muslims. However, he did not keep his promise to the Prophet.

Quraysh went out with the fighters they had gathered and took fifteen women with them to commemorate those killed in Badr, accompanied by musical instruments and wine. They spent tens of thousands of dinars to prepare for battle. The Quraysh army consisted of three thousand fighters, seven hundred soldiers wearing armor and two hundred horsemen, all led by Abu Sufyan. Wahshi, a slave of the Quraysh who was promised freedom if he killed Muhammad, Ali or Hamza, also accompanied them.

When the Prophet received the news of Quraysh's march, he ordered it to be kept secret in order to leave no room for the psychological warfare that might be practiced by the Jews and the hypocrites against the Muslims. He wanted to deprive them of the opportunity and thwart their potential plots. [304]

The army of Mecca continued its journey along the usual western main route. When they arrived at al-Abwa, Hind bint Utbah, the wife of Abu Sufyan, suggested that they dig up the grave of the Prophet Muhammad's mother. However, the commanders of the army refused this request and Abu Sufyan warned them that if they did so, the Banu Bakr and the Khazraj would dig up their dead.[305] Quraysh continued their march until they arrived at Dhi al-Hulayfa. The Prophet sent some companions, including al-Hubab ibn al-Mundhir, to observe them and ascertain their numbers and equipment. He said to him, "When you return, do not report to me in the presence of another Muslim unless you see me apart from them." Al-Hubab returned to him and reported to him alone. The Prophet ordered him to keep the information secret.

When the polytheists approached Medina, the Muslims posted guards, especially at the Prophet's mosque. The Messenger of God also gathered his companions to discuss an enemy army they had never fought before. The Prophet did not want to leave Medina, but a group of enthusiastic young men who had tasted victory in Badr insisted on going out, arguing that their staying in Medina would make the enemy consider them cowardly and attack them. The Messenger of God told them about a dream in which he saw cows being slaughtered and that his sword had a notch and that he was in a fortress. He interpreted the cows as a group of his companions who would be killed, the notch as a man from his family who would be killed, and the fortress as Medina. Ibn 'Ubayy said: "We will stay in Medina, and when the enemy comes, the children and women will throw stones at him, and the men will fight him on the paths." They said to the Messenger of Allah: "You had three hundred men on the day of Badr, and Allah gave you victory over them. But today we are a great number. " One of them said: "O Prophet of God, do not deprive us of Paradise; by the one who has my soul, I will enter it." The Messenger of God said to him, "With what?" He said: "That I love God and His Messenger, and that I do not flee from marching." He said to him, "You are right." One of the Ansar said to him, "When will we fight them, O Messenger of Allah, if we do not fight them at our valley?" Another said: "I do not want the Quraysh to return to their people and say, 'We besieged Muhammad in the fortresses and towers of Yathrib.' That would be a disgrace for us, and they have already entered our territory. If we do not defend our territory, why should we entrench ourselves in our fortresses?" Another said: "If the Quraysh stay close and gather the crowds in their valleys and the Al-Ahabish[1] follow them, then they will ride camels and horses until they reach us and trap us in our houses and castles. Then they will return unharmed. This will encourage them to attack us and carry out raids against us, destroy our houses and keep us under surveillance. And the Arabs around us will feel emboldened to attack us." Many people urged him to go out.

The Prophet was guided by the opinion of the majority and went into his house to put on his war clothes. Meanwhile, they repented their insistence on the Prophet and realized that he knows God better and knows what to do, as revelations are sent to him directly from heaven. When the Prophet came out to them in his war clothes to go to war with his companions against the Quraysh, they said: "O Messenger of God, stay as you have commanded us." He then declared: "It is not permissible for a prophet to return after he has put on the garb of war until he has fought." He then gave a sermon and appointed someone as a deputy in Medina. He prepared his brigades, gave the flag to Ali bin Abi Talib and set out with his army to fight the Quraysh.

The Prophet consulted the Muslims to calm their minds and win their love and trust without imposing his opinion on them. In the end, however, he makes the final decision as to whether he agrees with their opinion or not. It would have been better for them to submit to what the Messenger of God said instead of contradicting him or making suggestions to him. Ali was always in a position of obeying the Messenger of God and being satisfied with what he liked. It was the right decision to stay in Medina, as material losses are bearable, while the loss of human life is more difficult and painful. The Messenger of God would not have given up this correct opinion.

---

1 The name Al-Ahabisch goes back to a group of Quraysh, Kinanah, and Khuza'a, who formed an alliance at Mount Habashy below Mecca during the time of Jahiliyya.

The Prophet went with an army of a thousand men, including a hundred in armor and two knights, to Uhud via the mountain pass of Farewell (Thaniyyat al-wadā).

After the Prophet had taken his leave, he saw a large group in the army and asked, "Who are these?" They replied, "Abdullah bin 'Ubayy with a group of his Jewish followers." He said: "Have they converted to Islam?" They replied, "No, O Messenger of Allah." He then said: "Let them return, for we will not fight with the disbelievers against the idolaters." Ibn 'Ubayy returned with the hypocrites between Medina and Uhud, and there were three hundred men, and said: "Muhammad disobeyed me and he obeyed the ignorant. He will see. We do not know why we are killing ourselves and our sons here, O people." They returned. Jabir bin Abdullah Al-Ansari followed them and appealed in the name of God and the Prophet to return to the battlefield. Ibn 'Ubayy said: "If we had known that there would be a battle, we would have followed you. If you obey us, then come back with us." [306].

Allah mentions that the clash of the two armies took place with His permission in order to distinguish the believers from the hypocrites. When the hypocrites were asked to fight in the name of Allah, or at least to defend their women, they replied mockingly and argumentatively: "We see no battle, and if we saw a battle, we would take part in it. This is nothing but plunging ourselves into annihilation with this unbalanced war and ill-conceived plan." With this statement, they are closer to disbelief than faith, because by reducing the number of soldiers in the Islamic army, they are supporting the disbelievers. They claim faith outwardly, but they conceal disbelief in their hearts, and Allah knows best what they conceal.[307] This treachery came at critical and sensitive moments and had a negative effect on the morale of Muslims. It paved the way and gave the remaining hypocrites the excuse to flee at the most critical and dangerous moments for Islam and Muslims in general.[308] With the retreat of Ibn 'Ubayy and his group, the Islamic army was weakened, its numbers has shrunk to only 700 men. This situation caused concern among the Muslims, the drums of war were about to beat, and everyone was anxiously watching the rapid development of events. A group of Banu Haritha of the Aws and Banu Salamah of the Khazraj, who were on the flanks of the army, also began to think about retreating. There were heated discussions among them and they were on the verge of deciding to retreat, but at the last moments they changed their minds and decided to stay, trusting in Allah.[309]

When the Prophet reached the battle area, he chose to land on the side of Mount Uhud so that the mountain was behind them. He then lined up his companions and ordered them not to fight anyone until he commanded them to do so. On the Muslims' left was a mountain called Jabal Ainain, which had a gap in it. On it stood fifty archers under the leadership of Abdullah ibn Jubayr (See Figure 36). The Prophet instructed them to keep the horses away from behind so that they would not be attacked from behind. He ordered the archers to keep their place and protect the backs of the Muslims. And no matter what happened, that they should not leave their places. He told them not to support the Muslims with swords if they are killed and not to take the booty if the Muslims seize it.

Then the battle began and Abu Sufyan sent to the Ansar: "Let us be alone against our cousin. You need not interfere. We will withdraw from you as we have no need to fight you." They answered him with something he did not want to hear. Abu Sufyan incited Banu Abd al-Dar, the Quraysh flag bearers, to war and had the women beat tambourines and incited them with poetry. Then Talha bin Abi Talha, the Quraysh standard-bearer, challenged someone to a duel. Ali came to him. Talha asked: "Who are you?" Ali replied, "I am Ali bin Abi Talib." Talha said: "O Biter[1], you know that no one else challenges me." Then Ali hit him on the head so that he injured his head to the beard. Although Talha was still alive, Ali turned away from him. The Muslims called Ali and asked if he would not kill Talha. Ali replied that Talha had asked him to spare him for the sake of the children and that he knew that God would kill him. The Messenger of God rejoiced at this and said: "God is greatest[2]."

The two armies clashed and fierce fighting ensued. The Muslims were fighting to defend their religion and their homeland, on which all their interests and their future and existence depended. They fought against a relentless numeri-

---

1   When the Messenger of God stayed in Mecca, no one dared to do anything to him because of his kinship with Abu Talib. But instead, Quraysh sent their children to humiliate him by throwing stones and dirt at him every time he left the house. One day the Prophet Muhammad said to the young Ali: "May you be rewarded by Allah if you go outside with me". Ali answered him: "O Messenger of God, I am happy to accompany you". When they went outside together, they were again attacked by the boys. But this time Ali defended him and bit them in their faces, noses, and ears, so that they returned crying to their fathers and complained that Ali had bitten them. From that day on, Ali was known as "the biter".

2   Allahu Akbar in Arabic.

cally superior and better equipped group who wanted to avenge those killed in Badr. The companions of the Messenger of God fought against the Quraysh troops and struck them in the face until their ranks broke. Ali bin Abi Talib set his sights on the bearer of the Quraysh flag, followed him and killed him. Then his brother took over the flag and Ali killed him too. The flag was then taken over by seven others, one after the other, and Ali was able to kill all seven men one after the other. Finally, no one dared to carry the flag and it remained on the ground while the Quraysh retreated. A Quraysh woman finally took the flag and raised it, whereupon the Quraysh retreated to their banner. The Muslim archers on the mountain also attacked the Quraysh horses and forced them to turn back by throwing arrows at them. Ali went to the commander of the Quraysh army, Khaled bin Al-Walid Al-Makhzoumi, who was on the right side of the army. When Ali faced him, Khaled quickly undressed out of fear of him and remained naked to make Ali leave him alone. Ali averted his eyes from him and left him out of generosity.

Figure 35: From the middle of the Battle of Uhud.

When the Quraysh flag bearers were killed and the Muslim archers on the mountain attacked the Quraysh horses, the Muslims fought fiercely, with Ali, Hamza and Abu Dujana being the most influential fighters. The Quraysh army eventually retreated and became scattered groups. God sent down his victory over the Muslims. The Muslims pursued the Quraysh, slashing them with swords and plundering their army for booty.

The archers at the gap saw that the Quraysh had been defeated and the Muslims were taking booty. They argued about whether they should stay on the mountain or take the booty with the Muslims. The majority of them wanted to leave the mountain to take booty, while ten of them respected the order of the Messenger of God and wanted to remain in their positions. The Prophet had explicitly ordered the archers not to leave their positions on the mountain until someone is sent to them to give them the order to leave, even if the Muslims were defeated or are taking booty. However, the majority of the archers broke the Prophet's order and became disobedient. Therefore, they were deprived of God's support and victory. When Khaled saw the archers' descent from the gap and realized that the mountain was empty and the Muslims were busy with booty, he called in his horses and passed by with them, followed by Ikrimah in a group; they attacked those who remained behind in the gap; they killed them all and then fell on the Muslims from behind. The defeated Quraysh saw their men returning to the war and a woman of them - she is Umra Al-Harithiya - rushed over, picked up the banner of the polytheists which was lying on the ground, the polytheists gathered around it and shouted at each other until they gathered around the Muslims and stood for the battle and the Muslims were surrounded from the front and back.

The Muslims, preoccupied with the booty, were scattered and their ranks fell apart. They were no longer a solid unit that held each other together. They could not withstand this fierce attack and each of them was anxious to save himself. [310]

Allah has fulfilled the promise of victory to the Muslims. They had the upper hand at the beginning of the battle, they were the ones who overpowered their enemy, and the idolaters fled the battlefield until Allah tested the Muslims with the booty to see their compliance with their leader's instructions. They were not to leave the mountain no matter what, and their task was to protect the backs of the Muslims from any enemy maneuvers. But they quarreled over the booty after seeing the overwhelming victory. Most of them were out to make some worldly gains, while only a few stuck to the words of the Prophet and did not leave their posts. They believed that the reward that Allah has is better. [311]

Wahshi looked at Hamza as he relentlessly fought the polytheists around him with his sword, leaving none of them behind. Hamza wore a shirt with an ostrich feather on his chest. Wahshi hid behind a stone and lay in wait for him. He then approached Hamza from behind and thrust his spear into his back, causing him to fall and die a martyr's death. Wahshi came to him, took his spear and mutilated his body on the orders of Hind bint Utbah. Meanwhile, the Muslims were preoccupied with their defeat. Wahshi then returned to the army and informed Hind of this, which she rejoiced in and gave him her dress and jewelry and promised him ten dinars in Mecca.

Ibn Qami'ah, one of the Quraysh, wanted to attack Musab ibn 'Umair, thinking that he was the Prophet, and killed him. Mus'ab was holding the flag, and when he fell, his brother Abu al-Rum ibn 'Umair took up the flag. Ibn Qami'ah exclaimed, "Muhammad has been killed." This gave the Quraysh more courage and they rushed at the Muslims. The Muslims, unable to rally and organize themselves, were defeated. Nevertheless, the Prophet continued to fight in the chaos with the few who still held out. Ali held out alone with the Messenger and defended him. Fear and chaos broke out among the Muslims so that they were all defeated and some of them threw down their weapons and fled to the mountains to seek shelter without turning to the Messenger of God. The Messenger of God called them loudly and waved his hands, saying, "Come to me, O servants of God, come to me, servants of God, come to me." But no one descended to him and they did not turn around while arrows struck him from all sides. [312]

Allah reminds them: You were sad and distressed because you thought that if you followed the Prophet's orders, you would miss the booty. Know that when you disobeyed the Prophet's orders and left the mountain to seek the booty, you fell into this great sadness as a result of defeat and death, each of which is much greater than this sadness. Allah has given you this great sadness after your sadness so that you do not grieve over the loss of the booty and so that it is a deterrent for you. Allah knows all your deeds, intentions and motives and is able to reward them, whether good or bad. And this is one of the greatest deterrents for the servant to commit sins.[313]

The enemy reached the Messenger of God, his lip was wounded and his face slashed as stones were thrown at him until he fell into a ditch. But he did not move from his position and did not retreat a single step. He then said at this difficult moment, "O God, guide my people, for they know not what they do." The Muslims retreated as far as the mountain, including Abu Bakr, Omar bin Al-Khattab, Talha bin Ubaidullah, Saad bin Abi Waqqas and others. They climbed a rock at the top of the mountain. Othman bin Affan ran for three days to escape the war.

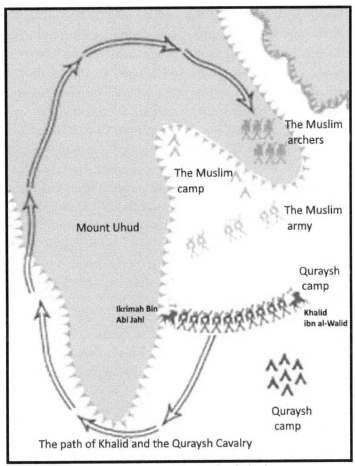

The Muslim archers

The Muslim camp

Mount Uhud

The Muslim army

Quraysh camp

Ikrimah Bin Abi Jahl

Khalid ibn al-Walid

Quraysh camp

The path of Khalid and the Quraysh Cavalry

Figure 36: Map of the Battle of Uhud.

The Prophet looked at a man among the Muhajirun who had thrown his shield behind his back as he fled and called out to him, "O owner of the shield, throw down your shield and flee to hell." The man threw his shield. When almost all the Muslims fled back, the Messenger of God became angry. He looked to his side and saw Ali and said: "What is the matter with you that you did not join the others?" He replied, "O Messenger of God, shall I become an unbeliever after becoming a believer? You are my role model." Ali bin Abi Talib followed the fleeing people carrying a handful of pebbles. He threw them in their faces and shouted loudly: "Man. May God make your faces black and disfigured. Where are you fleeing to?! To hell?! Have you sworn allegiance and then broken it? By God, you deserve to be killed more than who I kill." Omar bin Al-Khattab, who was afraid of him, said to him: "O Abu Al-Hassan[1], calm down, the Arabs sometimes stand firm, and sometimes flee. And steadfastness in battle can eliminate the disgrace of running away." The Quraysh battalions began to attack the Messenger of God, and he said: "O Ali, take this." Then Ali attacked them. He killed some and the rest scattered. Then another group came to attack the Messenger of God and he shouted, "O Ali, take this one." Ali attacked them and they scattered. Until a group from Banu Kinana came to him and the Prophet said to Ali, "O Ali, take this one. " Ali confronted this group when he was on foot. They were almost fifty horsemen. He struck at it with his sword until it broke away from him. Then he struck it again and again until he killed ten of them. Gabriel was astonished and said: "O Muhammad, this is indeed the consolation. The angels are amazed at the comfort this man offers." He said: "What hinders him if he is from me and I am from him." Gabriel said: "and I am from you." Then a voice was heard from heaven: "There is no better sword than Dhū l-faqār[2] and no better hero than Ali." The Prophet was asked about the voice. He said: "This is Gabriel."

No one stayed with the Messenger of God except Ali ibn Abi Talib and seven of the Ansar. When the rumor spread that the Prophet had been killed, one of the Muslims who were on the rock on the mountain said: "If only we had a messenger who would go to Abdullah ibn 'Ubayy and give us protection before they kill us." Some of the hypocrites said: "If he was really a prophet, he would not have been killed. Return to your original faith." A group of Muhajirun said: "We will surrender to them, for they are our people and our cousin." Anas ibn Nadir came to them and said: "If Muhammad was really killed, what will you do with your lives after that. Keep fighting as he fought and die as he died." Then he said: "O Allah, I apologize to you for what these (hypocrites) say, and I distance myself from what these (disbelievers) have brought." Then he fought until he was killed.

In the midst of the chaos, Ka'ab bin Malik saw the Prophet alive and exclaimed his joy. But the Prophet ordered him to remain silent as the situation was too critical and serious. Abu Dujana was the first to return with Asim bin Thabit and protected the Prophet from the arrows of the unbelievers until he himself was hit by arrows. The Messenger of God honored him by giving him a sword. Salman al-Farsi also protected the Prophet with his body and said: "My soul is a ransom for the Messenger of God." Umm 'Amarah, Nusaybah bint

---

1   Abu Al-Hassan: is Ali bin Abi Talib.
2   Dhū l-faqār: The name of the sword of Ali bin abi Talib.

Ka'ab, also fought and defended the Prophet with all her might when she saw that only a few were standing by him. She was wounded, but her son 'Amarah helped her and even killed a man. The Prophet said: "May Allah bless you, O Nusaybah," and he said: "The rank of Nusaybah is higher than the rank of Abu Bakr and Omar." Then the Prophet called out, "Who sells himself to seek the pleasure of Allah?" Then Ziyad bin Al-Sakan stood up with five of his Ansar companions. Then a group came and they separated the attackers from the Messenger of Allah and fought until they were all killed. Some Muslims were encouraged and returned to the Messenger of God as individuals or in groups. The Prophet urged them to fight. Although they were outnumbered, they fought bravely. However, most of the Muslims who were on the mountain did not leave their place and did not return. The prophet placed those who returned to their original positions by making the mountain behind them as per first plan.

Ali suffered nearly sixty wounds and blows and was exhausted. The return of the Muslims to their first positions and the reunification of their ranks frightened the Quraysh once again. The polytheists feared that the Muslims would do to them what they had done at the beginning of the war and withdrew peacefully. When the two parties separated, the Prophet came to the mountain pass but did not climb the mountain. The fighting stopped and the two armies watched each other with caution. Ali bin Abi Talib passed between the rocks on Mount Uhud and filled his jug with water. He then brought it to the Messenger of God, who used it to wash the blood from the Prophet's face. Abu Sufyan announced the end of the war and shouted "Glory be to Hubal[1]". The Prophet told Ali how to respond to Abu Sufyan, and Ali said: "God is higher and more majestic." Abu Sufyan said that the war had ended in a draw and that this day was like the day of Badr. Ali disagreed and said: "That is not true. Our martyrs are in heaven, your martyrs are in hell." Then Abu Sufyan asked if the Prophet had been killed, but the Prophet ordered the Muslims not to answer him. Omar revealed it to Abu Sufyan and said: "No, by God. He hears your words now." Abu Sufyan said: "You are more honest with me than Ibn Qami'ah[2] and more just." When Abu Sufyan was about to leave, he shouted, "O Muhammad, the appointment between you and us is the coming season of Badr Al-Safrah[3]." It is not clear why Omar revealed the truth about the

---

1   Hubal: was an important deity of the Quraysh tribe, the ruling tribe of Mecca.
2   Ibn Qami'ah was the one who spread the rumor in the war that the Prophet had been killed.

Prophet's life to Abu Sufyan and the Quraysh at such a critical and sensitive moment, even though the Prophet had forbidden it.

During the battle, Quraysh women came to the battlefield and mutilated the bodies of the Muslim martyrs. They cut off their noses, ears and organs and turned them into bracelets and necklaces. Hind, the wife of Abu Sufyan, did the same with the body of Hamza. She cut open his stomach and tried to eat his liver, but she did not like it. The Messenger of God sent Ali to the battlefield to see what the Quraysh army was doing. If they were riding camels and leading horses, they wanted to go to Mecca. If it was the other way around, then they wanted to go to Medina. Ali returned and reported that they were riding camels. This meant that Quraysh wanted to leave Badr and march to Mecca. After the end of the battle, Fatima washed the Prophet's wounds and bandaged them. When she saw that the water only increased the blood, she took a piece of cloth, burnt it and stuck it on the wound to stop the bleeding. The Messenger of God said: "The wrath of God intensified against the one who injured the face of his Prophet."

The Messenger of God then went to the battlefield, stood before the corpse of Hamza, wept bitterly and said: "May the mercy of Allah be upon you. You were always there for good and nurtured the bonds of kinship." Then he prepared him for burial. The dead were brought and laid next to Hamza's body. The Prophet prayed for them until he prayed seventy-two prayers for them and for Hamza especially with seventy takbirs. Then they were buried there. The number of martyrs was sixty-four from the Ansar and six from the Muhajirun, and seventy were wounded. This is what the Prophet had promised them in Badr. As many as thirty men from Quraysh were killed. [314]

On the day of the Battle of Uhud, the Jewish scholar Mukhayriq was also killed. Before the battle, he exclaimed: "O Jews, by God, you know that it is your duty to support Muhammad." They replied to him: "Today is the Sabbath." He replied: "There is no Sabbath." Then he took his sword and his equipment and said: "If anything happens to me, my wealth belongs to Muhammad, he can do with it as he pleases." He then went to the Prophet Muhammad and fought alongside him until he was killed. The Prophet said: "Mukhayriq is the best of the Jews." He owned seven gardens, which now belonged to the Prophet. [315]

---

3   Badr Al-Safrah: An area near Badr in the Hejaz, where a market is held in Dhu Al-Qi`dah.

After the Messenger of Allah finished burying the martyrs, he turned to his companions and said: "Line up so that I may praise my Lord, the Exalted." They lined up behind him and he said: "O Allah, all praise is due to You. O Allah, there is none who withholds what You have granted, and none who grants what You have withheld, and no guide for the one whom You have misguided, and no misguide for the one whom You have guided rightly, and no giver for what You have withheld, and no restrainer for what You have given. " [316]

Then the Prophet and the Muslims returned to Medina. The mother of Saad bin Muadh rushed to him, looked him in the face and rejoiced, saying, "May my father and mother be sacrificed for you, O Messenger of God, I can bear any calamity if it goes well with you." The Prophet condoled with her about her son. Another Ansar woman, whose husband, brother and father were martyred with the Messenger of God at the Battle of Uhud, received condolences from the Muslims. But she was mainly worried about the Prophet and asked how he was doing. The Muslims replied that he was fine, thank God. The woman then asked to see him to make sure that he was indeed well. When she saw the Prophet, she said a prayer for him and said that she would do anything as long as he was safe.

On the way to Medina, the Prophet and his companions passed Ansar houses where people were weeping for the dead of Uhud. The Prophet heard the weeping and shed tears and said: "But Hamza has no mourners for him". He ordered Saad bin Muadh to tell the women to mourn for Hamza first and then for their own dead. But he also advised them not to hit, scratch or tear their clothes in the process. These women had reached a deep understanding of the Prophet. For them, he was the most important thing in life, and as long as he was safe, everything else was insignificant. They comforted him with their money, their lives and their noble feelings. [317]

After the Islamic army returned from the Battle of Uhud, feelings were mixed. Some mourned their dead, while others, the hypocrites, secretly rejoiced at the Muslims' defeat. Some who fled in battle felt ashamed, and others were still scarred by the hardships of battle and their injuries. The Prophet Muhammad observed the tensions among the Muslims after the battle and wanted to unite hearts. He did not want the defeated Muslims who had abandoned him in battle to feel outcast and exiled. He did not want them to be branded as cowards, traitors and losers and lose their former status among the Muslims and with himself. This could cause them feelings of failure, sadness and a desire to distance themselves from the Islamic community. This was something the Prophet did not want. Therefore, he did not speak harshly and severely to them, but with gentle words and treated them with leniency and ease.

When the wife of Othman ibn Affan came to the Prophet while he and Ali ibn Abi Talib were cleaning their weapons, she asked, "What did Ibn Affan do? By God, you will not find him at the front." Ali replied, "Without a doubt, Othman has become the scandal of our time." Othman was among those who had fled in the battle of Uhud. He had fled far from the battlefield and did not return until three days after the end of the battle. The Prophet said to Ali: "Stop." Later, when Othman came to him with his companions, the Prophet only said to him, "You have gone far." Although Ali's words were true - Othman's escape would be remembered forever - the Prophet had forgiven them, especially because they came to him, showed their repentance and asked for forgiveness.

In any attempt to create a neutral historical work, an author strives for objectivity. Nevertheless, there are moments that move the just and fair author to speak his mind and express his admiration. One such remarkable moment is the attitude of Muhammad after the battle of Uhud. Despite the severe injuries he suffered from their betrayal, which almost cost him his life, he showed himself to be a caring father to the Muslims. He forgave them, treated them with gentleness and showered them with his affection to protect them and soothe their feelings. The best praise for him came from Allah Himself, who said: "By what great mercy Allah has granted you that you have such a good attitude, so that you are gentle with them and treat them with kindness, and if you were harsh, severe and heartless, they would turn away from you. So forgive them as Allah has forgiven them, and ask forgiveness for them in order to perfect their compassion and perfect their kindness. Consult them in important matters, and when you have decided and formed an opinion, then trust in Allah and leave the matters to Him. Allah loves those who trust in Him. The result of this trust is success and victory from Allah. Allah's power is over all powers, and if He wills good for a servant and wants his victory, support and defense, then no power on earth, no matter how great it is, is able to defeat him. And if Allah abandons you, who can help you but Him? Therefore, the believers should trust in Allah. [318]

However, not everyone in Medina mourned the martyrs of Uhud. The hypocrites and Jews rejoiced at the suffering inflicted on the Muslims. They claimed that the Prophet could not be a true prophet because he was injured and that he only sought power. Others claimed that the martyrs would not have been killed if they had stayed with them. Allah replies to them: "Tell them, O Muhammad, after you have refused to support your believing brothers, you now claim that you have insight into the unseen world and that you know about the future and its events. So if you are telling the truth, then ward off death from yourselves or choose for yourselves an honorable death if you are able. "[319] They even tried to unsettle the companions of the Messenger of God and advised them to leave him. Omar ibn al-Khattab heard what they said and asked the Prophet for permission to kill these hypocrites and Jews. "Do they not testify that there is no god but Allah and that I am the Messenger of Allah?" said the Prophet. Omar replied, "Yes, they do, but they only say it out of fear of the sword, and their plan has become clear. God, has revealed their hatred." The Prophet said: "I have been instructed not to kill those who confess this. And the Jews have a covenant, so I will not kill them." [320]

In addition to the shock of defeat in battle, the gloating of the hypocrites deepened the wounds of the Muslims and increased their pain. Allah said to them to ease their burden after what had happened in the battle, "Your determination should not be less than the determination of the enemies. Despite the heavy loss of life and property in Badr - where seventy of them were killed, many wounded and captured - they did not stop fighting you. They were not deterred from going to war against you. In this battle, they made up for what they had lost and compensated for their defeat. So if you have suffered a heavy defeat in this battle, you should not stop until you have made up for what you have lost. So why the weakness and why the sadness?".

Allah also told them: "There are sweet and bitter events in people's lives, but they are not permanent. Victories and defeats, strength and weakness, all these things change, all these things pass away, none of them last. No one should imagine that defeat in a single battle and its consequences are permanent things. It is necessary to evaluate and avoid the causes of defeat and its factors and turn defeat into victory. Life is an up and down, its events are in constant flux, and nothing of its conditions and circumstances remains. These changes serve to distinguish the true believers from those who only pretend to believe. If no painful events occur in the life of nations, the ranks are not distinguished and the bad is not distinguished from the good. You should know that this religion has not come to you easily, you have to face some martyrs in battle. Then Allah emphasizes that He does not love the unjust and will never support them against the believers.[321]

The battle of Uhud caused a great shock in the hearts of the Muslims and they could hardly cope with it. However, God did not abandon them in their sorrows but lightened their burden by forgiving them for what they did in the war. He also explained to them that what had happened had already been pre-destined by God. God wanted to take martyrs from among them through this incident and teach them useful lessons for the future so that the faithful could be distinguished from the hypocrites. [322]

Muawiyah bin Al-Mughirah bin Abi Al-Aas, the cousin of Othman bin Af-fan and a polytheist from the Quraysh, fled at the Battle of Uhud and entered Medina. He went to the house of Othman bin Affan. Othman said to him, sur-prised and rejecting his arrival, "You have destroyed me and yourself," and then hid him in his house and went to the Prophet to obtain safety for him. How-ever, the Prophet received knowledge of him through revelation and sent Ali to fetch him from Othman's house. Umm Kulthum, Othman's wife, showed the place where Othman had hidden him and Ali brought him to the Messenger of God. Othman was angry because of what his wife had done. He went to the Prophet and asked him to give him time, and the Prophet granted him a period of three days before he left the city. He threatened to kill Muawiyah if he found him in Medina or its surroundings afterwards. Othman then provided Muawiyah with a camel. But Muawiyah did not do this with innocent inten-tions; rather, he was tasked with spying on the Prophet and the Muslims in Medina and passing the information on to the Quraysh. He spent three days gathering information. The Prophet was already aware of his plan. [323]

The battle of Hamra al-Assad

One day after the Battle of Uhud, the Quraysh arrived in Al-Rawha'a, about fifty-six kilometers from Medina. There they argued with each other and planned to return to eliminate Muhammad and his companions. The Quraysh said: "You killed many of them and left almost nothing. But you have neither killed Muhammad nor acquired female slaves. Go back and finish them off be-fore they can reinforce themselves." Safwan bin Umayyah said: "Don't do that. Muhammad and his companions are now in great anger over what has hap-pened to them. I believe that when you return, all the people left behind by the Aws and Khazraj will gather, attack and overpower you. But now the victory is yours."

172

The Prophet was informed of this. He wanted to show the Quraysh his strength and scare them. But how could he obtain this information from a distance of more than fifty kilometers in one night, except through revelation? Based on a revelation, Prophet Muhammad set out for Hamra al-Asad, a place about thirteen kilometers from Medina. Gabriel appeared to the Prophet and said: "O Muhammad, God commands you to pursue the enemy and take only the wounded with you." The Prophet ordered his caller to invite only the wounded and proclaim: "Come, servants of God, to obey God's command. Let us pursue the enemy of God until we meet him and then show him our strength. For our departure will be terrifying to the enemy, and our news will resound." Muslims find it difficult to go to war again after the Uhud War. Allah has revealed to support them: "It is not fitting for you to weaken your resolve or to be sad because of what you have lost in victory over your enemies and triumph over them. If there is faith in you, then faith will surely lead to your elevation, for it goes hand in hand with piety and patience, and in them lies the core of victory and triumph. "[324] The Prophet set out with his wounded companions, of whom there were seventy horsemen. Ali carried his flag and Ibn Umm Maktum was left as a proxy in Medina. On the way, he informed them that the scout Muawiyah bin Al-Mughirah bin Abi Al-Aas was nearby. He then sent Ali and Ammar to find and kill him. When Othman ibn Affan learned of the death of his cousin Muawiyah, he took revenge on his wife Umm Kulthum because she had previously pointed out her cousin and revealed his affair. He beat her until she died as a result of the beating.

When the Muslims arrived in Hamra al-Assad, they also buried two Muslims who were killed by the Quraysh on the way to Mecca. The Prophet also arrested Abu Azza al-Jumahi, who had been captured in Badr. Because of his five daughters, the Prophet forgave him and released him on the condition that he would not return to the war against the Muslims and would not support anyone against them. However, he broke the agreement, incited tribes and took part in the Battle of Uhud. When the Quraysh left Hamra al-Assad, they left him sleeping and the Muslims arrested him and brought him to the Prophet. The Prophet ordered Ali to kill him, which he did. The Prophet wanted to show the Quraysh and their army the strength of the Muslims and terrify them. He therefore ordered the Muslims to light five hundred flames of fire and store them there. That way, anyone who saw the flames would think that the army was large.

Figure 37: The Muslims light the fire at the command of the Prophet.

A man who was on his way to Mecca passed by the Muslims and saw their preparations and the army. When he reached Abu Sufyan and his companions, he told them that Muhammad was looking for them in a gathering such as he had never seen and that Ali bin Abi Talib had come to the fore among the people. Those who were left behind had joined him because they regretted what they had done and they were angry and ready to fight.

Terror struck the hearts of the Quraysh, so Abu Sufyan instructed Na'im Ibn Masoud, who was on his way to Medina, to visit the Muslims' camp and frighten them. He was to tell them that the Quraysh would come with a large army to eliminate them and uproot them. Abu Sufyan promised to give him as many dates and raisins as he wanted. When the Prophet and the Muslims heard this, they were not frightened, but their faith was deepened and strengthened. [325]

Allah awarded great reward to a certain group who came with the Prophet because they showed perfect sincerity. When people tried to frighten them with the army of Quraysh, they remained steadfast and did not fear. Instead, this strengthened their faith and they said: "Allah is sufficient for us, and He is the best protector." Allah says to them: "This is only Satan, who appears in the form of Na'im ibn Mas'ud to frighten his followers in particular. But the stead-fast believers are not at all deterred by these whispers. "[326]

Abu Sufyan and his group hurried to return to Mecca. The Prophet then sent someone to tell them the truth about the situation. When they learned that the danger was over, they returned to Medina, blessed and favored by Allah, with their faith strengthened and no harm done to them. [327] The clash at Hamra al-Asad was a strategic move in the divine plan to bring psychological and media defeat upon the Quraysh and thwart the plans of the hypocrites and Jews in the city, especially after the Battle of Uhud and its aftermath. Moreover, it strengthened the authority of the Muslims in the city, promoted unity among the Muslims and raised their morale. [328]

625 - 626 AD

The fourth year after the Hijrah

Birth of Al-Hussein bin Ali

In the fourth year of the Hijrah, on the fifth Sha'ban, the second son of Fatima was born. The Prophet named him Hussein and prayed for him. He also slaughtered a ram for him and told his mother to treat him like his brother al-Hassan, shave off his hair and give the weight of the cut hair in silver as alms. The Prophet placed Hussein on his lap and wept. Asma bint Yazid Al-Ansariya was present and said: "May my father and mother be sacrificed for you, why are you crying?" Prophet Muhammad replied, "For my son, this one." She said: "He was born recently!" He said: "The apostate group will kill him after me. May Allah not grant them my intercession." Then he said: "O Asma, do not tell Fatima about what I have told you, for she has just given birth to her son." [329]

Speech of the Prophet on the month of Ramadan

On the last Friday of the month of Sha'ban, Prophet Muhammad delivered a sermon to the Muslims on the occasion of the beginning of the month of Ramadan. He said: "O people, verily the month of Allah, the Exalted is He, has come to you with blessings, mercy and forgiveness. A month that is the best month with Allah, whose days are the best days, whose nights are the best nights and whose hours are the best hours. This is a month in which you are invited to the hospitality of Allah, and you have been established among the people of worship. Your breaths in this month are praise, your sleep in it is worship, your actions in it are accepted and your supplications in it are answered..."

When he finished, Ali stood up and said: "O Messenger of Allah, what is the best action in this month?" He said: "O Abu al-Hassan, the best action in this month is to stay away from what Allah, Exalted and Revealed is He, has forbidden." [330]

The death of Fatima bint Asad

Fatima bint Asad and her husband Abu Talib acted as the Prophet's adoptive parents for fifteen years after he lost his mother. She was the first woman to pledge allegiance to the Prophet in Mecca after Khadija, and also the first woman to migrate with the Prophet from Mecca to Medina. Fatima bint Asad died in the fourth year of the Hijrah. The Messenger of God prayed for her, took care of her burial, took off his shirt and put it on her, lay with her in her grave and wept. He said: "May God reward you for being a good mother." He recited the Quran for her. When the dust was poured on her, he was asked the reason for his action at her death, and he said: "I dressed her to put on the garments of Paradise, and I lay with her in her grave to relieve her of the pressure of the grave." [331]

Badr al-Mau'id

Almost a year passed as the date set by Abu Sufyan approached. But Abu Sufyan was afraid of the consequences and did not want to go out. However, after consulting with Quraysh, he decided not to go out too far in order to preserve his self-respect. So he set out with the people of Mecca and camped in Majnah in the direction of Dhahran with 2,000 men and 50 horses.

There he met Na'im bin Masoud Al-Ashja'i, who came to Umrah and asked him to go to Medina and discourage the Muslims. Abu Sufyan promised him 10 camels which he had left with Suhail bin Amr. Abu Sufyan said: "It is a dry year. I prefer not to go out to them. But I don't want Muhammad to go out and not me, because that would strengthen their courage against us. I would prefer that they withdraw instead of me doing so." After Suhail ibn Amr had guaranteed the camels for Na'im, Na'im hurried to Medina. There he found the people preparing for the meeting with Abu Sufyan. He asked them and they informed him of their plan. He then said to them: "That's a bad idea. They will come to your home and only the fugitive will survive. Do you really want to go out when they have already gathered for you. By God, none of you will escape." He repeated these words to the Prophet's companions, so that the Prophet's companions no longer liked the idea of going out and believed Na'im's words. The hypocrites and Jews rejoiced at this and said: "Muhammad will not escape this gathering." When the Prophet heard about this and the news increased, he feared that no one would go out with him. So he swore: "By the One in Whose hand is my life, I will go out even if I am alone." Othman bin Affan told the Prophet: "You have seen how fear has been cast into our hearts, and I see no one who has any intention of going out."

After that, the cowards retreated and turned back, while only the brave ones prepared to fight with the Messenger of God. The Messenger of God appointed Abdullah bin Rawaha as the representative over Medina, and Ali bin Abi Talib carried the main banner when they went out with their goods and trade. The hypocrites said to them, "They have already killed you in front of your houses. How will it be when you come to their land and they unite against you? By Allah, you will never return." The believers answered them: "Allah is sufficient for us, and He is the best of guardians." They added that if they met Abu Sufyan, it is for this purpose that they went out, and if they did not meet him, they could sell their goods. When they approached Badr, the hypocrites said to them, "It is full of those who were gathered by Abu Sufyan to frighten and intimidate them." The believers said: "Allah is our protector and an excellent helper." When the Muslims reached Badr, they did not find the supposed army of Abu Sufyan, but they found markets where no one was competing with them. The Prophet spent eight days there waiting for Abu Sufyan and his army. The Muslims sold their goods in the Badr market and doubled their profits. People heard about their march and the fame of their army spread in all directions. God helped the Muslims defeat their enemy and they returned safely to Medina.

The polytheists received news that the Muslims marched to Badr and were numerous, and that they were the most traders in that season. Abu Sufyan was shocked and returned to Mecca. Safwan bin Umayyah said to Abu Sufyan, "I advised you not to make promises to the people, but you did not listen to me. They challenged us and saw that we broke our promise."

Abu Sufyan made a big mistake at the end of the Battle of Uhud and made a bad decision. He lacked insight and experience when he promised himself to meet the Muslims a year later at Badr al-Mau'id. But he realized his big mistake too late. Safwan ibn Umayyah had pointed it out to him, but he did not heed it.

Abu Sufyan now had to save face, even if it was only for appearances, but he failed to do so. Therefore, he was forced to resign and break his promise under the pretext of drought. Even the inhabitants of Mecca themselves made fun of what had happened and called their army, which was morally and psychologically defeated, the "Army of Sowiq". This means they went out to eat Sowiq[1] on the way, not to wage war and fight.

After going through several wars and experiencing many crises in several directions, the Muslims felt somewhat exhausted. They needed time to reorganize their situation. Therefore, the absence of war in Badr al-Mau'id had a positive impact on the Muslims. The commercial benefit that the Muslims derived from the Badr market on this occasion was a relief and brought joy and hope in terms of the possibility of improving living conditions. This was to give Muslims enough time to reorganize their agricultural seasons and rebuild economically in other areas of crafts, trade and other fields in an atmosphere characterized by peace, security and relative tranquility. But not long after, something unexpected happened when the Quraysh and their allies launched an all-out and far-reaching attack on Medina from various locations.[332]

Battle of the trench (Al-Khandaq)

When the Prophet expelled the Jews from Banu Al-Nadir in the third year of the Hijrah, they fled to Khaybar. A group of them went to Mecca to call on the Quraysh and their followers to wage war against the Muslims in revenge for what they had done to them. They went to Abu Sufyan and told him about their experiences. They asked him for support in the battle. Abu Sufyan asked: "So you are here because of him?" The Jews replied: "Yes, we have come to ask you to fight with us against Muhammad." Abu Sufyan said: "Welcome. Those who help us against Muhammad are the dearest people to us." When they heard this from him, they wanted a guarantee for his statement. They said to Abu Sufyan, "Let us choose fifty men from the tribes of the Quraysh, including you, and we will sit together under the curtains of the Kaaba. Then we will swear by Allah that none of us will betray the other and our word should be one against this man, as long as there is still one of us left." Then Abu Sufyan said: "We are

---

1   Sowiq is a type of food made from wheat flour that can be diluted with water to drink or eat. It was often used on journeys as provisions because it is long-lasting.

here for you. go out to Quraysh and call them to war and guarantee them the support and steadfastness until you eradicate him."

The Jews went to the Quraysh elders and called on them to fight against the Prophet. Then some men of Quraysh said to each other, 'The leaders of the people of Yathrib and the scholars of the first book have come to us. So ask them, Which of us is on the right path, we or Muhammad?" Abu Sufyan said to the Jews, "You are the people of the first book and of knowledge. Tell us who is right, we or Muhammad. We build the house, slaughter the camels, give water to the pilgrims and worship idols." The Jews replied: "O God, you worship this house and offer hospitality to the pilgrims. You sacrifice the camels and worship like your ancestors. Therefore, you are more right than Muhammad." They said to the Quraysh what they wanted to hear and the Quraysh were reassured. Then the Jews made an appointment with them and went out to Ghatafan and promised them that they would have dates of Khaybar for a year if they helped them against Muhammad. They asked the Arabs for support and incited the Al-Ahabish[1] against Muhammad. Then they turned to the Banu Salim. Banu Salim promised to go out with them when the Quraysh marched. Salim came and met them in Marr Dhahran[2] with seven hundred, and Banu Fazara went out with a thousand, and Ashjaa went out with four hundred, and Banu Murra also came out with four hundred. The army of the Quraysh, together with the Ghatafan, Asad and Salim, consisted of ten thousand fighters under the leadership of Abu Sufyan. They had three hundred horses and one thousand five hundred camels.

Quraysh landed in Brumah and Wadi Al-Aqiq, and Ghatafan landed in Al-Zaghaba on the side of Uhud.

When the armies of Quraysh started moving from Mecca and headed towards Medina, a group of horsemen from Khuzaa'ah quickly set out for Mecca to Medina and came to the prophet within four days and reported the matter to him. Then the messenger of Allah gathered the people and told them the news and consulted them about their affair. He commanded them to be serious and militant and promised them victory if they were patient and god-fearing. He commanded them to obey Allah and his messenger. Er discussed the war plan with them and said: "Should we go out of Medina to them. Or should we stay in it and dig a trench around it? Or should we stay nearby and leave the moun-

---

1   Al-Ahabisch Quraysh: A group of Quraysh, Kinanah, and Khuza'a gathered and allied at Mount Habshi below Mecca.

2   Marr Dhahran: A large valley of the Tihama valleys in the Mecca region, also called the Valley of Fatima.

tain behind us?" They had different opinions. Salman said: "O Messenger of Allah, a small group cannot put up a long resistance against a large group in war." The Prophet asked, "What should we do?" Salman replied, "We could dig a trench to create a barrier between us and them. That way you could fend them off in the siege and they wouldn't be able to attack us from all sides. When we, the Persians, were attacked by enemies in our homeland, we dug trenches. So the war was waged in familiar places." Gabriel came to him and confirmed Salman's opinion. The Muslims were enthusiastic about Salman's idea and preferred to stay in the Medina. The Prophet rode with a group of Muhajirun and Ansar to Mount Salaa, dismounted and then directed them to the site of the trench and started digging himself (See Figure 38). He called the people to work and informed them of the approach of their enemy and his camp. The aim of the trench was to prevent the soldiers and horsemen of the allies[1] from entering the city and to avoid a direct confrontation with them.

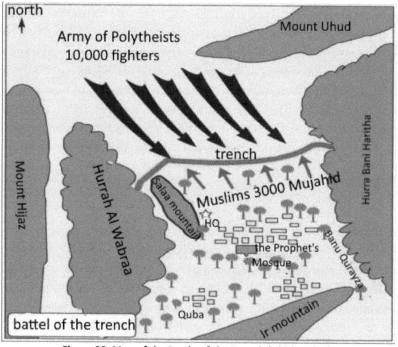

Figure 38: Map of the Battle of the Trench (Al-Khandaq).

To dig the trench, the Prophet borrowed some tools from the Banu Quraiza, such as shovels, axes and machetes. This help was granted in accordance with the

---

1   The Allies, the groupings or 'Al-Ahzab' in Arabic refer to the allied troops who attacked Medina and the Prophet Muhammad together with the Quraysh.

treaty with the Jews of Medina. The Prophet himself helped and prayed for forgiveness for the Muhajirun and Ansar. The Messenger of Allah dug with them until he was exhausted and then sat down to rest. His companions said to him, "O Messenger of Allah, we are enough. we will work for you." He replied, "I want to share in your reward."

While digging the trench, the Ansar happily recited poems emphasizing their allegiance to Prophet Muhammad and Jihad. All the Muslims took part in the work, and when a stone was too hard and a shovel broke, they informed the Prophet about it. Then the Messenger of Allah came and struck the stone with a shovel, and lightning radiated from it. The Messenger of Allah stood up and shouted Allahu Akbar (Allah is Most Great). The Muslims also said takbir. Then he struck it a second time in the same way. And then a third time too, until he was shattered. Salman asked the reason for the takbir and the Prophet explained that with the first takbir, the palaces of al-Hirah and the cities of Khosrau were illuminated for him. With the second takbir, the red palaces of the Byzantine Empire were illuminated and with the third takbir, the palaces of Sana'a were illuminated. Gabriel told him that his nation would be victorious over these lands, and the Muslims rejoiced at the prospect of victory. The hypocrites said: "Do not be surprised at Muhammad. He promises you lies. He claims that he can see the palaces of al-Hira and the cities of Khosrau and that they will open up for you, while you are only digging trenches out of fear and are unable to confront the enemy." Abu Bakr and Omar were present, and one of them said to the other, "He promises us the treasures of Khosrau and emperors, although none of us is able even to go to the latrine. "[333] The hypocrites looked at each other in astonishment and believed, along with some weakly believing Muslims, that what the Prophet said about victory and triumph was only deception and vanity. [334]

Not everyone liked working in the heat and sun. When the Prophet said to Othman bin Affan, "Dig.", Othman became angry and furious and said: "Is it not enough for Muhammad that we obey him and submit to Islam? Now he is also ordering us to work hard." Othman walked past Ammar bin Yasser while he was digging the trench so that the dust rose near him. Othman put his sleeve on his nose and walked past. Ammar recited:

"There is no comparison between someone who builds mosques,

And prays in them, practicing prostration and bowing.

And someone who avoids dust with his sleeve,

who defiantly turns away from it."

Othman turned to him and asked, "Do you mean me, you son of the black woman?" Then Othman went to the Prophet and said: "We have not come to have our dignity insulted." The Messenger of God then said to him: "I release you from your Islam, go. "

Allah reports in the Quran about what these people of weak faith carried in their hearts. They wanted to present their conversion to Islam as a favor to the Prophet, as if they had done him a favor by becoming Muslims. However, Allah answers them: "Do not make your conversion to Islam a boast to the Prophet, as if you had done him a favor. Rather, Allah's favor to you is that He has sent His Messenger, revealed His Book, and shown you the straight path, if you are sincere in your faith." [335]

Jabir bin Abdullah saw Prophet Muhammad working with the other people and the dust covering his thin body. Jabir asked for permission to go home and the Prophet allowed him. Jabir and his wife decided to make food and invite the Prophet and one or two men to join them. They prepared barley and a roasted sheep's neck and invited the Prophet to eat. The Prophet asked Jabir what he was preparing and he told him about it. The Prophet said: "It is much good." Then the Prophet called all the people in the trench and said to them, "Jabir has prepared a feast for you." The Muslims all went to Jabir. He said: "By God, this is a scandal." He then went to his wife and told her about it. She asked him whether he had invited them or the Prophet. Jabir replied, "No, he invited them." His wife then said: "Leave them, he knows better." The Prophet came and ordered his companions to come in groups of ten. They scooped from the food and ate until they were full without the food or bread diminishing. The Messenger of God said: "Eat and distribute the food, for the people are afflicted by a severe famine." The Muslims did this until all the people in the trench area had eaten and were full.

Work on the trench continued until it was dug in about twelve days. Its length was about two thousand five hundred meters, its width four and a half meters and its depth three and a half meters. The region of the trench is located in the area near Thaniyat Al-Wada in the northwest of the city of Medina until it ends at Mount Uhud. The western and eastern parts of the city are rugged areas of volcanic rock and are natural barriers. In the south there were date palms, in addition to the narrow buildings. Since some parts in the east and south were weaker than others, the Muslims fortified the city with buildings. So the Prophet closed the gaps through which the enemy could enter and built doors for the moat. He also placed guards at the doors. The prophet's participation in digging the trench was not symbolic participation, but real participation in the form of genuine suffering. This was a practical representation of equality between all social groups.

The Prophet prepared the army, which consisted of only nine hundred fighters. He rejected some and placed women and children in a fortified area. On the way to Medina, Huyay ibn Akhtab, the master of Banu al-Nadir, said to the Quraysh as he traveled with them that Banu Quraiza was with them and had seven hundred and fifty fighters. As they approached Medina, Abu Sufyan told him to go to his people and break the covenant between them and Muhammad. The Quraysh saw the trench and were surprised. They built themselves up on the trench and besieged the Muslims. When the Muslims saw the huge enemy army besieging the city, they were overcome with fear. The sounds of the enemy horses silenced them, and they saw nothing but the spears and swords flashing on the horizon. They stood still as if birds were sitting on their heads. The believers, however, when they saw the allies, said: "This is what Allah and His Messenger have promised us. There must be a confrontation with the enemy and there must be victory. Allah and his Messenger have spoken the truth." What they saw only strengthened their faith in Allah and their absolute devotion to His will.[336] The great difference in numbers and equipment between the Muslims and their enemies from the allies that came from all directions had a profound effect on the mental state of both armies. The pagan army saw itself as strong and superior and saw the Muslims as weak. The Muslims, on the other hand, believed that their existence was under threat and that they could be wiped out. They had to defend themselves in order to survive.

The Messenger of God called the enemy army to God and appealed to them on the basis of their kinship. However, the Quraysh refused. Abu Sufyan, the leader of the army of the pagans, wrote a letter to the Messenger of Allah: "You have killed our heroes, orphaned children and made women widows. Now tribes and clans have gathered to fight against you and erase your traces. We come to you and demand half of the city's date palms. If you comply with our request, you will be safe. Otherwise, be prepared for the destruction of the houses and the eradication of the roots." The Prophet replied: "In the name of Allah, the most gracious, the most merciful. The letter of the people of idolatry, hypocrisy and disbelief has arrived, and I have understood your words. By Al-lah, I have nothing for you but the blades of swords and the shafts of spears. Return, woe to you. From the worship of idols. Rejoice at the blow of the sword, at the cleft of the spear, at the destruction of the homeland and the dis-appearance of the traces. Peace be upon him who follows the guidance."

The Banu Quraiza had fortresses in Medina that were three kilometers away from the city. Ka'ab bin Asad Al-Qurazi was the clan chief of Banu Quraiza and had made a covenant with the Messenger of God. When Huyay ibn Akhtab came to Banu Quraiza, they were reluctant to receive him. He spoke to Ghazal ibn Samwal and said that the Quraysh had reached the Valley of Aqeeq and were near Uhud. However, Ghazal was suspicious and said that Huyay had brought the worst. Huyay then went to the door of Ka'ab bin Asad and asked to speak to him. Ka'ab said to him: "There is a contract between me and Muhammad which I will not break. For I have seen nothing but loyalty and sin-cerity from him." Huyay said: "Open the door, I want to talk to you." Ka'ab replied, "I won't do it." Huyay insisted until Ka'ab opened the door for him. Then he said: "Woe to you, O Ka'ab. I have great news for you. I have brought Quraysh and their leaders to you. They are now near Medina, and I have come to you with their help. They have promised me that they will not leave until they have wiped out Muhammad and his companions." Ka'ab refused and said: "You have brought to me misfortune and thunder and lightning in which there is nothing. Leave me and Muhammad in peace, I will not betray him, for I have learned from him only loyalty and truthfulness." Huyay insisted until he made him a promise and swore by God to be with him and return with him to his fortress if these masses returned disappointed and did not kill Muhammad, so that what would happen to him would also happen to Huyay. Ka'ab was con-vinced of his promises and broke what was agreed between him and the Mes-senger of Allah and was absolved of his obligations to him. They tore up the paper on which the contract was written. Ka'ab gathered the heads of his peo-ple and told them that he had broken the covenant.

An old man whose sight had gone, told them of a prophecy in the Torah that at the end of time a prophet would be sent to Mecca and emigrate to Med-ina. Huyay claimed that this prophet was from the Children of Israel and not from the Arabs. He also claimed that Muhammad was not a prophet but noth-ing more than a magician. Another reminded them of the covenant of the Mes-senger of God and intimidated them for their misdeeds. He told them that if they did not help him, they should leave him with his enemy. A group of them who refused to break the covenant finally went to the Messenger of God and embraced Islam. Ka'ab asked Huyay to take a guarantee from Quraysh and Ghatafan. They were to hand over hostages from them who would stay with Ka'ab if they returned and did not support him in the fight against Muhammad. The hostages were 90 men from the noble class. The agreement was fulfilled and the pact broken. When the Messenger of Allah heard this, he was deeply shocked and his companions panicked, which distressed the Messenger of Allah. He said: "Allah is sufficient for us and He is the best protector.".

The Prophet sent Saad bin Muadh, the leader of Al-Aws, and Saad bin Ubadah, the leader of Al-Khazraj, in a group to check whether the reports were true. He ordered them that if they indeed found treachery, they should inform him secretly without mentioning it openly in front of the people so as not to confuse the people and aggravate their suffering in the ongoing times of war. They then entered the fortress and called on the Jews to renew their covenant. However, Banu Quraiza said bad things about the Messenger of God, which angered Saad bin Ubadah, who cursed them. Saad bin Muadh said to him, "By God, we did not come here for this, and what stands between us is greater than an insult." Saad bin Ubadah called them and said: "You know what is between us, and I fear that you will suffer like the day of Banu Al-Nadir for worse." They then cursed him and he replied, "You should have said something better."

When Saad bin Muadh and Saad bin Ubadah returned to the Prophet and told him in code about the annulment of the treaty by Quraiza, they said to him upon their arrival: "O Messenger of Allah, 'Adal and Al-Qarah[1] want to betray Al-Rajee'." The Prophet said: "Allahu Akbar, rejoice, O Muslims, rejoice in God's victory and help." The Messenger of God ordered the Muslims to remain steadfast in their place and remain in their trenches. The polytheists looked at the trench and were afraid to go in. They circled it with their soldiers, horses and men and called out to the Muslims to fight and duel. But no one responded, and the Muslims held on to their positions as the Messenger of God had commanded.

---

1   'Adal and Al-Qarah were two Arab tribes. They had turned to the Messenger of Allah after the Battle of Uhud and asked him to send someone who teaches them Islamic Sharia and reads the Quran to them. The Prophet sent ten of his companions with them. However, when they set out with them and reached the water of Al-Rajee' in the Hejaz region, they betrayed the Prophet's companions. They killed them and took two of them captive, who they sold as slaves in Mecca. But the Quraysh also killed them. This event was a tragedy for the Prophet.

The polytheists took turns, so that one day Abu Sufyan came with his companions, the next day Khaled bin Al-Walid and then Amr bin Al-Aas. They came every day with their horses. They approached the companions of the Messenger of Allah, brought their men forward and threw stones and arrows at the Muslims across the moat. They besieged the city and there was no direct confrontation in battle between them except with arrows and stones. Saad bin Muadh was hit by an arrow in the arm. Saad prayed, "O God, if you allow the Quraysh war to continue, then keep me for it, for I would like to fight against a people who harmed your Messenger, expelled him and lied to him. O God, if you want to end the war between us and them, then let me die a martyr, and do not let me die until you have made me happy with the defeat of Banu Quraiza." When Saad was wounded, the Prophet ordered him to be taken to the tent of Rufaida, which she had set up in the Prophet's mosque, to treat the wounded.

The Muslims were afraid of the large crowds surrounding the Medina and wanted to pounce on them at every opportunity and destroy them from the outside. The treachery of the Banu Quraiza shook the Muslims' plan to fortify the city, made them vulnerable to invasion and increased their fear for their families in the city. The Prophet knelt on his knees, spread his hands, wept his eyes and cried out in a loud voice: "O Savior of the afflicted, O Hearer of the prayers of the afflicted, take away my sorrows and affliction from me, for You see my condition." [337]

Allah describes how the polytheists and Jews besieged Medina. The Jews of Banu Quraiza came from the east and the Ghatafan, while the Quraysh, the Banu Kinanah and those who had joined them from the Bedouins came from the west. The Muslims were filled with fear and fell into a state of confusion and astonishment. They lost their ability to think clearly and their hearts seemed to leap out of their chests in terror. They believed that Allah and His Messenger would not keep their promise of victory and that this was the end of this religion. The hypocrites believed that the Prophet's promises were nothing but lies and that the war would end with the defeat of the Muslims. In these difficult times, the faith of the believers was put to the severest test. They saw death coming before their eyes. This test was like a powerful earthquake that sighted them. Only the true believers remained steadfast. [338]

After almost twenty nights of siege and continuous fighting, the situation worsened for the Prophet and his companions. Many people turned away from him and spoke ugly words about the Prophet. There were also residents of houses on the outskirts of Medina who came to the Prophet and said: "allow us to return to our houses because they are on the outskirts of Medina and they are exposed to the enemy. We fear that the Jews would attack them." The Messenger of God allowed them to do so, and only three hundred of them stayed with him when most of them returned to their homes.

Other groups said among themselves: "Let us flee and go into the desert to seek refuge with the Bedouins. Because everything that Muhammad promised us is false." When the Prophet saw the suffering and fear of the people, he began to encourage them and proclaimed good news. He said: "I swear by God, in whose hand is my soul, that what you see of hardship will surely be removed from you. I hope that I will safely circumambulate the old house (the Kaaba), and God will give me the keys of the Kaaba. And God will defeat Chosroes and Emperor (Heraclius), and we will spend their treasures in the name of God." A man who was with him said to his companions, "Do not be surprised at Muhammad. He promises us to go round the old house and share the treasures of Persia and Rome, but here we are, and none of us feels safe to go out once. He promises us nothing but lies." Others said: "O people of Yathrib, there is no place for you here, so go back."

The hypocrites began to ask the Messenger of Allah for permission, saying, "Our houses are unprotected," that is, they are close to the enemy because they are outside the city and their walls are low. They feared that they might be stolen. "Allow us to return to our wives and children." The Prophet gave them permission, and that night only three hundred stayed with him. In time, most of the people left the Messenger of Allah at night. They sneaked out and went to their homes as if they had surrendered, and only twelve men remained with him.

Allah reveals the hidden intentions of these hypocrites. If the enemies were to enter from all sides of the city and attack them and then ask these people to deny their faith and return, they would immediately agree and not hesitate, even for a short time. These people are in a state of fear and terror that if they were asked to betray the Muslims and return to disbelief, they would do so without hesitation. Although they have made a strong promise and oath to their Lord that they will not flee the battlefield but will fight with the Prophet and sacrifice themselves for the defense of Islam, they should keep their promise and abide by it, for Allah will ask people about it and reward them accordingly.

Then Allah says: "Tell them, Muhammad, that fleeing the battlefield out of fear of death or killing will not help them, for death is inevitable and the remaining days of life are only a few in which they can have a little joy, and in the end their fate is death. Tell them, Muhammad, that they should understand one fact, and that is that Allah is in control of affairs and no one can avert Allah's judgment if he wants evil for you, and no one can prevent his good if he decides to pardon you and give you good, and they will not find anyone who can help them or avert evil from them except Allah, for the supporters fall before God and the helpers lose their abilities before God.

It is not hidden from Allah how the hypocrites prevent the weak Muslims from fighting in jihad by spreading lies and asking the Muslims to give up the fight and join them, and Allah knows that they only intervene in some cases in a fight that the Muslims are waging where it benefits them and serves their interests and protects their personalities from falling, so that they are not exposed before society and their identity becomes clear in hypocrisy, they are stingy with you with themselves and with victory for you and stingy with any good that returns to you, then when they are forced to be with the believers in a war or a battle, you see them when the hardship is great, they lose focus, where out of great fear they look at you, Muhammad, like someone who has lost his mind and it shows in his eyes that wander around worried and anxious, or like someone who is experiencing death, you see him in his death spasms, he faints and cannot speak, and this speech is in a state of distress, but in a state of ease and calmness and return of things to their normality, they are not silent, but direct the arrows of criticism and slander and try to hurt you with harsh and sharp words, and when there is booty, they quarrel to get their share, these have not believed and faith has not settled in their hearts, so Allah has invalidated their deeds, that was easy for Allah. [339]

After Saad bin Muadh was injured, the chiefs of the polytheists agreed to attack all of them. They searched for a place to cross the ditch and found a narrow place that the Muslims had neglected. Some of them were able to cross the ditch, including Ikrimah bin Abi Jahl, Nawfal bin Abdullah Al-Makhzoumi, Dirar ibn al-Khattab al-Fihri, Hubaira bin Abi Wahb and Amr bin Abdwud. The polytheists hoped that the entry of Omar bin Abd Wad and those who were with him would end the war. [340]

Death of Amr bin Abdwud

After this group took the gap and began to break through the trench, the Prophet ordered Ali to advance with those who were brave enough with him to take the position from them, saying, "Whoever fights you on this position, kill him." Ali went out and when he reached the gap, Amr bin Abdwud was approaching, masked with iron. He saw the Muslims who were with Ali and the horsemen accompanying him and shouted like a camel, "Is there a swordsman?" Amr ibn Abdwud was a knight of the Quraysh and was considered the equal of a thousand knights. He was never defeated in battle. The Messenger said: "Who among you will come out to Amr, and I will guarantee him paradise (heaven) from God?" But no one came forward. When the Prophet called out several times, Ali stood up and said: "I will challenge him, O Messenger of God." He ordered him to hold back and wait briefly until someone else comes forward. Amr repeated the call and the people remained silent, watching anxiously and fearing Amr and those with him and those behind him. Amr said: "O people, you claim that your dead are in heaven and our dead are in hell. Does not one of you like that he goes to paradise, or that he sent his enemy to the hell?" No one dared to confront him. But Ali stepped forward again and said: "I will do it, O Messenger of Allah." He ordered him to sit down. Amr charged forward and backward with his horse and the leaders of the allies came and stood behind the ditch and stretched their necks to watch, and when Amr saw that no one answered him, he said:

"My voice grew hoarse from shouting in their assembly:

'Is there a swordsman? - But no one stepped forward.

I stood there when the brave one was scared,

but I took the stance of a brave fighter.

I am ready to swing the swords,

My courage and generosity are well known."

Then Ali stood up and said again: "O Messenger of God, allow me to fight him." When Amr's request for a duel was repeated and Ali continued to stand up, the Messenger of God said to him, "Come closer to me, O Ali." Ali approached the Prophet and the Prophet handed him his sword (Dhū l-faqār) and took off his own turban from his head and put them on Ali's head and said: "Go to him." When Ali came to him, the Prophet prayed, "O God, help him." Then he accompanied Ali as if bidding him farewell and continued praying to the heavens while the Muslims around him were silent and afraid. Ali met him as a fighter on foot, while Amr rode a horse.

Amr mocked Ali when he saw Ali. Jabir bin Abdullah Al-Ansari accompanied Ali to see what was going to happen. Ali said:

"Do not hurry, for the answerer to you did not come helpless,

full of intention, insight and honesty without grief"

Figure 39: Ali cuts off the leg of Amr ibn
Abdwud.

The Messenger of God said as they stood facing each other, "All of Islam stands against all idolatry." Amr asked him, "Who are you?" Ali replied, "I am Ali bin Abi Talib." Amr said: "O son of my brother, is there not one of your uncles who is older than you. I hate to shed your blood." However, Ali replied, "But by God, I don't hate shedding your blood." Amr then angrily drew his sword and attacked Ali. But Ali blocked his attack with his shield and cut off Amr's leg, causing him to fall on his back. The dust rose and when it settled, Ali appeared, standing on Amr bin Abdwud and fixing him with his leg as if waiting for something. The Muslims shouted and demanded that Ali kill him immediately. Then Ali struck him down and killed him, so the people pronounced takbir. The Messenger of God heard the takbir and said: "By the one in whose hand is my soul, he has killed him." When the Prophet's companions heard the takbir, they rushed to see what had happened. Omar Ibn Al-Khattab was the first to reach the place and see that Ali had killed Amr. Omar said: "Allahu Akbar, O Messenger of God, he has killed him." Omar ibn al-Khattab and Dhirar ibn Amr had a fight, and Dhirar overpowered him. But when the spearhead touched Omar, Dhirar took the spear away from him and said: "This is indeed a grateful favor. Keep it, O son of al-Khattab. I had decided that my hands should never harm a Qurayshi, so I have spared you." Dhirar then returned to his companions.

The companions of Amr ibn Abdwud dispersed and their horses jumped over the ditch. Then Ali approached the Messenger of God with a radiant face. Omar ibn Al-Khattab asked him: "Did you take his shield? Because there is no comparable shield among the Arabs." Ali replied, "When I struck him, he exposed his private parts to prevent me from killing him, so I was ashamed to deprive my cousin." The Prophet asked Ali about his attitude before killing Amr. Ali replied, "He insulted my mother and spat in my face, and I was reluctant to strike him out of personal revenge. So I left him alone until I calmed down. Then I killed him for the sake of Allah." The Messenger of God said: "The striking of Ali on the Day of the Trench is better than the worship of the two worlds (mankind and the jinn)."

The morale of the Quraysh collapsed and they were disappointed after Amr bin Abdwud was killed. The Quraysh sent someone to the Messenger of God to buy the body of Amr bin Abdwud for ten thousand dinars. The Prophet Muhammad said: "It is yours, we will not take a price for the dead." After this incident, the Prophet said: "Now we will attack them, and they will not attack us." This statement surprised everyone present. This means that the Quraysh will not attack the Muslims in the future, but the Muslims will continue to fight against them, not only in this war but also in the future.

Na'im bin Masoud was known for passing on news that he had heard. One evening he was passing near the Prophet and the Prophet beckoned him over and asked, "What have you heard?" He replied, "I have heard that the Quraysh and Ghatafan have asked Banu Quraiza to come to them to fight you. Banu Quraiza agreed and asked the Quraysh to send hostages as a guarantee." The Messenger of God said to Na'im bin Masoud, "I am going to tell you a secret, so do not reveal it. Banu Quraiza has sent me a messenger to make peace and let Banu Al-Nadir return to their homes and return their wealth." Na'im bin Masoud deliberately went to Ghatafan and Quraysh to tell them this news. The Messenger of God said: "War is a deception. May God create something for us." Na'im went to Ghatafan and the Quraysh and informed them of what he had heard from Prophet Muhammad. Quraysh hurried and sent Ikrimah bin Abi Jahl and a group with him to Banu Quraiza to ask them to fight with them. The Jews argued that it was the Sabbath and demanded hostages as a guarantee of security, but they could not reach an agreement.

Then the Messenger of God was informed that Banu Quraiza sent a message to Abu Sufyan: "If you and Muhammad meet, we will support you against him." The Prophet then stood up and delivered a sermon and said: "Banu Quraiza told us that if we meet with Abu Sufyan, they will support us against the Quraysh." When Abu Sufyan heard about this, he said: "The Jews have betrayed us." He turned his back on them and left them. The Prophet worked through intelligent and deliberate media methods to sow doubt between the allies until he achieved what he wanted. He was thus able to thwart all their plans and undo all the efforts they had made to cooperate with each other.

The Quraysh continued to besiege the city and the Muslims suffered under the intensified siege. Therefore, the Prophet prayed to God: O Allah, Who sent down the Book, Who is swift in reckoning, defeat the allies, O Allah, defeat them. O Allah, I call upon You to fulfill Your promise. O Allah, if You will it, You will not be worshipped. O Allah, if this group perishes, You will not be worshipped on earth afterwards." The Prophet did not suffer from fear, as he himself was the source of peace, security and tranquility for the people. But he was concerned about the fate of this religion, its survival and what threatened its existence. So the Messenger of God prayed until a third of the night had passed, and Gabriel came down to him and said: "O Muhammad, Allah has heard your words and answered your prayer. He has commanded Al-Dabur[1] together with the angels to defeat Quraysh and the allies." On Saturday night, Allah sent a strong wind on the allies. This wind extinguished their fires, prevented them from seeing and sent upon them troops of angels who they couldn't see. They tore down their tents, causing them to panic. [341] That night, the angels' cries of "Allahu Akbar" filled the air around their army. Their number reached a thousand. These angels did not take part in the battle, but they re-

---

1   Al-Dabur: refers to a stormy wind that blows from the west, and "Al-Saba" is the east wind.

moved the tent poles, cut the tent ropes, extinguished the fires, overturned the pots and everyone there heard the sound of weapons clashing, but there was no battle. There was chaos, the horses ran in confusion and Allah cast terror into their hearts. They left hastily, leaving behind all their possessions.

Before leaving, Abu Sufyan wrote a message to the Prophet and said: "We marched to you with our allies. And we never wanted to return from you until we had wiped you out. However, I have seen that you hate our meeting and have built trenches and obstacles. What a wonder, who taught you that. If we turn our backs on you, you will see a day like the day of Uhud, when we will slit open the bellies of your women." Then the Prophet wrote to him: "Your arrogance towards God has already deceived you. What you mentioned, that you came to us with your congregation and that you will not return until you have wiped us out, that is God's command preventing you from doing so and gaining victory for us so that the remembrance of al-Lāt and al-'Uzzā will not remain. Your statement: 'Who taught you how to dig this trench.' Allah has inspired this to me to anger you and your companions. The day will come when you will only ward me off with your bare hand, and the day will come when I will destroy the idols of al-Lāt, Al-'Uzza, Manat, Asaf, Naeelah and Hubal, and I will remind you."

After Abu Sufyan sat on his camel, he beat it and walked away. Ikrimah bin Abi Jahl encouraged him to stay and not leave the people. He dismounted and stood still. Later, he, Amr ibn al-Aas and Khaled bin Al-Walid decided that it was necessary to stand in front of Muhammad and his companions in a group of cavalry, as they did not feel safe until the soldiers had left.

Many Muslims experienced that night as a terrifying nightmare, characterized by unexpected noises and surprises. Despite the natural fear that darkness brings, the presence of the Prophet, who unceasingly promised Allah's victory and succor, should have had a calming effect. If they had been firmly rooted in faith and had completely surrendered to Allah and His Messenger, the fear and terror should have receded from their hearts. The hypocrites were filled with fear and, due to their intense fear, could not believe that the armies of their enemies had already departed. They were overwhelmed by a terrifying nightmare, as if the armies of unbelief were constantly passing before their eyes, swords drawn and spears tipped, as they trembled in fear. They jumped up in fear when they heard the neighing of horses and the bellowing of camels, thinking that the armies of the allies had returned. [342] God, says that the hypocrites want to hide in the desert among the Bedouins to escape the Muslims and the Medina. They want to follow the news of the Muslims there to find out if the allies were getting too close to them. If they had not fled and stayed with the Muslims, they would not actively participate in the battle, with few exceptions. [343]

The allies returned, but with failure and defeat despite their mobilization of armies and equipment. They were at odds with each other and exhausted by the length of the siege and problems at the supply level. Disagreements shook the trust between the different allies and led to their failure. The killing of Amr, the knight of the allies, and his companions and the flight of the rest were the fatal blow to them and their hearts. Finally, the wind came to arouse more fear and dread in their souls, and the feeling of loneliness and isolation as everyone was busy protecting themselves from this destructive wind. All these factors had the greatest impact on the defeat of the allies and their failure. [344].

Battle of Banu Quraiza

One of the points of the Treaty of Medina was: "And the Jews have their issues and the Muslims have their issues, and between them is victory over those who fight the people of this document, and between them is counsel and advice and kindness without sin. "[345] That is, the Jews had to stand by the Muslims against the disbelievers of Quraysh and support the Muslims, or at least give them money and weapons if they did not want to fight with them themselves, and the Muslims had to support the Jews as well. There was also no clause in the treaty between them and the Prophet that allowed them to stay away from the battles that took place outside and around the city. The Jews of Banu Quraiza were among the Jews of Medina who swore to the Messenger of Allah that they would not help any enemy, but they broke the oath and did not help the Muslims in their battle against Quraysh in Badr, but helped the people of Mecca with weapons on the day of Badr and stood against the Muslims, and when the Prophet confronted them, they said: "We forgot and erred, so the Messenger of Allah forgave them and made a new treaty with them again," [346] but they broke their oath again and deceived the Messenger of Allah and conspired against him in the war of allies, so the Messenger of Allah sent Saad bin Muadh and others to them to find out the situation, and Saad tried to convince them to give up the idea of breaking the oath, but he heard from them what he did not want to hear. [347]

196

Allah makes it clear in the Quran that man's worth lies in his oath and in his word, and that those who have no oath are the worst creatures to walk the earth. He thus depicts the Jews of Banu Quraiza who had sworn to the Prophet to support him and not to fight against him and not to cooperate with his enemies against him, but they broke the oath more than once. Allah called them disbelievers because many of the Jews of Medina had proclaimed their love for the Prophet and their belief in him before his appearance, according to what they found written about him in their books, so they even invited people and prepared things for his appearance. But after he appeared and they found that their material interests were in danger, they denied him and showed a strong obstinacy in this matter until there was no hope for their faith. Then Allah teaches his Prophet the method of confronting these people and said: "O Muhammad, if you have arrested them in a war in which you have triumphed over them, then educate the others with the retribution from them so that those who are behind them may reconsider their accounts and learn from them and separate from them. And this matter was only enacted so that the other enemies, even the enemies in the future, may learn from it and avoid war against the Muslims and avoid oath-breaking, those who have treaties with the Muslims. O Muhammad, if you see signs of oath-breaking from those who have a treaty with you, give them back their treaty and tell them that you have invalidated it so that you and they are on the same level of knowledge that there is no treaty between you, and then march against them and harm them, and you should not march against them before informing them of the dissolution of the treaty, for that would be treachery and Allah does not love the treacherous." [348]

On Wednesday in the fourth year of the Hijrah, when the Prophet left the trench, entered the city and laid down his weapon, Gabriel came to him and there was dust on his wings. He told him that the angels who had fought against the allies had not laid down their weapons. Gabriel added: "We have driven them to Hamra al-Asad. God commands you to march to Banu Quraiza, for I will go to them and shake them." When Gabriel left the Prophet, one of the Muslims came to the Prophet and said to him, "May my father and mother be sacrificed for you, O Messenger of God." This is Dihyah al-Kalbi calling out to the people, "No one prays the afternoon prayer except in Banu Quraiza. The Prophet said: "This is Gabriel. Call Ali for me." Then Ali came and the Prophet said to him, "Call the people: Let no one perform the afternoon prayer except in Banu Quraiza." Not all Muslims understood the Prophet's instructions, although his words were clear. Some of them did not pray until they came to the Banu Quraiza, while others had already prayed. They gathered around the

Prophet at sunset, he did not rebuke any of them for this and forgave them for their misunderstanding of his statement. When they arrived, the Muslims found palm trees around the palace of Banu Quraiza, but no place to camp. The Prophet then pointed with his right hand to the palm trees, which pushed together, and with his left hand to the palm trees, which retreated. This made room for the Muslims to get out.

The Prophet sent Ali bin Abi Talib with thirty men from Khazraj and his banner to the Banu Quraiza to see if they had come down from their strongholds. When Ali was nearby, he heard bad words from them and returned to the Prophet to tell him about it. The Prophet said to Ali: "Leave them, for God will defeat them. The one who stood by you against Amr bin Abdwud will not let you down." Ali rushed to the wall of the Banu Quraiza fortress, and when they saw him, they shouted that the killer of Amr had come. Ali put up the banner at the fortress. Banu Quraiza insulted the Messenger of God and his wives. The Prophet besieged their fortress and called on them to submit to him. Only a few Jews converted to Islam and secured their lives and property. However, some of them remained with Judaism but were not willing to participate in the Banu Quraiza's deception of the Prophet. They remained neutral and left the city. When the Banu Quraiza lost hope of victory, they sent Nabash bin Qais to speak to the Prophet. He said: "O Muhammad, we will agree to what the Banu Al-Nadir have agreed to. You have the money and the weapons, and you spare our blood, and we will leave your land with wives and descendants, and our belongings that can be carried by camels." The Prophet did not accept their proposal and asked them to submit to his judgment. Nabash said: "You spare our blood and give us wives and offspring, and we do not need what camels carry." The Messenger of God said: "No, until you submit to my judgment." Nabash returned to his companions with what the Messenger of God had said.

Ka'ab ibn Asad said: "O assembly of the Banu Quraiza, by Allah, you know that Muhammad is a prophet of God. We were only prevented from joining him out of envy of the Arabs, because he did not emerge from the Banu Israel as a prophet. But he is where Allah has appointed him. I was against the abrogation of the treaty, but the plague and calamity of this man (meaning Huyayy ibn Akhtab) befell us and his people. Muhammad leaves no man behind except the one who follows him. Remember what Ibn Hauqal said to you when he came to you. He said: "I have given up wine, beer and gambling and have come to water, dates and barley." They asked, "What does this mean?" He said: "A prophet will emerge from this city. If he appears during my life, I will follow him and support him. If he appears after me, do not deceive yourselves about him, but follow him and be his followers and allies. You have believed in both books, the first and the last." Ka'ab added: "Let us follow him and believe in him so that we are safe with our blood, our women and our money, so that we are in the same position as those who follow him." They said: "We should not follow others, we are the people of the Book and prophethood, and we should not follow others." Ka'ab tried to persuade them. They said: "We will not leave the Torah, and we will not deviate from what we know." Ka'ab said excitedly, "Then let us kill our sons and wives and then go to Muhammad and his companions with swords in our hands to fight them." Huyay bin Akhtab laughed and said: "What have these poor people done?!" The chiefs of the Jews said: "There is nothing good in life after them (our families)" Ka'ab said: "There is only one opinion left, and there is no other opinion. If you do not accept it, then there is no way out for you." They said: "What is it?" Ka'ab said: "Tonight is Saturday, and it is very likely that Muhammad and his companions do not expect us to fight them. Let us go to them secretly to surprise them." They said: "Shall we violate our Sabbath?! Do you know what happened to us before?" Huyay said: "I invited Quraysh and Ghatafan to participate, but the Jews refused to violate the Sabbath. If the Jews wanted to, they would have done it then." The Jews shouted, "We do not break the Sabbath." Nabash bin Qais said: "How can we surprise them when you see that their situation is getting more difficult every day. At the beginning of the siege, they only fought during the day and returned at night, which meant that a night attack would have been good. Now, however, they attack both day and night, which has made it more difficult to surprise them. It's a disaster written on us." They were divided and regretted their decisions. The women and children wept.

The Prophet sent an army, led by his senior companions, to Banu Quraiza. But they were defeated. Then he sent Ali ibn Abi Talib , who vowed to either storm their fortress or suffer the same fate as Hamza. He approached them and then shouted, "O battalion of faith." Ali killed ten of their men. The Jews were afraid that Ali would attack them and they asked the Prophet to send Abu Lubaba to them to consult him on their matter. Abu Lubaba was an advisor to them because his property, his family and his son were in Banu Quraiza. The Prophet had bought him as a slave and then set him free. When he arrived with them, they wept and said: "We have no power today to fight with those who are with you." Ka'ab bin Asad stood up and said: "Abu Bashir, you know what we did in your affair and in the affair of your people on the day of Alhadaiq,

Baath[1] and in every war in which you were involved. The siege has intensified and we are almost at the end. Muhammad refuses to leave our fortress until we submit to his Judgment. If he grants us free passage, we will leave the country and move to Levant or Khaybar and never step on his land again. We will never again ally ourselves against him and never again fight against him." Then Abu Lubaba and Ka'ab bin Asad accused Huyay bin Akhtab of responsibility for what happened, whereupon Huyayy felt powerless and said sadly, "It is our fate that a misfortune has befallen us." Then they asked Abu Lubaba about his opinion on accepting the Prophet's judgment, and he said to them: "Yes, do it.", and he pointed to his neck, meaning that he meant slaughter. The Jews understood the message Abu Lubaba wanted to convey to them and decided to surrender on the condition that a person related to them should judge them. They chose Saad bin Muadh, the leader of the Aws, because the Aws were their allies. The Messenger of Allah agreed, and after that they came out of their fortress. 349

Abu Lubaba returned to the Messenger of Allah and told him about the surrender of the Jews of Banu Quraiza. The prophet said to him, "Do you think that Allah overlooked your hand when you pointed to your neck?" The Messenger of Allah surprised Abu Lubaba, as he had not expected the Prophet to find out about this. He regretted his betrayal and was shocked. The Messenger of Allah rejoiced at the news of the Jews' surrender and Ali's victory. He wanted to talk to his companions, and those who gathered around him were a group of distinguished and important companions from the Muhajirun and the Ansar; among them were Khaled bin Saeed and Abu Bakr. The Prophet said to them, "O assembly of the Quraysh. I commend to you a recommendation, keep it from me and take it seriously. I am giving you a command, do not lose sight of it. Ali ibn Abi Talib is your Imam after me and my successor among you. This is what my Lord has commanded me." After a few days, Prophet Muhammad returned to Medina and had the Banu Quraiza imprisoned in the house of Ramla bint Al-Harith Al-Ansariya. They spent the night studying the Torah and encouraging each other to remain steadfast in their religion and adhere to the Torah. The Messenger of God gave the order to his companions and said: "Give them fresh water to drink, feed them good food and treat them well." Then the Messenger of God ordered dates to be brought and scattered over the captives, after which they began to eat.

---

1   Wars before Islam between the Aws and the Khazraj.

When the Prophet was in a meeting, they brought the prisoners to him. Al-Aws also came and asked him to pardon their allies from the Banu Quraiza, just as he had pardoned Ibn 'Ubayy for seven hundred prisoners from the Banu Qaynuqa[2].

The Messenger of God kept silent and did not speak until they insisted on him a lot and spoke all the Al-Aws. Finally he said: "Will you not be satisfied if judgment on them goes to a man from among you?" They replied, "Yes." He then said: "So this goes to Saad bin Muadh." Saad was injured at the time and was being treated in the Rufaida tent in the Prophet's Mosque. A group of the Al-Aws went to Saad, carried him on a donkey and asked him to do good to his allies, just as Ibn 'Ubayy did for his allies. Ad-Dahhak bin Khalifa said: "O Abu Amr, your allies. Your allies. They supported you in all wars, preferred you to others and asked for your intercession." Salama bin Salam bin Waqsh added: "O Abu Amr, be kind to your allies. The Messenger of God loves to return favors. They helped you on the day of Baath, Alhadaiq and other wars. Do not be worse than Ibn 'Ubayy." Saad listened and didn't answer them at first, but when they pressed him too hard, he said: "It's time for Saad not to fear anyone for the sake of God." Ad-Dahhak bin Khalifah exclaimed, "O my God, my people." Mu'tab bin Qushayr said: "What a terrible morning." Hatib bin Umayyah Al-Dhafri said: "My people are gone forever."

When Saad came to the Messenger of God and the people were sitting around him, the Prophet ordered the Al-Aws to stand up for their master Saad bin Muadh. They stood up in two rows on their feet, saluted him and went to the Messenger of God. The Al-Aws who remained with the Messenger of God asked Saad to treat Banu Quraiza well and to take their suffering into consideration. They told him, "You are only destined to treat them well." Saad replied, "I ask you by God that the final judgment on them is what I judge." The Al-Aws agreed. Saad respectfully turned to the other side, where the Messenger of Allah was, and asked, "Does this also apply to those on this side?" The Messenger of Allah and his followers replied, "Yes." Saad then ruled: "Anyone who

---

2   At that time, the Prophet Muhammad accepted to the request of Abdullah ibn 'Ubayy not to kill the Banu Qaynuqa, but instead to expel them from Medina. They were allies of Ibn 'Ubayy' and had helped him in the past. He feared that circumstances could change and he might need their help in the future. The Prophet's response to Ibn 'Ubayy's request was necessary under these circumstances. The aim was to maintain the stability of the internal front and maintain good relations with the hypocrites in order to win as many of them as possible in the future.[495]

fought against the Prophet should be killed, while women and children should be taken captive and the wealth should be divided." The Messenger of God said: "You have indeed decided according to the judgment of Allah, the Exalted and Mighty, which comes from above the seven heavens." Then Saad decided that the houses should belong to the Muhajirun, not the Ansar. The Ansar said: "Our brothers, we used to live together." Saad replied, "I wanted them to get along without you." [350]

After that, the legal judgment was carried out by killing all those who had allied themselves against the Prophet and fought him. Their number amounted to forty fighters, and others were taken prisoner. Then the women, the children and the wealth were divided among the Muslims.[351] Allah narrated that it was he who brought down the Jews who had conspired against the Muslims from their fortresses and cast terror into their hearts. Then you, O Muslims, killed some of the fighters and captured others, and it is Allah who gave you their lands, their houses, their wealth and another land that you had not reached before, and Allah is capable of everything. [352].

An essay on slavery

Here we must briefly interrupt the narration of the story of Prophet Muhammad to clarify some historical facts about slavery, and then we will continue. Slavery or servitude is a condition in which one human being owns another human being. Slavery has occurred in many cultures since the beginning of civilizations and was legally allowed in societies. But in modern times, it became illegal and was therefore gradually abolished from the eighteenth to the twentieth century. Despite the widespread abolition of the old form of slavery, it unfortunately still exists today in various forms, often referred to as modern slavery, and these include: Human trafficking, forced labor, debt bondage, forced marriage and domestic slavery. [353]

When Islam emerged, slavery was recognized worldwide. It was an economic and social currency in circulation. No one denounced it or thought of changing it. Therefore, changing or eliminating this system took a very gradual and long time. Islam could not completely eradicate slavery at that time, as this depended not only on it, but also on its enemies, over whom it had no authority. The custom of enslaving or killing prisoners of war was widespread in ancient times. This custom existed for a long time, as shown by the Hammurabi

Stele, which dates back to the 18th century BC and contains laws regulating the relationship between slaves and their masters. Slavery was an inseparable part of human history in its various phases, and when Islam came, people were still living under this system. When wars took place between Islam and its enemies, Muslim captives were enslaved by the enemies of Islam. They were deprived of their freedoms, and the men among them were treated with arbitrariness and injustice. The women were mistreated and raped. At that time, Islam could not liberate those who fell into its hands. It is not good policy to encourage your enemy against you by releasing his captives while your people, your family and the followers of your religion experience fear and torment at the hands of these enemies. Reciprocity is the fairest or the only law that can be applied here.

When talking about slavery, the image of desperate people in chains, driven with whips, poorly fed and housed in dark rooms comes to mind, especially with European people. This may be true in Europe or America. But slavery in Islamic society was very different. Gustave Le Bon says: "The truth is that slavery was different among Muslims than among Christians in the past, and that the situation of slaves in the East was better than that of servants in Europe. Slaves in the East formed part of the family and could sometimes marry the daughters of their masters, as we saw in the past, and they could reach the highest ranks. And in the East they saw no disgrace in slavery, and the slave had more connection with his master than the laborer in our country. "[354] The essential difference between the East and the West in the treatment of slaves is based on one fundamental factor, namely society's view of this class. While slaves in Europe and America were seen as laborers and servants who had no right to express their opinions, had no civil rights and were treated cruelly as if they were second-class people, in Islamic society we find an effort to integrate this class of slaves into society by enacting laws that guaranteed and protected their rights, encouraged marriage to them and then empowered them to become free people who depended on themselves. This is why we find many who were slaves or born of slaves holding positions in their countries.

The way Islam dealt with slavery can be summarized in two axes: The first axis: the organization of relations and interactions with slaves and the establishment of their rights. And the second axis: the search for ways to gradually eliminate this phenomenon. The laws that the Prophet Muhammad issued and incorporated into Islamic doctrine were the first regulator of the lives of slaves. He said: "Your brothers are your servants. God has placed them under your hands. So whoever has his brother under his hand should feed him with what he eats and clothe him with what he wears, and not burden him with what is too much for him. And if you burden him with something, then help him. "[355] And when the Messenger of God was walking behind one of his companions - Abu Masud al-Ansari – and saw him beating his slave one day, he became very angry and said: "Know, Abu Masud, God has more power over you than you have over him." He turned around and saw the Prophet and said: "O Messenger of God, he is free for the sake of God." He said: "If you had not done that, the fire would have touched you."[356] The last instruction of the Messenger of Allah when he was close to death was: "Prayer, prayer, fear God in what you possess of slaves. "[357]

Islam not only proclaimed slogans to organize and eliminate slavery, but worked to implement them. The Messenger of God saw no difference between the free and the slave, just as he saw no difference between the Arab and the non-Arab. He appointed the leader of his army, Osama bin Zaid, whose father was a slave who was then freed. He married the daughter of his aunt Zainab bint Jahsh to a slave he had after he had set him free, and that was Zaid bin Haritha. Even Mary the Copt was a slave with the Messenger of God and he did not marry her and she bore him Ibrahim, and a Quran was revealed about her because of her high status, and she became one of the mothers of the believers like the other wives of the Prophet. We will learn more about these events in the biography.

Therefore, the slaves loved the Prophet and revered him because they sensed humanity in all his actions. They noticed that he was authentic and sincere in his actions, without any pretense or staging. He bore the humility of the weak and the suffering of the tormented and stood up for the oppressed classes. We will see from the story of Zaid how he refused to leave the Messenger of God and return to his father even though he was a slave to the Messenger of God. We will also read the story of Juwairiyah bint al-Harith, how she herself came to the Prophet to free herself from slavery because she knew that she would come to a righteous leader who would give her justice, and indeed it was so.

The issue of freeing the slaves is a fundamental axis in Islamic doctrine. God made the liberation of slaves an expiation for some sins, such as perjury, slander and murder. [358] Islam encouraged efforts to free the slaves[359] by paying money and alms for freedom of contract to free them. The Islamic legislator, as part of the educational role of man, made freeing the slaves one of the most

204

important good deeds directed towards serving people and helping the weak and needy, so that this person overcomes the punishments of the world and the desires of the soul in order to achieve spiritual elevation and purification of the soul. [360]

Having clarified the issue of slavery in this period, we can now understand how the Islamic army dealt with captives and slaves.

When the Messenger of God heard that Saad bin Muadh's condition had deteriorated and that he was close to death as his wound continued to bleed, he visited him with a group of his companions. They found him wrapped in a white cloth. The Prophet sat down by his head and placed it in his lap. Then he prayed: "O God, Saad has striven in your way, believed in your Messenger and fulfilled all that was asked of him. Take his soul in peace as you take the souls of all creatures." Saad opened his eyes when he heard this and said: "Peace be upon you, O Messenger of God. I bear witness that you have delivered his message." As the Prophet was about to leave, he lifted Saad's head from his lap and stood up and left sadly. An hour later, Saad died. No one felt his death until Gabriel descended and informed the Prophet of Saad's death and said that the throne of the All-Merciful was shaken by his death. The Prophet hastened to go to Saad. When he entered the house, no one was there. He began to walk on tiptoe. Later he was asked why he did this. He replied, "I could not enter the meeting until one of the angels folded his wing for me and I could sit down." The Messenger of God then said: "Congratulations to you, Abu Amr, congratulations to you, Abu Amr." Then Saad was washed and shrouded. The Prophet prayed for him. Saad was 37 years old when he was martyred.

The Jews of Banu Al-Nadir were in Khaybar and the Jews of Khaybar were waiting for the results of the siege of Banu Quraiza. When they learned of the events, they blamed Huyayy ibn Akhtab. Their women cried and tore their clothes, cut off their hair and held mourning ceremonies attended by Arab women. In their fear, the Jews turned to Salam ibn Mishkam and asked him for advice. He told them: "Muhammad has defeated the Jews of Yathrib and he will come to you. He will deal with you as he did with the Banu Quraiza." They asked, "What is the advice?" He replied, "We go to him with the Jews of Khaybar, for they are numerous. We take the Jews of Tayma, Fadak and Wadi al-Qura, and we do not seek help from the Arabs. You have seen what the Arabs did to you in the Battle of Khandaq (the Battle of the Trench) after you promised them the dates of Khaybar. They broke this promise and abandoned you. They asked Muhammad for dates from the Al-Aws and Al-Khazraj to turn away from him, even though it was Na'im ibn Masoud who had deceived them through Muhammad. Then we go to him in his homeland and fight him, because of this matter and old ones." The Jews said: "This is a good plan." Then Kinana ibn al-Rabi ibn Abi al-Huqayq said: "I have seen the Arabs. They are hostile to him. Our fortresses here are not like there (in Medina), and Muhammad will never come to us because he knows about our fortresses." Salam ibn Mishkam said: "This is a man who does not fight until he is seized by his neck."[361]

627-628 AD

The sixth year after the Hijrah

The battle of al-Muraysi

In the sixth year, in a region between Mecca and Medina in the south, near a well called al-Muraysi, the Messenger of Allah learned that al-Harith ibn Abi Dirar, the leader of the Banu Mustaliq, had called upon his people and other Arabs whom he could mobilize to go to war against the Messenger of Allah. They responded to his call, gathered together, bought horses and weapons and prepared for war and the march with him. The Messenger of God sent a scout to check this out, and when he returned, he confirmed the impending attack. It was now the duty of the Messenger of God to protect the Muslims and Medina from this coming invasion. He called the people and they rushed out. Seven hundred fighters followed him, including Ali, Abu Bakr, Omar bin Al-Khattab, Othman and Al-Zubair, Abd Al-Rahman bin Awf, Talha bin Ubaidullah and Al-Miqdad bin Amr. When they arrived, the Banu al-Mustaliq began to shoot arrows at the Muslims. The Messenger of God ordered the attack and they defeated their enemies, killing ten of them and capturing the rest. They also captured men, women and children as well as sheep and camels and then returned to Medina. [364]

On the way back, the people crowded around the water - and it was little - so the crowding around the water led to a quarrel between one of the poor Muhajirun named Ja'al bin Suraqa and one of the Ansar named Jahjah ibn Sa'id al-Ghifari - and he was an ally of Ibn 'Ubayy - and they fought; so each of them called his group for help. The people rushed to them and took up arms. When Abdullah ibn 'Ubayy came, he saw his companions and said: "Did we go along with Muhammad to cause problems ourselves! By Allah, our example and their example is like saying, 'Fatten up your dog, it will devour you one day.'" Then he proceeded to incite the Ansar against the Muhajirun. Then he said: "By Allah, when we return to Medina, the more honorable one will drive out the more humiliated one." By the more honorable he meant himself and by the more humiliated he meant the Messenger of Allah. Then he turned to those of his people who were present and said: "You have done this to yourselves, you have allowed them your land and shared your wealth with them. By God, if you stop providing Ja'al and his people with surplus food, they will not overpower you and they will be forced to move to another country. Do not give them anything until they turn away from Muhammad. "[365] It almost came to a discord and a fight between the Muslims if the people had not pursued the matter between them and settled the dispute.[366] One of them came to the Messenger of Allah and reported the news to him, and with him was Omar ibn al-Khattab. Omar said: "Let me strike his neck, O Messenger of Allah." The Prophet said: "Then many noses in Yathrib would tremble." He said: "If you do not want him to be killed by one of the Muhajirun, then order one of the Ansar." He said: "How, O Omar, if people would say that Muhammad kills his companions. But announce the departure." And that was at a time when the Messenger of Allah did not usually depart. So the people departed. And Abdullah ibn Abdullah ibn 'Ubayy learned what his father had done. He came to the Messenger of Allah and said: "O Messenger of Allah, I have been told that you want to kill Abdullah ibn 'Ubayy for what you have heard from him. If you want to do it, then order me to kill him and I will bring you his head. By Allah, the Khazraj knew that there is no man in them who was kinder to his parents than me, and I fear that you will order someone else to kill him, and I will not bear to see the murderer of Abdullah ibn 'Ubayy among the people; so I would kill him; and I would kill a believer with an unbeliever and go into the hell." The Prophet replied to him, "We are gentle with him and treat him well as long as he stays with us." When the Messenger of Allah left early with the Muslims, people wondered about the reason for the departure and what had happened of the discord and what Ibn 'Ubayy had done and that the Quran had been sent down about him. After the people learned what happened, they told Ibn 'Ubayy that severe verses were revealed about him and that he should go to the Messenger of Allah to seek forgiveness from Allah.[367] He said: "and what did I say?!" as he twisted his head mockingly. [368].

Juwairiyah in the house of the Prophet

Among the prisoners of the Battle of al-Muraysi was Juwairiyah, the daughter of the head of the Banu al-Mustaliq clan, al-Harith Abi Dirar. She came from a house of fame and honor, her life was by no means compatible with slavery and servitude. Juwairiyah was a slave of Thabit bin Qais bin Shammas. She wanted to buy her freedom and discussed with Thabit about her letter (agreement of manumission) to buy her freedom in exchange for money. Thabit agreed. She decided to go to the Messenger of God to ask him for help in providing money for her release. When she reached the Messenger of God, she said: "O Messenger of God, I am Juwayriyah, the daughter of al-Harith, the lord of his people. My affair has not remained hidden from you. I have become a slave of Thabit bin Qais bin Shammas, and I want to buy my own freedom. I am here to ask for your help." The Prophet suggested, "What do you think if I offer you something that is better for you?" She asked, "What would that be, O Messenger of God?" He replied, "I will pay the cost of writing your release and marry you." She accepted, and the Prophet guaranteed the sum of her letter, set her free and married her.

When the people heard that the Messenger of God had married Juwairiyah, they sent what was in their hands from the captives, freed them and said: "The in-laws of the Messenger of God should not be enslaved." Through this marriage, a hundred families were freed from Banu al-Mustaliq. Juwairiyah's pride caused her not to seek help from anyone except the Messenger of God. She recognized in him noble qualities and saw in him the man who was able to solve her problem humanely, justly and realistically, even though he was the same man who had led the army that had captured her and inflicted defeat on her people. [369]

Zainab bint Jahsh in the house of the Prophet

Zaid bin Al-Harith was bought as a slave in the Okaz market and given to the Prophet Muhammad by Khadija bint Khuwaylid, who raised him as a son. Zaid embraced Islam early, and when his father wanted to buy him back, the Prophet said: "He is free, let him go wherever he wants." However, Zaid refused to leave the Prophet, which led to his father Haritha declaring in front of the Quraysh people that he disowned Zaid and said that he was no longer his son. The Prophet then declared before the people that Zaid is like his own son. Zaid was also referred to as "Zaid son of Muhammad", but the Prophet asked the people to name him after his biological father.

When Zaid grew up and wanted to get married, the Prophet betrothed him to his cousin Zainab bint Jahsh. However, Zainab was initially unwilling to accept Zaid because she thought the Prophet would ask her to marry him. However, the Prophet confirmed his decision that Zaid was the right husband for Zainab, even though she had reservations due to her lineage and beauty status. "I am your cousin, O Messenger of God, I do not accept him for myself," she said. The Messenger of God said: "I have accepted him for you."

While they were talking, Allah revealed, "It is not permissible for a believer man or a believer woman to reject the judgment that the Prophet has made and ordered to be carried out. No one has the right to choose anything that contradicts the judgment of Allah and His Messenger." Then Allah declares that whoever disobeys the command of Allah and His Messenger and goes against them has gone astray in error and deviated from the truth.[370] Zainab accepted and left her affair to the Prophet, who married her to Zaid and gave her the bridal gift.

The reason for Zainab's refusal to marry Zaid was her arrogance towards him and her pride in herself and her lineage. Someone who is indignant and angry towards a matter that the Messenger of God has approved deserves discipline and needs education so that others can benefit from his lesson of obedience and submission to the Messenger of God. Zainab spent almost a year with Zaid, but she had no affection for him and he found it difficult to live with her. Intending to separate from his wife, Zaid sought the advice of the Messenger of God. The Prophet asked Zaid if there was any particular reason why he wanted to leave her, but Zaid explained that he had nothing negative to say about her. He only felt uncomfortable because of her arrogance and her words. The Messenger of God advised him to keep his wife and to fear God in his marriage. But the Prophet knew from God that Zaid would divorce his wife and that he would marry her later. However, the Prophet was embarrassed to reveal this as people might think that he wanted the wife of his adopted son. The adopted child was considered by the people as a real son, and therefore bonding with his ex-wife was not permissible. The Prophet feared that people's trust in him would be shaken and that they would not believe his prophethood, which could harm Islam. The Prophet's fear was not directed at himself, but resided in Allah. He hid within himself what he was hiding out of the perception that if he revealed it, people would rebuke and ridicule him and some of the hypocrites might attack him, which could affect the faith of the general public. This fear is not a reprehensible fear, but a fear in Allah. In reality, it is a fear of Allah. [371]

Zaid, however, could not reconcile with his wife Zainab and found it unbearable to live with her, so he divorced her. After her waiting period was over, the Prophet said to Zaid, "I find no one more reliable than you. Go to Zainab and tell her that God has given her to me as a wife." When the Prophet told Zaid this, he found it difficult to go to her. He went anyway and knocked on the door and stood with his back to the door. Zainab asked, "Who is there?" He replied, "Zaid." She asked: "What does Zaid want from me? Hasn't he already divorced me?" Zaid replied, "The Messenger of God has sent me." She said: "Welcome, Messenger of Allah." Then she opened the door for him and he entered while she was crying. Zaid said: "May Allah not wet your eyes with tears. You have really been a good woman, obedient to me, fulfilling my orders and following me. Allah has blessed you with something better than me." She asked, "Who is that?" He replied, "The Messenger of Allah." When Zainab heard that, she rejoiced and prostrated in gratitude and humility and decided to fast for two months.

The marriage of Zainab by Zaid was not because of any merit that she had earned, but because it was a decision that Allah had made to abolish the system of adoption. She was obliged to do this and it was imposed on her to overcome her arrogance. However, if she disregarded this, she would sin and lead herself astray, which would ultimately lead to her own undoing.

The Prophet acted in accordance with the divine command and married Zainab in the sixth year after the Hijrah. It is noteworthy that he collaborated with Zaid, Zainab's former husband, in arranging this marriage. Although this may be unusual for people, the Prophet showed through his purity and obedience to God that the truth and submission to God are more important than natural instincts and whims. In addition, the Prophet wanted to express to the believers the purity of Zaid's conscience as well as his piety.

Zainab was not at the level of the other wives of the Prophet in terms of her sincerity and behavior in the house of the Messenger of God. She did not care much about staying on the side of calmness and serenity and seeking what pleases God and His Messenger. Aisha, a courageous and ambitious woman, found in Zainab bint Jahsh a supporter and helper for some of her projects. She created an atmosphere that served both her immediate interests and her future. [372]

Drought in Medina

In the sixth year after the Hijrah, the people were struck by a severe drought and it stopped raining. The people asked the Messenger of God for help and he said: "People today believe in Allah but disbelieve in the heavenly bodies." People used to believe that the phases of the moon brought them rain. But the Messenger of God corrected this belief and explained that these are only causes and that the true creator of everything is God. The Prophet proclaimed what

God had revealed to him: "Among my servants there is one who believes in me and another who disbelieves. He who says, 'It has rained on us by God's grace and mercy,' believes in me and not in the heavenly bodies. But whoever says, 'It rained by the phases of the moon,' believes in the heavenly bodies and not in me." Then the Prophet prayed two rak'ahs together with the people in the mosque. He recited aloud in the first rak'ah Surah Al-Fatihah and Surah Al-A'la and in the second rak'ah Al-Fatihah and Surah Al-Ghashiyyah. He then turned his robe so that the drought would turn into fertility. Then he knelt down, raised his hands and said: "Allahu Akbar. O Allah, give us water and bless us with abundant rain and green fertility."

While they were still praying, clouds formed in the sky, merged and it began to rain. The people rejoiced and began to water their crops and livestock. The Messenger of God said: "If Abu Talib were still alive, he would be happy about this. Can any of you recite his poetry to us." Ali stood up and said:

"O Messenger of God, perhaps you would:

A white man, with his face, asking for rain,

A refuge for the orphans, a shelter for the widows.

The estranged of the Banu Hashim flee to him,

Find in his favor the support they need, No jest, no wrath.

By God's house, you speak lies,

Tell Muhammad to give in, but we'll keep him out.

With sword and force of arms, we defend him,

Remain faithful, support him, leave no profit."

The Messenger of God said: "Yes". Then a man from Kinanah recited a poem to mark the occasion:

"Praise and thanks be to You with those who gave thanks,

We were given rain for the Prophet's face.

He cried out to God, our Creator,

And made people's eyes wide.

And it was only the turning of the garment

And faster, till we saw the rain.

It was as his uncle said: Abu Talib: shimmering white[1].

Thus God waters us with clouds,

This is the proof of this incident.

He who gives thanks to God receives more,

And whoever denies God will receive lessons."

After the rain fell continuously for seven days and nights, the people returned to the Messenger of God and asked him: "O Messenger of God, the earth is flooded, the houses are destroyed and the roads are impassable. Pray to God to deliver us from this suffering." The Messenger of God smiled when he was in the pulpit, and he wondered at the quick boredom of the people. Then he raised his hands and said: "O God, let it rain around us and not on us, on the tops of the mountains, on the trees, in the valleys and on the hills." Then the clouds cleared over the city and the rain stopped. [373]

The Treaty of Al-Hudaybiyah

The Prophet had a dream in which he and his companions entered Mecca safely and entered the Kaaba, some with shaved heads and others with cropped hair[2]. He took the key of the Kaaba and performed Umrah. When he told his companions about this, they rejoiced and thought that they would visit Mecca in the same year. Then he told them that he was leaving for Umrah. The people prepared themselves and the Arabs from the surrounding desert tribes, including Ghifar, Juhaina, Muzaina and Aslam, also mobilized. Some of them are still polytheists.

---

1 White: The Arabs praise the honorable people with whiteness, and they do not want the whiteness of skin color, but they want purity from errors, while they call white (bright) skin red. (The title of the book is taken from these verses).
2 As part of the Hajj, male pilgrims shave their head hair (halq) or shorten it (taqsir).

In the month of Dhul Qi'dah, the Prophet set out for Umrah after washing himself[1], putting on two pieces of clothing and saddling his camel "Al-Qaswa".

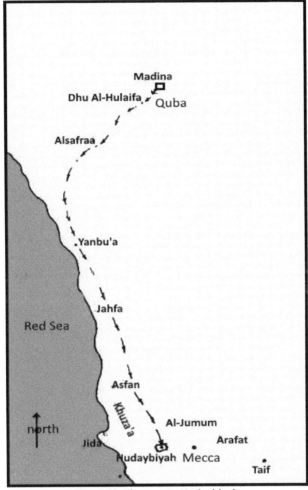

Figure 40: The way to Hudaybiyah.

Most of his companions also entered Iḥrām in Dhul Hulayfah after praying two rak'ahs there. Some of his companions from Al-Juhfa also entered Iḥrām[2] (See Figure 40).

---

1   The entry into the state of consecration (DMG iḥrām) is preceded by the great ritual washing (ghusl).

2   Iḥrām: refers to the state that a pilgrim must enter before performing the rites of the Hajj or the Umrah. It includes certain duties such as the declaration of intent, wearing the consecration garments, and avoiding certain actions such as hunting and sexual intercourse.

The Messenger had sent a scout of the Khuza'a from Dhu al-Hulayfah to observe the movements of the Quraysh and to be warned of their attacks. Women, Muhajirun and Ansar accompanied him, as well as the Arabs they met on the desert road, many of whom were late. The Muslims only carried the traveler's weapons. Omar Ibn Al-Khattab asked the Messenger of God, "Do you fear Abu Sufyan and his companions, and you did not take the war equipment with you?" The Messenger of God replied, "I do not like carrying weapons at Umrah." Then the Prophet took the route through Al-Baida[1] and brought seventy camels or cows with him as al-Hadī [2] and marked the sacrificial animals before praying the noon prayer in Dhu al-Hulayfah. The Muslims did the same, and the number of Muslims amounted to seven hundred men. Then he traveled on to Asfan. [374]

The fact that the Prophet went out as a pilgrim, honoring the house and visiting it, reassured the people of Mecca and the surrounding area. It also showed that he did not want war. This act also put pressure on the polytheists of Mecca, as the house should be open to all people and Muslims would come to visit it. How could they be pushed away and faced with war?! Especially since this measure would be during the holy months when fighting is forbidden. This would cast the Quraysh in a bad light among the Arabs and diminish confidence in them, while the Muslims would appear oppressed and deprived of their most basic rights.[375] The Prophet had entrusted Ibn Umm Maktum with the administration of the city in his absence. Although Ibn Umm Maktum was blind, his choice shows that his blindness did not prevent him from dealing with delicate matters.

The Prophet traveled between Mecca and Medina and met the Bedouin tribes of Banu Bakr, Muzaina and Juhaina. He tried to mobilize them, but the tribes refused and looked for excuses not to go with him. They said among themselves: "Muhammad wants to make us go against people who are equipped with weapons and men. Muhammad and his companions are only "Aklah Juzur "[3] , they will never return from this journey. They have neither weapons nor large numbers." But they did not tell the Messenger of Allah what they had discussed among themselves and what they had thought about him. But Allah ex-

---

1   The path of Al-Baida: It is a desert path that lies between Mecca and Medina.
2   al-Hadī: is an animal sacrifice performed by pilgrims on the 10th of Dhul Hijjah. It is a form of gratitude and the meat is distributed to people.
3   Aklah Juzur: is an Arabic expression and means, a group of men who have gathered to eat a single sacrificial animal, such as a camel. It is estimated that about a hundred men are needed to consume such an animal.

posed them and said: "These Bedouins who stayed behind will tell you that 'we were busy with our work, our families and our homes and had no one to take care of them, and it is not that we do not want to go with you because we doubt you or have no desire to obey you.' Then they will ask you to ask forgiveness for them to hide their faults and their lagging behind. But Allah rejects them and reveals what is in their hearts. Everything they said with their tongues is a lie. Tell them, Muhammad, that everything is in the hands of Allah and nothing can prevent what He wills. If you are in your homes and he wants to bring disaster upon you, he will do it and no one can help you. And if He wills good for you, no one can prevent it, even if you are on the battlefield. Allah knows all your deeds, both overt and covert, in all their details and He will call you to account and give you your reward. " [376]

In the previous days, the Muslims had gone through difficult times as they were subjected to repeated attacks from Quraysh, the tribes and the Jews, which made the situation dangerous and critical for them. But the Prophet was able to secure the area by sending military brigades before Hudaybiyah to eliminate the threat of these enemies. As for the Jews, the events of Banu Al-Nadir, Banu Qaynuqa and Banu Quraiza spread fear in the hearts of the Jews of Khaybar, so they began to avoid confrontations with the Muslims for fear of a fate similar to theirs. Therefore, there was no fear for Medina during the absence of the Messenger of Allah, even if his absence lasted a month or two. [377]

On his way, Muslims came to the Messenger of Allah who had a small bowl in his hands from which he performed ablution. He asked, "What is the matter with you?" The people replied, "O Messenger of God, we have no water for drinking or washing except what is in your bowl." The Messenger of God then put his hand in the bowl and let the water gush out between his fingers like springs so that they could drink and wash themselves. The showing of the divine gift by the Messenger of God was not an accidental matter, but a purposeful matter that served to strengthen hearts, preserve faith and prepare for upcoming trials.

When the polytheists learned that the Messenger of God had left Mecca, they were worried. They gathered and discussed whether Muhammad would invade them with his soldiers. They sent Khaled bin Al-Walid with two hundred horsemen to Karaa Al-Ghamim. They also mobilized those who obeyed them from the Al-Ahabish[1] and brought Thaqif with them. They erected domes and tents and took women and children with them. They camped there and planned to prevent the Messenger of God from entering Mecca and to fight against him. They sent observers to the mountains to monitor the Muslims.[378]

The scout whom the Prophet had sent to Mecca returned and reported the news from Mecca and the Meccans. He met the Messenger of Allah in Ghadir Al-Shattat behind Asfan and told him, "O Messenger of Allah, the Quraysh have learned of your march and are preparing for a long journey. They are wearing armor and are coming down in Dhi Tuwa. They swear by Allah that you will never enter Mecca. And Khaled ibn al-Walid has gone ahead with his horses to Karaa al-Ghamim." The Messenger of Allah said: "Woe to the Quraysh. They have been devoured by war. What harm will it do them if they leave me alone with the rest of the Arabs. If the Arabs were to defeat me, then that is what Quraysh want, and if God Most High were to grant me victory over them, then they would convert to Islam in droves. And if they did not, they would fight against me. What does Quraysh think. By God, I will continue to fight them to achieve what God has sent me to do until He leads me to victory or I die in battle."

On the way, the Prophet's caravan passed villages that were allies of Quraysh. The Prophet wanted to discuss with his companions this matter. He stood up among the Muslims and, after praising Allah and exalting Him, said: "Now then, you assembly of Muslims, Tell me. Do you think that we should turn towards these children and families of these tribes who have supported Quraysh against us to defeat them and take them as captives? If Quraysh sees this and does not move to help them, they will remain defeated and subjugated. And if they come to us to fight, we will have defeated them by defeating their allies. Or do you think that we should go to the Sacred House to perform the pilgrimage, and whoever stops us, we will fight him." The Messenger of Allah wanted to hear their opinions as to whether they wanted to attack the inhabitants of the villages on the way who had joined Quraysh to fight with them and had left their children without protectors and guarantors. Abu Bakr said: "Allah and His Messenger know best, O Messenger of Allah, we have come only as pilgrims, and we have not come to fight anyone. We believe that we should go on wherever we want, and whoever keeps us from the House, we fight him."

---

1   The name Al-Ahabisch goes back to a group of Quraysh, Kinanah, and Khuza'a, who formed an alliance at Mount Habashy below Mecca during the time of Jahiliyya

Asid ibn Hudair agreed with him on this matter. Al-Miqdad ibn al-Aswad said after Abu Bakr's speech, "By Allah, O Messenger of Allah, we will not say to you what the Children of Israel said to their Prophet: 'You and your master go and fight, we are sitting here.'[379] But you and your master go and fight, we are fighters with you." The Messenger of Allah said: "Go in the name of Allah." The Messenger of Allah did not consult them to know the right from the wrong, for he knew more than they did. But he consulted them so that people would know the intentions of each of them and be able to distinguish the sincere from the false. [380]

After the Messenger of God learned of the stance of the Quraysh, he decided to change the route of the caravan to avoid a clash with them during the holy months. He said: "Go the way to the right." and he led them through a bumpy path between the reefs. Khaled saw the tracks of the caravan and realized that they had changed course. He hurried to the Quraysh to warn them. The Messenger of God asked the Muslims to go to Thaniyet al-Marar and the people began to ascend. One of them said: "O Messenger of God, we are afraid that the Quraysh would see our fire." The Prophet replied, "They will not see you." When the Messenger of God arrived at Thaniyet al-Marar, his camel was sitting and the people thought it was exhausted. It refused to get up and the Muslims said: "The camel is resisting and does not want to get up." The Messenger of God explained: "The camel does not do this on its own, and this is not its habit, but someone stops it, just as he stopped the elephant[1] from Mecca." Then he said: "By the One in Whose hand is the soul of Muhammad, if the Quraysh asked me today about a plan involving the veneration of the sanctities of God and the maintenance of ties of kinship, I would agree with them." The Prophet shouted at the camel, which finally got up and took him to a well with little water in the remotest part of Al-Hudaybiyah. The polytheists reached Baladh first and took over the water sources. There was a well whose water had dried up. The weather was also hot. The people complained about the lack of water to the Messenger of God. He asked for a bucket of water from the well and performed ablution with water. Then he rinsed out his mouth, spat it into the bucket and said: "Put the bucket down and pour it into the well." When they did this, the water gushed out of the bucket until the well was full. The people began to draw from it until they had drunk the well empty. There was also a group of hypocrites there that day, including Abdullah bin 'Ubayy. Aws bin Khouli said to Abdullah bin 'Ubayy: "Woe to you, O Abu Al-

---

1   Refers to the raid of Abraha on Mecca in 570-571 AD. see p. 33.

Hubab[1]. Is it not time to see where you stand? Get over this matter." He replied, "I have already seen such a thing." Aws said: "Shame on you." Ibn 'Ubayy came to the Messenger of God and the Prophet asked him, "O Abu Al-Hubab, where did you see such a thing?" He replied, "I have never seen such a thing." He asked, "Why did you say that?" Ibn 'Ubayy replied, "O Messenger of God, ask forgiveness for me." His son Abdullah bin Abdullah bin 'Ubayy said: "O Messenger of God, ask forgiveness for him." The Prophet then asked God for forgiveness for him. When Omar heard this, he said to the Prophet, "Has Allah not forbidden you from praying and asking forgiveness for them?" The Messenger of God turned away from Omar, but Omar repeated his question. The Prophet said to him, "Woe to you, I have been given freedom of choice and I have chosen; Allah says: ❬ask forgiveness for them, or do not ask forgiveness for them; even if you ask forgiveness for them seventy times, Allah will not forgive them. This is because they have denied Allah and His Messenger. Allah does not guide the people of the wrongdoers.❭ [381]

The Prophet Muhammad camped in al-Hudaybiyah. Badil bin Warqa came to him with men from the Khuza'a, including: Amr bin Salem, Kharash bin Umayyah, Kharijah bin Karaz and Yazid bin Umayyah. They were among the trustworthy people of the Messenger of God in Tihama. Some of them are Muslims, and some of them are under an agreement with Muslims. When they came to the Messenger of God, they greeted him, and Badil bin Warqa said: "We come to you from your people, Ka'ab bin Lu'ayy and 'Amr bin Lu'ayy[2]. They have mobilized the Al-Ahabish against you, and those who obeyed them have come down in great numbers, bringing camels, women and children with them. They swear by God that they will not let you go to the house until you wipe them all out." The Messenger of God said: "We have not come to fight anyone, but we have come to circumambulate this house. Whoever prevents us from doing so, we will fight him. The Quraysh have been harmed and exhausted by the war. If they want, we will sign a treaty to which they would be safe, and they would leave me alone with what is between us and the other tribes - and the tribes are more than them. If the tribes strike me, that is what Quraysh wanted. And if my affair spread among the people, they would either enter into what the people entered into, or they would fight. And if they refuse,

---

1   Abdullah ibn 'Ubayy ibn Salul had a son from his wife Khawla bint al-Mundhir, whose name was Abdullah. Abdullah ibn Abdullah was called "Al-Hubab" by his father, but the Prophet Muhammad changed his name to "Abdullah".
2   Ka'ab bin Lu'ayy and 'Amr bin Lu'ayy are the ancestors of the Prophet and Badil meant Quraysh.

then, by God, I will fight over this matter until I die, or God will carry out his command." Badil understood what the Messenger of God was saying and said: "I will pass on to them what you have said:" and he rode back to the Quraysh. When he arrived in Mecca, some said: "This is Badil and his companions, and they want to tell you what happened, don't ask them about anything." When Badil saw that they were not asking him, he said: "We came from Muhammad, do you want us to tell you about him?" Ikrimah bin Abi Jahl and Al-Hakam bin Abi Al-Aas said: "We don't need to know, but tell him on our behalf: He will never come to us this year as long as one man of us is left alive." Urwa bin Masoud Al-Thaqafi advised them to listen to Badil, and if they liked it, they would accept it, otherwise they would leave it.

Safwan bin Umayyah and Al-Harith bin Hisham said to Badil and his group, "Tell us what you have seen and heard." Badil said to them, "You hurry to condemn Muhammad, he has not come to fight but he has come to perform Umrah." Then Badil told them the words of the Prophet. Urwa said aloud, "O people of Quraysh, am I a liar in your opinion?" They said: "No." He said: "Do I not belong to you?" They said: "Yes, you do." Urwa had a lineage in the Quraysh. He said: "Don't you know that I mobilized the people of Okaz to support you. And when they failed to do so, I mobilized myself, my children and those who obeyed me to support you." They replied, "Yes, you did. You are a confidant to us." He said: "I am your confidant and sympathizer, and I will never let you down. Badil has come to you with a great plan that no one should reject unless he accepts something worse. Accept his plan and send me to Muhammad so that I can bring his confirmation of the plan. I will be an observer for you and keep you informed of his news." The Quraysh then sent him to Muhammad.

When he arrived, he said: "O Muhammad, Quraysh has prepared for a confrontation with you. You are faced with one of two options: Either you invade your people, and become the first man to invade his own people, or your people abandon you and betray you. By Allah, I see no respectable faces or noble lineages, but only vile and unworthy people who might run away and betray you to be captured.What could be worse for you than that." Abu Bakr was there. When he heard this, he became angry and said: "How can you say that we will abandon him or flee in front of him." Then Abu Bakr insulted him. Urwa asked, "Who is this?" They said: "That is Abu Bakr." Al-Mughirah bin Shu'bah was also present and harassed Urwa, Urwa got angry with him and said: "How rude you are. Who is the one who cursed me? No one is worse than him!" The

Messenger of God smiled and said: "This is your nephew, Al-Mughirah bin Shu'bah." Urwa said: "You are a traitor. Your treachery was washed away from you only a short while ago on the Okaz. Because of you, there is enmity with Thaqif." Urwa observed the Prophet's companions listening to him and when he ordered them to do something, they obeyed him quickly and when he performed ablution, they almost struggled to take his water. They respected him and lowered their voices when he spoke to show him respect. [382]

However, the Muslims were not all equal in their beliefs and obligations. Some of them submitted to the Prophet without discussion, while others expressed their opinions and even objected to the Prophet. There were also those who did not observe etiquette in their speech in the presence of the Prophet. The Prophet sometimes rebukes or scolds them, but in order to save their face in front of the enemies and take the situation into consideration, he says nothing. [383]

The Prophet replied to Urwa just as he had replied to Budail ibn Warqa and suggested a truce to them. When Urwa had finished his talks with the Messenger of Allah, he returned to Quraysh and said to them, "O people, I have served as an Messenger to the kings like Khosrau, Caesar[1] and Negus, and by Allah, I have never seen a king who is obeyed by his companions as much as Muhammad is obeyed by his companions. By Allah, I have never seen a king who is as revered by his companions as Muhammad is by his companions. By Allah, when he spits, it falls into the hand of one of his companions, who then rubs it on his face and skin. When he gives them an order, they rush to carry it out. When he performs his ritual ablution, they almost fight to see who can get hold of some of it. None of his hair falls down without them picking it up. When he speaks, they lower their voices in his presence and do not look directly at him out of respect for him. None of them speak until he gives permission. When he gives permission, he speaks, and when he does not give permission, he remains silent. He has proposed a reasonable plan to you, accept it because this plan will grant you security. And know that if you ask them for the sword, they will give it to you. I have seen that these people do not care what happens to them if you prevent their leader. By Allah, I have seen women with him who would never, under any circumstances, hand him over to the enemies. So think about what you want to do, come to him, people, and accept what he proposes to you. For I am your advisor, but I fear that you will not support a

___

1 Caesar: Heraclius.

man who has come to this house as a visitor to honor it and slaughter the sacrificial animal and then leave."

The Quraysh said: "Do not say something like this, O Abu Ya'fur. What you say has already been said. We think that we will send him back this year and then he should come back the following year." He replied: "I believe that a catastrophe will befall you." He then left Mecca with his followers and went to Taif. Mikraz ibn Hafsa stood up and said: "Let me go to him." When the Prophet saw him, he said: "This man is a sinner," and did not speak to him, and he returned with no result. Halis ibn Alqamah Al-Kinani, who was the leader of Al-Ahabish at that time, stood up and said: "Let me go to him." They replied, "Go to him." When he approached the Prophet, the Prophet said: "This is Halis, a man who respects sacrificing, send the sacrificial animals to him." They sent him the sacrificial animals so that he could see them. When he saw them grazing on the hills of the valley, he was seized by the voice of tenderness for the homeland. The people welcomed him while reciting the pilgrim formula (at-talbya)[1]. They had already spent half a month, and their appearance had changed due to the long wait, their hair had become dusty. "Oh my God. No one should stop these people from visiting the house. Has God allowed the tribes of Lakhm, Judham, Kindah and Himyar to make the pilgrimage and denied Ibn Abd al-Muttalib. No one should turn them away from the House. By God, Quraysh have failed in their decision. The people have come for Umrah," said Halis. The Messenger of God said to him from a distance, "Yes, O brother of Banu Kinanah." But when he saw this, he did not go to the Prophet and was ashamed of what he saw.

He returned to the Quraysh and said: "I saw something that cannot be prevented. I saw the sacrificial animals with their necklaces, and they had eaten their hair while they were locked up. I also saw that the men were getting dusty and exhausted because of the long wait to be allowed to go around this house. By God, we have not made any covenant or contract with you that says you should turn anyone away from the house. Everyone who comes to it should respect its sanctity and fulfill its rights. I ask you, by the one in whose hand is my soul, to allow him to do what he has come for, otherwise we will rise with the Al-Ahabish against you." They said: "Leave us alone, Halis, until we take for

---

1   attalbya: the hearing / obeying of a command. The Talbiya or attalbya comes as a term in relation to the Hajj. The Talbiya consists of words of praise, expressing the submission of the praiser and the exaltation of Allah.

ourselves what we are satisfied with. You are just a Bedouin who has no idea. Everything you have seen is a conspiracy of Muhammad." [384]

Here Allah mentions that the disbelievers were seized by the arrogance of ignorance (Jāhilīya). They were partial to themselves and became angry about it and did not think and did not surrender to the truth and did not listen to the words of the Prophet and that he came with the Muslims as pilgrims. This was too difficult for them and they did not accept it. So Allah sent down calm upon His Messenger and the believers and strengthened them and tightened their hearts so that they were able to endure and overcome the difficult conditions despite the provocations. Their Lord made them the people of piety who fear Allah and His punishment and hope for His reward and do whatever is required of them. Since Allah's knowledge encompasses all things, He knows the secrets of things and their subtleties, He knows who is worthy of piety and who is able to endure it. [385].

The Prophet wanted to send a messenger from himself to Quraysh with a sign confirming their true intentions and that his arrival in Mecca was not a warlike initiative. So he sent to Quraysh Kharash ibn Umayyah on his own camel called "The Fox" to convey to the nobles of Quraysh the reason for his arrival in Mecca. But when Kharash was walking on the camel, he was detained and beaten by a group of Quraysh and Ikrima ibn Abi Jahl slaughtered the Prophet's camel, and they wanted to kill Kharash, but Al-Ahabish prevented them and they let him go until he came to the Messenger of Allah and told him what torture he had experienced and how they had killed the camel. The Prophet did not give up and wanted to try again to clarify the peaceful nature of their movement to the Quraysh. The Prophet wanted to send a man from his companions to them. He called Omar bin Al-Khattab, but the latter feared for his own life and had no one among the Banu Uday who could protect him. Finally, Omar suggested sending Othman bin Affan, who was more powerful than him in Mecca and had more protection. The Messenger of God called Othman and instructed him to go to the Quraysh and tell them that they had not come to fight but to perform Umrah. He also asked him to invite them to Islam. He ordered him to go to the believing men and women in Mecca, visit them and give them the good news of victory. He was to tell them that Allah would soon reveal his religion in Mecca so that the believers there would no longer be persecuted. Othman set off and met Aban ibn Sa'id, who greeted him and gave him shelter. Aban said: "Do not hesitate to express your needs." Then Aban dismounted from the horse he was riding and allowed Othman to mount the saddle. He fastened him firmly and rode with him to Mecca. Othman went to the respected members of the Quraysh, one by one, and they rejected him, saying, "Muhammad will never enter Mecca while we are here." Othman replied, "The Messenger of Allah has sent me to you to invite you to Islam and to the worship of Allah, the Exalted. You should all join Islam, for Allah will spread His religion and make His Prophet victorious. You should stop opposing the Prophet. If someone else comes and tries to challenge the Prophet himself and triumphs over him, then that is exactly what you want. But if he is defeated, you have a choice: either you join the people in converting to Islam, or you oppose the Prophet and fight him. At that time, you will be able to do so. The war has weakened you and the best of you have left. The Messenger of Allah informs you that he has not come to fight anyone, but he comes as a pilgrim, to slaughter the sacrificial animals and then return."

They said: "We have heard what you say, but this will never happen and it will not be imposed on us by force. Go back to your companion and tell him that he will not reach us." Othman entered a group of believing men and women who were oppressed in Mecca and said: "The Messenger of Allah said: 'I will protect you so that from today no one in Mecca will have to be afraid because of their faith.' " They rejoiced at this and said: "Give our regards to the Messenger of Allah."

The companions of the Messenger of Allah were instructed to keep watch at night and not to light a fire so as not to be discovered by the enemies. They were three men: Aws bin Khouli, Abbad bin Bishr and Muhammad bin Maslama. They took turns to keep watch at night. One night, Muhammad bin Maslama was on guard duty when the Quraysh sent fifty men to watch and attack the Prophet. The Muslims alerted the Prophet, who then deployed his men to fight. On that day, Ali Ibn Abi Talib carried the banner, and they captured the attackers and brought them to the Prophet. Ten men among the Muslims had secretly entered Mecca with the permission of the Messenger of Allah. Quraysh learned about them and captured them. Then thirty armed men went to the Muslims' camp and attacked them until they shot at them with arrows and stones. The Messenger of Allah prayed to God against them, then Ali ibn Abi Talib attacked them with a group, captured them and brought them to the Prophet. The Prophet asked them, "Have you come to us in the protection of someone else? Has anyone given you security?" They replied, "No." The Prophet forgave them and released them. Finally, eighty men from the side of Jabal Al-Tanaim attacked the Messenger of Allah and his companions, but due to the intervention of Ali Ibn Abi Talib, they were captured and pardoned by the Prophet.

Allah has revealed that He sees everything you do, whether it is peace or something else, and He will reward you for it. It is He who prevented a battle from taking place between you and the disbelievers in Mecca on the Day of Hudaybiyah after He gave you the upper hand over them. You took them as captives and then you forgave them while you were in their land, and so you defeated them. [386]

The Muslims had captured twelve other polytheists and only one Muslim was killed. The Quraysh then sent Suhail bin Amr, Huwaytib bin Abdul Ezza and Mukariz bin Hafs to free the fifty captives. When Suhail bin Amr, one of the Quraysh nobles, arrived and the Prophet saw him, he said to his companions, "Your affairs are relieved." The Prophet was optimistic about Suhail's name because it was derived from Sahil, which means "easy". Suhail said: "O Muhammad, those who imprisoned your companions and who fought against you did not do so with the approval of our decision-makers. We were even against these acts when we came to know about them, and we knew nothing about them. It was the act of some of our fools. Please send back to us our companions who were captured the first time and those who were captured the last time." The Messenger of Allah was in a position of strength and imposed his will on his enemy, forcing them to admit that Quraysh were the aggressors and oppressors. The Messenger of Allah said: "I will not release them until you release my companions." In response, the Quraysh said: "You have treated us fairly." Omar ibn al-Khattab said to the Messenger of Allah: "O Messenger of Allah, pull out his teeth so that he may never again appear as an orator against you." But the Prophet rejected this brutal suggestion without justification and said: "Let him, Omar, may he rise to a position for which we praise him[1]." So Suhail and his companions were sent back to Quraysh, and they sent back Othman and the ten captives they had with them. The Messenger of God then sent those whom he had captured.

In the meantime, some slaves and oppressed people of the Quraysh joined the Muslims. The Quraysh wrote to the Messenger of God to bring them back, claiming that they had not gone to him out of desire for his religion, but to escape slavery. The Prophet refused their request and said: "They are God's

---

1 This prophecy was fulfilled after several years, after the death of the Prophet, where Suhail played a role in quelling a rebellion.

freedmen. " Suhail also asked the Prophet to send back some of their sons and slaves who had defected to the Muslims because they had no understanding of the religion and had fled from them. Some of the Prophet's companions who were present with them said: "They are speaking the truth, O Messenger of God, send them back." The Messenger of God became very angry at this until his anger was evident on his face. He said: "I do not see you stopping, O people of Quraysh, until God sends to you a man whose heart God has tested for faith and who strikes your heads for it." He refused to give them back. Some of those present asked, "O Messenger of God, is Abu Bakr that man?" He replied, "No." Then they asked, "Is he Omar?" The Prophet said: "No, but he is the one who is repairing the shoe in the chamber." The people rushed into the chamber and found Ali bin Abi Talib repairing the shoes of the Messenger of God.

The Prophet showed his strong anger in support of the weak people who were oppressed by their masters by denying them their right to freedom of belief and religion. Therefore, the Messenger of Allah did not want to bring them back to them or help them, because that would be an attack on them and a confiscation of their freedoms. It became his duty to defend them and protect them from injustice and enslavement, and he did so. [387]

Al-Ridwan's oath of allegiance

The Messenger of Allah went to the camps of Banu Mazen ibn al-Najjar who were camped in a district of al-Hudaybiyah, and he sat in their tents under a green tree. Then he said: "Allah, the Exalted, has instructed me to hold the pledge of allegiance ceremony." The pledge of allegiance is the making or renewing of a covenant, and the renewal is aimed at confirming the commitment to it and enforcing the obligation to fulfill it. This is only required of those who are suspected of treachery and who are accused of treason and lack of loyalty. The herald of God's Messenger called out, "O people, swear allegiance, the Holy Spirit has descended, go forth in the name of God." Thereupon the people came to swear allegiance to him until they crowded there and stepped on the belongings of the Banu Mazen. Some carried weapons, despite the fact that they had few of them.

Abu Sinan al-Asadi said to the Messenger of God: "Stretch out your hand and I will swear allegiance to you." The Messenger of God asked: "What do you want to pledge allegiance to me for?" Abu Sinan replied: "For what is in you." The Prophet then asked: "What is in my soul?" Abu Sinan replied: "I will strike with my sword with you until God makes you victorious or I am killed." Then Abu Sinan swore allegiance to him, and the people swore allegiance to the Prophet like Abu Sinan's oath of allegiance.

Salamah ibn al-Akwa pledged allegiance to the Messenger of God in the first gathering and the people pledged allegiance to the prophet one by one. Salamah ibn al-Akwa stood among the people. When the Messenger of God saw him, he said: "Pledge allegiance, O Salamah." Salamah replied, "I swore allegiance to you, O Messenger of God, among the first people." He swore allegiance to him again. The Prophet saw him unarmed and gave him a leather shield. When the Prophet saw him standing by the last group that swore allegiance, the Prophet asked him for the third time, "Will you not swear allegiance to me, O Salamah?" Salamah replied, "O Messenger of God, I have sworn allegiance to you among the first people and in the midst." Salamah then swore allegiance to him for the third time. The Prophet asked: "Where is the shield I gave you?" Salamah replied, "My uncle Amer met me and I gave it to him." The Messenger of God smiled and said: "You are like the one who first said: 'O God, help me to seek a friend who is dearer to me than myself." Salamah ibn al-Akwa kept the Messenger of God's gift to himself for only a short time. Then he renounced it and gave it to his uncle. Meanwhile, there were people who felt blessed by the Prophet's water of ritual purification, his hair, his stick and everything related to him. Therefore, one wonders why Salamah renounced this precious gift.

Despite repeated calls for the pledge of allegiance and the participation of the believers, there were hypocrites among the people in Hudaybiyah who failed to pledge allegiance. The pledge of allegiance of Al-Ridwan was a neces-sary matter to clarify the facts and intentions before the enemies, to strengthen the resolve of the Muslims, to purify their souls and to renew their covenant. It happened because of the numerous incidents that took place in Al-Hudaybiyah. The Quraysh were clearly determined to prevent the Prophet from performing Umrah and visiting the House of God. They even hinted at killing him by at-tacking his messenger Kharash bin Umayyah. There were skirmishes between them and the Muslims, capturing and killing some of them. The Quraysh re-jected all methods of dialog and negotiation. Moreover, the Prophet felt that the hypocrites were secretly planning a dangerous betrayal. [388] Allah announced to the believers the glad tidings of His satisfaction with this oath, praised them, guided them and sent down Sakīna upon them. Allah promised them a near conquest that would bring them many political and material gains, which they would attain. [389]

When Suhail bin Amr, Huwaytib bin Abd al-ʿUzzā, Mukariz bin Hafs and those who were sent by the Quraysh saw how quickly the people pledged allegiance and prepared for war, their terror and fear intensified and they quickly informed the Quraysh about the matter. The opinion leaders among them said: "There is nothing better than making peace with Muhammad so that he leaves us alone this year and does not come to the House until those who have heard of his journey among the Arabs learn that we have stopped him. Then he will return next year, stay three days and slaughter his sacrificial animals and then leave us again." They agreed on this.

When the Quraysh agreed to peace, they sent Suhail bin Amr, Huwaytib and Mukariz to Muhammad and said to Suhail: "Go to Muhammad and make peace with him. And leave it in the treaty: 'He will not enter this year', for by God, we do not want the Arabs to say that he entered Mecca by force." So Suhail came to the Messenger of God, and when the Prophet saw him, he said: "The people wanted reconciliation when they sent him." Revelation was sent down on the Prophet to command him to agree. The Messenger of God sat cross-legged in a group of his companions, and Suhail sat on his knees and spoke to the Messenger of God. They talked for a long time and argued, and their voices rose and fell. Abbad bin Bishr said to Suhail, "Lower your voice in the presence of the Messenger of God." And so it came to pass that Treaty was signed. The terms of the Treaty of peace were:

1- The war between them will cease for ten years.

2- The people will trust each other.

3- Muhammad will return this year, and when the next year comes, they will allow him to enter Mecca so that he can stay there for three days. All the Quraysh will leave Mecca except one man who will stay with Muhammad and his companions.

Figure 41: An imaginary depiction of Suhail ibn
Amr, as he reads the terms of the peace treaty.

4- Muhammad shall not enter Mecca except with the traveler's weapon.

5- Whoever comes to Muhammad from the Quraysh without the permission of his guardian - even if he belongs to the religion of Muhammad - will be returned to his guardian.

6- Whoever comes to the Quraysh from the followers of Muhammad will not be sent back to him.

7- Whoever of the companions of Muhammad comes to Mecca for Hajj, Umrah or trade, his blood and property will be safe. Also the one who travels from the Quraysh on the way to Egypt or the Levant to seek trade and comes to Medina, his blood and property are also safe.

8- Islam will be visible in Mecca, and no one will be forced to change his religion, nor will he be harmed, nor will he be rebuked.

9- It is a binding contract between them and Muhammad that should not be betrayed or violated.

It was of utmost importance for the Quraysh to secure their vital trade routes through Medina, and the binding treaty confirmed that there would be no aggression or attacks on the interests of either party for ten years.

The Prophet then ordered Ali to write at the beginning of the Treaty of Hudaybiyah: "In the name of Allah, the Most Gracious, the Merciful." Suhail bin Amr said: "I do not know this, but write 'In the name of Allah'." Then the Prophet said: "Write: 'In the name of Allah'." So Ali erased the first sentence and wrote it down, and said to the Prophet, "If I did not have to obey your command, I would not have erased it." The Prophet also ordered him to write: "This is what Muhammad, the Messenger of Allah, agreed with Suhail ibn Amr." So he wrote it down, and Suhail bin Amr objected again and said: "If we had known that you were the Messenger of Allah, we would not have fought against you or stopped you. But write down your name and the name of your father." Then the Prophet ordered Ali to erase it. Some of the Prophet's companions stood up and said: "We only write 'Muhammad, the Messenger of Allah'." Ali also refused what Suhail asked him to do. The Messenger of God said to Ali: "O Ali, I am truly the Messenger of God, and I am Muhammad bin Abdullah, and my prophethood will not be erased from me if I write to them: 'From Muhammad bin Abdullah. Write it down and erase what they want to erase. You will have the same and accept it while you are oppressed."[1]

The argument between the companions and Suhail intensified, and they grabbed Ali's hand to prevent him from writing. The Prophet then waved his hand for them to be quiet and tried to calm them down. Huwaytib bin Abdul Ezza and Mukariz were astonished at what the Prophet's companions were doing. He said: "I have never seen a people so careful about their faith as these people." The Prophet then asked Ali to show him the word with his hand. When Ali did this, the Prophet erased it with his hand. Ali Ibn Abi Talib wrote the treaty and a group of Muslims witnessed it.

Meanwhile, Abu Jandal bin Suhail bin Amr came from the south of Mecca in handcuffs and threw himself among the Muslims. His father Suhail had tied him in irons and locked him up. After escaping from prison, he walked along the road, rode through the mountains and reached Al-Hudaybiyah, where the Muslims greeted him and congratulated him. When his father Suhail saw him, he stood up and hit him in the face with a thorny branch, grabbed him by the collar and said: "O Muhammad, the first thing I ask of you is that you send him

---

1   The meaning of the expression: (while you are oppressed), which was reported in the history of arbitration in the year 37 after the Hijra between Ali and the people of Levant, where they asked him not to address him with the commander of the believers, and he agreed to settle the dispute and unify the opinions.

back." The Messenger of God replied, "We have not yet concluded the treaty." Suhail said: "By God, I will never reconcile with you." The Prophet said: "Grant him permission." He replied, "I will not give him permission." The Prophet said: "Yes, do." He replied, "I will not do it." Then Mukariz and Huwaytib said: "Yes, we have given him permission." They took him and brought him to their tent. They really did not give him permission, but they kept his father away from him. Abu Jandal said: "O Muslims, I am being sent back to the idolaters even though I came as a Muslim. Do you not see what I have been through?" He had been severely tortured. Then the Messenger of God raised his voice and comforted Abu Jandal, saying, "Be patient, for God will grant you and those who are oppressed relief and a way out." In this crucial situation, Omar ibn al-Khattab approached Abu Jandal, stood next to him and said to him: "Be patient and trust in God. For they are polytheists and their blood is the blood of a dog." Omar brought the sword closer to him, hoping that Abu Jandal would take the sword and strike his father Suhail with it. But what would have happened if Abu Jandal had treacherously killed his father, as Omar aspired to do. Wouldn't that have wasted all the efforts and jihad of the Messenger of God and led back to a point zero or something worse.

Some Muslims rejected the terms of peace and were angry about it. But when they agreed and only the document remained, Omar Ibn Al-Khattab jumped to the Prophet's side and, while overcome with tension and confusion, said: "O Messenger of Allah, are you not truly the Prophet of Allah?" The Messenger replied, "Yes, I am." Omar asked further, "Are we not in the right and they in the wrong?" The Messenger replied, "Yes, it is true." Omar continued, "Aren't our dead in heaven and their dead in hell?" Again the Messenger replied, "Yes, that is true." Omar then asked, "Why do we allow humiliation in our religion. Why do we turn back when God has not yet passed judgment between us and them?" To this the Messenger of God replied, "I am God's servant and His Messenger, I am not disobedient to Him and He will not abandon me. He is my supporter." Omar said: "Didn't you tell us that we will actually come to the house and go around it." The Messenger replied, "Yes, I said that, but did I tell you that you will come to the House this year?" Omar said: "No." The Messenger then said: "You will go to the house and go around it. O Omar, don't you see that I agree while you refuse." Omar angrily and impatiently went to Abu Bakr and said: "O Abu Bakr, is this one not a true prophet of God?" He replied, "Yes, he is." Omar asked further, "Are we not in the right and they in the wrong? And are not our dead in heaven and their dead in hell?" Abu Bakr replied, "Yes, that is true." Omar asked further: "Then why do we allow humili-

ation in our religion? We turn back even though God has not yet passed judgment between us and them." Abu Bakr replied, "O man. he is the Messenger of
God, and he is not disobedient to his Lord. so abide by what he says until you
die, for he is truly on the right path." Omar said: "I bear witness that he is the
messenger of God." Omar further asked, "Didn't he tell us that we will come to
the house and go around it?" Abu Bakr replied, "Yes, he did say that." Abu
Bakr asked, "Did he tell you that you will come to it this year?" Omar replied,
"No, he did not say that." Abu Bakr said: "Then you will go there and go
around it." Omar was greatly affected by these events and began to doubt his
faith and argue with the Messenger of God. Abu Obeida bin Al-Jarrah said to
him: "Do you not hear, O Ibn Al-Khattab, what the Messenger of God says?
Seek refuge in God from Satan, blame your self." Omar then sought refuge in
God from Satan when he was afflicted and wanted to do good deeds to atone
for what he did. [390]

Then the Khuza'a came and said: "We are in covenant with Muhammad
and his treaty." Banu Bakr came and said: "We are in alliance with Quraysh and
their treaty." The Quraysh were angered by the Khuza'a joining the alliance of
the Messenger of God. One of the negotiators, Huwaytib bin Abdul Ezza,
turned to Suhail bin Amr and said: "Your uncles have started hostilities against
us, they have been hiding from us and joined the alliance of Muhammad and
his treaty." Suhail said: "They are like everyone else, they are our relatives and
our flesh, they have entered into a cause with Muhammad that they have chosen for themselves. What should we do with them." Huwaytib said: "We will
deal with them by leading our allies Banu Bakr to victory over them." Suhail
said: "Don't let Banu Bakr hear this from you because they are evil people. If
they attack Khuza'a, Muhammad will be angry for his allies, and break the alliance between us and him." Huwaytib said: "By God, you favor your maternal
uncles in every way." Suhail said: "Do you think that I prefer my maternal uncles to Banu Bakr. But by God, when the Quraysh want something, they enforce it. If Banu Bakr attacks Khuza'a, then I am a Quraysh man, and although
Khuza'a are my relatives on my mother's side, Banu Bakr is closer to me because of my ancient lineage. and I know Banu Bakr, and we have experienced
many situations from them that were not good, including the day of Okaz."

The acceptance of these concessions by the Prophet's companions was a
difficult task and a test for which not all were prepared. Some objected, while
others became angry. The noise and uproar that ensued helped us realize the
true motive behind the Al-Ridwan's pledge of allegiance. As mentioned earlier,

the pledge of allegiance is renewed when one fears an internal enemy, not an external enemy. The Messenger was fully aware of the circumstances of the events and prepared his companions both spiritually and psychologically for this trial so that they could remain steadfast and patient in their faith.

While the Muslims were encamped in Hudaybiyah near Mecca after being prevented by the disbelievers from entering Mecca to perform Umrah, Allah mentioned that there are believing men and women in Mecca who have hidden their faith from the people of Mecca. You do not know them either. If it had come to a fight, you would have endangered the lives of these weak believers. You could have harmed them with your own hands by killing or injuring them because they did not reveal their faith. Thus, the believers would have killed other believers - without knowing it - and would have had to pay blood money to their families, while at the same time the lives of devout monotheists would have been lost. This is why Allah forbade fighting in Mecca. The mercy of Allah manifested itself in the preservation of this group of believers. If the believers had differed from the disbelievers and separated from them, fighting would have ensued and the result would have been mass killing of polytheists and a painful punishment. [391]

The Prophet wanted to provide the people of Mecca with some of the sacrificial animals that he wanted to slaughter in order to familiarize them with Islam and break down the barriers that the Quraysh wanted to build between the people and him. Therefore, the Messenger of Allah sent twenty camels from his al-Hadī to be slaughtered in his name in al-Marwa. After the Messenger of Allah had finished, he said to his companions, "Sacrifice your animals and shave your heads." Some of them hesitated and said: "How should we slaughter and shave our heads when we have not yet made the tawaf (circumambulation) around the house and have not yet walked between al-Safa and al-Marwa." The Messenger of Allah was saddened because they refused to do what he had ordered them to do, and he complained about this to Umm Salama. She said: "O Messenger of Allah, you, slaughter the sacrificial animal and have yourself shaved." The Prophet did so and threw his hair on a nearby tree, from where people distributed it among themselves. Umm 'Amarah, Nusaybah bint Ka'ab washed strands of his hair for a sick man who got better as a result. The Muslims shaved each other's heads until some of them could almost kill themselves with grief. Some shaved their heads completely, while others only shortened their hair. Then the Prophet took his head out of his tent and said: "May God have mercy on those who are shaved." One group also slaughtered with the

Prophet and then contentedly shaved their heads. Another group, however, did not obey the Prophet's command as they doubted his decision. They hesitated and argued before finally realizing that they had to end the Iḥrām. However, instead of shaving completely, they only cut their hair out of stubbornness towards the Prophet's orders. The Messenger of Allah said: "May Allah have mercy on those who shave." They asked, "And those who do not shave completely, O Messenger of Allah?" The Messenger of Allah replied: "May Allah have mercy on those who shave." They asked again, "And those who do not shave completely, O Messenger of Allah?" The Messenger of Allah repeated: "May Allah have mercy on those who shave." They asked again, "And those who do not shave completely, O Messenger of Allah?" The Messenger of Allah replied, "And those who do not shave completely." They said: "O Messenger of Allah, why did you mention in the prayer only those who have shaved their hair and not those who have their hair cut?" The Messenger of Allah replied, "They did not doubt."When the Prophet Muhammad set out from Al-Hudaybiyah, he made a stopover in Al-Dhuhayran and then in Asfan. The people complained about the lack of food and that they were hungry and tired. They said: "O Messenger of Allah, we will slaughter a camel and use the fat from it and make shoes from the skins." The Prophet allowed this. When Omar ibn al-Khattab heard about this, he came to the Prophet and said: "O Messenger of Allah, do not do this. If there are herds of camels among the people, then it is better. How will we meet our enemy tomorrow if we are hungry and weak. But if you ask the people to gather their leftover provisions and pray for their blessings, Allah will answer us to your request." The Prophet called on the people to bring their leftover food and they spread out a cloth. The people brought a handful of food and more on top of it, and the one who brought the most brought a sack of dates, and so the people's food was collected on the cloth, the amount of which was equal to a goat, and there were 1,400 people. The prophet prayed to God and then the people ate until they were full. They filled their bowls and there was still enough left. The Prophet laughed and said: "I bear witness that there is no god but Allah and that I am His Messenger. Allah will not punish a believing servant with these two things."

As they continued walking to Kara'a Al-Ghamim[1], people wondered why people were walking so fast. Some of them asked each other, "What is wrong with the people?" They replied, "It was revealed to the Messenger of Allah." The Messenger of Allah was on his camel in Kara'a Al-Ghamim, and the people

---

1 Kara'a Al-Ghamim is a place in the Hejaz region, located between Mecca and Medina. It is a valley that is about 13 kilometers before Asfan.

gathered around him, and he said: "A verse was revealed to me at noon that is dearer to me than the whole world, so he recited to them. ❴Indeed, We have bestowed on you a clear victory so that Allah may forgive you what is past of your sin and what is to come, and that He may complete His favor on you and guide you to a straight path, and (that) Allah may help you with mighty help.❵[2]
392

A man from among the Prophet's companions said: "Is this a victory?" He replied, "Yes, by the One who holds my soul in His hand, it is a victory." Then Gabriel came to congratulate the Messenger of Allah. The people said to the Messenger of Allah: "Congratulations, O Messenger of Allah. Allah has shown you what He will do with you. What will he do with us?" Then it was revealed: ❴That He may admit the faithful, men and women, into gardens with streams running in them, to remain in them [forever], and that He may absolve them of their misdeeds. That is a great success with Allah.❵ 393

Allah has supported His Prophet with an obvious victory through the Treaty of Hudaybiyah. For the first time, the Quraysh has recognized Islam as a religion and Muslims as an active force. Allah has forgiven you, O Muhammad, for your sin among your people because you abandoned their gods and their religion and embraced another religion. After the treaty and the clarification of the matter, they understood what they thought was a sin and forgave it to you. The forgiveness was attributed to Allah because it was Allah who facilitated this victory, so it was metaphorically attributed to Him. Allah has granted you this victory to show the religion and to elevate His word, and to guide you to the straight path that leads you to Allah and His satisfaction. We will soon see the fruits of this treaty.394

This peace treaty showed that Prophet Muhammad's wise policy was not to break family ties. He had no interest in aggression and injustice. His concern was to put an end to injustice and arbitrariness. He treated even his worst enemies with forbearance, forgiveness and mercy. His primary concern and greatest concern was the guidance of people and the spread of Islam.

When the Messenger of God returned, a man among the Prophet's companions said: "This was no victory. We were turned away from the House, and our al-Hadī was turned away, and the Messenger of God sent away two men of the believers who had come to him before." After the Messenger of God heard

_____

2   Later we will understand the full meaning of these Quran verses. See page 305.

about this, he said: "This is nonsense. In fact, this is the greatest victory. The polytheists drove you out of their land with their bare hands. They asked for a truce and wanted security. They were afraid of you. But God, gave you victory over them and brought you back safely and rewarded you. This is the greatest victory. Remember the day of Uhud. Where you go up and do not turn around, and I call you from behind. And in the battle of the trench. {When they came to you from above and from below, and when the looks became uncertain and the hearts reached the throat and you had different opinions from Allah.}[395] The Muslims said: "God and His Prophet speak the truth. It is the greatest victory. By Allah, O Prophet of God, we have not contemplated what you have contemplated. For you are better informed about God and affairs than we are."

When the hypocrites loosened their tongues and questioned the victory, complaining that they had not cut or shortened their hair, God revealed a verse to confirm that the Prophet's vision was a God-made, true reality. You will surely enter the Sacred Mosque, shorten your hair, and therein lies a lesson for the people to join their affairs with God. God has also promised them another victory soon.[396]

After the conclusion of the treaty of Al-Hudaybiyah, some women migrated from Mecca to Medina, so the Quraysh asked the Prophet to return them. But he refused, explaining that the Treaty of Al-Hudaybiyah did not contain any provisions regarding women.

So the Messenger of God made them swear that they were not leaving out of hatred for their husbands, nor out of love for other men, but only out of desire for Islam. Then the Messenger of God gave their husbands their dowries and what they spent on them.[397] A number of women also left Medina and returned to Mecca voluntarily, so the Messenger of God gave their Muslim husbands the dowries of their wives. This reconciliation made the Muslims safe from the Quraysh so that they could devote themselves to spreading Islam among all the tribes. Islam spread rapidly in Mecca and entered every home, and the Muslims in Mecca practiced their rituals without fear or persecution. What he had achieved in this reconciliation was many times greater than what he had achieved in his defensive wars against the Quraysh and others. [398]

The problem of Khawla bint Thalabah

When the Prophet was in Medina, Khawla bint Thalabah, the wife of Aws ibn al-Samit, came to him and reported an argument with her husband. Her husband became angry with her and said to her: "You are like my mother's back to me". In pre-Islamic times, this statement was considered a divorce. This practice continued until the advent of Islam. He later regretted his words. Khawla complained to the Messenger of God and said: "O Messenger of God, my husband Aws ibn al-Samit married me, and I had money and a family at that time. But when he used up my money, I grew older and left my family. Then he said to me: 'You are like my mother's back to me'." The Messenger of God replied to her: "God has not sent down a book in which I can judge between you and your husband, and I do not want to judge according to my opinion." Khawla wept and complained: "I complain to God about my poverty, my need, my sorrow and my little boys. If I leave them with him, they will be lost, and if I keep them with me, they will starve." While she was in this state, the face of the Messenger of God changed when Gabriel revealed the words of God: ﴾Allah has certainly heard the speech of the one who argues with you, [O Muhammad], concerning her husband and directs her complaint to Allah. And Allah hears your dialogue; indeed, Allah is all-hearing, all-seeing.﴿ Allah informed him that this statement is invalid in Islam and how to atone for this sin. [399]

The Messenger of Allah called the woman and she came to him. He said to her, "Bring your husband." She brought him to the prophet, and he asked him, "Did you say to your wife, 'You are forbidden to me like my mother's back'?" He replied, "Yes, I said that to her." Then the Messenger of God said: "God, the Blessed and Exalted is He, has sent down a Quran über you and your wife." He recited the verses to them. The Prophet then said to him, "Free a slave." He said: "I have no financial means." The Messenger of God said: "Fast for two consecutive months." He said: "If I do not eat twice a day, all my sight will be lost." The Messenger of God said: "Then feed sixty poor people." He said: "I have nothing to eat unless you assist me with your help." The Messenger of God said: "I will give alms for you." He gave him dates to feed sixty poor people, and he said: "Go and give them alms." He said: "By the One who sent you with the truth, I do not know anyone in Medina who needs it more than me and my children." The Messenger of God said: "Go, eat, feed your children and

take your wife to you, for you have said something wrong and God has forgiven you, so do not repeat it." The man went away and took what the Messenger gave him, and he regretted what he had said to his wife. [400]

To Khaybar

In Hudaybiyah, God announced to the Muslims through the Prophet
Muhammad that He would soon grant them a nearby victory in Khaybar that
would bring them political and material benefits.In the sixth year, three months
after the peace treaty of Hudaybiyah, the Messenger of Allah ordered his companions to set out for Khaybar. They were eager to do so and mobilized those
around them who had witnessed Hudaybiyah to go to war with him. Those
who had not followed him in Hudaybiyah came to go out with him in the hope
of booty. Then the Messenger of Allah said: "Go with me only if you desire jihad, but not for booty." Then he ordered a herald to announce this and he proclaimed it. He appointed someone to take over the administration of the city
during his absence and the Muslims prepared to leave. The Prophet took his
wife Umm Salama with him again.

While preparing the army, Abu Al-Abbas bin Jabr came to the Prophet and
asked him for help as he had no money, food or clothes to go with them. The
Prophet gave him a piece of clothing. The Muslims marched to Khaybar, a region three days' walk from Medina, on the left of the pilgrims' route from Levant. There are many farms, palm trees, castles and fortresses there, the largest
of which are Naam, Al-Saab, Al-Zubair in the Al-Nitat area, Ubi and Nizar in
the Shaq area, Al-Qamus, Al-Wateh and the Al-Salalem in the Al-Katiba area.

On the way to Khaybar, the Prophet said: "Whoever rides a camel that is
weak or difficult to drive should go back." Some people returned, but one man
refused to follow the Prophet's orders and incited others against him. He rode a
hard camel in the night and died in an accident. When they brought the dead
man to the Prophet, he asked, "What is the matter with your friend?" They told
him what had happened to the man, and he said: "O Bilal, did you not announce to the people that anyone riding a weak or hard-to-ride camel should go
back?" Bilal replied, "Yes." The messenger of God then refused to pray for
him. He ordered Bilal to call out to the people three times: "Paradise is not permitted for the disobedient."

The march continues, and the Messenger of God saw a man in front of them, he asked, "Who is that?" they said: "Abu Abas bin Jabr" The Prophet said: "catch up with him." They reached Abu Abas, who thought that an order had come down from God on his behalf. The Messenger of God asked him, "Why are you walking in front of people and not going with them?". Abu Abas replied that his camel mare was active. The Prophet asked him about the clothes he gave him and Abu Abas explained that he sold them for eight dirhams and left two dirhams for his family. He bought a Bedouin dress for four dirhams. Thereupon the Messenger of God smiled and said: "By Allah, O Abu Al-Abbas, you and your companions are poor. I swear by Allah, if you make it and live for some time, your wealth will increase. You will leave more for your family, and your wealth and slaves will increase. All that is good for you will come."

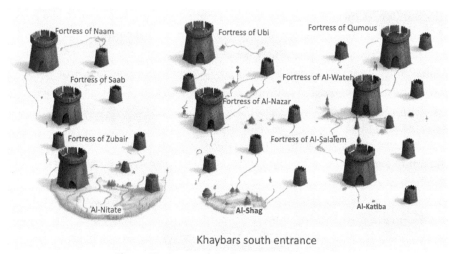

Figure 42: A map of the fortresses of Khaybar.

In Al-Sahba, a place near Khaybar, the Messenger of Allah arrived and performed the Asr prayer. After they had rested and eaten, the prayers of Maghrib and Isha were performed. They then continued their journey. Then the Messenger of God said to Husail, "O Husail, go on until the valleys surround us, until you reach between Khaybar and the Levant, so I would cut them off from the Levant and their allies from Ghatafan." Husail said: "Well, I will take you there." He landed at a place with several paths and said: "O Messenger of God, there are several paths here." The Messenger of God said: "Name them to me." Prophet Muhammad favored good omens and names and abhorred pessimism and bad names. Husail said: "There is a way called Hazan, a way called Shash and a way called Hatib." The Messenger of God said: "Do not take these." Husail continued, "There is another way called Marhab." The Messenger of God said: "Take this one." When they reached a valley, the people shouted the takbir in a loud voice: "Allahu Akbar, Allahu Akbar, la ilaha illa Allah.[1]" The Messenger of God said: "Be quiet. You do not call a deaf or absent person, you call a hearing, near one, and He is with you." It was important to maintain composure and prudence in order to see things and capabilities in a realistic and balanced way and to stay away from unrealistic and exaggerated expectations, especially on the way to war. The journey with the Messenger of God continued as he enriched his companions with knowledge that would benefit them in their religion and in the world. He said to a man walking behind him, "Shall I tell you a word from the treasury of Paradise?" The man replied, "Yes, O Messenger of God, may my father and mother be sacrificed for you." The Messenger of God said: "There is no power and no strength except with Allah.".

They reached Khaybar and dawn broke. The Messenger of Allah said to his companions, "Stop." And so they stopped. Then he said: "O God, Lord of the seven heavens and what they cover, Lord of the seven earths and what they bear, Lord of the demons and what they seduce, Lord of the winds and what they spread, we ask You for the good of this village and the best of its people. We seek refuge in you from its evil and the evil of what is in it. Go forth in the name of God."

Abdullah bin 'Ubayy already sent someone to the Jews of Khaybar to warn them that Muhammad will come to them. He told them to arm themselves, secure their money in their fortresses and fight against him. The Jews of Khaybar then sent a delegation to Ghatafan to ask for help. Uyaynah ibn Hisn[1] came to Khaybar with an army and entered the fortresses of Al-Nitat with the Jews three days before the arrival of the Messenger of God. When the Messenger of God arrived in Khaybar, he sent Saad bin Ubadah to them while they were in the fort. Saad reached the fort and called out to them, "I want to speak to Uyaynah bin Hisn." Uyaynah wanted to bring him into the fort, but Marhab said: "Do not let him in, for he would see our weaknesses and know the areas from which he might come. You should go to him." Uyaynah said: "I wanted him to come in and see the strength of our building and our great numbers." But Marhab refused to let him enter, so Uyaynah went out to the gate of the

1 In English: „Allah is the greatest. There is no god but Allah."
1 One of the leaders of the Arab tribes (the Adnan tribes), and he had ten thousand men who obeyed him.

fortress. Saad said: "The Messenger of God sent me to you and said: 'God has promised me Khaybar. Go back and stop what you are doing. If we defeat them, we will give you khaybar dates for a year.'" Uyaynah replied, "By God, we would not give up our allies. We know what you have and how much energy you have. These people are the owners of impregnable fortresses, have many men and weapons. If you fight them, you and your companions will die. If you want to fight, they will come at you with their men and weapons. They are not like the Quraysh or other peoples, they will prolong the war against you until you are tired." Saad bin Ubadah said: "I bear witness that he will imprison you in your fortress until you ask for what we have offered you. We will then give you nothing but the sword. You saw, O Uyaynah, how we defeated the Jews of Yathrib when they confronted us. We tore every piece of them apart."

Saad returned to the Messenger of God and told him what Uyaynah had said. Saad said: "O Messenger of Allah, Allah will fulfill what He has promised you and prevail His religion. Do not give him a single date, O Messenger of Allah. If we take him with the sword, they will surrender and flee to their land, as they did once before on the day of the Battle of the Trench." The Messenger of Allah then ordered his companions to go to the fortress of Ghatafan, which was a Naam fortress in Al-Nitat. Then the herald of the Messenger of God called out that the army should leave in the morning for the Naam fort where the Ghatafan were. Ghatafan were terrified day and night and heard a cry that they did not know from heaven or earth: "O people of Ghatafan, your people, your people. Help, help, in Haifa no land nor money." This happened three times and a group of Ghatafan ran away terrified. The Messenger of God then went on until he came to Al-Manzala, the marketplace of Khaybar, where he stayed for an hour at night.

The Jews did not think beforehand that the Messenger of God would attack them because of their strength, their fortresses, their weapons and their numbers. They went out every day with thousands of fighters to show their ranks. They said: "Muhammad is attacking us. Impossible. Impossible." The Jews of Medina had said that Khaybar is the most difficult for the Messenger of God. If he had seen Khaybar, its fortresses and its men, he would have returned before reaching them. The fortresses were high up in the peaks of the mountains and the water in them had never stopped. These people were very conceited about themselves and believed that the Prophet would not come to fight them. They imagined that he thought like them and was afraid of being outnumbered and amassed by soldiers. But when they woke up from this sleep, they were suddenly confronted with reality. They put their children, their money and their men in what they thought was the strongest fortress and placed some of their men in the first fortress they expected to attack the coming army. They hoped to save these fortresses from capture by the attackers and exploit them.

Figure 43: Above is a computer-generated depiction of the fortress of Al-Qamus, below is a real picture of the remains of the fortress of Al-Qamus, one of the fortresses of Khaybar.

When the Prophet marched to Khaybar, he appointed Ali as the leader of the army and said: "Whoever enters the palms is safe." When the Prophet said this, Ali exclaimed it and the Prophet looked at Gabriel laughing and asked, "Why are you laughing?" Gabriel replied, "I love him." The Prophet said to Ali,

243

"Gabriel says he loves you." Ali replied in astonishment: "Have I managed to make Gabriel love me?" The Prophet replied, "Yes, and who is better than Gabriel, God." The Prophet then ordered some palm trees to be cut down for war needs. When the Muslims arrived, they landed in an inappropriate place near the enemy. The people complained to the Prophet about this. The Prophet was aware of the danger but did not want to break the Muslims' enthusiasm or show the Jews that there was hesitation in the Muslims' decisions. One of them told the Prophet about it, and the Prophet decided to fight during the day and move in the evening. When the Messenger of God reached the place of the Jews at night, the Jews did not agree on their war plan and did not attack that night. Normally, the Messenger of God does not attack a people when he arrives at night, but waits until morning. However, when he hears the call to prayer, he stops attacking, and if not, he attacks in the morning. In the evening, his camel got up and wanted to run away. The companions tried to bring it back, but the Prophet ordered it to be left alone and said: "Leave it alone, it has a mission." The camel mare knelt down by a rock. The people joined him and set up camp in that place to separate the people of Khaybar from Ghatafan who were supporting the Jews. The Prophet built a mosque there and prayed there during his stay in Khaybar.

With the dawning of day, the hearts of the Jews were pounding with intense fear. They opened their fortresses and brought their shovels and vessels made of wool and leather to carry seeds and fruits. When they saw the messenger of God, they immediately turned and fled to their fortresses. The Jews shouted in shock: "Muhammad with the army." The Muslims were praying the morning prayer in Khaybar and did not hear the call to prayer. The Prophet said: "Allahu akbar, Khaybar is conquered. If we camp in a people's courtyard, their mornings will be bad." Then the Prophet lined up his companions, encouraged them and forbade them to fight until he gave them permission. But a man from Ashjaa deliberately attacked a Jew and was killed. The people said: "The man was martyred." The Prophet asked, "Did this happen after my prohibition of fighting?" They replied, "Yes." The Prophet ordered a companion to announce to the people, "Paradise is not permitted for the disobedient. " Then the Prophet gave a speech to them before the battle and said: "Do not wish to meet the enemy and ask God for well-being, for you do not know what awaits you from them. Sit on the ground, and when they cover you, stand up and say takbir." [401]

When he finished, he authorized the battle and asked the Muslims to be patient. He gave Othman bin Affan the task of guarding the women's houses,

244

where the wounded would also be treated. The Prophet's main flag was white and bore the name Al-Oqab, and he gave it to Ali bin Abi Talib. After the Muslims had set up camp, they laid siege to the first fortress, which was called Naam. The Jews began to shoot at it with arrows, while the Muslims also carried arrows and shot back at them. Then a fierce battle broke out between the two parties until Allah conquered the fortress for the Muslims. Then they went to the fortress of Al-Saab bin Moaz, and there the clashes between Jews and Muslims began. Amara bin Uqba Al-Ghafari challenged one of the Jews to a duel, saying proudly, "Take this, I am Al-Ghafari man." Amara struck the Jew down. The people denounced his boastfulness and said: "His jihad was in vain." When the Messenger of God was informed of this, he said: "There is nothing wrong with him, he will be rewarded and praised."

The Jews launched a campaign and some of the Muslims were overwhelmed until they returned to the Messenger of God. Ali bin Abi Talib held his position and continued to fight against them. The believers were encouraged to wage jihad by the Prophet Muhammad. He informed them that Allah promised him victory in Khaybar and that they would take many booty. All the fighters then returned to their leader and gradually moved closer. The Jews withdrew and locked themselves in the fort. They began to throw stones at the Muslims from the fort. The Muslims retreated but later returned and fighting broke out at the gate of the fort. Three companions of the Prophet Muhammad were killed and the Jews carried their dead into the fort. Finally, Ali ibn Abi Talib led the Muslims who brought the Jews into the fort and followed them. Fighting ensued and some Jews were captured while the rest fled to the fort of al-Zubair Castle. The Muslims climbed the walls of the fort and rejoiced in their victory. The siege of the fortresses of Al-Nitat lasted several days, so that food became scarce among the Muslims. Eventually there was a famine and they had nothing left to eat. Among them were Arabs from the tribe of Aslam who had come with the Messenger of God for booty and did not expect jihad. They decided to send one of them to the Prophet on the assumption that the Prophet of God was saving food for himself and favoring himself. Some of them said to a man from their tribe: "Go to the Messenger of God and greet him on behalf of the tribe of Aslam and tell him that we are exhausted and suffering from hunger." Buraydah bin Al-Hasib Al-Aslami was outraged by their request and scolded them, saying, "By Allah, I have never seen anyone among the Arabs who would do such a thing!" However, one of them said: "I hope that this Messenger to the Messenger of Allah will help us." The man then went to the Prophet and conveyed the message: "O Messenger of Allah, the tribe of Aslam greets you and asks for help because we are hungry and weak." The Prophet replied: "I have nothing with which I can strengthen them. I know their condition and I know that they have no strength." Then he prayed to God to help them and said: "O Allah, open for them the greatest fortress in which there is plenty of food and Ghee."

On the sixth night, the Prophet changed the night watch and appointed Abbad bin Bishr to watch the camp. Abbad caught a scout during the night and brought him to the Prophet for questioning. Omar bin Al-Khattab wanted to have the scout executed, but Abbad had granted him safety. The scout asked for a meeting with the Prophet. They brought him to the Prophet and the Prophet asked him, "What do you have behind you?" He replied, "Do you grant me security, O Abu al-Qasim." The Prophet said: "Yes." He said: "I have come from the fortress of Al-Nitat, where people slip out of the fortress secretly this night." The Prophet asked, "Where are they going?" He replied, "They are going to Al-Shaq, they are taking their children there and preparing for battle." The Prophet then ended the siege of Al- Nitat and moved on to the fortress of Al-Shaq. The Muslims began to fight with the Jews and killed some of them, but the Jews refrained from further fighting. The Muslims shouted "Allahu Akbar" and attacked the fortress. They entered it, opened the gates and collected booty. The surviving Jews fled to the fortress of Nizar and barricaded themselves in. The Prophet and his companions approached the fortress of Nizar and fought against the Jews, who pelted them with arrows and stones. The Prophet took a handful of pebbles and threw them at the fortress. It shook and eventually collapsed, allowing the Muslims to capture their enemies.

Most Muslims were mainly interested in booty and foodstuffs such as ghee, honey, sugar, oil, dates, livestock and goods that they could find in the fortresses. However, the Prophet had another mission to fulfill, which he shared with his faithful companions. The Prophet Muhammad told his companions in battle, "The devil has come to the Jews and told them, 'Muhammad is fighting you for your wealth. Call them and say, 'Say, 'There is no god but Allah,' and your wealth and your blood will be protected and your account will be with Allah." It was a clear promise from the Prophet that they would be satisfied with this declaration without being persecuted or investigated in search of hidden meanings in their utterances, despite all that they had accused him of violating treaties, incitement and conspiracy. Their reckoning would be with Allah alone. and the Prophet Muhammad did not claim for himself wealth or power or the like. The Jews, however, rejected the offer, saying that they would not leave the religion of Moses and that the Torah was still with them.

When the Prophet and his companions saw the resistance of the Jews of Khaybar to surrender, even after the fall of the fortresses of Al-Nitat and Al-Shaq, the Muslims moved towards the fortresses of Katiba. Those Jews who had surrendered had retreated to a group of fortresses in Qatiba. The largest of these fortresses was Al-Qamus, an impregnable fortress and the largest fortress in Khaybar. The Jews barricaded themselves in the fortress of Al-Qamus and locked themselves in there. When the siege of the fortress of Al-Qamus began, the Messenger of God sent Omar ibn al-Khattab with the army on the first day, but they were defeated and could not gain access to the fortress. On the second day, he sent Abu Bakr, but he was also defeated and could not take the fortress. On the third day, he sent Omar ibn al-Khattab again, but he was also defeated and returned with his companions to the Messenger of God. They argued with each other and claimed that Omar was a coward, while he said that the companions who were with him were cowards themselves. The Prophet was displeased and angry with what was happening and said: "What is wrong with people who return defeated and accuse their companions of cowardice?" He added angrily, "Is this how the Muhajirun and the Ansar behave?" He repeated this question three times. Their defeat was not justified and was due to negligence and cowardice on the part of the Companions. The flight that took place was ugly and abominable.

The Messenger of God preached to the people and then said: "I will hand over the banner tomorrow to a man whom God will never abandon, who loves God and His Messenger, and God and His Messenger love him." When the people heard the statement of God's Messenger, they became eager to conquer and fought over who would receive the banner. The next morning, they rushed to the Messenger of God, hoping to be chosen. Buraydah stood up and raised his head in the hope that he would be allowed to carry the banner. Omar said: "I have never liked leadership as much as I did that day.". He therefore stuck his head out of the crowd so that the Prophet could see him and choose him. Omar thought that whoever carried the banner would have power and leadership. Finally, the Messenger of God asked, "Where is Ali?" The people replied, "He is in the tent grinding grain." The Prophet asked, "Could none of you grind the grain except him?" Ali was indeed in the tent and had eye inflammation due to the smoke rising from the fortress. However, he had continued to grind to feed the soldiers. Some of the people said: "As for Ali, you got rid of him, he is blind." Others said: "He has been complaining about his eye problems." When Ali heard about the Prophet's calling, he considered the call and the authorization of the Prophet to him as a divine honor, with which God favors whom He wills. He said: "O God, there is no giver for what you have withheld, and no one withholds what you have given." Salama led Ali to the Prophet. Some were angered by his arrival as they did not want him to compete with them for this honor and status. When Ali arrived, he sat down next to the Prophet. His eyes were covered with a cloth. The Messenger of God asked, "What happened to your eyes?" Ali replied, "They are smeared so that I cannot see what is in front of me." The Prophet ordered Ali to come closer to him. He put Ali's head in his lap and spat in his hand and rubbed Ali's eyes with it. Immediately, Ali's eyes were healed as if he had never been in pain.

Then the Messenger of Allah mounted him on his camel and put a turban on Ali. He dressed him in his clothes, gave him the banner and led him to the fortress. He said to him, "Go and fight them until God grants you victory, and do not turn back." Ali ran and took a few steps, and then he stopped short without turning around to ask a question, then he said: "Why should I fight them. Do I fight them so that they are like us?" Ali ibn Abi Talib's question surprised many of the Companions who were around the Messenger of God. Most of them were fighting for booty, positions, fame, the love of leadership or to enforce Islam through violence and oppression. The Prophet said: "Fight them until they testify that there is no god but Allah and that Muhammad is his servant and messenger. If they do that, then they will have kept you away from their blood and their money, except what is rightfully yours, and their reckoning will be with God." He continued, "Carry out slowly until you come down in their courtyard. Then invite them to Islam and tell them what is incumbent upon them in terms of the rights of God and the rights of His Messenger. By God, it is better for you if God guides a man through you than to have red camels." Then he prayed for him and Ali set off for their fortress. The Messenger of God had instructed him to offer the Jews three options: Either they enter Islam, and they have what the Muslims have, and they have the same obligations as the Muslims, and their money is theirs. Or they accept the payment of Jizya and make a peace, and they are granted security, and their money is theirs. Or they choose war."

The companions of the Messenger of God were aware of the strength of the resistance of the Jews and the bravery of their warriors in this fortress, as they had experienced in the previous failed campaigns. They complained to the

Prophet that one of their fighters named Marhab was of great stature and none of them dared to confront him. They asked the Messenger of Allah to send Ali to him. The Messenger of Allah said: "Ali, take Marhab."

When the Muslims reached the gate of the fortress, they were met by Judean soldiers. Ali called them to Islam, but they refused. Then he called on them to pay the jizya, but they refused that too. Finally, Ali had no choice but to attack. The first to come out of the fortress was al-Harith Abu Zainab, Marhab's brother, who was known for his bravery. The Muslims were so intimidated by him that they retreated, but Ali stood firm and fought him until he killed him. When al-Harith died, his companions returned to the fortress and fled to the door of the fortress, which consisted of a stone with a hole in the middle. Ali placed his left hand in the hole while holding his sword in his right hand. Then he pulled the door towards him and the rock holding the door collapsed and the door fell into his left hand.

Figure 44: A symbolic depiction of Imam Ali, carrying the gate of a fortress in Khaybar

The Jews attacked Ali. He used the door as a shield and pushed against them. Then he threw the door behind him and continued forward. Marhab came out roaring like a camel and said:

"Khaybar knows that I am Marhab an experienced warrior armed from head to foot.

now piercing, now slashing as when lions advance in the rage."

When Ali saw him, he ran towards him. However, Marhab paid no attention to him and denied him until Ali reached him and said:

"I am the one whose mother named him Haidara,

like a ferocious lion at hunt.

massive and stiff armed,

like a lion of the forest with terror-striking stare.

on the enemies as fast as the whistling wind blows,

I will kill you all with the sword in masses.

I will strike you a strike that exposes the spine,

and I will leave behind a land in peace for a century.

I strike with a sword the neck of disbelievers,

the strikes of honorable and mysterious young man.

Whoever forsakes the truth, proves their insignificance,

I will kill seven or 10 of them.

There are all people of defiance and lies."

Ali entered into a duel with him and they alternated two strikes at each other until Ali struck a blow, the sound of which could be heard from across the camp. This blow split Marhabs head open and he fell face down. The Jews ran in panic to their fortress while shouting, "Marhab is killed. Marhab is killed." [402]

Gabriel was astonished and came down from heaven. The Prophet asked him, "What are you surprised about?" Gabriel congratulated the Prophet on the killing of Marhab by Ali and said: "The angels are proclaiming in the towers of the mosques of heaven: There is no hero like Ali and no sword like Dhū l-faqār." On that day, people heard a takbir from the sky. After the killing of Marhab, the people joined Ali. Yasser, the brother of Marhab, came to avenge Marhab's death. Ali came against him and killed him too, and the Jews fled back and were defeated.

When the Prophet heard about the conquest of Khaybar, he was very pleased. He received Ali, embraced him and kissed him between the eyes and said: "I have heard of your praiseworthy message and your work. May God be pleased with you, and I am pleased with you." Ali wept when he heard the Prophet. The Prophet asked him, "What makes you weep, O Ali?" Ali replied, "I am happy that God and His Messenger are pleased with me." The Messenger of God told him, "By the One in Whose hand is my soul, if it were not for a faction of my nation saying what the Christians said about Jesus, the son of Mary, I would have said so much about you today that every Muslim who passes by you would take some of the dust from your feet and the rest of the water of your ablution to be healed with it. But it is enough for you that you are from me and I am from you. You inherit me and I inherit you, and you are to me as Aaron was to Moses, except that there will be no prophet after me."

Hassan bin Thabit asked the Messenger of God for permission to recite poetry on the occasion of this special event, and he was granted permission. He then recited:

"Gabriel proclaimed loud and clear,

and the war is not over yet.

The Muslims have gazed around the sent prophet.

'There's no sword but Dhul-Fiqar and there is no fighter but Ali.'"

When the Messenger of God defeated the people of Khaybar, he agreed with them that they and their families would leave and the Prophet would receive money and weapons. They also promised not to hide anything from him. However, if they did, there would be no security for them. The Judean family of Abi Al-Haqiq owned many pieces of jewelry that they treasured. Kinana and Al-Rabee bin Abi Al-Haqiq were brought to the Prophet and he asked them, "Where are your vessels that you lent to the people of Mecca?" They replied, "We fled and spent our money on our expenses and needs, we had nothing left of our money." He said skeptically, "The Time is short, and the money is plentiful!" Then the Messenger of God said to them, "If you two hide something from me and I discover it, then I have the right to shed your blood and take your descendants." They said: "Yes." Then God revealed the location of the treasure to His Messenger. The Prophet said to Kinana, "You are making fun of heavenly matters." The Messenger of God then ordered a man from the Ansar to go to the place mentioned in the revelation and dig next to a palm tree to find the treasure. The man brought the money and the objects, including bracelets, anklets, earrings, gold rings, necklaces of jewels, emeralds and necklaces of nails strewn with gold. The Jews had lied and the death penalty was imposed and their families were taken. Although they could read about this prophet in their Torah and see miracles and signs, including Ali uprooting the door of their fortress to use it as a shield and passageway for the fighters, they did not consider this and did not believe it. They fought the god on earth where they could not fight him in heaven. Their knowledge of the truth of this prophet should have prevented them from lying to him, for they know that God informs his prophets of their conspiracies and exposes their lies.

Banu Fazara[1] of Ghatafan were among those who came to help the people of Khaybar. On that day, the Messenger of God told them not to help the Jews and asked them to leave. He promised them a reward from Khaybar, but they refused. When God conquered Khaybar and the Messenger of God collected the booty, those from Banu Fazara came to him and said: "We want our share and what you promised us." The Messenger of God said: "Your share is Dhul Raqiba." Dhul Raqiba is a mountain from the Khaybar Mountains. They said: "Then we will fight you." He said: "Your date is in Haifa." It was as if the Messenger of God, reminded them of the cry they had heard before, which frightened them because they did not know where the voice came from. He made them realize that this matter was predestined by God and that they had no power to fight against God and His Messenger. When they realized that the case was so decided, they were frightened and fled.

Ali took a slave woman named Safiya bint Hayy, called Bilal and gave her to him, saying, "Only give her into the hands of the Messenger of Allah so that he can express his opinion about her." The Messenger of Allah gave her the choice between being released so that she could return to her relatives, or embracing Islam and becoming his wife. She chose Islam and married him. He freed her and stipulated her release as her dowry. Through this victory, Khaybar was conquered and about ninety Jews were killed, while less than half of the Muslims died. Half of Khaybar was conquered by war, so one-fifth of the booty belonged to the people of al-Chums[2], while the remaining four-fifths were for all Muslims. The other half was obtained through a peace treaty and belonged to the Messenger of Allah.

---

1   Banu Fazara is an Arab tribe, a branch of the Dhibyan tribe from Ghatafan.
2   al-Chums is divided into two halves. One half is given to the Imam or in his absence a Mujtahid (a qualified expert, scholar) to use it for the spread of Islam, the other half is given to the needy, mu'min Sayyids.

252

After the Messenger of God finished with Khaybar, he held up a flag and waved it. Then he said: "Who can take it. We will send him to the farms of Fadak." Fadak was a village in the Hejaz, two days away from Medina, where a Jewish community lived. Al-Zubair stood up and said: "I am." The Prophet then said: "Go away from it." Then Saad bin Abi Waqqas stepped forward. The Prophet said: "Go away from it. I swear by the one who honored the face of Muhammad, I will give it to a man who will not flee." Then he said to Ali, "O Ali, get up and take her." Ali took the flag and went to Fadak. There he concluded a peace treaty with the inhabitants without fighting, whereby he received half of their harvest and their wealth. In this way, the Fadak farms were declared as Fay'a and belonged exclusively to the Messenger of God. Then Gabriel came down and said: "God, the Mighty and Majestic, commands you to give the relatives what is due to them." The Prophet asked: "O Gabriel, who are my relatives and what is their right?" Gabriel replied: "Fatima, give her the land of Fadak and everything in it that God and His Messenger have in it." Thereupon the Messenger of God called Fatima to him and wrote her a certificate of ownership for it. [403]

After his return from the campaign of Khaybar, the Prophet came to his wives. They asked him to give them some of what he had captured in Khaybar, but he explained that he had divided it among the Muslims according to God's instructions. His wives were annoyed and said: "Perhaps you think that we will not find suitable men among our people if you leave us?" Zainab bint Jahsh said: "You are not righteous, and you are the Messenger of God?!" He replied, "May your hands become dusty[1], if I were not righteous, who will be?!" She said: "You prayed to God to cut off my hands?!" He replied, "No, only to get dusty." Hafsa said: "If you leave us, we will find suitable men among our people." Allah was angered by what they said to the Messenger of God and ordered him to withdraw from them. After about a month, God revealed to his Prophet, "O Muhammad, tell your wives that if they desire the worldly life and its pleasures and enjoyments, then come, I will give you appropriate money and dismiss you in a way that will not cause harm. But if you do not desire the worldly life and its joys and pleasures and instead choose faith in God and His Messenger and the Hereafter, then God has prepared a great reward for the good among you. This is the reward for those who choose God and His Messenger and the Hereafter and are among the good." This shows that being close

---

1   The man is 'covered with dust' or dusty: He has been hit by dust. And 'his hands are covered with dust': He is impoverished, he is literally sticking to the dust due to his poverty. The Arabs also use this phrase to express affection.

to the Prophet - through marriage - does not grant them an additional level of favor that enables them to enter Paradise, but it is the goodness that offers them what God has prepared. [404] When the Prophet returned to them, he informed them of what God had commanded him. Then Umm Salama stood up and said: "I have chosen God and His Messenger." Then they all stood up, embraced him and said the same.

The arrival of Ja'far from Abyssinia

Before his march to Khaybar, the messenger of God had sent Amr ibn Umayyah al-Damri to the Negus, the king of Abyssinia, and asked him to send Ja'far and his companions to him. The Negus provided Ja'far and his companions with good equipment and transported them in two ships. The group consisted of sixteen people, apart from those who had previously died or returned. The Negus sent his nephew with them to the Messenger of God to serve him.

Figure 45: Ja'far ibn Abi Talib arrives from Abyssinia.

Ja'far ibn Abi Talib arrived from Ethiopia immediately after the conquest of Khaybar. The Messenger of Allah sent one of his companions to receive him. When the Prophet saw him, he stood up and greeted him. Ja'far ran to him and the Prophet hugged him to his chest, kissed him between the eyes and wept with joy at seeing him. He said: "I don't know which I am happier with, the conquest of Khaybar or the arrival of Ja'far." The Prophet spoke to him and then mounted the camel, with Ja'far riding behind him. As the camels moved with them, the Prophet turned to him and asked, "O Ja'far, brother, shall I fa-

254

vor you? in anything else. Should I give you something. Shall I favor you." The people thought he was giving Ja'far some of the money or lands he had conquered in Khaybar. Ja'far said: "Yes, may my father and mother be sacrificed for you." Then the Prophet taught him the prayer known as the Ja'far prayer.

Seventy men in woolen garments came from the people of the monasteries, sixty-two of them from Abyssinia and eight from the people of the Levant. The Messenger of God recited Surah Ya-Seen to them, they wept and embraced Islam and said: "How similar this is to what was revealed to Jesus!" The Prophet served them himself. His companions said to him, "We are enough, O Messenger of God, you do not need to work yourself." He replied: "They have always treated our companions with respect and taken care of them." The Messenger of God considered the coming of Ja'far as significant and valuable as the victory in Khaybar or even more so. Ja'far, however, was no ordinary man. He embodied the Islamic faith deeply in his existence and being, and his entire existence was united with Islam. He returned victorious from a country that professed Christianity after persuading the king to convert to Islam.

Asma bint Umays, the wife of Ja'far ibn Abi Talib, came with her husband from Ethiopia. She visited Hafsa, the wife of the Prophet. While she was with Hafsa, Omar, Hafsa's father, came. When Omar saw Asma, he asked, "Who is this?" Hafsa replied, "This is Asma bint Umays." Omar then provocatively said to Asma, "We were the first to emigrate, we have a greater right to the Messenger of God." Asma became angry and said: "No, by Allah, Omar. You were with the Messenger of Allah to satisfy your hunger and to teach the ignorant among you, while we were in the distant and foreign land of Abyssinia for the sake of Allah and His Messenger. I swear by Allah, I will not eat or drink anything until I have told the Messenger of Allah and asked him about what you have mentioned. I will not lie and I will not deviate from the truth." When the Messenger of God came, she said to him, "O Prophet of God, some men are arrogant towards us and claim that we are not among the first immigrants (Muhagirun)." He asked, "Who says that?" She replied, "Omar said that." And she told him everything that Omar had told her. The Messenger of God said: "I did not say that. He has no more right to me than you do. He and his companions have undergone one migration and you - the people of the ship - have two migrations. You migrated to the Negus and then to me." .

Among those who came with them from Abyssinia was Umm Habiba bint Abu Sufyan. She was one of those who had emigrated to Abyssinia with her husband Abdullah bin Jahsh. He renounced Islam, converted to Christianity and died. She, however, stuck to her Islam. When the news reached the Prophet Muhammad, he sent Amr ibn Umayyah al-Damri to Negus in the seventh year to ask him to marry Umm Habiba to the Prophet Muhammad. [405]

After Khaybar battle, the Messenger of God prepared some brigades to secure the area around Khaybar. The brigades were a call to God, and some of them were tasked with surveillance and spying so that the Muslims were not surprised by enemies. In one of the campaigns that the Prophet sent to some Jewish villages to invite them to Islam, there was a Jewish man named Mirdas bin Sulaym. When Mirdas saw them, he gathered his camels and money on the mountainside. He said: "I bear witness that there is no god but Allah, and that Muhammad is the Messenger of God." Osama bin Zaid passed by him, killed him and took his camels.

Then they returned to the Messenger of God and told him about it. They saw that the Messenger of God was very upset. He had heard about the expedition before. Astonished, the Messenger of God asked them: "Did you kill him to take what he had with him?" Osama replied: "O Messenger of God, he only said it to escape death." The Prophet replied: "Couldn't you have opened his heart to find out whether he was telling the truth or lying?" And he recited to them a verse from the Quran addressed to the believers, saying, "O you who believe, when you go out on expeditions or reconnaissance missions and meet some people and are uncertain whether they are disbelievers or Muslims, do not be hasty in your decisions and do not assume that everyone you meet is a disbeliever and kill him. Instead, you should verify the truth before making a decision. And do not say to anyone who greets you with the Islamic greeting - peace be upon you - or surrenders to you that he is not a believer and is lying. For these words are sufficient in Islam and are enough to be recognized as a believer. And do not say that he is not a believer with the intention of shedding his blood and taking his property out of greed for some worldly gains from the booty. Know that God knows the secrets of the hearts and sees your deeds and will call you to account for them. "[406] Osama said: "O Messenger of God, ask forgiveness for me." The Messenger of God replied sadly, "What about 'There is no god but Allah'?" and repeated it three times. Osama repented deeply and wished he had become a Muslim that day.

A man named Husail bin Nuwayrah, from Ashja tribe , came to the Messenger of Allah and was his guide to Khaybar. The Prophet asked him, "Where did you come from, Husail?" He replied, "I came from Jinaab." The Prophet asked, "What is behind you?" He replied, "I left a group of Ghatafan in Jinaab. Uyaynah told them, 'Either come to us or we will come to you.' They wrote to him, 'Come to us so that we can all go to Muhammad.' They want to attack either you or the outskirts of the city." A pre-emptive strike had to be carried out to ward off evil from the Muslims. The Messenger of Allah sent them three hundred men. Then the people fled, their gathering was dispersed and the Muslims met no resistance.

Uyaynah fled on his horse. His ally Al-Harith ibn Awf al-Murri asked him to stop. But he could not and said as he ran, "No, I cannot, Muhammad and his companions are behind me." Al-Harith said to him, "Can't you see what you are about to do? Muhammad has conquered the land, and you are totally somewhere else." Then Al-Harith stepped back from the spot where he expected the horses to pass to see if they were still following Uyaynah or not. He stayed at the spot from noon until nightfall, and no one came by or looked for him. But the fear that had gripped him made him feel that way. Then Al-Harith told him about it, and he admitted that he did not want to be found for fear of being captured. Al-Harith said to him, "O man, you witnessed what happened to the Banu al-Nadir, at the Battle of the Trench, with the Quraiza and before that with the Qainuqa. And in Khaybar; they were the most powerful Jews in all of Hejaz, known for their courage and generosity. They possessed impregnable fortresses and palm trees. By Allah, even the Arabs used to seek refuge with them. Did you see how the Al-Aws asked the Jews for help and allied themselves with the Banu Al-Nadir and the Banu Quraiza to help them. They helped them against the Al-Khazraj. But did you see how Muhammad defeated the Jews of the Banu Al-Nadir and Quraiza?" Uyaynah said: "Yes, by God, I did. But my soul would not allow me." Al-Harith said: "Go with Muhammad." Uyaynah asked, "Shall I be a follower?! A people preceded me in Islam and they humiliate those who came after them by saying, 'We fought in Badr and other battles. We are more honorable than you." Al-Harith replied: "It all depends on your own conscience. If we had been there earlier, we would have done the same as them. Your people have agreed on a truce with Muhammad in Mecca, he will attack them when he has the chance." Uyaynah said: "I understand, by God." Al-Harith and Uyaynah did not succeed in converting to Islam early on, so their conversion was delayed. Despite the reason and insight of Al-Harith ibn Awf. It also arouses astonishment that Uyaynah ibn Hisn justified his reluctance to embrace Islam by saying that he did not want to be submissive.

In that year, the angel Gabriel came to mourn the death of the Negus. The Messenger of God wept over him and said: "Your brother Al-Asham has died." Then he went to the cemetery, prayed for him and said takbir seven times. Every hill was flattened for him until he saw his burial, even though the Negus was in Abyssinia. The hypocrites said: "Look at this man praying for a Christian Abyssinian, although he has never seen him and has not practiced his religion. [407]

Messages from the Prophet to the kings

When the Quraysh's hostility towards the Muslims subsided, the prophet sent letters to six rulers and emperors of his era, who had power over world's nations, calling them to Islam. He asked some of his companions to carry these letters. His decision astonished them, and out of fear of these kings, they avoided the task.

The Messenger of God went out to his companions and said: "O people, God has sent me as a mercy for all people, so pass on my message, may God have mercy on you. And do not be divided about me as the disciples were divided about Jesus the son of Mary, and do not go and do like the messengers of Jesus the son of Mary." The Prophet wrote to Abyssinia, the Romans, the Persians, Egypt, the Levant and Al-Yamamah, and the messengers set off with the books. So he sent to Khosrau, the king of Persia: "In the name of Allah, the most Gracious, the Merciful. From Muhammad, the Messenger of Allah, to Khosrau, the Great of Persia: Peace be upon those who follow guidance, believe in Allah and His Messenger, and testify that there is no god but Allah alone, without partners, and that Muhammad is His servant and Messenger. I call you with the call of God, for I am the Messenger of God to all people {so that anyone who is alive may be warned, and that God's verdict may come due against the disbelievers.} [1] [496], If you become Muslim, you will be safe. If you refuse, you will bear the sin of the Majūs[2]."

---

1 The meaning of the verse is: This Prophet or this Quran came to warn those who have an open mind, analyze things, and come across truths, to believe and do good. He also came to confirm the punishment for the unbelievers who have strayed from the path and do not believe in God.
2 Majus: Followers of Zoroastrianism or Mazdaism especially priests or Magi or "Magicians".

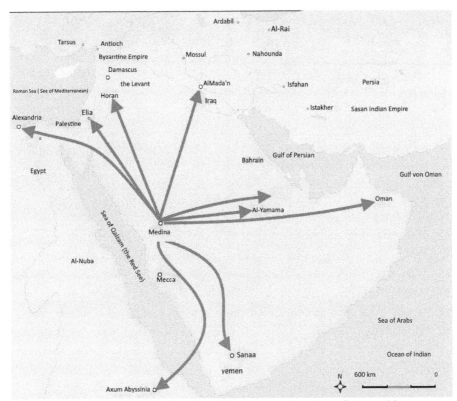

Figure 46: Diagram of the Prophet's envoys to the kings of the world.

Khosrau summoned those who could read the letter to him, and as he read: "From Muhammad, the Messenger of God, to Khosrau, the Great of Persia," Khosrau became angry because the Messenger of God began with himself. Khosrau shouted and took the letter and tore it up before he knew what was in it, saying, "He is writing this letter to me while he is my slave!" When Prophet Muhammad heard about this, he said: "Khosrau has torn up his kingdom." Later, Khosrau went back and rectified the matter by sending a gift with some earth to the Messenger of God. The Messenger of God said to his companions, "May Allah tear up his kingdom as he tore up my letter. Indeed, you will tear up his kingdom. And he sent me earth as a sign that you will possess his land." Khosrau II was one of the most tyrannical and arrogant rulers. He wrote to his agent in Yemen (Bazan) to go to the Messenger of God and order him to apologize. Bazan sent two men with Khosrau' letter to Prophet Muhammad and ordered him to march with them to Khosrau. A message reached the Messenger of God from heaven that God had instigated the son of Khosrau, and he killed his father. The revelation told the prophet the exact date of his death. That was in the year 628 AD When the two messengers came to him, the Prophet said to

259

them, "My Lord has killed your Lord by inciting Shirouh against him." He told them when he was killed.

The two messengers returned and came to Bazan and told him what had happened. He said: "By God, these are not words of the kings. I see him as a prophet, let us see." It was not long before Bazan received a letter from Shirouh telling him about the death of Khosrau and telling him, "You know the man who wrote to you Khosrau about him, do not disturb him until I give you further instructions." When Bazan realized the truth of Prophet Muhammad, he embraced Islam with those who were with him in Yemen. He sent a message that he and his people had converted to Islam to the Prophet of God.

At the same time, the Messenger of God also wrote a letter to the Emperor, the Great of Rome, inviting him to Islam: "In the name of Allah, the most Gracious, the Merciful. From Muhammad bin Abdullah, to Heraclius, the great leader of the Romans. I call you with the call of Islam: enter Islam and you will attain safety. Allah will give you your reward twice over. But if you turn away, you will bear the sin of the Arians.[1] And {come to a word that is the same between us and you: that we serve none but Allah and do not associate anything with Him, and that some of us do not take others as masters besides Allah. But if they turn away, then say: "Bear witness that we are devoted to Allah." [497]

The Jews and the Christians (Ahl al-kitāb) believe that their religion is based on monotheism and that their practices do not contradict the principle of monotheism. Therefore, God commands His Prophet to invite them to a just and fair word that unites him with them and forms a common meeting place that reflects the unity of all. This word calls for the worship of one God, namely Allah, and belief in His uniqueness in terms of His essence and attributes, without associating other persons in His worship. If they respond to the Prophet's call, it is to be hoped. And if they turn away and do not accept what has been presented to them, then they should at least testify, O Muhammad, that you are Muslims who adhere to this monotheistic faith. [408]

Emperor Heraclius honorably and generously sent back the Prophet's Messenger and presented a gift to the Messenger of God. claiming that he had accepted and believed in Islam and that he had called upon the Romans to believe

---

1 The Arians were followers of Arius (256–336 AD), the bishop of Alexandria, which was a foundation of Alexander the Great and next to Rome the largest city of antiquity. Arius earlier believed in pure monotheism and denied the Trinity and considered Christ as one of the sincere servants of God.

in the Prophet Muhammad, but they refused. When Emperor's letter came to the Messenger of God, he said: "God's enemy lied, he is not a Muslim." The Prophet also sent a letter to al-Muqawqis[2] who was a Christian: "In the name of Allah, the All Gracious and Merciful: From Muhammad bin Abdullah to al-Muqawqis, the great of the Copts: peace be upon those who follow guidance. I invite you to Islam. If you become a Muslim, you are safe, may God reward you twice. And if you refuse, you will have to bear the sin of the Copts. and {Come to a word that is the same between us and you: that we serve none but Allah and add nothing to Him, and that some of us do not take others as masters besides Allah. But if they turn away, then say: "Bear witness that we are devoted to Allah." [409]

The Egyptian king Muqawqis responded to the Prophet Muhammad's letter by sending gifts without accepting Islam, he wrote: "I have honored your Messenger and sent you two female servants who are of high rank in Egypt." These two servants were Mary and her sister Sirin, who later converted to Islam. The Prophet Muhammad later chose Mary to live with him as a slave.

The Messenger of God also sent a letter to the third Negus, the king of Abyssinia, and a letter to the Roman governor in Aelia in Jerusalem. They refused the Prophet's request, just as Heraclius and Khosrau had done before. The reason for this was that they did not want a new religion to spread among their people. They were intent on preserving their rule and did not want to make room for anyone else to take part in it. [410]

---

2 Al-Muqawqis is often identified with Cyrus, the Patriarch of Alexandria, who administered Egypt on behalf of the Byzantine Empire. The meaning of the name could derive from the Arabic term for "Caucasian".

628 - 629 AD

The seventh year after the Hijrah

The battle of Dhat al-Riqa

In the seventh year, someone came to Medina and said that the tribes; An-mara, Thalaba and Ghatafan had gathered crowds to attack the Muslims. When the Prophet heard this, he appointed Abu Dhar al-Ghifari as his representative over the city and set out in the month of Muharram with four hundred men until he came to Wadi al-Shaqra. He stayed there for a day, dispersed the patrols, and then they returned to him at night. They told him, "They have not seen anyone." The Prophet walked with his companions until he came to the place of the assembled tribes. When they saw his army, they fled from the Muslims and hid in the mountains, clinging to their peaks and some of them sought refuge in the valleys. There were only women left whom the muslims took without a fight. Then the Prophet returned to Medina and sent one of his companions to Medina to give good news to the people of Medina about his safety and the safety of the Muslims.

On the way, a man grabbed a baby bird, whereupon one of the parent birds flew up and threw itself into the hands of the man who had taken its young. The people were astonished. Then the Messenger of God said: "Are you astonished at this bird? You have taken his young and he has given himself out of compassion for his young. By God, your Lord is more merciful to you than this bird is to its young." The Prophet used this incident to explain the mercy of God and left a deep impression on the hearts of the people through this practical illustration.

Jabir was riding a slow camel on the journey and was the last in the group. The Prophet passed him and asked, "Who is that?" He replied, "Jabir bin Abdullah." The Prophet asked, "What's wrong with you?" Jabir said: "I am riding a slow camel." The Prophet asked, "Do you have a stick?" Jabir replied, "Yes." The Prophet said: "Give it to me." He gave him the stick and the Prophet hit the camel with it. From that moment on, Jabir rode at the front of the group.

The Prophet said: "Sell it to me." Jabir said: "No, it is for you, O Messenger of God." The Prophet said: "Better sell it to me. I bought it for four dinars and you can use it until we reach Medina." Then the Prophet said: "O Jabir, have you married yet?" Jabir said: "Yes, O Messenger of God." The Prophet said:

"Widow or virgin?" Jabir said: "No, a widow." The Prophet said: "Why didn't you marry a virgin so that you could play with her and she could play with you?" Jabir said: "O Messenger of God, my father was killed on the day of Uhud and he left behind seven daughters. I married a woman who can take care of them." The Prophet said: "You have done the right thing, God willing. When we reach Sarar[1], we will slaughter a camel and stay there for the day, when your wife will know of our arrival, she will prepare the house for your arrival and will lay pillows for rest." Jabir said: "By God, O Messenger of God, we have no cushions." The Prophet said: "You will have them. When you arrive, do a good deed." Then the Messenger of God said to him, "O Jabir, what have you done with your father's debt?" Jabir said: "O Messenger of God, I have been waiting for him to harvest his dates." The Messenger of God said: "When you harvest, please inform me." Jabir said: "Yes. " The Prophet said: "Who is your father's debtor?" Jabir said: "Abu Al-Shahm, the Jew, owes my father 120 kilograms of dates." The Messenger of God said to him, "When will you harvest?" Jabir said: "Tomorrow." The Prophet said: "O Jabir, when you gather them, sort the Ajwa dates apart from other types of dates" When they reached Sarar, the Messenger of God ordered a camel to be slaughtered and they stayed in that place and spent the day there. When evening came, they entered Medina. Jabir went to his wife and told her what the Messenger of God had told him. She said: "Accept it and listen and obey." The Prophet entered the mosque. Jabir came afterward and entered the mosque with his camel. He fed the camel in the courtyard area and said: "O Messenger of God, this is your camel." So the Prophet went out and rode the camel and said: "The price and the camel are yours." He gave him four dinars and added one carat.

**Figure 47: Jabir ibn Abdullah goes
with the Prophet on a camel.**

---

1   Sarar: A place that is five kilometers from Medina.

The next day, Jabir had harvested the palms and isolated their varieties as the Messenger of God had told him. Jabir informed the Messenger of God about what he had done. The Messenger of God set off with his companions and entered the farm. Abu Al-Shahm was also present. When the Messenger of God looked at the sorted dates, he said: "God bless them." He came to the ajwa dates and touched them with his hand. He sat down among the Baskets, then said: "Call your debtor here." Abu Al-Shahm came. The Messenger of God said: "Cradle." He took his right from a Basket of ajwa dates and left the rest of the dates untouched. When the Jew finished, the Prophet asked, "O Jabir, are there any debts left from your father?" He said: "No." Jabir later recounted what happened: "And the rest of the dates remained. We ate them for a long time and sold them until the harvest reached the next year. If I had sold the first harvest, it would not have covered my father's debt."

The Messenger was a close companion to his Followers and cared for them lovingly, understanding their needs and challenges. He showed them compassion and comfort and regularly asked about their well-being. Sometimes he also visited those who were in difficult situations to help and support them. In this way, he shared the sweet and bitter lives of his followers and created an atmosphere of trust and affection between them. [411]

The performance of Umrah

It has now been a year since the peace of Hudaybiyah. The Prophet Muhammad had made an agreement with the Quraysh that he would be allowed to enter Mecca one year after Hudaybiyah, but without any weapons other than those of the travelers, namely swords. He was not allowed to stay longer than three days and was to leave on the fourth day. These and other conditions were agreed by him with the Quraysh at Hudaybiyah. The Prophet decided to perform Umrah according to the agreement. On the first day of Dhul-Qi'dah in the year 7, the Prophet ordered his companions to prepare for Umrah and that none of those who participated in Hudaybiyah should stay behind. A group of those who did not attend Hudaybiyah also joined them. Two thousand Muslims performed Umrah.

Ja'far bin Abi Talib was one of those who accompanied the Prophet, and he was one of those who did not witness Al-Hudaybiyah because he was in Abyssinia at that time. A man who wanted to participate in the Umrah said: "O

Messenger of God, by God, we have no provision and we have no one to feed us." So the Messenger of God ordered the Muslims to spend in the way of God, to give alms and not to hold back their hands so that they would not perish. They asked: "O Messenger of Allah, with what should we give if one of us has nothing?" The Prophet replied, "With what you have, even half a date."

During this Umrah, the Prophet brought sixty camels and put necklaces on them to mark that they were sacrificial animals, and he appointed someone to take care of them. He appointed Abu Dhar as a representative in Medina and carried weapons, shields and spears with him. He appointed someone to guard them. The Prophet led a hundred horsemen under the leadership of Muhammad ibn Muslima. When they reached Dhul Hulayfah, The Prophet sent the horses ahead of him. They said to him: "O Messenger of God, you have brought weapons, and they have stipulated that we must not enter it armed except with the weapons of a traveler." The Messenger of God replied, "We will not allow them to enter the sacred region armed, but the weapons will be near us. If there is an uprising from their side, the weapons will be close to us."

The Messenger of God began the Iḥrām from Al-Shajara Mosque (Dhul Hulayfah) (See Figure 48), and all those who came with him from Medina began the Iḥrām. Muhammad ibn Maslamah rode on with the horses, and when he was in Marr Al-Dhahran (Fatima Valley), he found a group of Quraysh. They asked him what was behind him and he said: "This is the Messenger of God, he will come to Mecca tomorrow, God willing." The group also saw many weapons and quickly went back until they came to the Quraysh, and they told them what they had seen of horses and weapons. The Quraysh panicked and said: "We have not broken the treaty, and we are still committed to him and his term, so why is Muhammad invading us with his companions?" The Quraysh sent Mukariz bin Hafs with a group of Quraysh to the Prophet, and they met him in the Valley of Yajij (before Al-Taneem) and said: "By God, O Muhammad, you are not known for treachery, young or old. You enter the sanctuary with weapons against your people, and you have stipulated that you will not enter it except with the traveler's weapon?!" The Prophet said: "I do not enter it with a weapon." Mukariz said: "These are your qualities in righteousness and loyalty." Then Mukariz quickly returned to Mecca and said: "Muhammad does not enter with weapons, and he is committed to the condition he has set for you."

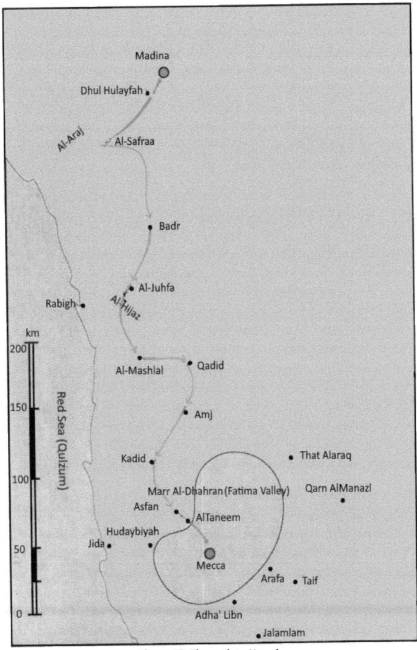

Figure 48: The path to Umrah.

When the Quraysh learned of his departure for Umrah, their leaders, including Khaled ibn al-Walid, left Mecca. They did not want to see the Prophet and his followers circumambulate the Sacred House. Their actions were characterized by hostility, hatred and envy of the Messenger of Allah. The Messenger of God and his companions entered Mecca on the morning of the fourth Dhul-Hijjah riding on his camel Al-Qaswa, with Ibn Rawaha holding his reins. His companions stared at him, carrying swords and reciting the Talbiya[1]. The Prophet said as he entered Mecca, "O God, do not let our death be here." He left the weapons in the valley of Yajij, a place near the shrine, and he left two hundred Muslims at the weapons to guard them. When those who were with him finished their rituals, two hundred of them came and replaced them so that they could also perform their rituals.

A group of polytheists sat on Mount Qainuqa and looked at the Prophet and his companions as they circumambulated the house, and the disbelievers of Quraysh said: "The fever of Yathrib has weakened the Muhajirun." God informed His Prophet of what they said: whereupon the Prophet said: "May God have mercy on anyone who shows them strength from himself." The Messenger of God ordered his companions to run the three laps to show the polytheists that they were strong. Out of kindness and so as not to overburden them, he ordered them not to jog all the laps. Then the polytheists said: "Those you claim are weakened by the fever. They are braver than we thought. They jump like an antelope." The Prophet came to the house while he was sitting on his camel, and he touched the corner of the Sacred House with his stick, and Abdullah bin Rawaha held the reins of it and he recited:"Desist, you sons of the disbelievers,from his path, For all the good is on this ridge.O Lord, I believe in his words,Recognize God's right, in his words.We fought you for Quranic interpretation,And for revelation with zeal and passion in every encounter."

But Omar Ibn Al-Khattab did not like this, so he said angrily, "O Ibn Rawaha, In the presence of the Messenger of God and in the sanctuary of God you speak poetry." The Messenger of God immediately silenced him and said: "O Omar, I am listening." Then the Messenger of God slaughtered the sacrificial animals between Safa and Marwa and shaved his head at Marwa. He put on the pilgrim's robe and uncovered his right upper arm, and the companions did the same. When the Messenger of God had finished his rituals, he entered the sanctuary and remained there until Bilal called for noon prayer over the Kaaba in accordance with the command of the Messenger of God. The Qurayshites were in great pain when they saw Bilal, the black-skinned man, the slave, the

---

1 Talbiyah (in Arabic): Labbayka-llāhumma labbayk (a), inna l-ḥamda wa-n-ni'mata, laka wa-l-mulk (a), lā sharīka lak!

poor man and the strange Abyssinian. They saw him above the Kaaba, the greatest thing they cherish.

Ikrimah bin Abi Jahl said: "God honored my father by not hearing this servant say what he wanted to say." So did Safwan bin Umayyah. Khaled bin Usayd said: "Praise be to God who killed my father and he did not witness this day when Bilal Ibn Um Bilal roars over the Kaaba." Suhail bin Amr and the men with him covered their faces when they heard this. Khaled bin Saeed bin Al-Aas said: "Praise be to God who honored my father so that he did not live to see this day." Al-Harith bin Hisham said: "Woe to him. I wish I had died before this day, before I heard Bilal shouting over the Kaaba." Al-Hakam bin Abi Al-Aas said: "This is indeed a great event. A slave of Banu Jamh is standing on the house of Abi Talhah and shouting with all his might." The Messenger of Allah asked the polytheists to allow him to enter the Kaaba, but they refused, saying, "This was not in the contract."

The Prophet and his companions spent three days in Mecca. After completing the Umrah, Ja'far ibn Abi Talib arranged Prophet Muhammad's marriage to Maimunah bint al-Harith al-Hilaliyya, who became his last wife. When Maimunah learned of the engagement and sat on her camel, she said: "The camel and what is on it belongs to God and His Messenger." The Messenger of God wanted to marry her in Mecca. He did not enter under the roof of one of the houses of Mecca, but a tent made of leather was erected for him in the Al-Batha neighborhood of Mecca, and he stayed in it until he left Mecca. When the three days of the agreement for Umrah were over, Huwaytib bin Abdul Ezza came to Prophet Muhammad along with Suhail bin Amr when he was in a gathering of the Ansar and was talking to Saad bin Ubadah. They said: "Your term has expired, so go away from us." The Prophet said: "What harm would it have done you if you had left me with you until I got married and prepared food and invited you to join me?" They said: "We do not need your food." We ask you by God and the covenant that you leave our land, for the three days have passed." Saad bin Ubadah heard their words to the Prophet, became angry and said to Suhail, "You are lying, you have no right to this land, neither does it belong to you nor to your father. By Allah, no one will leave it without being satisfied and against his free will." The Messenger of God smiled and then said: "O Saad, do no harm to the people who visited us in our tents." Then the Prophet ordered them to leave and said: "None of the Muslims will spend the night there."

The Prophet rode until he came down in Saraf, and all the people came with him. The cavalry joined him and brought the weapons that were in the valley of Yajij. At night the Prophet left Saraf and went on to Medina. After his return to Medina, the Prophet continued to administer the affairs of the Muslims, secure the surrounding areas of Medina and spread Islam. [498]

When the Messenger of God left Hudaybiyah, there was no one left among the Khuza'a who had not embraced Islam. The Messenger of God wrote a letter for them in which he said: "In the name of Allah the Most Gracious and Merciful, from Muhammad, the Messenger of God, to Badil, Bishr and Sarawat Banu Amr. Peace be upon you, I thank God for you. There is no god but Allah. I appreciate your status and do not underestimate you, and the most honorable of Tihama are you for me, and the most merciful of them are you, and those who follow you are among the righteous. I consider those of you who have emigrated, just as I consider myself - even if you have emigrated to your country - not as residents of Mecca, but rather as immigrants to Mecca for Umrah or Hajj. I have not acted rashly to reproach you. Instead, I have chosen patience and forbearance. If you embrace Islam, I will not reproach you. So you should not be afraid or apprehensive of me." This letter showed the love, respect and appreciation the Prophet Muhammad had for these faithful people when he granted non-residents of Mecca and non-immigrants the same rewards and privileges that an immigrant receives. [499]

The event of the cloak

In that year, the Messenger of God went to his wife, Umm Salama, and his daughter Fatima was with her. He greeted her and said: "O Fatima, I feel tired and weak." Fatima answered him, "I seek refuge in God, Father, from weakness." He said: "Bring me the Yemeni cloak and cover me with it." She brought it to him and covered him with it while looking at his face in amazement, as if he was shining like the full moon. Then Fatima brought him a bowl of soup. He said to her: "Call your husband Ali and your two sons Hassan and Hussein." They came and greeted the Messenger of God. They sat down with him and ate the soup while Fatima sat with them. The Messenger of God took the excess cloth and covered them with it. Then he took out his hand and turned his hands to the sky and said:

Figure 49: The Prophet covers his family with the cloak.

"O Allah, these are the people of my household[1], remove all impurity from them and make them completely pure. O Allah, these are the people of my household, remove all impurity from them and make them completely pure." Here Gabriel descended and said: "The Most High greets you and says that I have not created an erect sky, a spread out earth, a shining moon, a shining sun, a circling star, a flowing sea or a floating ship except for your sake and out of love for you. He has given me permission to enter with you. Do you allow me, O Messenger of God." The Messenger of God said: "Peace be upon you, O Messenger of God's Revelation. Yes, I have given you permission."

Then Gabriel entered with them under the cloak, and God revealed this verse: {Indeed Allah desires to repel all impurity from you, O People of the Household, and purify you with a thorough purification.}[412] The members of the household are Muhammad, Ali, Fatima, Hassan and Hussein. God willed for the members of this household that He would purify them, honor them, and protect them from all sins and offenses.

Umm Salama was praying in her room when she heard what was happening and wanted to join them. She came into the room where they were gathered, lifted the cloak to go with them, and asked, "Shall I not be with you too, O Messenger of Allah?" But the Messenger of Allah withdrew the cloak from her hand and did not allow her to enter with them. He said to her, "You are good,

---

1 People of the Household: Ahl al-Bait is an Arabic expression that literally means "family of the house" and refers to the direct family of the Prophet Muhammad, including his daughter Fatima, his son-in-law Ali, and their descendants, including Hassan and Hussein.

you are good." On this occasion, those who were gathered under the cloak, Muhammad, Ali, Fatima, Al-Hassan and Al-Hussein, were called the people of the cloak. God chose them for the verse of purification among the people. [413]

629 - 630 AD

The eighth year after the Hijrah

In the eighth year of the Hijrah, Khaled bin Al-Walid and Amr bin Al-Aas came to the Messenger of God, declared their Islam. They were considered among the greatest of Quraysh and its leaders. [414]

Battle of Mu'tah[1]

In the same year, the Messenger of God sent the first messenger from the Arabian Peninsula to the Levantine lands that belonged to the Romans. The Prophet sent Al-Harith bin Umair Al-Azdi with a letter to the king of Busra[2]. When he reached Mu'tah, he met Sharhabil bin Amr Al-Ghassani, one of the princes of emperors over the Levant. Sharhabil asked him: "Where are you going?" Al-Harith replied: "To Levant." Sharhabil asked, "Are you perhaps one of Muhammad's envoys?" He said: "Yes, I am the messenger of the Messenger of God." Sharhabil then ordered him to be captured and executed. He thus became the first messenger of the Messenger of God to be executed.

When the news of al-Harith's assassination reached the Messenger of God, he was saddened and grieved. He gathered the people and told them about the assassination and who was responsible for it. The people hurried, went out with him and camped in Al-Jurf. The Messenger of God did not inform them of his plan. Al-Jurf is about five kilometers from Medina in the direction of the Levant, and the Prophet followed them. He led the noon prayer for the Muslims at this place and then appointed the commanders of the army. The Messenger of God held a white banner for them and gave it to Ja'far bin Abi Talib He said to them, "If Ja'far is wounded, then Zaid bin Haritha is your commander. And if Zaid is wounded, then Abdullah bin Rawaha is your commander." Then the Messenger of God set out to accompany the army towards Mu'tah until they reached Thaniyyat al-Wada'. He stopped and they gathered around him. He said: "I advise you to fear Allah and be good to the Muslims who are with you. Go to battle in the name of Allah, for the cause of Allah, against those who deny Allah. Do not betray, abuse or kill children, and when you meet your enemy among the polytheists, invite him to do one of the following three things. Whatever they choose, accept it from them and stop harming them. Invite

---

1   Mu'tah: A well-known place near Al-Karak in Jordan.
2   Busra is about 140 kilometers south of Damascus, known for its Roman ruins.

274

them to move from their land to the land of the migrants, and if they do, tell them that they have the same rights and duties as the Muhajirun. If they refuse to move, tell them that they will be like the Bedouins of the Muslims, under the rule of Allah, who rules over the believers. In terms of war booty, they will have nothing except if they fight together with the muslims. If they refuse, then ask them for the jizya. If they agree, accept it from them and leave them alone. If they refuse, seek help from God against them and fight against them. If you besiege a fortress or a city and you want to give them the protection of God and His Messenger, do not give them the protection of God or His Messenger. Instead, give them your own protection and the protection of your fathers. If you violate your protection and the protection of your companions, it is easier than violating the protection of God and His Messenger. Intervene in the name of God and fight against the enemy of God and your enemy in the Levant. You will find men in the monasteries, isolated from the people. Leave them alone. You will also find others who have the devil in their heads. Fight them with swords. Do not kill women, animals or old men. Do not approach the palm trees. Do not cut down trees or demolish houses." [415]

The Prophet was observing all the movements of his enemies and was aware of the colonial plans of the Romans in the region. He was aware of the large army of Romans gathered and their intention to invade the entire Hejaz region to eradicate the call of Islam and possibly occupy the entire Arabian Peninsula. It was of vital importance to prevent this large army from advancing towards the Medina.

When the Messenger of God bid farewell to Abdullah bin Rawaha, Ibn Rawaha said: "O Prophet of Allah, tell me something I remember from you." He said: "You will come tomorrow to a city where prostration (in prayer) is rare, so make many prostrations." Abdullah bin Rawaha said: "O Messenger of God, advise me more." He said: "Remember God, for He will help you in whatever you ask of Him." He got up, went away then came back and said: "O Messenger of God, God is one and loves monotheism."

The Prophet replied: "O Ibn Rawaha, if you are unable to do something, do not be too weak to do at least one thing well, even if you have done ten things wrong." Ibn Rawaha said: "I am satisfied with that and do not ask you for anything after that."

**Figure 50: An imaginary representation
of Abdullah ibn Rawaha.**

On that day, the number of Muslims did not exceed 1500, but the Prophet of Allah sent messengers to the Arabs to warn them of the danger of the Romans and to call them to fight in Levant, which increased the number of the army to about 3000. The people prepared for war and then got ready to move out. The people gathered to bid farewell to the commanders of the Messenger of God. Abdullah bin Rawaha was crying here. They said: "What makes you cry, Ibn Rawaha?" He said: "By God, it is not for the love of this world, not even for a little bit, but I have heard the Messenger of God recite a verse from the Book of God in which he mentions the Hellfire: {And there is none of you except he will come to it. This is upon your Lord an inevitability decreed. } [416] I do not know how to return after I have arrived.[1] " The Muslims said: "May God accompany you, protect you and bring you back to us righteously."

---

1   Abdullah ibn Rawaha referred in his words to the two verses from the Surah Maryam: {And there is none of you except he will come to it. This is upon your Lord an inevitability decreed. Then We will save those who feared Allah and leave the wrongdoers within it, on their knees.}. This means that there is none among you people - whether pious or unjust - who will not see and experience Hell on the Day of Resurrection. This is an inevitable and final matter with your Lord. Then God will save those who were God-fearing, and leave the wrongdoers in it on their knees due to their injustice. It was reported from the Prophet Muhammad that he said about this verse: People will see the fire and then be led away from it according to their deeds. The first will be as fast as lightning, then like the wind, then like a galloping horse, then like a rider on his journey, then like a running man, then like a walking man. Ibn Rawaha expressed his concern, which comes from his faith, that he might not be led away from this scene due to his deeds. [417]

Of the three leaders, Ja'far and Zaid were stronger, more insightful and braver than Ibn Rawaha to oppose this matter. The Prophet gave Ibn Rawaha advices that gave him strong spiritual impetus and enabled him to fulfill an extremely sensitive task. The Prophet told him that he should not rely on his own abilities because his self might fail him at the most critical moments. There is no remedy for this matter except through the remembrance of Allah, in which that soul feels His Lordship over it and His ownership of it, and that He is the Preserver, the One Who manages it and is the Most Merciful to it. Moreover, Ibn Rawaha should not allow the feeling of helplessness despite repeated defeats and should try again and again, even if he fails ten times. After all, failure does not prevent him from succeeding again and achieving a great victory the next time.

The prolonged wars between the Byzantine and Persian empires in the period from 602 to 628 AD had exhausted both sides without changing the territory of either empire. In 629 AD, the Battle of Mu'tah took place, in which the number of Roman soldiers was estimated at ten thousand fighters [418] camped in Al-Balqa' and some Arab tribes loyal to the Romans joined them. The Muslims moved on until they reached the borders of al-Balqa'. Then the enemy approached and the Muslims moved to a village called Mu'tah. The Roman army mobilized its troops under the leadership of Theodore, the brother of Emperor Heraclius, as he was informed of the movements of the Islamic army through his spies. They laid an ambush for the Muslim army. When the Islamic army arrived at Mu'tah, the Roman army attacked them unexpectedly, the Muslims panicked and were confused. The Roman troops fought against the front of the army where the three commanders were. [419]

At the beginning of the battle, the flag was in the hands of Ja'far bin Abi Talib. He fought resolutely until his right hand was severed. He then held up the flag with his left hand, but this was also severed. Nevertheless, he hugged the flag to keep it visible so that the Muslims could continue fighting. Eventually Ja'far was killed and Zaid bin Haritha took over the flag and fought until he too died. Abdullah bin Rawaha then took the flag and carried it on his horse. He hesitated for a moment, but then he attacked with his sword and fought until he was also killed. The flag fell from his hand and the Muslims and polytheists mingled in battle. Some of them fled. Qutbah bin Amer then shouted: "O people, it is better to be killed while advancing than to be killed while fleeing." After Abdullah bin Rawaha was martyred, Khaled bin Al-Walid took the initiative, seized the flag, turned back and fled with it, followed by the rest of the army. It was a defeat, and twelve Muslims were killed, and the polytheists followed them.

Meanwhile, the Messenger of God told his companions in Medina what happened in Mu'tah when it happened. He said: "God, raised the earth for me until I saw its battlefield." When the Prophet told the people that the three leaders had been killed, the companions of the Messenger of God wept. The Prophet said to them, "What makes you weep?" They said: "And why should we not weep when our best, our nobles and the virtuous among us have gone?" The Prophet said to them, "Do not weep, for the parable of my community is like that of a garden whose owner watches over it and tends it by tending its date stalks, erecting its buildings and pruning its palm leaves. Every year it produces a new group. Perhaps the last harvest will be the best variety and the best fruit. Perhaps the best man in my community will be the one who comes at the end. By the one who sent me as a prophet with the truth, Jesus, the son of Mary, will find a successor in my community.[1]"

When the fleeing army, led by Khaled, approached Medina, they were met by the rushing boys, and the Messenger of God came with the people and said: "Take the boys and carry them and give me the son of Ja'far." So they received the Messenger of God and the Muslims threw dust on the army and said: "O fugitives, you have fled in the way of God." The Messenger of God said: "They are not fleeing, but they are brave attackers, God willing." The people of Medina criticized them so much that a man of them went to his house and his family, and when they knocked on the door, he refused to open the door for them, and they said: "Why did you not advance in battle?" The older ones among the companions of the Messenger of God remained sitting in their houses out of shame until the Prophet sent men to them who said to them, "You are the victorious fighters in the way of Allah." Only then did they go out, while the Messenger of God was present and watching, without holding anyone responsible for what he had done, nor did he show anger. In this way of mitigation, he wanted to deal with the negative aspects of the defeat.

Fleeing from the advancing enemy in battle is considered impermissible in the Quran. Muslims are expected to stand firm and face the confrontation. Whoever flees from battle and is defeated will return with the wrath of God and his punishment, and his fate will be hell. Exceptions to this rule are the

---

1 Although the prophecy for this statement has not yet been fulfilled, it will happen in the future.

fighters who change their location to deceive the enemy, or those who leave their location to go to a group or faction to seek their help or aid them. This fact was clear to the Muslims in the city, for everyone knew what it meant to flee in a war. [420] Therefore, the Prophet Muhammad regarded the fugitives as if they had joined a faction so that they would not be among the fugitives and would be included by the Qur'anic verse. The Prophet said to them, "And I am your faction." This means that he considered them to be part of a faction in the war, namely the Prophet Muhammad. He said this to them as a metaphor to give them relief, not in a literal sense, because there is nothing in their apparent state at the time of their flight to indicate that they intended to join a faction with this flight. Their main concern was to save themselves.

Then the Messenger of God approached Asma bint Umays, Ja'far's wife, and said: "Bring me the sons of Ja'far." Asma did not yet know what had happened. She brought them to him, and he hugged them, smelled them, and his eyes shed tears. Asma asked anxiously, "O Messenger of God, may my father and mother be sacrificed for you, why are you crying. Have you heard anything about Ja'far and his companions?" He said in tears, "Yes, they were injured today." She stood up and screamed. The women gathered around her. The Messenger of God said to her, "O Asma, do not speak falsely and do not beat your chest." He went out to his daughter Fatima, and she said with sorrow, "O my uncle." The Prophet said: "For a man like Ja'far, let the mourners weep." Then he said: "Make food for the family of Ja'far, for they are busy with a disaster." A group of Muslims also came to the Messenger of God, including Khaled bin Al-Walid and Saad bin Ubadah. The daughter of Zaid bin Haritha burst into tears in front of the Prophet's face, whereupon Prophet Muhammad wept until he sobbed. Saad bin Ubadah said to him, "O Messenger of God, what is this?!" The Prophet said: "This is the longing of the beloved for his beloved."

The plan of the Messenger of God in Mu'tah was to resist until the martyrdom of the leaders. Then the war would continue, and the Muslim army would stand firm, even for an hour, the leaders of the Roman army, headed by the Roman emperor who was experienced in war, would have realized then that the war with the Muslims have no end. And the emperor would think that it is necessary to calculate things in a different way, which could lead to withdrawing and ending the war, also it could lead to reconsidering the matter of this religion and studying its teachings and facts. [421]

The slander in the house of the Prophet

In the Islamic community, the Prophet's wives enjoyed a unique position. They were regarded by Islam as "mothers of the believers", which earned them high esteem and respect in the community. However, this motherhood was of a spiritual and intellectual nature, as the Prophet was regarded as the moral and spiritual father of the Ummah (the community of believers).[422] The effects of this spiritual connection were limited to maintaining respect for the Prophet's wives and the sanctity of their marriage during his life and after his death.

Islam endeavored to regulate the treatment of the Prophet's wives in a way that preserved their dignity and status. For this reason, there were special laws for the Prophet's wives that did not apply to all women. For example; it was common in Arab society and among many people in that simple society that if they needed something, they would borrow it from their neighbors until they could own it themselves. The Prophet's house was no exception to this practice, and people would come to him, whether the time was appropriate or not, and ask the Prophet's wives for something.[423] Hence, the Qur'anic verses came to clarify to people the proper way to treat the Prophet's wives. Muslims were instructed that if they wanted something from the Prophet's wives, they should ask for it from behind a curtain to take into account the special circumstances of the Prophet's wives. The curtain in the Quranic verses does not refer to the women's clothing, but is an additional rule that applies specifically to the Prophet's wives and does not refer to the commonly known hijab[1] for all women. Also, the Prophet's wives were not to appear before people and show themselves in such matters, even if they were veiled. Of course, this regulation does not apply to other women, who must adhere to the Islamic dress code.

The instructions also went so far as to specify the etiquette for entering the Prophet's houses. The Quran emphasized the need to ask permission before entering the Prophet's houses and not to linger there, which could make the Prophet uncomfortable. Nevertheless, some hypocrites in the city wanted to insult the Messenger of Allah. Some of them even expressed this openly. Thus Talha ibn Ubaidullah said in objection to these instructions: "When Muham-

---

1 The hijab is the garment worn by Muslim women that covers their bodies, including their heads.

mad dies, I will marry Aisha." When the Messenger of Allah heard his words, he was saddened by them.[424] Allah forbade marriage with the Prophet's wives after his death in order to preserve the sanctity of the Prophet and Islam. The Prophet's wives were obliged to live without marriage after the Prophet Muhammad's death, even though this was difficult for some of them.

Sometimes important issues are raised in a person's life where sacrifice and selflessness must be shown, and one must give up some rights, especially when great achievements come with great responsibilities. The Prophet's wives have gained unparalleled pride and honor by marrying the Prophet. Acquiring this honor requires such a sacrifice. For this reason, the Prophet's wives were treated with great respect and dignity by the Muslim community after his death and were very pleased with their condition. They considered it minor in comparison to the achievements they had acquired. On the other hand, the hypocrites could have used the association with the Prophet's wives to achieve their goals and gain a prestigious social status. Or they could have started to denigrate Islam by marrying the Prophet's wives, assuming that they had exclusive information from inside the Prophet's house. Therefore, the Prophet's wives had to accept this victimization with an open heart.

The hostile attitudes towards the Prophet's house continued in order to defame his image in the Muslim community. They spread rumors accusing this pure house. The hypocrites wanted to attack the Prophet personally and tarnish his reputation. They were determined to do this as revenge against the Prophet and as an insult to his sanctity, and they wanted to strike a blow against his existence in this way.

In the eighth year after the Hijrah, some hypocrites accused Mary al-Qibtiyya, the Prophet's slave woman (ama)[1] of secretly cheating on him with one of her relatives. No greater plot was hatched against the Muslims than this rumor. It was a fabricated rumor that shook the Prophet's house for a whole month. It caused unrest throughout the city of Medina and shook the entire Muslim community and was part of a series of conspiracies against the message and an attempt to defame its symbols because the enemy knew that this religion

---

1   In Islam, slave women (al'imā') can be taken intimately by their owner without a marriage contract, witnesses, or dowry. They are not wives, but the relationship between a man and his slave woman should be public and not secret. This is because certain rules apply due to this announcement, including possible children between them

was only based on the model and example. Hence you see the hypocrites continue to spin conspiracies and spread war of doubt, of suspicion.

Mary was a good, pious, virtuous and kind woman, and the Prophet took care of her. She lived an ordinary, quiet life in her house, free from any exciting and extraordinary event. One of her relatives named Mabur (Grig) al-Qibti joined her and helped her with some things and entertained her. Mary's qualities and beauty and the Prophet's interest in her aroused jealousy in Aisha. The Prophet had taken Mary to a house belonging to Haritha ibn al-Nu'man, so she became a close neighbor of Aisha and Hafsa. Mary suffered from the attacks of Aisha and Hafsa, so the Prophet decided to take her to al-'Alya so that she could have peace, but they did not stop hurting her.

A group of people who were connected to each other and to Aisha and Hafsa, the wives of Prophet Muhammad, conspired to spread rumors about Mary. They did this for political reasons and personal interest. Among those who conspired with them to slander Mary were Hassan bin Thabit, Mustah bin Athatha, Rifa'a bin Zaid, Abdullah bin 'Ubayy, Hammna bint Jahsh and others. Allah says that those who have spread this falsehood have brought it forth from themselves and they are a group among you. You Muslims should not think that this conspiracy is bad for you, on the contrary, it is good for you because it has removed the mask from the hypocritical elements who are trying to tarnish the Prophet's reputation through some of his wives. Every individual from this group has his share of sin and disobedience, depending on how involved he is in it. And as for the one who was the main perpetrator of this incident and spread and publicized it, he will suffer a great punishment. [425]

The Prophet used to be just between his wives with regard to spending the night. On the day the Prophet spent the night with Hafsa, she visited her father, and the Prophet called Mary to him. She then came to Hafsa's house. However, Hafsa was not present when Mary arrived. When Hafsa returned and found out what had happened, she was furious and asked the Prophet, "O Messenger of Allah, are you doing this in my house on my day?" Hafsa was furious with Mary and accused her of infidelity to her husband and infidelity with another man. She fabricated these accusations against her in collusion with Aisha. This led the Prophet to reflect on Mary's fidelity. The Prophet said to Hafsa: "She is forbidden to me, don't tell anyone about it." But Hafsa could not keep the secret to herself and told Aisha. There was nothing immoral about what the Prophet had done with his wife Mary, and Mary was innocent of the accusations leveled against her. Allah admonishes His Prophet for restraining himself from what Allah has permitted him to do.[426] And God exposed Hafsa for revealing the secret that the Messenger of Allah had entrusted to her. When he told her about her misbehavior, she asked in astonishment, "Who told you this?" believing that Aisha had informed him. But he surprised her by telling her that Allah had informed him. Allah reprimanded them for their bad behavior and told Hafsa and Aisha to repent and turn to Allah. Allah also declared that He could divorce them from him and give him better wives than them. [427]

When the Prophet learned of the conspiracy that his wives were plotting against him and Mary, he regretted leaving Mary and returned to her. But the jealousy and hatred in the hearts of his wives remained. When Mary became pregnant, the prophet took care of her and even accompanied her at the birth of her child. This increased Aisha and Hafsa's hatred of Mary and they harmed her. A few months later, Ibrahim, the Prophet's son from Mary, died. The Prophet was very sad about the death of his son. Aisha asked out of resentment: "Why is he so sad? He is the son of the Coptic Grig." With these words, she wanted again to sow doubt about Ibrahim's descent from the Prophet and about Mary's honor and chastity. When the Prophet heard these words from her, he was very hurt and ordered Ali to kill Grig. Ali went to him with his sword, and Grig was in the garden. Ali knocked on the door of the garden and Grig came to open the door for him. When he saw Ali, he recognized the evil in his face and retreated, and did not open the door. Ali jumped to the wall and descended into the garden, and he pursued him while Grig fled from him. Fearing he would be seized by him, he climbed a palm tree and Ali followed him. When he got close to him, Grig jumped off the palm tree and his genitals became visible. It turned out that he was not a man and had no female attributes, which meant that he had been castrated.

When Ali saw this, he returned to the Prophet and asked, "O Prophet of Allah, have you instructed me in this matter so that I should be like a hammered nail or should I act?" The Prophet replied, "Act." Ali said: "By the One who sent you with truth, he has neither what men have nor what women have." The Prophet replied, "Praise be to Allah, who has diverted evil from us, the people of the house." In this way, Ali proved Mary's innocence of these accusations. Prophet Muhammad did not actually give an order to kill him. But he decided to use this incident to show Mary's innocence in a clear way and to convey to people the truth and the real purpose of these events. This is a denigration of the reputation of the prophetic house.

The Prophet did not impose a punishment on those who conspired against him and his wives. This is because carrying out such a punishment could lead to great corruptions and serious dangers that could threaten the building of Islamic society and the future of the Islamic mission. Therefore, he preferred to refrain from retaliating against them. This was also his approach in other situations; he refrained from carrying out punishments against some of the leading figures when the general good of avoiding them was greater than the benefit of punishing them. For example, he did not impose punishment on Khaled bin Al-Walid for what he did at the Banu Jadhimah, and he did not punish Ibn 'Ubayy for his deeds, and many other situations. [428]

The Battle of Dhat al-Salasil

The dangers facing Islam and the Muslims are not yet over, as the hatred, envy and ambitions of the Arabs around the city continue to increase, and their plans to eliminate the Prophet Muhammad and his message continue.

Figure 51: The inhabitants of the valley of al-Yabis.

In the eighth year, the inhabitants of the valley of al-Yabis agreed not to abandon or betray each other, not to abandon anyone and never to give up until they all die or kill Muhammad and Ali ibn Abi Talib. About twelve thousand horsemen and fighters gathered. Gabriel came to the Prophet, told him about the matter and ordered him to send Abu Bakr with four thousand horsemen of the Muhajirun and Ansar. The Prophet turned to the people and told them what Gabriel had told him about the people of Wadi (valley) al-Yabis.

He ordered them to prepare for the march on Monday with Abu Bakr. When the time for the march came, the Prophet ordered Abu Bakr: When he sees them, he should offer them Islam. If they would follow him, he should leave them alone. Otherwise, he should fight them, kill their fighters, take their wives and children and take their wealth. Abu Bakr walked with them on an easy path until he came down close to them. Two hundred heavily armed horsemen came out to him and asked, "Where have you come from? And where are you going?" Then they asked to meet their leader. Abu Bakr went out to them. They asked him and he told them why he had come to them. The group from Tal al-Yabis said: "We swear by al-Lāt and al-ʿUzzā. If not for kinship and compassion, we would have killed you and all your companions. And you would be a story for those who come after you. Turn back, you and your companions, and hope for safety. For we only want your companion himself and his brother Ali ibn Abi Talib." Abu Bakr said to his companions: "O companions, the people are many times more than you and better equipped than you. Let us go back and inform the Messenger of God about the situation of the people." They all said: "O Abu Bakr, you have disobeyed the Messenger of God and violated what he commanded you. So fear God and fight the people and do not contradict the words of the Messenger of God." He said: "I know what you do not know. The witness sees what the absent one does not see." They returned to the Prophet. The Prophet angrily declared on the pulpit that Abu Bakr had disobeyed his command and that when Abu Bakr heard their words, he was terrified from them. The Messenger of God continued: "Gabriel commanded me in the name of God to send Omar to them in his place among his companions with four thousand horsemen. Go, Omar, in the name of God, and do not do as Abu Bakr, your brother, did, since he disobeyed God and me." He commanded him as he had commanded Abu Bakr, and so he went with them and followed their path until he came close to the people and two hundred armed men went out to him, and they said to him and his companions the same as they had said to Abu Bakr. He went, and the people went with him, and his heart almost flew away at what he saw of the people's equipment, and he turned back to flee from them. Gabriel came down and told the Prophet Muhammad what Omar had done. The Prophet told the Muslims what Omar had done and that he had also disobeyed his command. When Omar came, the Prophet said: "O Omar, you disobeyed God on his throne, and you disobeyed me and my words and acted according to your opinion. So may God put your opinion to shame." .

Then he mentioned that Gabriel had ordered him to send Ali with the four thousand and that God would grant him and his companions victory." The Prophet called Ali and told him this. Ali went out and walked with his companions on a different path from that of Abu Bakr and Omar, for he was so violent with them that they feared that they would perish with their animals from exhaustion. Ali said to them, "Fear not, for the Messenger of God has commanded me to do something and told me: God will grant me and you victory. So be glad, for all will be well." They rejoiced, and continued their arduous march until they landed near them. The same armed men went out to him, and when Ali saw them, he went out to them with a group of his companions. The people of Tal Al-Yabis asked, "Who are you? Where do you come from. And where are you going?"

Figure 52: Ali's surprise attack on Wadi al-Yabis.

He said: "I am Ali bin Abi Talib, the cousin of the Messenger of God, his brother and his messenger to you. I invite you to testify that there is no god but Allah and that Muhammad is His servant and His Messenger. And you have the rights of Muslims and you have the duties that they have." They said to him, "We wanted you and you sought us and we listened to your speech. Get ready for a hard fight, for we will fight you and your followers. The appointment between us and you is tomorrow morning, and the warner is excused." Ali said to them, "Woe to you, you threaten me with your multitude and your gathering?! I seek refuge in Allah, His angels and the Muslims against you. There is no power and no strength except with Allah." They went to their positions and Ali went back to his place. As night fell, he ordered his companions to take good care of their animals and saddle them.

When dawn broke, he prayed silently with the people and then attacked them with his companions. They did not notice until the horses reached them. They were taken by surprise and their fighters were killed, their descendants were enslaved. Ali took the prisoners and the money with him. Gabriel descended and informed the Messenger of God about what God had granted Ali and the group of Muslims. The Prophet ascended the pulpit, praised God and told the people what God had granted the Muslims and informed them that only two men were injured. Before the arrival of the armies of Islam in Medina, Surah Al-Adiyat was revealed, and on the same day the Messenger of God led the people in the morning prayer and recited Surah Al-Adiyat: In the name of Allah the All-Merciful the Merciful {By the charging steeds that pant and strike sparks with their hooves}

Allah swears by the horses of the Mujahidin[1] who run fast in the name of Allah and exert themselves, and they breathe heavily and loudly, which shows their exertion in fighting the enemy. And Allah swears by the horses that run fast so that fire and sparks fly from their hooves. And Allah swears by the horses that attack in the morning and surprise the enemy and take them unawares. The movement of these horses stirs up dust in the morning, which astonishes and surprises the enemy, and he loses control of his territory, while the horses of the mujahidin break through the ranks of the enemy and find themselves in the midst of the enemy army and defeat them. Allah swears by all these heroic moments of the mujahidin. The response to this oath is that man takes the path of ingratitude and disbelief and forgets his Lord and does not thank Him for His favors. And this person testifies to himself and admits through his words and deeds that he is ungrateful for the benefits of Allah, and this is obvious and clear, and he will also testify to this truth on the Day of Resurrection when he is confronted with irrefutable evidence. And this is what Allah has sworn by, that this person loves money very much and forgets to thank Allah for His benefits. Does this person not know that when the Day of Resurrection comes, the dead will come out of their graves and be called to account, then the great catastrophe will occur and this person will be exposed to the greatest and most terrible dangers.[429]

When he had finished his prayer, his companions said: "This is a surah we did not know." The Messenger of God replied, "Yes, Ali has prevailed over the enemies of Allah and Gabriel has announced this to me this night." He descended and went out to receive Ali among all the Muslims of Medina until he

---

1   Mujahed, pl. Mujahidin: someone who practices Jihad.

met him a few kilometers away from Medina. When Ali saw him coming, he dismounted from his mount and the Prophet dismounted. The Prophet hugged him and kissed him between the eyes. He accepted the booty and the captives and what God had given them from the people of the Valley of al-Yabis. [430]

The massacre of Banu Khuza'a

Enmity and wars between Banu Bakr and Khuza'a continued until the Prophet Muhammad was sent. When Islam came, the wars between them were prevented and the people were preoccupied with Islam. But enmity still remained in their hearts. When the peace treaty of Al-Hudaybiyah was made between the Prophet Muhammad and the Quraysh, one of its conditions was: "Whoever wishes to enter the treaty of the Prophet Muhammad shall enter, and whoever wishes to enter the treaty of the Quraysh shall enter." Khuza'a then entered the treaty of the Prophet Muhammad, which angered her rival from the tribe of Banu Bakr.

In the month of Sha'ban, two years after the treaty of Hudaybiyah, one of the Banu Nafatha mocked the Messenger of God in Mecca, and one of Khuza'a warned him to stop, but he did not stop. Then al-Khuza'i struck him. The man from Banu Nafath then asked his people for help. This aggravated the situation and Banu Nafatha and Banu Bakr went and spoke to the nobles of Quraysh to help them with men and weapons against their enemy of Khuza'a, reminding them of those who were killed by Banu Khuza'a before Islam. They appealed to the Quraysh for kinship and reminded them that they were their allies and that Banu Bakr had already entered into the treaty with the Quraysh and that they, like Quraysh, had not embraced Islam and that Khuza'a had entered into the treaty of Muhammad and his covenant. The Quraysh encouraged them to do so and hastened to help them, but Abu Sufyan bin Harb was not consulted about this and knew nothing about it. The Quraysh, Banu Bakr and Banu Nafatha supported the action with weapons and men. They kept this secret carefully to ensure that the Khuza'a would not be warned. According to the provisions of the Hudaybiyah agreement, the Khuza'a were also under the protection of Islam at that time.

The Quraysh agreed to allow Banu Bakr and Banu Nafatha to come to Al-Wattir, a place below Mecca, the home of the Khuza'a. Among them: Suhail bin Amr, Safwan bin Umayyah, Ikrimah bin Abi Jahl, Huwaytib bin Abdul Ezza,

Shaybah bin Othman and Mukariz bin Hafs. They conspired against the Khuza'a at night while they were sleeping in safety, and most of them were boys, women and weak men. They attacked and killed them in their sleep and pursued them until they reached the borders of the sanctuary. The companions of Nawfal bin Muawiyah, who is from Banu Nafatha, said to him while he was killing among the Banu Khuza'a without mercy, "O Nawfal, your god, your god. you have entered the sanctuary." He replied, "I have no god today, O sons of Bakr. By my life, you are robbing the pilgrim in the sanctuary. Will you not take revenge on your enemy? We will not take revenge too late after this day."

When the Khuza'a reached the shrine, some of them entered the house of Badil bin Warqa and the house of their slave named Rafi' Al-Khuza'i. The Quraysh leaders also entered their houses, thinking that the news had not spread and that this would not be conveyed to the prophet Muhammad. The Khuza'a died at the door of Badil bin Warqa and Rafi' Al-Khuza'i. Twenty men were killed that day. Suhail bin Amr said to Nawfal bin Muawiyah, "You saw what we did to them and who among the people were killed. You harvested them and you want to kill the rest as well, but that is something we cannot agree to. Leave them alone then." He left them alone and they went away. The Quraysh regretted what they did and knew that there might be a breach of covenant between them and the Messenger of God. Al-Harith bin Hisham and Abdullah bin Abi Rabi'ah came to Safwan bin Umayyah, Suhail bin Amr and Ikrimah bin Abi Jahl and blamed them for what they had done. They said: "There is a treaty between you and Muhammad, and you are breaking it."

On the morning of the day on which the massacre took place, the Messenger of God said to Aisha, "O Aisha, something has happened in Khuza'a." Aisha asked, "O Messenger of God, do you think the Quraysh dare to break the covenant between you and them after they are exhausted from war?" The Messenger of God replied: "They are breaking the covenant for something that God wants." Aisha asked, "O Messenger of God, is it good?" He replied, "Yes, it is good.".

The Quraysh regretted helping Banu Nafatha and said: "Muhammad will invade us." Abdullah bin Abi Sarh said: "I am of the opinion that Muhammad will not invade you until he argues with you and gives you a choice in all matters that are easier for you than his attack." They asked, "What are these?" He said: "You will be asked to pay the blood money of the Khuza'a dead who were twenty-three, or you deny the alliance with those who broke the peace treaty and they are Banu Nafatha, or he breaks the treaty with you. What do you think of these options?" Suhail bin Amr said: "I don't think there is anything easier for us than to be released from our alliance with Banu Nafatha." Shaybah bin Othman Al-Abdari said: "You protected your maternal uncles and took care of them." Suhail said: "Who from the Quraysh was not born from Khuza'a?" Shaybah said: "But it is easier for us to pay the blood money of the deads' from Khuza'a." Qurza bin Abd Amr said: "No, by God, we do not pay the blood money, and we do not break the covenant of Banu Nafatha, but we break the treaty with Muhammad." Abu Sufyan said: "This is nothing, and the opinion is nothing but denial of this matter. that the Quraysh committed a breach of treaty or broke a term, as the Quraysh did not know that the people had made this decision, as they had made it without our consent or advice. So it is not our fault." They said: "This is the best opinion and there is no other opinion."

While the Messenger of God was among his companions, he said: "It is as if Abu Sufyan had come to you and said: 'Renew the covenant and extend it to tighten the treaty and extend the term.' And he will return without achieving what he wants."

In the meantime, Al-Harith bin Hisham and Abdullah bin Abi Rabi'ah went to Abu Sufyan bin Harb and said: "This matter must be settled. Otherwise, Muhammad will attack you with his companions." Abu Sufyan said: "Hind bint Utbah had a nightmare which she detested, found horrible and was afraid of its evil." They said: "What is that?" He said: "She saw blood flowing from Mount Al-Hajun until it stopped for a while at Mount Al-Khandama, then this blood disappeared." When the two heard the vision, they were pessimistic. They talked about the fall of Banu Nafatha and what happened to Khuza'a. Abu Sufyan said: "This, by God, is something that I did not witness. They will hold me responsible for it. and by God, they did not consult me about it, and I did not accept it when I knew about it. By God, Muhammad will attack us if my suspicions are true. There is no harm in my coming to Muhammad and talking to him about extending the peace treaty and renewing the covenant." They said: "By God, you are right."

Abu Sufyan set off for Medina, accompanied by one of his servants on two camels. He rode quickly and saw that he was the first to go from Mecca to the Messenger of God. He met Badil bin Warqa in Asfan. Abu Sufyan was afraid that Badil had gone to the Messenger of God. Abu Sufyan asked Badil and his companion, "Tell us about Yathrib. When did you visit it?" They said: "We have not been there." So he knew they had kept it quiet. "Do you have dates from Yathrib? Yathrib dates are the best Tihama dates." he asked. They said: "No." Abu Sufyan was not reassured, so he said: "O Badil, did you go to Muhammad?" He replied, "No, I did not, but I went from this coast to the land of Banu Ka'ab and Khuza'a, and there was a person among them who was killed. I have successfully mediated between the two parties." Abu Sufyan discussed goods with him and Badil and his companions left later. Abu Sufyan came to the place of their tents and smashed their camel dung and found in it the kernels of Ajwa dates, which are the well-known Medina dates: Abu Sufyan said anxiously, "I swear to God, the people have gone to Muhammad."

Abu Sufyan arrived in Medina five days after the massacre of Khuza'a. He entered the house of his daughter Umm Habibah, the Prophet's wife. When he wanted to sit on the bed of the Messenger of God, she folded the bed and did not allow him to sit on it.

He said: "O daughter, don't you want me to sit on this bed?" She said: "It is the bed of the Messenger of God and you are an impure polytheist. I do not want you to sit on the bed of the Messenger of God." He said: "My daughter, you are not well." She said: "No, but God has led me to Islam. And you, O father, master and leader of the Quraysh, how can you fail to enter Islam. How can you worship a stone that neither hears nor sees?" Then he got up and left her.

He came to the Messenger of God while he was in the mosque and said: "O Muhammad, I was absent during the Hudaybiyah peace treaty, so I ask you to confirm the treaty and extend the period of peace." The Messenger of God said: "Is that why you came, Abu Sufyan?" He said: "Yes." The Messenger of God said: "Have you done anything to break the treaty?" He said: "For God's sake, we honor our covenant and our treaty on the Day of Hudaybiyah. We do not change or break it." The Messenger of God said: "We are also committed to the term of our peace treaty on the Day of Hudaybiyah, and there is no need for us to change anything." Abu Sufyan repeated the request to the Messenger of God, but the prophet did not answer him.

Then he went to Abu Bakr and talked to him and said: "Can you talk to Muhammad. Or ask people to give me security?" Abu Bakr said: "My protection is the protection of the Messenger of God." Then he went to Omar ibn al-Khattab and asked him, just as he asked Abu Bakr. But Omar also rejected him. Then he came to Othman bin Affan and said: "There is no one among the people who is closer in lineage than you. Extend the term and renew the covenant, for your friend will never refuse your request." Othman said: "My protection is the protection of the Messenger of God." Abu Sufyan came to Ali and said: "O Ali, you are one of the closest people to me in the family line, and I came with a need, and I will not return disappointed as I came. Speak to Muhammad for me." He said: "Woe to you, Abu Sufyan. By God, the Messenger of God has decided something that we cannot talk to him about."

Then he came to Saad bin Ubadah and said: "O Abu Thabit, you are the master of Yathrib, ask the people for safety for my sake and extend the duration of the truce." Saad said: "My protection is the protection of the Messenger of God, and no one gives protection and security contrary to the opinion of the Messenger of God." He came to the nobles of the Muslims who all said the same thing and none of them offered him security contrary to the Prophet's decision. Desperate, he then entered the house of Fatima. Al-Hassan was still a young boy at the time. Abu Sufyan said: "O daughter of Muhammad, can you give me security?" Fatima answered him according to his logic and understanding and said: "I am just a woman.[1]" He said: "Your sister Zainab[2] did that for Abu Al-Aas bin Al-Rabea, and Muhammad agreed to it." She said: "It was a matter for the Messenger of God. When Zainab gave Abu Al-Aas bin Al-Rabea security, she only wanted to prevent people from attacking Abu al-Aas until the Prophet had decided on his matter and passed judgment on him. But she did not want to prevent the Messenger of God from carrying out God's judgment on him." He replied, "Look to your son, Hassan ibn Ali, if he can give security, and he will be the ruler of the Arabs forever." She said: "By God, he is still a child, and he cannot do such a thing. And no one here offers security in that which contradicts the Messenger of God." He said: "Then talk to Ali." She said: "You speak to him."

Then he spoke to Ali. And Ali replied, "O Abu Sufyan, none of the companions of the Messenger of God would do anything without the advice of the Messenger of God." He said to Ali: "O Abu Al-Hassan, I see that it has become difficult for me, advise me." Ali said: "By God, I don't know anything that could benefit you, but you are the master of Banu Kinana." Abu Sufyan

---

1   She meant: „according to your conception, a woman has no right to deal with such a matter. Why do you want to push me into something you don't believe in?!"

2   Zainab, the wife of Abi Al-Aas bin Al-Rabee, is not the sister of Fatima, and he called her, her sister according to what was circulating among the people at that time.

said: "You are right, and so am I." Ali said: "Get up and ask the people for safety, then go back to your country." Abu Sufyan said: "Do you think that will do me any good?" Ali said: "No, by God, but I can't find another way for you." Abu Sufyan stood up in the mosque and said aloud, "O people, I have sought refuge among the people, and by God, I do not know if anyone will offer me safety." Then he entered the Messenger of God and said: "O Muhammad, I have asked the people for safety." The Messenger of God said: "You say such a thing, O Abu Hanzala!¹" He rode his camel and returned.

In fact, Abu Sufyan wanted to renew the covenant between him and the Muslims in order to cover up the Quraysh massacre, but he did not succeed.

When the Messenger of God got up at night to perform ablution, his wife Maimunah heard him say during his ablution, "At your service, at your service, at your service, you will be victorious, you will be victorious, you will be victorious." She said: "O Messenger of God, I heard you say during your ablution: At your service, at your service - three times. You will be victorious - three times - as if you were talking to someone. Was someone with you?" He replied, "That was Amr bin Salem, who asked for my help. He claims that the Quraysh supported Bakr bin Wael against them." Amr bin Salem al-Khuza'i traveled with forty horsemen from Khuza'a to the Messenger of God to tell him about the events and to ask for help. The Messenger of God was sitting in the mosque among the people, and Amr bin Salem was the head of the Khuza'a. After they finished their conversation, Amr bin Salem stood up and recited, "O Lord, I appeal to Muhammad with the old covenant of our father and his father. "⁴³¹ The Messenger of God replied with tears in his eyes, "It is enough for you, O Amr." The Messenger of God was very angry about what had happened to the Banu Ka'ab² . He said: "May God not help me if I do not help the Banu Ka'ab." Then he continued: "By the one in whose hand my soul is, I will protect them from what I protect myself, my family and my house from." Just as he finished, a cloud came and thundered. The Messenger of God said: "This cloud heralds the victory of Banu Ka'ab." Then he turned to Amr bin Salem and his companions and said: "Go back and disperse in the valleys." Then the Messenger of God asked, "Whom do you accuse?" They replied, "The Banu Bakr." He asked, "Are they all Banu Bakr?" They replied, "No, only Banu Nafatha, and the head of the people is Nawfal bin Muawiyah al-Nafathi." The

---

1 Abu Hanzala is another name for Sakhr ibn Harb ibn Umayyah ibn Abd Shams. He is also known as Abu Sufyan and Abu Hanzala, named after his son Hanzala.
2 Part of the Khuz'a tribe.

Prophet said: "This is a part of Banu Bakr, and I will send someone to them in Mecca to ask them about this matter and offer them three options."

The three options were; to pay the blood money for the killed Khuza'a, to break the alliance with the Banu Nafatha or the Prophet breaks the treaty with them himself.

Abu Sufyan returned late and his absence lasted a long time. Therefore, he was accused of treason by Quraysh that he was an apostate of their religion who secretly followed Islam and concealed his conversion.

At night he came to his wife Hind. Hind said: "You were late until your people accused you of embracing Islam, and if you brought them good news with this delay, then you are the man." He approached her and sat next to her. She asked, "What did you do?" He told her what had happened and said: "I didn't bring anything except what Ali told me." She hit him on the chest with her leg and said: "You are a failed messenger of the people and have brought nothing good." In the morning, Abu Sufyan shaved his head at Asaf and Naila[1] and slaughtered a sacrificial animal for them. This was to absolve him of the accusation and prove to the Quraysh that he still stood by his religion.

When the Quraysh saw him, they came to him and said: "What do you have with you? Have you come with a letter from Muhammad or with an increase in the deadline to protect us from an invasion by Muhammad?" He said: "By God, he refused. When things got tighter for me, Ali told me, 'You are the master of Banu Kinana, ask the people in public for safety,' so I called for safety. By God, I don't know if that did anything for me or not. And Muhammad said to me, 'You say that, O Abu Hanzala. He said nothing else." They said: "You have settled without satisfaction and brought something that is of no use to either of us. By God, it will not bring us safety, and when you asked them for help, it was humiliating. Ali has brought us nothing but that he played with you." He said: "By God, I have found nothing else."

When Damra, the messenger of Prophet Muhammad, came to Mecca, he bent his camel at the door of the mosque, entered when the Quraysh met, told them that he was the messenger of the Messenger of God and told them what the Messenger of God commanded him to do.

---

1 Asaf and Naila are two idols that were erected at the Kaaba in pre-Islamic times.

Qurza bin Abd Amr Al-Ama said: "The Banu Nafatha have committed many killings against them. Therefore, we will not pay the blood money for the dead, otherwise we will have no more money. As for rejecting the alliance with Banu Nafatha, there is no Arab tribe that performs the pilgrimage to this house more reverently than the Nafatha. And they are our allies. That is why we will not break their alliance so as not to lose our trade and our money. But my opinion is to break the alliance with Muhammad." With this decision, the Messenger returned to the Prophet and told him the news. [432]

The conquest of Mecca

Shortly after the departure of Abu Sufyan, the Prophet decided to move to Mecca. He did not react immediately so as not to give the impression that he was planning to move to Mecca, as this might spoil the surprise. He said to Aisha, "Prepare us and keep our affairs secret." "O God, let them see us suddenly and hear about us suddenly by closing their eyes and ears," he said.

Abu Bakr came to Aisha as she was preparing some things of the Messenger of God and said: "Has the Messenger of God ordered you to prepare?" She said: "Yes, prepare yourself." He said: "Where do you see him going?" She said: "By God, I don't know." He said: "It is not the time to attack Banu Al-Asfar[1], where is he going?" She said: "I don't know." He went to the Messenger of God and asked, "O Messenger of God, do you want to travel?" Messenger of God said: "Yes." Abu Bakr said: "Shall I prepare myself?" Messenger of God said: "Yes." Abu Bakr said: "Where do you want to go, O Messenger of God?" Messenger of God said: "To the Quraysh. Keep it a secret, Abu Bakr." Abu Bakr said: "O Messenger of God, isn't there no treaty between you and them?" Messenger of God said: "They have committed treason. Haven't you heard of what they did to Khuza'a? Keep what I have told you a secret."

The people did not know exactly where the Messenger of God was going. Some thought he was going to Levant, others thought he was going to Thaqif and still others thought he was going to Hawazin. The Prophet Muhammad ordered a group to camp in the mountain passes to prevent the news from leaving Medina. He also sent messengers to the inhabitants of the desert and the surrounding Muslim communities with the message: "Whoever believes in Al-

---

1   Banu Al-Asfar refers to the Romans.

lah and the Last Day should come to Medina in Ramadan." He sent messengers to every region to come to him. He invited the leaders of each group, Muslims and non-Muslims, to come to him and mobilized them to come to Medina. He did not explain to them the reason for this request or the purpose of their presence. He also sent a stealth force to the region of Batn Idam[1] to confuse the people and give them the impression that the Messenger of God was going to that region and not to Mecca.

Despite the Prophet's efforts to keep his plan of movement and his work strictly secret, and despite his recommendation to keep the news secret from the Quraysh, Hatib bin Abi Baltaa sent a letter to the Quraysh informing them of the Prophet's plan of attack. Hatib bin Abi Baltaa had converted to Islam and emigrated to Medina, but his children were still in Mecca.

To ensure that the letter reached the Quraysh safely, Hatib bin Abi Baltaa gave the letter to a woman and asked her to take it to Mecca in return for payment. He said to her: "Hide it as well as possible and do not take the usual route, as it will be guarded." She hid the letter in her veil and tied her hair ribbon to it. She took a different route to leave the city. The Quraysh feared that the Messenger of God would attack them. For this reason, they approached Hatib's family and asked them to get Hatib to ask for the latest news about Muhammad. The news of what Hatib had done reached the prophet Muhammad from God. The Prophet immediately called Ali to him and said to him, "Some of my companions wrote to the people of Mecca to inform them of our plan, and I had asked God to hide our news from Quraysh. A black-skinned woman has the letter and she has taken an unconventional path. Take your sword and follow her. Take the letter from her and let her go, and if she refuses, strike her on the neck." Then he summoned Al-Zubair bin Al-Awam and said to him, "Go with Ali bin Abi Talib in that direction."

They continued walking and took a different path, and they overtook the woman. Al-Zubair went ahead of her and asked her about the letter she had with her. Al-Zubair said: "O Abu Al-Hassan, I don't see any letter with her. Take us back to the Messenger of God and tell him of her innocence." Ali said to him: "The Messenger of God has informed me that she has a letter with her, and he has ordered me to take it from her. And you say: she has no letter with her?!" Then he drew his sword and approached her and said: "By God, if you

---

1 Batn Idam: is located between Dhi Khashab and Dhi Al-Marwah in the north of Medina, about 40 kilometers away.

don't take out the letter, I will expose you and then I will cut off your head." She said: "If it is to be, then turn your face, O son of Abi Talib, away from me." He did so. She took off her veil and took out the letter from a lock of hair. Ali took the letter and let her go and he took it to the Prophet. The Prophet ordered that it be called out, "The prayer will be performed together." The Muslims then gathered in the mosque until it was full.

The Prophet ascended the pulpit, took the letter in his hand and said: "O people, I had asked God to hide our news from the Quraysh, and one of you wrote to the people of Mecca to inform them of our news. Let the writer of the letter stand up, otherwise the revelation will expose him." No one stood up. The Messenger of God repeated his words again and said: "Let the writer of the letter stand up, otherwise the revelation will expose him." Hatib bin Abi Baltaa stood up, trembling like a palm tree on a stormy day, and said: "O Messenger of God, I have written the letter. I have no hypocrisy after my conversion to Islam. I have no doubts after my faith." The Prophet said to him, "Why did you write this letter?" He said: "O Messenger of God, I have a family in Mecca, and I have no clan there. I feared that the Quraysh would prevail over us. Then my letter will be a reason to protect my family from them. I did not do this because I doubted the religion." Omar Ibn Al-Khattab stood up and said: "O Messenger of God, order me to kill him, for he is a hypocrite." The Messenger of God said: "He is from the people of Badr. Perhaps God has forgiven them after seeing them. Take him out of the mosque." The people pushed him from behind until they brought him out. As they did so, he looked back at the Prophet to seek his intercession. The Messenger of Allah ordered him to be sent back and said to him, "I have forgiven you and your deed. Seek forgiveness from your Lord and do not commit the same thing again."

Allah has forbidden the believers to make the enemies of Allah and their own enemies their protectors and not to make them friends and confidants or to treat them with love and reveal to them the secrets of the Muslims and their plans. This is because they have denied the Prophet who was sent to them and what came to them from the Quran sent down from their Lord. And how can a believer put together faith in God and His Messenger with affection for those who deny that. They expelled the Prophet and the Muslims from Mecca, and all this because of the Muslims' belief in Allah and what came from him.

Then Allah says: "O believers, if you went out from Mecca to fight for my faith and seek my satisfaction, then do not turn to my enemies and your enemies. Some of you secretly communicate to my enemy and your enemy their love for them, and Allah knows the apparent and the hidden and nothing is hidden from Him. Whoever of you shows his love to the unbelievers or makes them his allies has turned away from the straight and true path and has lost the right way. Know, O believers, that when they meet you in war or in peace, they will treat you as enemies and will show you no mercy or consideration, but their hands will strike you with violence and blows and killings, and their tongues will strike you with insults and humiliation, and they will wish you to disbelieve and return to what you used to be of idolatry. Know that the traitor who supports the enemy of Allah will not be helped by his family or his children on the Day of Resurrection, when matters will be decided and Allah will judge with His righteous judgment and give credit for what he has done. Every deed that man does is under the supervision of Allah, He knows it and observes its doers and will call all of them to account and give them their reward. And you had an example in the Prophet Abraham and those who believed with him, and how they faced the idolaters and they are an example to follow and you must follow their way, for they said to their idolaters that we should turn away from you as idolaters and from what you worship besides Allah, We have denied your faith and your religion, and there is enmity, hatred and aversion between us and you, you idolaters, and it will always remain so until you believe in Allah alone and stop worshipping idols, for they do no harm and do no good. [433]

The Messenger of Allah went out fasting on Wednesday after the afternoon prayer, on the tenth day of the month of Ramadan, and announced: "Whoever wishes to fast, let him fast, and whoever wishes to break his fast, let him break it." He placed a hundred horsemen at the front to be in front of the Muslims. When they were between the valley of Al-Arag and the well of Al-Tulob (see Figure 48), they intercepted a scout from Hawazin. The Messenger of God interrogated him. The scout said that Hawazin had gathered against him, and Thaqif supported them. They sent a messenger to Jerash - a place in Yemen - to seek help and make Al-Dababa[1] and catapults. The Prophet said: "Allah is our sufficient protector, and He is the best helper." Then the Messenger of God ordered Khaled bin Al-Walid to imprison him so that he would not go and warn the people. The people did not know where the Messenger of Allah

---

1 An "Al-Dababa" is a war machine that is made of wood and leather. The wood is made in the form of a large box in which the men stand in the middle and push it. It is covered with thick leathers to protect it from blows and fire. It approaches the fortresses and digs underneath, while the roof protects them. It is only used to attack fortresses and is not suitable for battlefields.

wanted to go, whether to the Quraysh or to the Hawazin or to the Thaqif. They wished to know. When the Messenger of Allah came down to Al-Arag, he was sitting with his companions and talking. Then Ka'ab ibn Malik said: "I will go to the Messenger of Allah and inform you where he wants to go." He came and sat next to the Messenger of God and recited a poem to him to make him reveal his destination. The Messenger of God smiled and said nothing. The people said: "By God, the Messenger of God has not revealed anything to you. We do not know whether he is going to the Quraysh or the Thaqif or the Hawazin.".

Then Uyaynah came to Prophet Muhammad and said: "O Messenger of God, I have heard of your departure and of those who will meet with you. I came quickly, and I could not gather my people, for we would have had a great commotion. I see no war uniforms, I see no troops and I see no banners. Do you want to do the Umrah. I see no Iḥrām clothes, Where are you going, O Messenger of Allah?" He said: "Wherever Allah wills." When the Prophet reached Qudaydah, Salim's tribe met him there. He organized the troops and the banners and distributed them to the tribes that were with him. Most of the tribes had gone out with him.

People from all the tribes joined him so that those who remained in the land would not be a threat. The Prophet knew the region and the tribes living in it very well. When Uyaynah saw the tribes taking the banners, he bit his fingertips. Abu Bakr said: "What do you regret?" He said: "To my people who fled with Muhammad. Where is Muhammad going, Abu Bakr?" He said: "Where Allah wills." On the way, one of the Muslims came to the Messenger of God and said to him, "O Messenger of God, do you like light-skinned women and white camels from Banu Mudlaj?" The Prophet said: "God did not allow me to do so because of their respect for their fathers and their observance of the rules of slaughtering camels." The Prophet was offered to attack Banu Mudlaj under strong temptation in two directions: one is the temptation of sex, because the women of Banu Mudlaj have fair skin. And the other is the temptation of money, because Banu Mudlaj has the most expensive camels; the white camels. But the Messenger of God rejected this because Islamic law does not allow attacking others arbitrarily and without regulation. As for the Banu Mudlaj, it is not permissible to attack them because they maintain their kinship ties, honor their parents and slaughter camels correctly according to their Sharia.

People were perplexed about where the Prophet of God wants to take them, and they did not know whether they were going to Mecca, Thaqif or Hawazin. This is because all these options require such a large gathering of fighters. Moreover, they are all in one area and in nearby places, and the way there from Medina is the same way that the Prophet took to Qudaydah. The Muslims continued on their way to Mecca without the Messenger of God publicly revealing to the Muslims the destination of the journey and their true goals. The news was also blinded from the Quraysh, and not a single word informed them of the path of the Messenger of God, and they did not know what he was doing. They then camped in Mar Al-Dhahran[1] for dinner in the company of ten thousand Muslims. The Prophet ordered his companions to light ten thousand fires.

In the meantime, Abu Sufyan bin Harb went for a walk to hear the news, accompanied by Hakim ibn Hizam. They met Badil bin Warqa and joined him. Together they went out to look for current events and to check if they saw anyone approaching or heard anything important. When they reached the bushes of Mar Al-Dhahran - and this was in the evening - they saw the soldiers, the domes and the flames. They looked like the fires of Arafat, and they heard the neighing of horses and the moaning of camels, and that made them very afraid. Badil bin Warqa said: "These are Banu Amr (Banu Khuza'a) who are going to the war." Abu Sufyan said: "Banu Amr are less than that, but maybe these are Tamim or Rabia." They said: "Does Hawazin want to go to our land. By God, we don't know, this military is like the pilgrimage of the people."

Al-Abbas had mounted the gray mule of the Messenger of God and left the camp. He recognized Abu Sufyan's voice and said: "Abu Hanzala?" Abu Sufyan also knew him and said: "Yes, Abu Al-Fadl, may my father and mother be sacrificed for you." Al-Abbas said: "Woe to you. This is the Messenger of God with ten thousand!" Abu Sufyan panicked and said: "O my God, by God, may my father and mother be sacrificed for you, what do you command me to do. Is there any trick?" He said: "Yes, ride on the back of this mule, and I will take you to the Messenger of God and ask him for safety for you. By God, if one of them were to catch you without the safety of the Messenger of God, he would kill you." Abu Sufyan said: "By God, I can see that too." Al-Abbas said to them, "Declare your Islam, for I will protect you among the Muslims until you reach the Messenger of God, for I fear that you will be killed without the safety of the Prophet." They said: "We are with you." Abu Sufyan rode behind Al-Abbas and he took them to the Messenger of God. Every time they passed by a fire from one of the Muslims, the Muslim said: 'Who is that?'", and when they saw the mule of the Messenger of God and Al-Abbas on it, they said: "This is the uncle of the Messenger of God on his mule," until they passed by the fire of Omar Ibn Al-Khattab. When Omar saw them, he stood up and said: "Who is this. Al-Abbas?" then he came and saw Abu Sufyan behind him and said: "O enemy of God. Praise be to God, who made you fall into our power without treaty or agreement."

They met at the door of the tent of the Messenger of God. Al-Abbas asked permission to enter: "O Messenger of Allah, Abu Sufyan bin Harb, Hakim ibn Hizam and Badil ibn Warqa, whom I have granted safety, wish to come to you." The Messenger of God said: "Bring them in." Omar followed him and said: "O Messenger of Allah, this is Abu Sufyan, whom Allah has put into our hands without treaty or covenant. Let me strike his neck." When Omar insisted on what he said: Al-Abbas said: "Wait, Omar, by God, if he were from the men of Banu Uday bin Ka'ab, you would not have said that, but you knew that he was from the men of Banu Abd Manaf." They stayed with him all night and the Prophet of Allah advised them and invited them to Islam. They said: "We bear witness that there is no god but Allah." The Messenger of Allah said: "Bear witness that there is no god but Allah and that I am the Messenger of Allah." Badil testified, and Hakim bin Hizam. But Abu Sufyan said: "I do not know, by God, but against this there is still something in the soul, postpone it." Then it was said to Hakim bin Hizam, "Swear allegiance to the Messenger of God."

Hakim said: "I swear allegiance to you standing and will not prostrate or bow down to you." The Messenger of God said: "From our side, we do not ask you to prostrate yourself, but you can swear allegiance standing up." Hakim believed that the Prophet was a king like all other kings in Persia and the Romans, and that people must submit or kneel to him as much as they can as soon as they see him to greet him. He wanted to distinguish something for himself, namely that when he saluted and swore allegiance to the Prophet, he did not prostrate or kneel down, but saluted him standing up. However, the Prophet's reply to Hakim has made it clear that there is no submission in Islamic law that amounts to bowing and prostration to the Messenger of God, as bowing and prostration are only for God.

It was also said to Abu Sufyan: "Pledge allegiance." He asked, "What do I do with al-Lāt and al-ʿUzzā?" Omar ibn al-Khattab said - while he was outside the tent - "fuck it. by God, if you had been outside the dome, you would not have said it." Abu Sufyan said: "Who is this?" They said: "Omar bin Al-Khat-tab. " Abu Sufyan said: "How obscene you are. O Omar, what troubles you with my words and the words of my cousin!" The Prophet said: "Be a Muslim, you will be safe. O Abu Sufyan." He said: "O Abu Al-Qasim[1], how generous you are. And how honorable you are." The Prophet said: "Be a Muslim, you will be safe." Abu Sufyan said again, "How generous you are. And how honor-able you are." Then the Messenger of God said: "O Al-Abbas, bring him to your tent, and when morning comes, bring him to me." Al-Abbas took him to his tent, and it was near the tent of the Messenger of God. As he sat in the tent, he regretted coming with al-Abbas and said to himself, "Who has done to him-self as I have done. I came and extended my hand, if I had gone to Mecca and gathered al-Ahabish and others, I would have defeated him." The Messenger of God heard what he said and called him out of his tent and said: "Then God will put you to shame."

When morning came, all the soldiers answered the call to prayer. Abu Su-fyan was startled by their call to prayer and said: "What are these people doing?" Al-Abbas said: "The prayer." Then Abu Sufyan saw the people crowd-ing around the water of ablution of the Messenger of God to seek blessings from him. Abu Sufyan said: "I have never seen a king like him, neither the king of Persia nor the emperor. O Abu Al-Fadl. By God, your nephew has become a mighty king!" Al-Abbas said: "It is not kingship, but it is prophethood." . He said: "Or that." When the Messenger of God finished, he said to him, "O Abu Sufyan, has not the time come for you to know that there is no god but Allah?" He said: "May my father and mother be sacrificed for you, how generous you are. And how great is your forgiveness. If there had been a god with Allah, he would have given me something on the day of Badr and the day of Uhud. I sought the help of my God, and you sought the help of your God. By God, ev-ery time I met you, you defeated me. If my God was right and yours was wrong, I would have defeated you."

Then the Prophet said: "Woe to you, Abu Sufyan, is it not time for you to realize that I am the Messenger of God?" He replied, "May my father and mother be sacrificed for you, how patient and generous you are, and how great is your forgiveness. But by God, there is still something in my heart that I can-not express." Then he returned to the tent, and after a while Al-Abbas came to the Prophet and said: "Abu Sufyan wants to come to you, O Messenger of God." The Prophet said: "Bring him." When he entered, the Prophet said: "Is it

---

1 Abu Al-Qasim is the Prophet Muhammad.

not time to become a Muslim?" Al-Abbas said to him, "Say it or he will kill you." He said: "I bear witness that there is no god but Allah and that you are the Messenger of God." The Prophet laughed and said: "Bring him back to you." Al-Abbas said: "Abu Sufyan loves honor, honor him." The Prophet said: "Whoever enters the house of Abu Sufyan is safe." He said: "My house will not suffice." Then he said: "Whoever enters the house of Hakeem bin Hizam is safe, and whoever enters the mosque is safe." Abu Sufyan said: "The mosque cannot accommodate everyone." The Prophet said: "And whoever closes his door is safe." Abu Sufyan said: "That would suffice."

The Prophet wanted to maintain respect for the sanctuary of God and the dignity of his house, for therein lies the protection of Islam. Therefore, he proclaimed protection for the people of Mecca so that not a drop of blood would be shed in the sanctuary of God. Although the Messenger of Allah granted this favor to Abu Sufyan and bestowed a certain honor on him, he took it away from him with the other hand in a discreet manner that made people realize immediately: it was only a formal procedure with no honor content. Not only did Abu Sufyan not receive what he wanted in terms of respect and glory, but he was also deprived of what he had taken unjustly. And this is because the Messenger equated entering the house of Abu Sufyan with entering the house of any person in Mecca. He even equated it with anyone who took a non-combatant position, thus degrading the position that Abu Sufyan had taken for himself and making him like any other person from Mecca.

Then Abu Sufyan and Hakim bin Hizam said: "O Messenger of God, you have brought the lowest people known and unknown to your family and clan." The Messenger of God replied, "You are unjust and immoral. You have broken the treaty of Hudaybiyah and shown your hostility towards the Banu Ka'ab in the sacred sanctuary of Allah." Hakim and Abu Sufyan said: "You are right, O Messenger of God. " Then they said: "O Messenger of God, endeavor to devise a plan against Hawazin, since they are not your relatives and they are the most hostile to you." The whisperings of Abu Sufyan and Hakim ibn Hizam to the Messenger of God against the Hawazin were not aimed at establishing the truth or spreading the religion. Rather, it was an unjust tribal argument, as they claimed that Hawazin were distant relatives and to harbor a particularly strong enmity towards him. The Messenger of God said: "I hope that my Lord will give me all this: The conquest of Mecca, the strengthening of Islam there, the defeat of the Hawazin and the conquest of their wealth and their progeny." [434]

More than twenty years have passed since the mission of the Messenger of God, of which the Prophet spent thirteen years in Mecca. During this time, he showed them the teachings of Islam, explained its doctrines and rules to the people and read the Quran to them. Yet they show in their actions and words what indicates a serious error in the basis of their view of him and his teachings. This is evident from the fact that what they see in Muhammad is kingship and not prophecy.

The Messenger of God would not force people to believe. But someone like Abu Sufyan, who commits the crime of fighting the truth, fighting Allah and His Messenger and killing the believers, can only escape a just punishment for his aggression if he abandons his stance. When Abu Sufyan got up to leave, the Messenger of God said to Al-Abbas, "Hold him in the valley until the soldiers of God pass by him." Al-Abbas caught up with him and imprisoned him. Abu Sufyan said: "Treason. O Banu Hashim?" Al-Abbas said: "The people of prophecy do not betray, but I need you on one thing." Abu Sufyan said: "Can you start with that?"

The Messenger of Allah gave a banner to Saad ibn Ubadah, who stood at the forefront of the battalion. As Saad passed by with the Messenger of Allah's banner, he called out to Abu Sufyan and said, "Today is the day of battle, today sanctity will be violated, today Allah will humble the Quraysh." When the Messenger of Allah passed by Abu Sufyan, he asked, "O Messenger of Allah, have you ordered the killing of your people?! Do you not know what Saad ibn Ubadah said?!" The Messenger of Allah inquired, "What did he say?" Abu Sufyan told him what has Saad said and said: "I implore you by Allah concerning your people. You are the most just, the most compassionate, and the most connected among people.

It appears that Saad ibn Ubadah uttered those words out of his fervent emotions, intending to intimidate Abu Sufyan. However, the Prophet was keen on maintaining peaceful movements to preserve Allah's sanctity. He responded, "Saad is lying, O Abu Sufyan. Today is the day of mercy, the day when Allah honors the Kaaba, the day when the Kaaba is covered, the day when Allah exalts the Quraysh." The Messenger of Allah then sent Ali ibn Abi Talib to Saad, instructing him, "Catch up to him, take the banner, and be the one to carry it into the city. Enter peacefully." Ali took the banner from Saad and added it to his own standard. Thus, he entered Mecca with two banners. The Prophet feared that Saads could be distressed or his mood might change, so he ordered it to be handed over to his son Qais. However, Saad worried that his son might act violently, so he requested the Messenger of Allah to take it back. At that moment, Zubair took it.

Taking the banner from Saad was not meant to humiliate him or diminish his status. It was taken from him to be given to someone more deserving—Ali ibn Abi Talib—to carry it peacefully into Mecca. This decision avoided any provocative or challenging situations and ensured that Qais ibn Saad would place it at Al-Hujun. Giving the banner to the son pleases the father and preserves his honor.[502]

The Muslims continued their march until they reached Dhu Tuwa. There they stopped and waited for the Messenger of God until the people gathered there. The Messenger of God came in his green brigade on his white camel "Qaswa", he humbly bowed his head before God and read Surah Al-Fath: In the name of Allah the most Gracious, the most Merciful {And We have bestowed upon you a clear victory, that Allah may forgive you of your sins, what was before and what will be after, and that He may complete His favor upon you and guide you to a straight path. }[435] The sin mentioned in the verse refers to what the polytheists regarded as his sin, namely his call to Islam and his rejection of the religion of the Quraysh and the wars against them and the killing of their men. But then came the conquest of Mecca, which broke their power and enabled them to enter the religion of God. Out of their own interest, they began to proclaim that they were wrong and he was right. Therefore, they forgave him his sins.

The day of the conquest of Mecca is the day on which injustice was removed and the day of declaring war on corruption and the oppressors, and it is the day of worshipping the Kaaba. The Messenger of God marched from Adhakhar and camped north of Mecca. He ordered Al-Zubair bin Al-Awam to enter one side of the highest point of Mecca from Kada' and to raise his banner in Al-Hujun and not to leave it until he comes to him. He also ordered Khaled bin Al-Walid to enter from the lower side of Mecca, from Al-Lait (see Figure 53). He ordered all his leaders to hold back their hands and attack only those who attack them.

"O Allah, the true life is the life of the Hereafter," said the Prophet as he entered Mecca. People expected to see the prestige of the king, the pride of the sultan and the appearance of determination, victory and strength in the Messenger of God, but they saw a different manifestation of servanthood to God and a marvelous image of submission and reverence to Him, so this victorious conqueror bowed his head in humility before God when the conquest of Mecca and the great number of Muslims saw. In this situation, the Prophet did not expect the support of the people before God, but stood alone before God. He pleaded with God alone, without a partner. He asked God to grant victory to him and those who were with him. He had no desire to win through them.

When Khaled bin Al-Walid entered as commanded by the Messenger of God, he found a group of polytheists preventing him from entering. They brandished their weapons and threw arrows at him, saying, "Do not enter by force." He shouted at his companions and fought them, killing twenty-four men of Quraysh and four of Hudhail. The rest escaped everywhere. A group of them made their way over the tops of the mountains, and the Muslims followed them. When the Messenger of God entered Mecca, he saw some of the polytheists fleeing from Khaled's army while carrying weapons and said: "What are these weapons. Did I not stop you from fighting?" The Messenger of God scolded Khaled and said to him, "You fought, and you were forbidden to fight!" Khaled said: "O Messenger of God, they are the ones who started fighting us and shot at us with arrows. I restrained myself as much as possible and called them to Islam and called them to join what the people have entered into. But they refused. Even if I had found nothing else to do but fight them, I had to fight them. God gave us victory over them and they fled in all directions." The Prophet said: "Stop chasing them.".

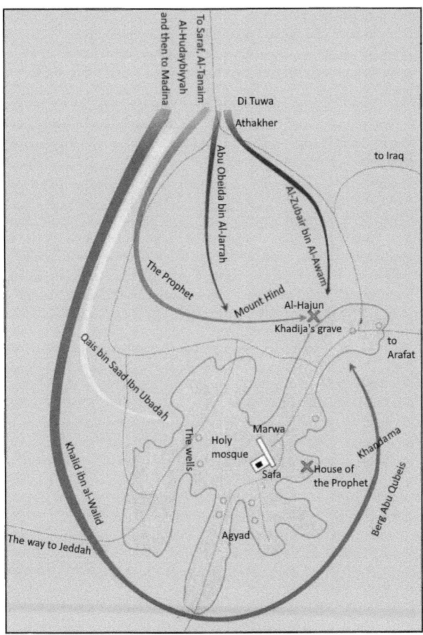

Figure 53: Plan of the Conquest of Mecca.

In fact, Khaled had killed many of them, even though there was no real resistance from their side, and had thus violated the Prophet's orders. A group of them even fled to the sea, into the mountains and towards Yemen, but Khaled continued their persecution until the Prophet ordered him to stop for the second time.

Abu Sufyan rushed and entered Mecca along with Hakim bin Hizam, both shouting loudly, "O people of Quraysh, this is Muhammad who has come with an unstoppable army that you are no match for. Whoever enters the house of Abu Sufyan is safe." Then Hind bint Utbah stood up, grabbed him by the moustache and said: "Kill the one with the fat belly and thin legs, who has no good, uglier than anyone in his community." The people of Mecca said: "Allah fight you, what good is your house to us." Abu Sufyan said: "Whoever enters his house is safe, whoever enters the mosque is safe, and whoever lays down his weapon is safe." Then the people dispersed to their houses and to the mosque and began to lock it and put their weapons on the paths for the Muslims to take.

Thousands of Muslims flocked to Mecca from all directions. Allah said: {And say, 'The truth has come, and falsehood has vanished. Indeed falsehood is bound to vanish.'} That is, say, O Muhammad: The truth has come, and it is Islam that carries the truth in its beliefs, judgments and laws. After the appearance of truth, no trace of falsehood remains. The false was dead from the beginning because it leads to death and carries death within it. Therefore, there is no survival for it, but its fate and its share is disappearance.[436] Thus Mecca was shaken by the words of the companions of the Messenger of God: {And say, 'The truth has come, and falsehood has vanished. Indeed falsehood is bound to vanish.'}

The Messenger of God pitched his tent in Al-Hajun in Wadi Abi Talib and refused to stay in one of the houses of Mecca. When he approached Adhakhar and saw the houses of Mecca, he stood up and thanked God and praised Him and looked at the position of its dome and said: "This is our home, O Jabir, where the Quraysh have conspired against us." Here Jabir remembered a speech he had heard from him earlier in Medina: "Our home, when God opens Mecca for us, is the hillside in front of Banu Kinana, where the disbelievers of the Quraysh have conspired against us." He then came to Umm Hani bint Abi

Talib[1] and said: "Do you have any food for us?" She replied, "I only have dry pieces of bread, and I am ashamed to give it to you." He said: "Bring them here." He broke them in water. She brought salt and he asked, "Is there any soup for dipping?" She replied, "I have nothing, O Messenger of God, only some vinegar." He said: "Bring it," then he poured it on the bread and ate it. Afterwards he thanked God and said: "Vinegar soup is good, Umm Hani. No house will be poor from soup dip if there is vinegar in the house."

The Messenger of Allah entered Mecca without Iḥrām and continued to carry his sword and helmet. Then he asked for his camel and went with the horses and set off with them. He reached the Kaaba and saw it with the Muslims. He touched the corner of the Kaaba with his stick and said the takbir. The Muslims said the takbir like him until Mecca shook. The Messenger of God signaled them to be silent while the polytheists on the mountains looked on. He circled the house and then went to the black stone, touched it. There were many idols around the Kaaba. He would point to one of the statues every time he passed by, poke it in the stomach or eye with his stick and say: {And say, 'The truth has come, and falsehood has vanished. Indeed falsehood is bound to vanish.'} The idols fell on their faces without being touched, and the people of Mecca said: "We have never seen a more magical man than Muhammad."

In this crowd was one who wanted to assassinate the Prophet by taking advantage of the large gathering of people around him. His name was Fadalah. As he approached him, the Messenger of God said: "Fadalah?" Fadalah replied, "Yes." The Prophet asked, "What were you thinking?" Fadalah replied, "Nothing, I was thinking about God." The Messenger of God laughed and then said: "Ask God for forgiveness." The Prophet then placed his hand on Fadalah's chest and reassured him.

After completing the circumambulation, the Prophet turned to Maqam Abraham and prayed two rak'ahs. He then came to the idols above the Kaaba and said: "O Ali, get on my shoulders and destroy the idols." Ali replied, "O Messenger of God, go up. You are more honorable than me, so I will not climb higher than you." The Prophet said: "You cannot bear the burden of prophethood, go up." Ali climbed up. The Messenger of God asked, "What do you see, Ali?" Ali replied, "I see that God has honored me with you. Even if I want to

---

1 Fakhta, daughter of Abu Talib, is also known by her nickname, with which she became famous, namely Umm Hani. She is the cousin of the Prophet and the sister of Ali ibn Abi Talib.

touch the sky, I would touch it." The Messenger of God said: "Blessed are you that you work for the truth, and blessed am I that I carry for the truth." He then took the idols from the Kaaba and threw them down.

After the circumambulation, he sent Bilal to Othman bin Talha to get the key of the Kaaba from him. Bilal came to Othman and said: "The Messenger of God commands you to give the key." His mother said: "No. By al-Lāt and al-ʿUzzā, I will never give it to you." This delayed Othman and the Messenger of God waited for him. He was sweating and asked, "What is stopping him? Let a man run to him and see what is stopping him." When they finally brought the key, the Messenger of God took it and opened the Kaaba. He called Omar Ibn Al-Khattab to him and said: "This is the fulfillment of my vision." It seems that Omar ibn al-Khattab still doubted the veracity of the vision of the Messenger of God, even though his vision was a revelation.

Then the Messenger of God returned to Othman and said: "Take the key forever, and no one will take it away from you except an oppressor. O Othman, God has entrusted his house to you, eat lawfully of what comes to you from this house." When Othman turned around, the Prophet called him back and said: "Wasn't that what I told you?" The Messenger of God mentioned what he had told him before the emigration (Hijrah) in Mecca: "Perhaps one day you will see this key in my hand, and I will put it wherever I want."

Figure 54: An imaginary representation of the Prophet preaching in front of the Kaaba.

Then the Messenger of God entered the Kaaba and proclaimed the praises of God in its corners and prayed two rak'ahs. He then ordered the removal of the images in the Kaaba. Then he opened the door and the people gathered around him, sitting around the Kaaba.

He said aloud, "There is no god but Allah, alone without partners. He has fulfilled His promise, made His servant victorious and defeated the parties(al-Ahzab) alone. O people of Quraysh, what do you say? What do you think I am doing to you?"

They said: "We say everything is good, and we think it is good. A generous prophet, a generous brother and a generous nephew, and the decision is yours." The Messenger of God said: "I say, as my brother Yusuf said: {No reproach shall come upon you today. Allah forgives you, for He is the Most Merciful of the merciful.} [437], Go, you are free[1]." The Messenger of God granted them the freedom to act like free people and did not enslave them as he does with slaves. Then the Messenger of God said: "God has taken away from you the fanaticism of the Jāhilīya, it's arrogance and it's pride in their fathers. You are all from Adam and Adam is from dust." He recited the verse: { O mankind, indeed We have created you from male and female and made you nations and tribes that you may know one another. Indeed, the most noble of you in the sight of Allah is the most righteous of you. Indeed, Allah is Knowing and all-aware.} [438]

Then he sat down and said: "O people, people are divided into two groups: a reverent, honorable believer and a wretched, mean unbeliever who is worthless in the sight of Allah. Indeed, Allah has made Mecca sacred since the creation of the heavens and the earth. It is therefore forbidden (No one may enter it with a weapon.) because it is Allah's sanctuary and it was not permissible for anyone before me and will not be permissible for anyone after me. It was only allowed to me for one hour a day, and it is forbidden until the Day of Resurrection." Then he began to counsel them and teach them the religious regulations until he said: "I speak these words and ask God's forgiveness for me and for you."

The Messenger of God went to the side of the mosque after his sermon and brought a bucket of zamzam water and washed his face with it. People hurried to seek blessings with the water of the Prophet's ablution. He sat in an area called Misfalah in Mecca so that the people there could pledge allegiance to Islam. Adults and children, men and women, came to him and swore allegiance to him on faith in God and the testimony that there is no god but Allah and that Muhammad is His servant and messenger. When he had finished with the men, the women began to swear allegiance to him, including Hind bint Utbah, the wife of Abu Sufyan, who was veiled and disguised out of fear. When she

---

1   Since then, they are called the Released (Al-Tulqaa in Arabic).

approached the Messenger of God, the Prophet said: "Swear allegiance that you will not associate anything with God." Hind then raised her head and said provocatively, "By God, you ask of us what you do not ask of men!" He said: "And don't steal." She replied, "By God, I had taken some money from Abu Sufyan, and I didn't know whether it was lawful or not." Abu Sufyan said - and he witnessed what she said - "What happened in the past, you are free from that, may God forgive you." Then the Prophet continued, "Do not commit adultery." Hind said: "O Messenger of God, does a free woman commit adultery?!" The Prophet continued, "And do not kill your children." Hind expressed doubt about what the Prophet said and said: "We raised them young and you killed them when they were old. You know best about them." Omar bin Alkhatab laughed and the Messenger of God smiled when she assumed that he had not recognized her. Then he said: "Do not bring forth slander that you invent between your hands and feet.[1]" She said: "By God, committing slander is ugly, and some forgiveness is better." Then he said: "Do not be disobedient in good.[2]" She said: "By God, we have not gathered with you to disobey you." Although this woman said hurtful words to the Prophet, he ignored her and did not comment on her words. He then asked for a Bucket of water. He put his hand in it and took it out again. He then said: "Dip your hands in this water, for this is the oath of allegiance."

He then climbed up the Safa until he saw the house. He raised his hands and began to praise God and pray to him. The Ansar were among him, and some of them said to each other, "The man has a longing for his city and pity for his clan." The revelation came, and the Messenger of God called out, "O Ansar." They said: "At your service, O Messenger of God." He said: "You said: 'The man has a longing for his city and pity for his clan.'" They said: "That is what we said: O Messenger of God." He said: "No, I am the servant of God and His Messenger. I have emigrated to God and to you. Life is your life and death is your death." They came to him weeping and said: "By God, O Messenger of God, we have not said what we said except that we wanted to keep God and His Messenger to ourselves out of avarice. "

The Messenger of God said: "God and His Messenger excuse you and believe you." Then the Prophet stood on Mount Safa and said: "O sons of Hashim, O sons of Abd al-Muttalib, I am the Messenger of God to you. I am

---

1 Meaning: Do not be disobedient to God, and in doing good for people.
2 This means that they committed adultery, then became pregnant and falsely attributed the pregnancy to their husbands.

concerned about you. Do not say: 'Muhammad is one of us. By God, my followers are neither you nor others, but the God-fearing. I will not recognize you if you come to me on the Day of Resurrection carrying the world on your shoulders while other people carry the Hereafter. Indeed, I have warned you and urged you to be cautious and left you no excuse in what lies between me and you and in what lies between God, the Exalted, and you. I have my work and you have your work." [439]

Punishment of the criminals

The Prophet Muhammad issued the sentence of retribution against some criminals and murderers. He said to the muslims: "Provide security for all people except these. Kill them even if you find them on the curtains of the Kaaba." The number of them was about twenty people, both men and women. The death sentence was imposed for their offenses, including murder, waging war against Allah and His Messenger, and inciting enmity against Muslims through words and deeds.

When these criminals learned of the sentences issued against them, some of them fled, while others turned to their relatives for protection and intercession. However, most of them returned to the Messenger of Allah, and since they became Muslims, he forgave them and granted them safety. This was because the crimes they committed, though atrocious, were on a personal level and could be transcended, and forgiveness was warranted for the sake of greater causes. Among them were:Wahshi ibn Harb, who killed Hamza, the Prophet's uncle, and then converted to Islam. He was forgiven.Abd al-'Uzzā ibn Khatal, who killed a follower of the Prophet and then apostatized from Islam, was executed for it.Muqays ibn Sababah, who also killed a follower of the Prophet, was executed for it.Hind bint Utbah, who gave the order to kill Hamza and ate his liver, converted to Islam and was forgiven.Zuhayr ibn Umayyah, the brother of Umm Salama, the Prophet's wife, converted to Islam and was forgiven.Hubaira bin Abi Wahb, the husband of Umm Hani, fled and died as an unbeliever.Safwan ibn Umayyah, who fought the Prophet and plotted to kill him, converted to Islam and was forgiven.

Ali learned that Umm Hani, the daughter of Abu Talib, was harboring some wanted people from Banu Makhzum, including Al-Harith bin Hisham and another man, to protect them from the rest of the fighters until they could come to the Messenger of God and he could judge them. Ali walked towards their house, armed with iron armor, and shouted, "Bring out those whom you harbor." They began to tremble before him. Umm Hani came out to him - she did not recognize him - and said: "O servant of God, I am Umm Hani, the cousin of the Messenger of God and the sister of Ali bin Abu Talib, leave my house." Ali replied, "Bring her out." She said: "By God, I will complain about you to the Messenger of God." Ali took off his helmet, she recognized him and said: "May I be sacrificed for you, I have sworn to complain about you to the Messenger of God." He said to her, "Go, fulfill your oath, for he is up in the valley."

She went to the Prophet, who was bathing in a tent, and Fatima was covering him. When the Messenger of God heard her words, he said: "Welcome, Umm Hani." She said: "May my parents be sacrificed for you, I complain to you about what I have witnessed from Ali today." She told him everything. The Messenger of God said: "I have given protection to those to whom you have given protection." Fatima said: "Have you come, Umm Hani, to complain about Ali because he frightened the enemies of God and the enemies of His Messenger?!" The Messenger of God said: "God has thanked Ali for his efforts, and I have given protection to those whom Umm Hani has given protection." Then the Messenger of God took a garment, wrapped himself in it, prayed eight rak'ahs.

The sentence was only carried out against four or five of criminals who had personally committed murders against Muslims. Abd al-'Uzzā ibn Khatal was executed because he had killed a Muslim from the Ansar, although he had previously been sent as a messenger by the Prophet. Abd al-'Uzzā had treacherously murdered him and stolen the money entrusted to him by the Prophet. Abd al-'Uzzā then fled to Mecca and tried to foment war against the Prophet with the help of two indecent singers. Although Abu Uzza held to the curtains of the Kaaba, the Prophet did not hesitate to exact just retribution on him. This punishment was part of respecting and cherishing the Kaaba by practicing justice and bringing criminals to justice.

Sufyan ibn Umayyah, Akrama ibn Abi Jahl, and those who were involved in the massacre of the Banu Khuzay'a fled when the Prophet conquered Mecca. However, they later returned as Muslims and the Prophet forgave them. Hind bint Utbah, who killed the Prophet Muhammad's cousin Hamza, came to him when he was on the ground of the shrine. She professed Islam and said: "Alhamdulillah (Praise be to Allah), Who has revealed the faith that He has chosen for Himself. Let your mercy touch me, O Muhammad. I am a woman who believes in God." Then she unveiled her face and said: "I am Hind bint Utbah." Prophet Muhammad replied, "Welcome." She said to him, "My husband Abu Sufyan is stingy and does not give me and my children enough to live on, except for what I have secretly taken from his property, of which he knows nothing." The Prophet Muhammad replied: "Take what is sufficient for you and your children, but act within the bounds of what is permissible (Ma'ruf)." [440]

After the conquest of Mecca

The Messenger of God appointed Itab bin Usayd as ruler of Mecca. Itab had just converted to Islam and was eighteen years old. Since Attab was from Quraysh and lived in Mecca, the elders of Quraysh were less envious of him and less sensitive towards him. Subsequently, the Messenger of God sent some companions to destroy the important idols in the region that were worshipped instead of Allah. Khaled bin Al-Walid was sent to destroy Al-Uzza, Amr bin Al-Aas to destroy Suwa, and Saad bin Zaid Al-Ashli to destroy Manat.

The Prophet of God then sent some brigades to the surrounding tribes of Mecca to call them to faith in Allah and His Messenger and to persuade them to abandon their worship of stones and idols. Some of them converted to Islam, while others remained hostile.

Among these tribes was Banu Jadhimah. The Prophet sent Khaled bin Al-Walid to them to call them to God. Khaled was not sent as a fighter. When the people saw him, they took up their weapons. Khaled asked, "What is going on?" They replied, "We are Muslims, we have prayed and we have built mosques in our courtyards. We called for prayer there." Khaled asked: "Why are you carrying these weapons?" They replied, "We have enmity with an Arab people, and we feared you might be them. That is why we took up arms." They said: "O Khaled, we have not taken up arms against Allah and His Messenger. We are Muslims. If the Messenger of Allah has sent you to collect alms, then these are our camels and sheep. Take them." Khaled replied, "Lay down your weapons." They said: "We fear that you might take revenge on us because of the disputes from the pre-Islamic era that Allah and His Messenger have wiped out." Khaled had a hostile relationship with them because they had killed his uncle in the pre-Islamic era. After they laid down their weapons, Khaled's companions turned away from them and they camped nearby. Khaled and his companions then attacked them, killing some and capturing others. He then ordered his soldiers: "You all have to execute your captives." They killed the prisoners. When they reached the Messenger of God and told him the news, the Prophet was shocked and said: "Was there no merciful man among you?!"

Khaled bin Al-Walid came to the Prophet. But the Prophet turned away from him and became angry with him for his actions towards Banu Jadhimah. Abd Al-Rahman bin Awf criticized Khaled for what he had done. He said: "O Khaled, did you act according to the pre-Islamic mentality? Did you kill them because of the death of your uncle Al-Fakih." Omar bin Al-Khattab supported him against Khaled. Khaled explained: "I killed them out of revenge because they killed your father." Abdul Rahman said: "You are lying, by God. I killed my father's murderer, and Othman bin Affan witnessed his killing." Then Abdul Rahman turned to Othman and said: "I ask you by God, did you know that I killed my father's murderer?" Othman said: "Yes, by God." Abd al-Rahman then said: "Woe to you, Khaled. If I had not killed my father's murderer, would you kill people who are Muslims because of my father?" Khaled asked, "Who told you that they had embraced Islam?" Abdul Rahman replied: "All the members of the brigade told us that you saw them. They have built mosques and embraced Islam. You attacked them with the sword." Kahled said: "The Messenger of the Messenger of God came to me to order me to attack them because they refused to accept Islam." Abdul Rahman replied, "You lied to the Messenger of God."

Then the Prophet called Ali and said: "O Ali, go to these people, see their condition and put the affairs of the Jāhilīya under your feet." Ali went to them, brought money that the Messenger of God had sent, and paid them the blood money for the dead as well as compensation for the loss of money and property. He even paid blood money for the dogs. He left nothing of blood or money that was not paid. Ali asked them when he had finished, "Do you have any money left that has not been paid?" They replied, "No." He said: "I'll give you some of this leftover money that neither we nor you know about, just to be on the safe side." He did so and returned to the Messenger of God to tell him the news. The Prophet said: "You have done well." Then the Messenger of God stood up, looked towards the direction of the prayer, raised his hands and in tears he said: "O God, I declare my innocence to you of what Khaled bin Al-Walid has done." He repeated this three times.

Khaled bin Al-Walid exonerated himself from retribution by claiming that he thought the Banu Jadhimah were infidels when he killed them. Thus the retribution fell away from him and he was only obliged to pay the blood money of those killed and compensate them for all that they had lost. The messenger of God stayed away from Khaled for a while, but Khaled kept trying to speak to him. He swore that he had not killed them out of revenge or enmity and that he had not heard them profess Islam. The Messenger of God was very sad about what Khaled bin Al-Walid had done. But he was relieved to know that Ali had judged them according to God's judgment and compensated them for their losses. The Messenger of God said to Ali: "What you have done is dearer to me than red camels." Ali had given Banu Jadhimah money so that they could rejoice as much as they were sad. Even if some money was left over, he gave it to them to calm the fears of their wives and children. He said to the Messenger of God, "I had some left over and I gave it to them so that they would be pleased with you, O Messenger of God."

Despite his sadness, the Messenger of God's joy at what he heard from Ali was great. He said to him, "O Ali, you have given them so that they may be pleased with me. May Allah be pleased with you. O Ali, you are to me what Aaron was to Moses, except that there will be no prophet after me." Then the Prophet said: "You are the leader of my nation. Happy is the one who loves you and follows your path. Unhappy is the one who denies you and turns away from your path until the Day of Resurrection." [441]

Battle of Hunayn

When the Messenger of God conquered Mecca, the nobles of Hawazin and Thaqif marched towards each other. They were tyrannical and combative. They feared that the Messenger of God would attack them. They decided to mobilize and said: "Muhammad is no longer busy elsewhere and there is nothing to keep him away from us. It seems better to us if we attack him before he attacks us." Hawazin made her decision, and Malik bin Awf bin Saad bin Rabi'a al-Nasri, who was thirty years old, gathered them - all the Thaqif, Nasr and all the Jashm, Saad bin Bakr and people from Banu Hilal. But Ka'ab and Kulab were not among them.

When Hawazin decided to fight against the Messenger of God, they asked Duraid to lead this war. Duraid bin Al-Samma, who was 120 years old and blind at the time, was an experienced old man known for his courage and chivalry. He said: "What is this? I am blind and can no longer ride a horse. But I will come with you and give you my opinion on the condition that you do not contradict me. If you do not accept my advice and oppose me, I will stay here and not go with you." They said: "We will not contradict you." Malik bin Awf came to him and the people gathered around him. They said to him, "We will follow your instructions."

Duraid said to Malik, "O Malik, you are fighting a noble man who has sub-jugated the Arabs. The non-Arabs and those in the Levant fear him. He ex-pelled the Jews from Hejaz, some of them were killed and some were expelled and humiliated. The day you meet Muhammad, you will have nothing like it." Malik said: "I hope that tomorrow you will see what makes you happy." Duraid said: "My house is where you can see it. So, when you gather the people, I will come to you." When he left, Malik concealed from him that he wanted to take children, women and money with him.

Their total number was thirty thousand, and they gave Malik ibn Awf the leadership. Malik's army marched with women and children until they reached Awtas, where they set up camp. Then people flocked from all directions to join the Hawazin army. Duraid bin Al-Samma arrived in a small howdah[1] that was guided by people due to his old age. When the Sheikh descended, he touched the ground with his hand and said: "Which valley are you in?" They replied, "In Awtas." He said: "Yes, it is an easy terrain for horses. It is neither steep nor soft ground. Why do I hear the crying of the little ones, the wailing of the camels, the neighing of the donkeys, the bleating of the sheep and the mooing of the cattle?" They said: "Malik has taken the children, the animals and the money." Duraid said: "He promised not to contradict me. He did not listen to me. I will go back to my family and leave this behind." Duraid was then asked, "Will you meet Malik and talk to him?" Malik was called to him and Duraid said: "O Ma-lik, you have become the leader of your people and this is a day to come and there will be no day like this. Why do I hear the crying of babies, the wailing of camels, the braying of donkeys, the bleating of sheep and the mooing of cows?" Malik said: "I have taken the children, livestock, the women and people's money with me." Duraid said in astonishment: "Why?" He replied, "I wanted to make sure that every man had his family and property behind him so that he

---

1 howdah is a platform or seat that is mounted on the back of an elephant, camel, or other large animals to transport people.

could fight for them." Duraid interrupted him and said to himself, "He's a fool, by God. He knows nothing about war!"

Duraid angrily slapped one hand on top of the other and said: "Can the defeated accomplish anything? If you want to win the battle, it will only benefit you if a man fights for you with his sword and spear. If you are going to lose, it will be a disaster for your family and property. O Malik, you have done nothing by leaving the women and children of Hawazin to the enemy's horses. Put the money, the women and the offspring away from the enemy and in the fortresses of your country. Face the people with your horses and let the men advance between the ranks of the horses or stand in front of the horses. If victory is yours, those behind you will catch up and follow, and if you lose, you have already secured your family and your property. " Malik bin Awf said: "By God, I will not do it, and I will not change my decision that I have made. You have grown old and your spirit is weak." He laughed at what Duraid was saying. Duraid became angry and said: "This is not the right opinion for you either, O people of Hawazin. He will hand over your women and children to the enemy. He will give your enemy the upper hand over you. And he will retreat to the fortress of the Thaqif and leave you. Turn away from him and leave him."

Malik drew his sword and fixed it in the ground, then he said in a loud voice: "O people of Hawazin. By God, obey me or I will lean on this sword until it comes out of my back." They came together and said: "By God, if we do not obey Malik, he will kill himself, and he is a young man, and we will stay with Duraid, who is an old man, and there will be no battle." They then agreed with Malik. Duraid saw that they did not agree with him. He asked, "O people of Hawazin, what have Ka'ab and Kulab done?" They replied, "They will not take part in the war." He said: "The wise men are not participating. If it had been a day of victory and honor, they would not have stayed behind. O people of Hawazin, turn back and do as they have done." They refused his request. Duraid said: "Which one of you will join the war?" They said: "Amr bin Amer and Awf bin Amer.[1]" He said: "These two tribes are from Banu Amer, their presence will neither benefit nor harm." Malik asked Duraid, "Is there any opinion other than this?" Duraid said: "Yes, if you lay an ambush, they will help you. If the people attack you, the ambush will come at them from behind, and you can then attack them from the front. And if the campaign is yours, none of the people will escape." Duraid said: "Who is at the head of Muhammad's

---

1   Awf bin Amer bin Rabia'a was one of the nobles of the Hawazin tribe. He and his brother Amr bin Amer participated in the Battle of Hunayn.

army?" They said: "Banu Salim." He said: "This is not a new habit for them. May my camel keep me away from the arrows of their horses." Then he stepped back.

In their war against the Messenger of God, Hawazin did not want to achieve right or wrong, and they did not want to defend a soul or freedom or dignity, nor did they want to defend human values. Rather, it was a war of disobedient and tyrannical aggressors.

When the Messenger of God heard the news of Hawazin, he reflected and did not hasten to make a decision to attack them, but sent Abdullah bin Abi Hadrad and ordered him to go among the people and stay with them, and he said: "Share with us their knowledge." Abdullah reached the tent of Malik bin Awf and found the chiefs of Hawazin there. He heard Malik say to his companions: "Muhammad had never fought against any people before this time. Rather, he faced ignorant people who had no idea of war, and triumphed over them. When dawn comes, line up your cattle and your women behind you, then line up. This is the first campaign for you. Break your sword pouches and attack together with twenty thousand swords, like a single man's attack. Know that the one who attacks first wins."

Abdullah went back to the Messenger of God and told him the news. The Messenger of God said to Omar Ibn Al-Khattab, "Do you not hear what Ibn Abi Hadrad says?" Omar said: "He lied." Ibn Abi Hadrad said: "By Allah, you accuse me of lying, O Omar, you have always lied about the truth." Omar said: "O Messenger of God, do you not hear what Ibn Abi Hadrad says?" The Messenger of God said to Omar, "You were misguided, then God guided you, and Ibn Abi Hadrad is honest." Then the Messenger of God gathered the tribes, encouraged them to jihad and promised them victory. He told them that Allah had promised them the property, wives and children of the enemy as booty. He prepared the army and borrowed armor and weapons from Safwan bin Umayyah and three thousand spears from his cousin Nawfal bin al-Harith.

The Messenger of God encouraged the people to go out and they went out with their banners. The main banner was given to Ali bin Abi Talib. In addition, whoever came to Mecca with a banner was to carry it. He then went out with twelve thousand men. The Messenger of God went to Hunayn at the beginning of the month of Shawwal, and with him the people of Mecca. None of them left him, neither horsemen nor soldiers. Even the women went out with him, who went with him without religious ties, to watch and hope for booty.

They had no objection to the attack being directed at the Messenger of God. The army marched with the Messenger of God until they held the prayer of noon in the afternoon. A man came in haste on his horse and said: "O Messenger of God, I have gone out before you and climbed a mountain. There are the Hawazin who have come with their children, their cattle and their wives. They have gathered together." The Messenger of God smiled and said: "Tomorrow, God willing, this will be the booty for the Muslims." He then turned to his companions and wanted to secure the camp for the next day's battle. He asked, "Who will guard us tonight?" It was Tuesday, the tenth day of the month of Shawwal.

Malik bin Awf had gone ahead of the Muslims and entered this valley at night into his army and dispersed them along the paths and entrances. He sent three spies to gather news about the Muslim army. But they returned quickly, frightened. He said: "Woe to you, what is the matter with you?!" They said: "We have seen white men on white horses. By God, we panicked and couldn't bear what we saw. By God, we are not fighting against the inhabitants of the earth, but only against the inhabitants of the heavens. And if you obey us, you will return with your people. For when people see what we have seen, what has happened to us will happen to them." He said: "Damn you, you are the most cowardly of the people in the army." He decided to lock them up as he was worried that terror would spread among the soldiers. He then said: "Show me a brave man." They unanimously agreed on one man, and this man also went out, but returned to Malik and was beset by what beset those before him. Malik said: "What did you see?" He said: "I saw white men on white horses. It was unbearable to look at them. By God, I did not hold on until what you see hit me." This did not deter Malik from his goal.

When the night was already two-thirds of its course, Malik bin Awf went to his companions and took them to Wadi Hunayn, a hollow valley with narrow reefs and paths. He dispersed the men there. He instructed them to carry out a single joint campaign against the Messenger of God and his companions. Malik bin Awf said to his people, "Let each of you put his family and money behind his back. And break the sheaths of your swords and ambush in the reefs of this valley and in the trees, and when it is in the dawn of the morning, conduct a joint campaign and destroy the people, for Muhammad did not meet anyone who knows how to fight." The Messenger of God prepared his companions, lined them up at dawn, distributed the banners, put on his armor and helmet. He rode his mule and circled the ranks of soldiers while encouraging them to fight and giving them the good news of victory if they are honest and patient. He placed Khaled bin Al-Walid in Banu Salim and the people of Mecca at the forefront and made the army a right, a left and a center in which was the Messenger of God. Malik bin Awf, on the other hand, placed the horses first, then the fighting men, then the women on camels, then the camels, then the cows. Then he said to the people: "If you see me advancing to attack, then advance with me in a group attack."

When the Muslims saw themselves, their gathering, their own equipment and weapons, they thought that they would not be defeated. They had not reached this number and level of equipment before. Abu Bakr was impressed by the abundance that day and said: "We will never be defeated today because our army is large." This made the Messenger of God dissatisfied with what Abu Bakr had said and he was hurt by this word. Just as al-Abbas was boasting about the abundance of soldiers, the Prophet stopped him and said: "Do you seek victory with the marauders of the people?!" They were impressed by their gathering and thought that large numbers were the criterion for victory, not divine support and trust in God. Therefore, God put them to shame and blamed them, declaring that they had relied on their abundance and thought it would be enough for them.

The Quraysh leaders in the Prophet Muhammad's army claimed to have converted to Islam, but in reality they remained firmly rooted in paganism. They were full of resentment against the Messenger of God. They plotted to overthrow the Muslims through an elaborate plan and then assassinate the Prophet Muhammad. Therefore, they gathered on a hill on the side of the polytheists, including Abu Sufyan and his son Muawiyah, Safwan bin Umayyah and Hakim bin Hizam with Al-Nadhir bin Al-Harith[1]. They watched and waited to see who would be victorious so that they would attack the Muslims with the polytheists.

After the Muslims prayed the morning prayer and as soon as the light of the sun rose, Malik began his attack. When the Muslims and the infidels clashed, the front of the Muslim army suddenly escaped and the ranks were disorganized. Then the remaining ranks fled along with the front. Banu Salim conspired with the people of Mecca to defeat the Muslims and they sympathized with the Hawazin. They ran to the hills, and the Quraysh leaders fled the battle

---

1 Al-Nadhir bin Al-Harith: the brother of Al-Nazir, who was killed after the Battle of Badr.

with their soldiers. Abu Bashir al-Mazni al-Ansari saw them fleeing and said: "O Ansar, may my father and mother be sacrificed for you, are you turning away from the Messenger of God?!" The freedmen (Al-Tulqaa) of Mecca said to each other as they ran, "Abandon him, for this is the time!" They meant the Prophet. They withdrew from the front first, then the people followed. The Messenger of God took the right side and said loudly, "O people, come to me. People, come to me. I am the Messenger of Allah, I am Muhammad bin Abdullah!" Umm al-Harith Al-Ansariya held the reins of her husband's camel and said: "O Harith, are you leaving the Messenger of Allah alone?! Most of the people have left him!" And she did not leave his side. When Omar ibn Al-Khattab passed by her while he was fleeing from the battle, she said: "O Omar, what is this?!" He said: "God's order."

The Messenger of God shouted loudly, "O servant of God, I am the servant of God and His Messenger. O people, I am the servant of God and His Messenger." But they did not speak to him and did not return to him. Only a few believers remained with him, including Ali bin Abi Talib. In these difficult moments, God did not abandon His Prophet. He lowered the sakīna on his Messenger and on Ali and those who remained steadfast with them, and supported them with armies that no one but the disbelievers could see.

The non-Muslims of Quraysh, who were on the hill, took advantage of the confusion and collapse of the Muslim forces, while the Prophet was supported by only a few. They dispatched Al-Nadhir bin Al-Harith ibn Alaqah to take advantage of this situation, overpower the Prophet in a moment of carelessness and assassinate him. Al-Nadhir went to him and saw him on a gray mule surrounded by men with bright faces. He walked straight towards him and they called out to him in a loud and rough voice: "Go away!" Al-Nadhir was terrified, his limbs trembled and he backed away fearfully, unable to do anything.

In the meantime, a group of Quraysh who were part of the Islamic army gathered and made fun of the Prophet Muhammad while rejoicing at his defeat or possible death. Abu Sufyan bin Harb, while watching and carrying lottery sticks (Azlam[1]) in his quiver, said: "The Muslims will be defeated before they reach the sea." Jabala ibn al-Hanbal exclaimed, "Today is the day, the magic ends." Safwan said to him, "Shut up, may God break your teeth. By God, I prefer that a man from Quraysh be my leader, rather than a man from Hawazin. "

---

1 The "Azlam" are small arrows that people used in the time of Jahiliyya to determine fate.

A Quraysh man passed by Safwan bin Umayyah and said: "Rejoice at the defeat of Muhammad and his companions. By God, they will never recover from this." Safwan angrily replied to him, "Are you rejoicing over the Bedouin winning. By God, I prefer the leadership of a Quraysh man to that of a Bedouin man."

The defeat worsened so much that almost the entire Muslim army was forced to flee, except for a small number of them. Prophet Muhammad rode his gray mule and raised his hand to the sky and said: "O Allah, thanks be to You and to You is my scream. You are my support." Then Gabriel came and said: "O Prophet of God, you prayed as Moses prayed when the sea was parted for him and he was saved from Pharaoh." When the Messenger of God saw the defeat of his people, he said to Al-Abbas, "Call the people and remind them of the covenant." Al-Abbas called out in a loud voice: "O people of the pledge of allegiance of Al-Shajarah[1], O people of Surah Al-Baqarah, where are you fleeing to? Remember the covenant you promised to the Messenger of God." However, the people kept running away.

The Messenger of Allah began to run towards the disbelievers with his mule, while Al-Abbas held the bridle of the Messenger of Allah's mule to prevent it from running too fast, and the Messenger of Allah did not care if he ran towards them too fast. He repeated, "I am the Prophet and I do not lie. I am the son of Abdul Muttalib."

Figure 55: An image depicting the attack of the polytheists on the Prophet in the Battle of Hunayn.

1   The oath of allegiance of Al-Shajarah is the oath of allegiance of Al-Ridwan.

Abu Sufyan bin Al-Harith took the stirrup from the Messenger of God. Then the Messenger of God said to Abu Sufyan bin Al-Harith, "Give me a handful of pebbles." He gave it to him and the Prophet threw it in the faces of the polytheists and said: "May the faces be disfigured." The Prophet raised his head to the sky and said: "O God, if this group perishes, you will not be worshipped, and if you do not want to be worshipped, then you will not be worshipped." He raised his hands to God in supplication and said: "O God, I beseech you for what you have promised me. O God, they should not overpower us." There were only ten people left with the Prophet: nine were from Banu Hashim and the tenth was Ayman bin Umm Ayman. Ayman was killed. The nine Hashemites held out, and they were Ali bin Abi Talib in front of him, who struck with the sword, and Al-Abbas bin Abdul Muttalib, on the right of the Messenger of God. Al-Fadl bin Al-Abbas is on his left. And Abu Sufyan bin Al-Harith is holding the stirrup of his mule. And Nawfal bin Al-Harith, Rabia bin Al-Harith, Abdullah bin Al-Zubair bin Abdul Muttalib, Utbah and Mu'tab, the sons of Abu Lahab, around him.

The Prophet and the few who were with him stood firm and fought against the unbelievers. At this moment, Shaybah bin Rabi'ah sneaks up from behind to kill the Prophet Muhammad as revenge for his father and uncle in the Battle of Badr. He approached him from behind and raised his sword to strike. But suddenly he was seized by a tremor and could not bear it. Out of fear, he retreated and told them that he could not hit him because Muhammad was immune.

This was their condition until the day passed and night fell upon them. The Messenger of God was in the valley. And the polytheists came out to him from the paths of the valley and had drawn their swords, their spears and their bows.

The Messenger of Allah looked at the people on the hills in the darkness, and his face lit up for them as if it were the full moon. Then he called out to the Muslims in a loud voice, "Where is that which you promised Allah?" Everyone heard him, and some of them descended from the hill where they were.

The progress of the Hawazin army was clear. With the retreat of thousands of Muslims, the chance of victory against the unbelievers diminished. But the few believers represented by the Messenger of God and Ali bin Abi Talib did not lose hope in Allah and His promise of victory for Islam and the Muslims.

They remained steadfast against the unbelievers. Ali bin Abi Talib went to the enemy army and rushed to their standard-bearer Abu Jarul, who was riding a red camel in front of Hawazin. He struck the camel on the hips. The camel fell on its hind legs. Ali jumped on the man and killed him. Al-Abbas turned around and did not see Ali bin Abi Talib among those who remained around the Prophet. He said: "Damn! In such a situation, Ibn Abi Talib prefers himself to the Messenger of God. And he is famous in wars!" His son al-Fadl said: "Don't say that about your nephew, O father." He said: "What do you mean, Fadl?" Al-Fadl said: "Don't you see him in the forefront. Do you not see him in the midst of the enemy masses?" He said: "Show him to me, son." He said: "He is the one with the scarf." Al-Abbas said: "and what are these sparks?!" Al-Fadl said: "That's his sword. He cuts the warriors with it." Al-Abbas said: "Right-eous! Son of Righteous!, may his uncle be sacrificed for him!" On that day, Ali killed forty swordsmen. He cleaved them all, and his blows were innovative.

Figure 56: A symbolic representation of the attack by Ali ibn Abi Talib on the army of the polytheists in Hunayn.

The death of the standard-bearer and the fall of the flag from his hand disrupted the movement of the army and caused great loss and frustration to many of its members. This could lead to an actual defeat. When the soldiers of Malik drove the Muslims to flee, they encountered the owner of a mule. It was the Messenger of Allah. Between him and them were men with bright, beautiful faces on white horses. They called out to them in a threatening tone: "Hey you, turn back!" And so they turned back in fear.

Then the Messenger of God took pebbles and dust, threw them in the faces of the unbelievers and said: "Be defeated. By Allah, the Lord of Muhammad!" As soon as he did this and hit them, their eyes and mouths were filled with dust and they became weakened and disoriented. They heard a clanging from the sky, similar to the sound of iron. The people were defeated, and Allah killed some of them, while those who were defeated fled. Allah rewarded His Messenger by granting them their property, their wives and their children.

The Ansar were encouraged when they heard the call of Al-Abbas. they came down, brandishing their swords, saying, "At your service." They passed by the Messenger of God and were ashamed to return to him. They caught up the flag. The Prophet asked Al-Abbas ibn Abd al-Muttalib, "Who are they, Abu Al-Fadl?" He said: "O Messenger of God, they are the Ansar." The Messenger of God said proudly and joyfully, "Now the battle has reached its climax." Then he turned to the right and said: "O Ansar, I am the servant of God and His Messenger." They said: "At your service, O Messenger of God, we are with you." Then he turned to the left and said: "O Ansar, I am the servant of God and His Messenger." They replied, "To you, O Messenger of God, we are with you."

He said: "O Ansar of Allah and Ansar of His Messenger, O Banu al-Khazraj." He ordered Al-Abbas ibn Abd al-Muttalib to tell this to the people on the mountain. When they heard about the return of the Muslims, they hurried to him. A hundred of them gathered, stood in front of the enemy army and fought against them. They said: "O Banu Abd al-Rahman, O Banu Abd Allah, O Banu Ubaidullah, O horses of Allah." The Messenger of God called his horses the horses of Allah, while the emblem of the Muhajirun was Banu Abd al-Rahman and the emblem of the Aws was Banu Ubaid Allah and the emblem of the Khazraj was Banu Abdullah.

When they returned from the mountains, they found the captives bound around the Messenger of Allah without having shot arrows, thrown spears or fought with swords. But they were furious with the polytheists and killed them until the killing reached the descendants of the polytheists. The Messenger of God was informed of this and he said: "What is the matter with people whose killing has reached the extent that it affects the offspring?! Do not kill the descendants, do not kill the descendants!" he said three times. Usaid bin Al-Hu-

dair said: "O Messenger of God, are they not the children of the polytheists?"
The Messenger of God said: "Every soul is born with an innate nature, until its
tongue expresses itself, then its parents make it a Jew or a Christian."

Safwan sent a boy of his to check the battlefield and inform the unbelievers
of the Quraysh who were on the hill about the outcome of the battle. He said:
"Listen, what emblem is being proclaimed?" The boy went down and then came to him and said: "I heard them saying, O Banu Abd al-Rahman, O Banu
Ubaidullah, O Banu Abdullah." Safwan said: "Muhammad won!"

A group of muslims at the beginning of the battle, acted so quickly that they
reached Mecca. and told the people of Mecca about the defeat of the Messenger of God. One of them said: "The Arabs will return to the religions of their
fathers, and Muhammad has been killed. His companions have dispersed." Etab
bin Usayd said: "Even if Muhammad is killed, the religion of Allah will remain.
That which Muhammad worships lives and does not die." In the evening of the
same day, the news arrived: "The Messenger of God has defeated Hawazin."
Etab bin Usayd and Muadh bin Jabal rejoiced.

Many people in Mecca converted to Islam, but not out of obedience to what
governed their thoughts out of love for the truth. Rather, their conversion to
Islam was a submission to violence and a reaction to their temptations, as they
saw the victory of Allah, His Messenger, and how Allah supported His Messenger and strengthened his religion. They believed that such events affected them
and that they had to benefit from them in order to gain advantages and wealth.
Allah reminded the Muslims of his favors for them. He said: "Allah has supported you in many situations where there were battles; such as Badr, Uhud and
the Battle of the Trench. But on the day of Hunayn, you were deceived by your
strength and numbers and said: 'We will not be defeated today because of small
numbers,' and you relied on the obvious reasons, forgetting Allah and His
power. But that multitude fell and did not achieve victory or avert defeat. In
fact, in defeat, the world felt narrow to you despite its vastness, because of the
intense fear and panic. Then, after that state, you returned defeated, you suffered a great failure. Then Allah sent down upon His Messenger and the believers sakīna and serenity and mercy and stability of the soul, and also sent down
forces that you did not see - and the polytheists saw them and were afraid and
terror entered their hearts, so they were defeated - and then things turned back
in favor of the Muslims and you were victorious and Allah punished the disbelievers with killing and imprisonment and that is the punishment of the disbe-

lievers because of their disbelief and their ingratitude and their distance from Allah. [442]

Malik bin Awf and some of his nobles of Hawazin fled until they reached the fortress of Taif. The Muslims continued their search for polytheists. The polytheists were very frightened. Some of them who were in the fortress of Taif even believed that the Muslims were on their trail and entered the fortress. A man came to Duraid bin Al-Samma and killed him. The Messenger of God heard about this and said: "May he go into the fire. What a miserable fate for a leader of disbelief. If he does not help with his hand, he will help with his opinion." The companions of the Messenger of God passed by a woman who had been killed and wounded at the front. They stopped and stared at her in amazement until the Messenger of God reached them on his camel and they made way for him. The Messenger of God stood there and said: "This woman was not meant to fight." He said to one of them, "Go to Khaled and tell him, 'Do not kill the descendants and the slaves.'"

Hudhail tribe had sent Ibn al-Akwa' before the Hunayn War to spy on the Prophet to find out his knowledge and he would come to Hudhail with his news. But he was captured on the day of the Hunayn. Omar bin Al-Khattab saw him and turned to a man from the Ansar and said: "This is the enemy of God who spied on us. And now he has become a prisoner. Kill him." The Ansari then struck him in the neck. This reached the Prophet and he was disturbed by what happened and said: "Did I not command you not to kill a prisoner?" Similarly, Jamil bin Muammar bin Zuhair was killed when he was a prisoner. The Prophet sent angrily to the Ansar and said: "What made you kill him when the Messenger came to you with the command: Do not kill a captive?" They said: "We killed him because Omar told us to." The Messenger of God turned away until Umair bin Wahb spoke to him to forgive him for this.

It is astonishing and regrettable that the Messenger of Allah forbade the killing of prisoners, children and women, but Omar ibn al-Khattab and Khaled ibn al-Walid disobeyed the Prophet's command. Did Omar take pleasure in killing prisoners? And where was his bravery in the battles when the Prophet alone called the defeated. [443]

After Taif

Awtas (Autas) is a valley in Hawazin and a place near Mount Hunayn in the direction of Taif. The Hawazin and Thaqif camped there first, then they and the Muslims encountered Hunayn. The Muslims fled first and then returned after divine support arrived.

The Prophet did not change the distribution of the soldiers he started from Mecca. He kept Khaled at his front, which consisted of the people of Mecca and Banu Salim, and they were a thousand men.

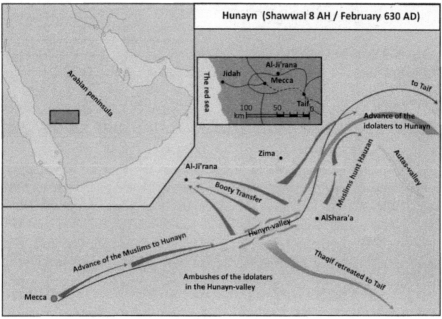

Abbildung 57: Schematische Darstellung der Schlacht von Hunayn.

The Prophet Muhammad did not change the formation of the army so as not to give the Muslims the impression that the presence of the people of Mecca in the Muslim army was a kind of flattery to the leaders of Mecca and did not stem from their personal conviction. It was to avoid that their withdrawal from their positions would cause people to doubt the faith or develop fears that would prevent them from thinking about entering Islam. Therefore, it was necessary for the war to end and for the people of Mecca to remain in their places.

At the end of the battle, Prophet Muhammad sent Abu Amer al-Ashari along with Abu Musa al-Ashari in a group of cavalrymen to disperse the remaining enemy groups and prevent them from reassembling and attacking the Muslim army.

The Messenger of God took a route called Al-Dayqa[1]. He asked for their name, and it was said: Al-Dayqa. He changed the name out of optimism and said: "No, it is called 'Easy'." Then the Prophet arrived in Taif. He set up camp there. He also built a mosque there and prayed in it. He had Umm Salama and Zainab bint Jahsh from his wives with him. He built two domes for them, and he prayed in the two domes during the siege of Taif. He sent Khaled bin Al-Walid to the fortress. When Khaled arrived at the fort, he shouted, "Who will fight a duel?" No one came out to him. He repeated the call twice and no one came down to him. One of the polytheists shouted, "No one will come down to you. We will stay in our fortress, and we have gathered in it what is enough for us for years. So, if you stay until this food is consumed, we will all come to you with our swords and fight to the last of us."

The Thaqif were guarding their fortress and preparing their weapons. They shot arrows and catapults from their fortress and threw red-hot pieces of iron at anyone who approached the fortress. They shot arrows at the Muslims fiercely so that some Muslims were injured and twelve men were killed. The Messenger of God fought them by also firing catapults at them. The siege lasted for forty days. The Messenger of God spread two rows of thistles around their fortress. The Muslims crawled under the Al-Dababa protection to the fortress wall to dig it out. But the Thaqif threw red-hot iron and set fire to the Al-Dababa, injuring some Muslims. The Muslims came out from under it and some of them were killed by spears and arrows from Thaqif. The Prophet also ordered their vines and date palms to be cut down and set on fire to put pressure on them and force them to surrender.

Jabir said to the Prophet while watching what was happening to his companions, "O Messenger of God, Thaqif has burned us with fire, pray to Allah against them." The Prophet replied, "O Allah, guide Thaqif rightly and bring them to us. " The Muslims' attempts to break through the fortress failed due to

---

1 Al-Dayqa means; difficult and narrowed.

the enemy's resistance. They complained to their leader about the difficulty of the task and asked him for help. Uyaynah ibn Hisn came to the Prophet and said: "Allow me to go to the fortress of Taif and talk to them." The Messenger of God gave him permission in the hope that he could convince them to submit to the Prophet's judgment and convert to Islam. Uyaynah approached them and asked, "If I come to you, will I be safe?." They said: "Yes." Abu Muhjan recognized him and said: "Come closer." So Uyaynah entered to them and said: "May my father and mother be sacrificed for you. By God, I was pleased with what I saw of you. There is no one among the Arabs except you. Do not give up and do not be affected by the cutting down of these trees. Muslims will not stay long. You have plenty to eat, and your water is plentiful. You need not be afraid that it will run out" When he left, Thaqif said to Abu Muhjan, "We regretted letting him in. We are afraid that he will tell Muhammad about a shortage in us or in our castle if he sees one." Abu Muhjan said: "I know him very well, and even if he is in Muhammad's army, no one is more hostile to Muhammad than him." .

Uyaynah returned to the Messenger of God and said: "I told them: Enter Islam, for by God, Muhammad will not leave your home until you come down. Ensure your safety!" I thwarted them as best I could. The Messenger of God said to him, "You lied, you said something other than that." A group of the companions admonished him. He said: "I ask God for forgiveness, and I repent, and I will never do the same thing again." These people still harbor idolatry in their hearts and wage war against the Prophet while flaunting false love and loyalty. All their endeavors and efforts were aimed at thwarting this religion and destroying it, which actually happened in the war of Hunayn and is still being repeated in Taif and elsewhere.

The Prophet did not give up and pursued various ways to persuade the enemy to surrender. He had his herald proclaim that any slave who leaves the fortress and comes to them will be free. Thereupon forty men descended from the Thaqif fortress to the Messenger of God, and this made it difficult for the people of Taif, and they were angry with their servants. The Messenger of God freed them. The Prophet distributed them to the Muslims. They embraced Islam, and the Messenger of God ordered the Muslims to read the Quran to them and teach them the Sunnah[1].

---

1 The Sunnah in Islam refers to the way of action, traditions, and exemplary behavior of the Prophet Muhammad.

The siege of the fortresses of Taif continued for a long time, about 40 nights, without the Muslims being able to break into them and open them, so the Muslims wondered whether it would be wise to continue the siege and stay. The men and women among the Muslims repeatedly turned to the Prophet to find out how long they would stay. In this context, Khawla bint Hakim al-Sulamiyyah came to the Messenger of God and said: "O Messenger of God, if God gives you victory over Taif, give me the jewelry of some of the women of Thaqif." He said to her, "And if we were not given permission in Thaqif, O Khawla?" When she had finished her conversation with the Prophet, she went out and met Omar ibn al-Khattab. She told him what the Prophet had just told her. Omar then went to the Prophet and asked, "O Messenger of God, what is this conversation that Khawla has told me about. She claims that you said it?" The Prophet said: "I said it." Omar asked, "Didn't permission come in their case?!" The Prophet replied, "No, we were not authorized to fight them." Omar asked in surprise, "How can we attack a people when God has not given us permission?!" Then he said: "Shall I ask the people to leave?" The messenger of God replied, "Yes." Omar then gave them permission to leave.

We do not know exactly who Omar ibn al-Khattab is objecting to! Is he contradicting God because he did not give permission to attack the people of Taif? Or does he contradict the Messenger of God because he brought the Muslims to a people whom God did not allow to fight against them? Despite the knowledge of all that the Prophet is infallible, is guided by revelations and acts only in accordance with the will of Allah, and he follows the orders given by Allah. The Prophet of Allah called for departure as soon as Ali returned from his campaigns, which the Prophet had sent to destroy the idols. When the Prophet saw Ali, he praised God for the victory and took him by the hand. He withdrew with him and talked to him for a long time. Then Omar ibn al-Khattab came to the prophet and said angrily, "Do you talk to him alone and withdraw with him without having us with you?" Abu Bakr expressed a similar opinion to Omar ibn al-Khattab. The Prophet then said: "Omar, I did not choose him for a conversation, but Allah chose him for a conversation. " Omar turned away and said angrily, "This is exactly what you told us before Hudaybiyah: {You will certainly enter the Sacred Mosque, God willing, in safety and without any fear,with your heads shaved and [hair] shortened} [444] We did not enter it, and we were prevented from doing so." The Prophet called out to him, "I did not say: you will enter it this year."

The Prophet then said to his companions as they were about to leave: "Say: There is no god but Allah alone, without partners. He fulfilled his promise, helped his servant, honored his soldiers and defeated the parties alone." When they set out, he told them to say, "We will return to God, God willing, repentant to our Lord, worshipping Him and praising Him."

The Messenger of God did not want to tell the people that the people of Taif had written to him to ask him to leave their fortress so that they would come to him as surrendering Muslims and thus save face. Therefore, he contented himself with saying, "He was not authorized to fight them." For if they had informed him of their intention to surrender, then God did not allow him to continue fighting them. Rather, the way was to be prepared for them to carry out what they had set out to do. When Thaqif converted to Islam, their leaders, including Al-Harith ibn Kalada, spoke about those who had been set free. They wanted to return them to slavery. In response, the Prophet said to them, "These are the freedmen of Allah, there is no way to return them."

The Prophet continued until he came to Mecca and a group of Muslims from Thaqif came to him. However, the people refused to obey him in the prayer and zakat. The Prophet was angry when he heard this and said: "O people, I am ahead of you[1] and your appointment is by the pond. I commend my family to you well. There is nothing good in a religion in which there is neither bowing nor prostration. By the one in whose hand my soul is, They should perform prayer and pay the zakat, otherwise I would send them a man who is like me. He would behead the fighters and take their descendants captive." The people saw that he meant Abu Bakr or Omar. He then took Ali's hand and said: "He is that man." The Prophet said: "Whenever the people of a kingdom or nation rebel against me, I shoot them with the arrow of Allah." They said: "O Messenger of God, what is Allah's arrow?" He replied, "Ali bin Abi Talib. Every time I saw him being dispatched in a brigade, I saw Gabriel on his right, Michael on his left and an angel in front of him. A cloud protected him until Allah, the Exalted, granted him victory and success." When the people of Taif reached their people, they told them what they had heard from the Messenger of Allah. They obeyed him in prayer and do what he had said. [445]

---

1 Meaning: "I am ahead of you and I will precede you in Paradise, and you will return to me at the pond on the Day of Resurrection."

Distribution of the booty

The captives and the booty of war were gathered in Al-Ji'rana (see Figure 57). Prophet Muhammad appointed a person in charge of distributing the booty and the captives on the day of Hunayn. The booty included four thousand knights, twelve thousand camels, and other booty that was not specified. Among the captives was al-Shayma bint al-Harith ibn Abd al-'Uzzā, the milk sister of the Messenger of God. She was led with the captives and was an old woman. She grew tired and began to say, "By God, I am the sister of your companion." But they did not believe her. A group of the Ansar took her and brought her to the Messenger of God. She said: "O Muhammad, I am your sister." The Messenger of God recognized her and stood up, spread his robe and said: "Sit on it," and welcomed her. His eyes filled with tears. He asked her about her mother and father, and she told him that they had passed away.

His sister al-Shayma spoke to him about Malik bin Awf. He said: "If he comes to me, he will be safe. I will give him back his family and his money and give him a hundred camels." He said: "If you want, stay with us as an honored lady, and if you want to return to your people, I will drive you and you will return to your people." She said: "I would rather return to my people." She converted to Islam. The Messenger of God gave her three slaves and a servant and ordered one or two camels for her and said to her, "Go back to Al-Ji'rana and you will be with your people, for I am going to Taif." She went there and the Prophet followed her later. He gave her camels and sheep and everyone who came from her household.

When Malik was informed of what the Messenger of God had done to his people and what the Messenger of God had promised about him, he met him in al-Ji'rana. The Messenger of God gave him back his family and his money and gave him a hundred camels. Malik accepted Islam, and said delightedly: "Among all the people I have ever seen,there was none like Muhammad, that is true.His word filled hearts with light, He was a role model,a man of weight. In war he stood ready like a lion, on guard,always vigilant. But in peace he was full of kindness and mercy,a prophet who taught us what counts in this world.".

The Prophet appointed him as his representative over his people, who had just converted to Islam, and over the tribes of Hawazin, Fahm, Salamah and Thamala. On the way to al-Ji'rana, Suraqa bin Jusham saw the Messenger of God and went towards him. The people walked in groups in front of him. He was standing among the horses of the Ansar. When they saw him, they frightened him with spears and said: "Go away. go away. who are you?" They didn't recognise him. When the Prophet saw him, he said: "This is a day of loyalty and righteousness, bring him closer. Bring him closer to me." The Messenger of God gave him the letter of safety. Suraqa had a special role during the Prophet's migration to Medina when he turned away those who sought the Prophet from Quraysh. He converted to Islam and asked, "O Messenger of God, do you see the lost camels that came to the water troughs that I filled for my camels. Will I get any reward from God if I water them?" The Messenger of God said: "Yes, there is a reward for every thirsty animal that you give water to drink."

The Messenger of God waited in al-Ji'rana for over ten nights for the Hawazin delegation to come to him before he started distributing the booty. When the Hawazin delegation caught up with the Messenger of God in al-Ji'rana and they had embraced Islam, they said: "O Messenger of God, we have a clan, and we have been afflicted by a calamity that is already known to you. So be kind to us from what Allah has bestowed on you."

The Messenger of Allah said: "With me is what you see, and the speech I love the most is the most truthful. You have two options, either slavery or money. For I have been waiting for you."

A preacher among them, Zuhair bin Sard, stood up and said: "O Messenger of God, if Al-Harith bin Abi Shamr or Al-Nu'man bin Al-Mundhir ruled over us as you are in power now, they would be merciful and sympathetic to us. But you are the best of those who have ruled. Now your aunts, your aunts' daughters, those who raised you and nursed you, are in the tents. We do not ask you for money, but we ask you to give us these women." And they said: "O Messenger of God, you have given us the choice between our families and our money. Therefore we say to you: We prefer our children and our wives. We are not talking about a sheep or a camel." The Messenger of Allah said: "What belongs to me and the sons of Abd al-Muttalib belongs to you. When I pray among the people, show your Islam and say, 'We are your brothers in faith and we ask for the intercession of the Prophet with the Muslims and ask for the intercession of the Muslims with the Messenger of Allah.' For I will grant you that and ask the people for you."

The Prophet had taught them the Tashahhud[1] and how they should speak to people. After he had performed the noon prayer with the people, they stood up and asked the Prophet for permission to speak, which he granted them. They then spoke well and asked the people to return their captives. When they finished, the Messenger of God stood up to support them. He praised God and said: "Your brothers have come to us repentant, and I have decided to return their captives to them. Whoever wants to do this favor, can do it, and whoever of you wants to keep his share so that we may compensate him for it from the first Fay'a booty when Allah provides us with some good, can do it." The men present agreed with him and said: "We will return our captivity, O Messenger of Allah. " The Messenger of God said to them, "We do not know which of you have been given permission and which have not, return until your matter is brought to us by your leaders." The people returned and spoke to the heads of their clans, and they told him, "They gave us permission." The Messenger of God said: "What is for me and for the sons of Abd al-Muttalib, it is for you." The Muhajirun said: "What is ours is for God and His Messenger." The Ansar said: "What belongs to us is for God and His Messenger." Al-Aqra' bin Habis said: "As for me and Banu Tamim, no." Uyaynah bin Hisn said: "As for me and Banu Fazara, no." Al-Abbas bin Mirdas said: "As for me and Banu Salim, no." Banu Salim said: "What belongs to us is for the Messenger of God." Al-Abbas bin Mirdas said: "You have weakened my opinion." The Messenger of God said: "Whoever of you clings to his right, we will give him six portions for each person from the first fay'a booty that God will grant us." So the Muslims re-turned the people to their wives and children, and none of them refused to re-turn those except Uyaynah bin Hisn, for he took an old woman and refused to return her, although neither Uyaynah nor anyone else had a right to those cap-tives. Rather, it should be for the Prophet. Since it was a "fay", it became the exclusive property of the Prophet. Nevertheless, the Prophet spoke to them as if they had a right to it, out of generosity and mercy.

---

1 The Tashahhud (Shahada) is a testimony of monotheism and the prophethood of Muhammad. The wording of the Tashahhud is: "I bear witness that there is no god but Allah and I bear witness that Muhammad is the Messenger of Allah" ['ašhadu 'ann llā 'ilāha 'illa'i Allah wa'ašhadu an muḥmdan rasūlu Allah]. For a person to become a Muslim, they must first pronounce the Shahada.

When the Messenger of God finished distributing the booty of war and brought back the captives of Hawazin, he rode on his camel. The people followed him and said: "O Messenger of God, give us our share in the booty." Until they forced him to a tree and took off his cloak. "O people, give me back my cloak. By the One in Whose hand is my soul, if I had the number of Tihama trees as booty, I would divide them among you. You did not take me for a miser or a liar," he said. Then the Messenger of God stood beside his camel, took a hair from its hump, put it between his two fingers and said: "O people, by God, I have nothing of your booty, not even this hair, except a fifth of it, and this fifth will be returned to you. Present what you have taken from the booty so that we may distribute it, and beware of treachery, for treachery is a disgrace on the Day of Resurrection." A man from the Ansar came with a bundle of hair threads and said: "O Messenger of God, I have taken these threads to make a cover for the back of my camel." The Messenger of God said: "As for my right to it, it is yours." The man said: "If the matter has gone this far, I don't need it." Then he threw it out of his hand.

A Bedouin came to the Prophet, pulled him tight, and said angrily, "Give me some of God's wealth that you have!" The Messenger of God turned to him laughing, then ordered a gift and a robe for him. The Prophet had distributed the booty, giving most of it to those from almu'lfa qalūbhm[1] from Quraysh and the rest of the Arabs. Each man of them received a hundred camels, giving nothing to the Ansar. Then a man came where they were gathered and greeted the people, but he did not greet the Prophet and said angrily, "O Muhammad, you have seen what you have done on this day?!" The Messenger of God said: "Yes, how did you see it?" He said: "You did not act fairly. Be just!" The Messenger of God became angry and said: "Woe to you. If justice is not with me, where would it be?!'" The Prophet continued angrily, "Don't you see that I divided all the sheeps until I had no more sheeps. Have I not divided the cows until there is not a single cow left with me? Have I not divided the camels until there is not a single camel left with me?" Omar Ibn Al-Khattab said: "O Messenger of God, let me kill this hypocrite." The Messenger of God said: "May Allah prevent people from saying that I would kill my companions. Leave him in peace, for he will have followers." The Prophet narrated, "This man and his companions recite the Quran, but it is not beyond their throats (not understanding and implementing the teachings). They only hold on to it superficially.

---

1 almu'lfa qalūbhm (those whose hearts need to be won): are those to whom alms were given by the hypocrites and weak Muslims to win their hearts to Islam, ward off evil from them, or strengthen their faith.

They abandon religion with heresy and misguidance as quickly as an arrow flies from a bow. They only appear at moments when people turn away from their unity. God will kill them at the hands of the Beloved of Creation after me."[1]

The distribution of the booty angered some of the Ansar, so there was much discussion and objection among them until one of them said: "May God forgive the Messenger of God. This is strange that he gives Quraysh and leaves us, and our swords are still dripping with their blood. We would like to know who it was from. If it is from the command of God, we will be patient, and if it is from the opinion of the Messenger of God, we reproach him."

A man from the Ansar said to his companions: "I have always told you that if things were settled, someone else would be preferred to you. You should confront him and discuss it with him fiercely." Saad bin Ubadah went to the Messenger of God and said: "O Messenger of God, this neighborhood has become angry with you." He said: "Why?" Saad said: "Because you distributed this booty among your people and among the rest of the Arabs and they had none of it." The Messenger of God said: "What do you think, Saad?" He said: "I am just one of my people." The Messenger of God then said to him, "Gather your people for me in this tent." He sent for the Ansar and gathered them without inviting anyone else. When there was no one left from the Ansar who had not gathered, Saad came to him and said: "O Prophet, this group of Ansar has gathered as you commanded me." Then the Prophet came, followed by Ali ibn Abi Talib, and sat in their midst. Then he said to them, "Sit down, and let no one but you sit with you." When they had sat down, the Prophet stood up and gave a speech. He praised God and glorified him. Then he said: "O Ansar, I ask you about one thing, answer me." They said: "Speak, O Messenger of God." He said: "Have you not gone astray and Allah has guided you through me?" They said: "Yes, thanks be to Allah and His Messenger." He said: "Were you not on the edge of a pit of fire and Allah saved you through me?" They said: "Yes, thanks be to Allah and His Messenger." He said: "Were you not few, and Allah has increased you through me?" They said: "Yes, thanks be to Allah and His Messenger." He said: "Were you not enemies, and Allah has reconciled your hearts through me?" They said: "Yes, thanks be to God and His Messenger."

Then the Prophet was silent for a while and then said: "Don't you tell me what is wrong with you?" They said: "How can we answer you. May our fathers

---

1 This prophecy was fulfilled more than thirty years after the death of the Prophet.

and mothers be sacrificed for you, we have answered you that you are the one who has done us a kindness and favor." The Messenger of Allah said: "Or if you had wished, you would have said: 'And you came to us in flight, and we sheltered you, and you came to us as rejected, and we helped you, and you came to us as denied, and we believed you!'." Thereupon they burst into tears and their elders and leaders stood before him and kissed his hands and feet and then said: "We are pleased with Allah and His Messenger, and this is our wealth in your hands. If you wish, distribute it among your people. Only those of us said this without hatred or malice in their hearts, but they thought that you were angry with them because of their negligence. And they asked God for forgiveness for their sins, ask forgiveness for them, O Messenger of God."

Figure 58: A depiction of Al-Ansar, crying and showing repentance in the presence of the Prophet.

The Prophet said: "The Quraysh have not long converted to Islam, and they are not far from the era of Jāhilīya. I wanted to encourage and win them. Have you, O community of the Ansar, neglected what Allah has entrusted to you because of the worldly wealth that I have used to support a recent convert to Islam? Would you not be satisfied, O community of the Ansar, that people go to their homes with sheep and camels and that you take the Messenger of Allah to your tents. And you keep him in your homes. By God, what you take is better than what they take." The people wept until their beards became wet, and they said: "We are pleased with God and His Messenger." The Prophet said: "The Ansar are my trust and my helpers. If the people had taken a valley and the Ansar had taken a valley, I would have taken the Ansar valley. O Allah, forgive the Ansar."

Unfortunately, the problem was not a fleeting matter that had arisen at the hands of ignorance and indiscretion of young men without experience. Rather, it was a conviction that took root in the minds of many wise people and their leaders, even Saad bin Ubadah, the leader of the Khazraj, let alone the rest of the people.

When they gathered their opinions and accused the Messenger of Allah, God lowered their light. And God laid down in the Quran a portion for those of Quraysh from almu'lfa qalūbhm. What was required of them was absolute devotion, even if the money belonged to them in reality. For the Prophet is more worthy of the believers than they themselves. Let alone that the money belonged to him in the first place. [446]

630 - 631 AD

The ninth year after the Hijrah

Campaigns and missions

The Prophet of God did not stop sending messengers and campaigns to call to God and to purify the Arabian Peninsula from manifestations of polytheism and backwardness. He sent Khaled bin Al-Walid with an army to the people of Yemen to invite them to Islam. Khaled took some captives after a battle and wrote to the Messenger of God, "Send us someone to take a fifth (al-Khum) of them." Among the captives was a maidservant who was one of the best captives. The Messenger of God sent Ali to Khaled to divide the booty, saying, "If there is a battle, Ali is the leader." Ali conquered some strongholds there. He divided up a fifth of the booty. He chose this captured woman for himself. Buraydah bin Al-Hasib said: "O Abu Al-Hassan, what is this. Have you not seen the maidservant who first belonged to the fifth, then became part of the family of Muhammad, and finally became part of the family of Ali?" Khaled wrote to the Messenger of God and wanted to tell him what Ali had done. Khaled summoned Buraydah and said: "O Buraydah, you know what Ali has done. go to the Messenger of God with my letter."

Buraydah walked until he reached the Prophet's door, and Omar met him and asked him about the status of the raid and why he had come now. He told him: He came to complain about Ali because Ali had chosen a servant from the fifth for himself. Omar said to him, "Go on with what you have come for. He will become angry for his daughter because of what Ali did." Buraydah visited the Prophet at his house, read the letter and told him what had happened. The Prophet's face changed. Buraydah said: "If you allow people to do such a thing, all their booty will disappear." Buraydah spoke to the Messenger of Allah about Ali and accused him of being unfair. When he finished, he lifted his head and saw that the Messenger of God became very angry. He saw such anger only on the day of Quraiza and al-Nadir. The Messenger of God said: "By the One in Whose hand is my soul, Ali's share of the fifth is better than this servant. If you love him, then increase your love for him." The Prophet held Buraydah's hand and said: "O Buraydah, do you hate Ali. O Buraydah, love Ali, for he does what I command him." Buraydah said: "I seek refuge in God from the wrath of God and the wrath of His Messenger. I am only a messenger."

After six months of intensive efforts by Khaled to convert people to Islam, no one from Yemen has responded to him. Khaled failed in the task entrusted to him by the Prophet. He was himself the obstacle that prevented people from converting to Islam. The Prophet ordered him to return, and he sent Ali bin Abi Talib in his place and told Ali: "Whoever of the companions of Khaled wants to join you can stay, and whoever wants to come back can come." Ali went with a group to Yemen, and when they approached the people, they came to meet them. Ali called them to Islam and advised them. Hamadan as a whole then converted to Islam. Ali read the letter of the Messenger of God to them, and later he wrote to the Messenger of God about their conversion to Islam. When the Messenger of God read the letter, he rejoiced greatly and prostrated himself, then raised his head and said: "Peace be upon Hamadan, peace be upon Hamadan." Then he said: "The best among the neighbors is Hamadan, how quickly she comes to victory."

In the month of Rabi' al-Akhir of the ninth year, the Messenger of Allah sent Ali bin Abi Talib with one hundred and fifty men from the Ansar on one hundred camels and fifty horses and with him a black flag to Al-Fils to destroy it, which is an idol of the Tai clan and those around it. He destroyed their idol and returned with the booty.

When the Thaqif embraced Islam, they sent Abed Yaleel bin Amr and Amr bin Umayyah to the Messenger of God and asked him about their idol called Al-Rabe, and they said: "What should be done with the Al-Rabe." The Messenger of God said: "Destroy it." They said: "Impossible. If Al-Rabe knew that we were planning to destroy it, it would wipe out our people." Omar Ibn Al-Khattab said: "Woe to you. O Abed Yaleel, what a fool you are. Al-Rabe is just a stone and do not know who worships it and who does not." Abd Yaleel said: "We have not come to you, Omar." They said: "O Messenger of God, let it stand for three years and do not destroy it." But the Messenger of God did not accept. They said: "Two years," but he refused. They said: "One year." And he did not accept it either. They said: "One month." But he refused to give them time. Their only goal was to leave the Al-Rabe behind because some of the believing men, women and children of their people were holding on to it. They did not want to frighten their people by destroying it now, but to let it until Islam was firmly established in their hearts. They asked the Messenger of Allah to spare them from its destruction and said: "O Messenger of Allah, you do it. For we will never destroy it." The Messenger of Allah said: "I will send Abu Sufyan bin Harb and Al-Mughirah bin Shu'bah to destroy it."

344

The delegation then returned and told their people about the decision on Al-Rabe. A sheikh from Thaqif said: "By God, this is proof of what stands between us and him. If he can destroy it, he is right and we are invalid, and if he couldn't do it, then ... there is still something (doubt) in the soul about it." Othman bin Abi Al-Aas said: "By Allah, your soul was wrong and pride has deceived you. Al-Rabe, by Allah, does not know who worshipped it and who did not." Abu Sufyan bin Harb, Al-Mughirah bin Shu'bah and their companions set out to demolish Al-Rabe. Al-Mughirah said to his companions who came with him, "I will make you laugh in Thaqif today." All the Thaqif gathered: men, women and children and mourned their idols. They did not believe that their idols could be destroyed as they thought they were untouchable.

Al-Mughirah bin Shu'bah stood up and mounted a camel with an axe in his hand, accompanied by the Banu Mu'tab, who were also armed. Al-Mughirah struck with the axe and then fell to the ground unconscious. The people of Taif were shocked and shouted: "Oh dear. Mughirah. Al-Rabe has killed him! They claimed that the goddess is not invulnerable, but she defends herself indeed!" They were pleased when they saw him fall and said: "Which of you would like to try and endeavor to destroy it. By God, he will never succeed?" Al-Mughirah bin Shu'bah jumped up and shouted, "May God curse you, O people of Thaqif, it is only stones and mud. Accept the grace of God and do not worship it." Then he struck the door and broke it. After that, he and his companions destroyed the wall stone by stone until they razed the temple to the ground. The servant of the temple said: "If they destroy the foundations of the building, they will be swallowed up." When Al-Mughirah heard this, he dug up the foundation and destroyed it and they found ornaments, perfumes, gold, silver and clothes that were inside and they took them away.

Destroying the idols was the most effective means of eliminating belief in them and exposing their myths and counterfeits. Therefore, the Messenger of God ordered the destruction of the idols that were worshipped in these areas. This posed a great challenge to the tribes who had devoted themselves to the worship of these idols for decades and attributed a certain power to them.

In the month of Ramadan, the Messenger of God sent Ali to Yemen again, as there were still areas there that had not yet converted to Islam. He held a banner in his hand and circled it while saying to Ali: "Go, O Ali, to the people of Yemen. Teach them the faith and the Sunnah and guide them according to the Book of God." He said: "Go ahead and don't look back." Then he added:

"When you enter their courtyard, do not attack them unless they attack you. Ask them to say: There is no god but Allah and Muhammad is the Messenger of God. If they say it, order them to pray. If they respond, order them to pay zakat. Do not ask them to do anything else. By God, it is better that God leads a person to Islam through you than that everything on which the sun rises and sets belongs to you."

He continued: "O Ali, I advise you to make frequent supplications, for they will be answered. Be grateful, for gratitude leads to more blessings. Beware of breaking or assisting in breaking a covenant. And I warn you against deception, for deception only affects those who practice it. And I warn you against committing treachery, for Allah will help those who have been betrayed."

The Prophet tapped Ali on the chest and then said: "Go, for God will guide your heart and strengthen your tongue." The Messenger of God gave him advice and prayed for him, for Ali was sent on a new mission to make judgments between people. It was a mission that required knowledge and experience. Ali set out with three hundred horsemen, whose horses were the best. When they encountered a group of polytheists, he called them to Islam. But they refused and threw arrows and stones at his companions. When he saw that they wanted to fight, he lined up his companions and attacked them. He killed twenty of them until they were scattered and defeated. They were taken prisoner and they took booty. They left their banner. Ali stopped pursuing them and then called them to Islam. They embraced Islam. A group of their leaders came forward and swore allegiance to Islam. They said: "We are representatives for our people. Here are our donations, take the share of Allah from it." [447]

The delegations to the Messenger of God

After the spread of Islam in the Arabian Peninsula, delegations spontaneously came to the Messenger of God to meet him and talk to him. Some had questions and were looking for answers. Others declared their conversion to Islam, and others asked for the blessing of the Prophet of God. The people believed that the Prophet would be able to heal their sick, solve their problems and even provide them with food.

When the delegation from Banu Thalabah came, there were four of them and they stayed in the house of Ramla bint Al-Harith. Bilal came to them and asked, "Is there anyone else with you?" They replied, "No." He then left, and after a short while he brought them a bowl of soup with yogurt and ghee, and they ate until they were full. Then they went out and saw the Messenger of Allah left his house and his head was dripping with water, he took one look at them and they rushed to him. In the meantime, Bilal called to prayer. They greeted him and said: "O Messenger of Allah, we are messengers and representatives of our people. We have embraced Islam. Our people in their work and with their livestock, and we have been told, O Messenger of God: there is no Islam for those who do not have hijrah." They were referring to the migration of the Prophet and the Muslims from Mecca to Medina. Some of the Muslims who took part in this migration boasted about it to other Muslims, seeing it as a source of pride.

Figure 59: Some Arab delegations on their way to the Prophet.

Then the Messenger of Allah replied: "Wherever you are and you fear Allah, it will not harm you (it is sufficient). " Bilal finished the call to prayer and the Messenger of God led them to midday prayer. Then he went to his house, entered and shortly afterward he went out to them after praying two rak'ahs in his house. He called them and said: "Where are your families?" They said: "O Messenger of God, they are near this tent." He said: "How is your land?" They said: "Fruitful." He said: "Praise be to God." So they stayed for days and learned the Quran and Sunnah. They were overwhelmed by his hospitality. Then they came to bid him farewell and he said to Bilal, "Reward them as you give delegations." Then he brought silver coins and gave each man five uqiya (one uqiya equals 40 dirhams) and said: "We have no dirhams." Then they left for their country.

The delegation of Abdul Qais, a tribe living in Bahrain and the outskirts of Iraq, came to the Prophet. Omar stood up and walked towards them. They were thirteen horsemen. Omar said: "Who are these people?" They said: "From Banu Abdul Qais." He said: "What brings you here. Trade?" They said: "No." He said: "The Prophet just mentioned you and said good things about you." The Prophet had looked at the horizon on the morning of the day they came and said: "A caravan will come from the east. They are not forced into Islam, they are tired of traveling, their food is running out and their leader has a sign. O God, forgive Abdul Qais. They came to me and ask no money from me, they are the best people of the East." Then they went with Omar until they came to the Prophet. Omar said to the people, "This is your companion you are looking for." .

They threw themselves from their horses, and some of them walked, and some of them jogged, and some of them ran, until they came to the Prophet and greeted him. They kissed the hands and feet of the Messenger of God. The Messenger of God asked them, "Which one of you is Abdullah Al-Ashaj?" Abdullah Al-Ashaj said: "Me, O Messenger of God." Al-Ashaj did not have an attractive appearance. The Messenger of Allah looked at him and said: "One is not judged by his external appearance, but what matters are the least parts of a person: his tongue and his heart." Al-Ashaj said: "O Messenger of Allah, I have a sick man with me. Pray to God for him." He said: "Where is he? Bring him to me." Then he slapped his back and said: "Out, enemy of God." A jinn[1] was in possession of this man who harmed him, and the Messenger of God removed him from him. The man became well. And they saw that the man did not look as he was. The Prophet made him sit beside him and prayed for him. He said: "Welcome to the people who have come without shame or regret.[2]" They said: "O Messenger of God, we come to you from a great distance. and between us and you lies this disbelieving tribe of Mudar. And we only reach you in a holy month. Tell us something important. If we do, we will enter paradise." He said: "I command you to follow four things and forbid you to do four things. I command you to believe in God alone. Do you know what faith in God is?" They said: "Allah and His Messenger know best." He said: "The statement that there is no god but Allah and that Muhammad is the Messenger of Allah, to perform

---

1 A Jinn is in the Islamic conception a being that is created from "smokeless fire", has reason, and populates the world alongside humans, Satans, and angels with other Jinn.

2 This means that they did not hesitate to convert to Islam, and there was no resistance. They were not captured or enslaved, nor was there anything similar that they would be ashamed of or regret. This is a demonstration of their honor, as they obediently joined Islam, without disgrace.

the prayer, to give zakat, to fast the month of Ramadan and to give the fifth share of the booty. And I forbid you four things: al-Dabaa, al-Hantam, al-Muzaffat and al-Naqir[1]. Remember these and pass it on." They said: "O Prophet of God, how do you know al-Naqir?" He said: "Yes, a stem that you drill and throw some dates into it - then you pour water into it. And when it is boiled, you drink it."

Then he said: "O people of Abdul Qais, why do I see that your faces have changed?" They said: "O Prophet of God, we are in a rugged land where no grass grows, and we used to take from these alcoholic drinks, which makes this situation easier for us. And it was the circumstances that forced us to do so, when you stopped us, our faces changed." The Messenger of Allah said: "Circumstances make something neither permissible nor forbidden, but all intoxicant consumption is forbidden. You should not sit and drink until your veins are alcoholized and then brag until one of you jumps on his cousin with a sword and leaves him paralyzed." They said: "How do we drink, O Messenger of God?" He said: "In leather containers[2] whose mouths are knotted."

They said: "O Messenger of God, our land is full of rats, and there are no watering cans left in it." The Prophet of God said: "Even if the rats ate from it two or three times." Al-Ashaj said: "O Messenger of God, our land is heavy and rugged, and if we do not drink these drinks, our colors will turn pale and our stomachs will swell. Allow us this." - He pointed with his palms. The Prophet said: "O Ashaj, if I allow you to drink something like this" - and he pointed like this with his palms - "would you drink it in something like this" - then he spread his hands and spread them out. It means more than it is - "until one of you, when he gets drunk on his drink, confronts his cousin and stabs him in the leg with a sword." Al-Harith dropped his clothes when he heard it from the Messenger of God to cover the blow to his leg. But God showed it to his prophet.

Then the Messenger of God told them about the dates they had. He said: "You have one kind of dates that you call such and such, and dates that you call such and such." And he told them about all the kinds of dates they had. A man from among them said to him, "May my father and mother be sacrificed for you, O Messenger of God, if you had been born in Hajjar, you would not be

---

1 The mentioned terms refer to traditional vessels for making sweetened and fermented mixtures of dates or raisins and water, which are then drunk.
2 All leather containers for water and milk, which are wrapped with a rope.

more knowledgeable than you are now. I bear witness that you are the Messenger of God." The Prophet said: "Your land has been elevated for me since you sat down with me, and I have looked from its lowest to its highest. So the best dates among you are the Barni dates, which remove diseases." The Messenger of God made Al-Ashaj sit next to him and asked him, "Pledge allegiance to yourselves and on behalf of your people." They said: "Yes." Al-Ashaj said: "O Messenger of God, you will not find anything more important to a person than his religion. We pledge allegiance to you for ourselves, and we send to our people whoever calls them to allegiance. Whoever follows us is one of us, and those who leave us is against us." The Prophet said: "You are right. You have two qualities: Forbearance and patience." Al-Ashaj said: "O Messenger of God, did I acquire them or has God created these two qualities in me?" The Prophet said: "No, rather God has created in you a willingness to act with these two qualities." Al-Ashaj said: "Praise be to God who created me with two qualities that God and His Messenger love." He gave them gifts, as was customary with the delegations before them, and then they returned to their country. [448]

The Prophet had written a letter to the people of Najran[1] inviting them to Islam. He said in this letter: "In the name of the God of Abraham, Isaac and Jacob. From Muhammad the Prophet to the Bishop of Najran and the people of Najran: If you embrace Islam, I thank you to the God of Abraham, Isaac and Jacob. I invite you to worship Allah and abandon the worship of other people, and I invite you to place yourselves under the guardianship of God rather than under the guardianship of servants. If you refuse, then pay the jizya. If you refuse, I have warned you of war. Peace."

When Bishop Abu Haritha bin Alqamah read the letter from the Prophet, he was terribly shocked. He sent to the scholars of the people of Najran to consult them. They said to him: "You know that God promised Abraham prophethood in the descendants of Ishmael. Do you believe that this man is the one?" The bishop then ordered the bell to be rung and the fires were lit in the temples. The people of the valley gathered. The bishop read them the letter of the Messenger of God and asked for their opinion. The decision-makers decided to send a delegation to discuss the letter with the Prophet Muhammad.

---

1 Najran is a large land near Sana'a, between Aden and Hadramout, and the people in Najran were of two types: Christians and Ummiyyun (neither Christians nor Jews).

In the tenth year, a delegation of Christians traveled from Najran to Medina to meet the Prophet Muhammad. The delegation consisted of sixty horsemen, including fourteen men from their elite. Among them were the leader of the people, whose name was Abd al-Masih, the leader of their caravan, whose name was Al-Ayham, and their bishop Abu Haritha bin Alqamah. The delegation set off until they arrived in Medina and took off their traveling clothes. They wore jewelry and clothes which and were sealed with gold. They went to the court-yard of the mosque in Medina to the Messenger of Allah. Those who saw them were astonished at their appearance. When they stood up to pray in the mosque of the Messenger of God, the people wanted to prevent them from doing so. The Messenger of Allah said: "Let them. " Then they came to the Messenger of God and greeted him, and he returned their greetings. Abd al-Masih and Abu Haritha bin Alqamah said: "We have embraced Islam, O Muhammad." He said: "You have not embraced Islam." They said: "Yes, we converted to Islam before we came to you." He said: "You are lying. If you like, I will tell you what is keeping you from Islam." They said: "Tell us." He said: "Love of the cross, drinking alcohol and eating pork." They asked, "O Muhammad, what do you say about Jesus?" He said: "He is the Spirit of God, His Word, the servant of God and His Messenger." They were not convinced and said: "No, He is not so. Have you ever seen a human being who was created without a father?" The Messenger of Allah bowed his head and was silent, then Allah revealed: {Indeed, the example of Jesus[1] to Allah is like that of Adam. He created Him from dust; then He said to him, "Be," and he was. The truth is from your Lord, so do not be among the doubters.} [449].

When it was morning, they returned to him and he recited the verses to them, but they refused to believe. Allah ordered his Holy Prophet to invite them to Mubahala[2]. God said: {Should anyone argue with you concerning him, after the knowledge that has come to you, say, 'Come! Let us call our sons and your sons, our women and your women, ourselves and yourselves, then suppli-cate earnestly [together], and call down Allah's curse upon the liars.' } [450]

Then the Messenger of Allah called them to the Mubahala and said: "Allah has commanded me that I must invite you to the Mubahala if you do not accept

---

1 Jesus ('Īsā ibn Maryam): is a prophet in the Quran, who is considered an immediate word of God and refers to Jesus of Nazareth.

2 Mubahala is a religious rite in Islam, in which both parties are called to a curse competition in a solemn appeal to God to prove the truth. The rite was historically used in various contexts, especially in debates between Muslims and Christians.

this." They said: "Give us three days," whereupon they exchanged views among themselves and discussed it. The leader of the people, Abd al-Masih, said: "By God, O Christians, you have known that Muhammad is a sent prophet, and if you curse him, the earth will swallow you up and uproot you. No people have ever cursed a prophet without suffering consequences for it, both the older and the younger." They said: "What is your opinion, Abu Maryam?" He said: "In my opinion, I should ask him to judge in our matter, because I see a man who will never exercise arbitrariness."

Al-Ayham said: "If you want nothing but to keep your religion and stick to your decision regarding Christ, then reconcile with the man and return to your homes." But they agreed to confront and challenge the Prophet and go to the Mubahala. At the Mubahala, their chiefs said: "If he comes to the Mubahala (curse competition) against us with his people, then he is not a true prophet. But if he comes to the Mubahala with the members of his household, we will not challenge him, for he never comes out with the members of his household unless he speaks the truth."

When the time was up and the day of the Mubahala arrived, the people of Najran arrived for the Mubahala and waited for the arrival of Prophet Muhammad. The Prophet came, wrapped Hassan and Hussein in his cloak, Fatima walked behind him and Ali behind her. The Prophet said to his family: "When I pray, you say amen." The Bishop of Najran, who was watching the Prophet and his family, said: "I see faces, if they asked God to remove a mountain, He would do it. Do not join the Mubahala, or you will be destroyed and there will be no Christian left on earth until the Day of Resurrection. By God, you know his prophethood and he has come to you with a convincing argument concerning Jesus. By God, no nation has ever challenged a prophet without being destroyed. If you do not want to give up your religion, then bid farewell to the man and leave." They turned to the Prophet and said: "Abu al-Qasim, we will not curse you." The Prophet said: "Then become Muslims and you will have the same rights and duties as Muslims." They refused. The Prophet said: "Then I will fight you." They said: "We are not in a position to wage war against the Arabs. But we can make a treaty with you." They made a treaty with him and he said: "By the One who holds my life in His hand, punishment would have come upon the people of Najran, and if they had participated in the Mubahala, they would have been turned into apes and pigs, and the valley would have burned above them, and God would have wiped out Najran and its people, up to the birds on the trees. "

After they refused to participate in the mubahala and the jizya was established for the people of Najran, they withdrew. When the next day came, he wrote them a letter. When the bishop received the letter, he asked permission to return to his people and those who were with him. They received permission and withdrew.

The delegations kept coming until the tenth year, among them was a delegation from Muharib in the tenth year, they were ten men, including Sawa bin al-Harith and his son Khuzaima bin Sawa. They were accommodated in the house of Ramla bint al-Harith and Bilal brought them lunch and dinner until one day they sat with the Prophet from noon until the afternoon. They converted to Islam and said: "We are representatives of our people." Among the delegation was a person from Muharib whom the Prophet knew, because when the Prophet was in Mecca presenting his message to the tribes during the Hajj season and inviting them to God and to his support, a group with coarse and harsh language met him and among the delegation was a man from among them whom the Prophet recognized and looked at him for a long time. When the Muharibi saw that the Prophet was looking at him for a long time, he said: "It seems, O Messenger of God, that you know me." He said: "I have seen you." The Muharibi said: "Yes, by God, you have seen me and spoken to me, and I have said the ugliest words to you in Okaz while you were going around." The Prophet said: "Yes." The Muharibi said: "O Messenger of God, no one among my companions that day was harsher towards you and further away from Islam than me. I praise God who kept me alive until I believed in you. Those men who were with me died in their religion." The Prophet said: "These hearts are in the hand of God." He said: "O Messenger of God, ask forgiveness for my behavior with you." The Prophet said: "The Islam erases what was unbelief before it." When they were about to leave, the Prophet raised his hands, looked towards the Qibla and prayed for them, then he gave them gifts as he does with other delegations, and they went back to their families. [451]

Battle of Tabuk

The Messenger of God received reports about King Akidar bin Abd al-Malik al-Kindi, who had a kingdom in the Levant regions. Akidar threatened the

Messenger of God and his companions to attack them, kill them and destroy their land. Because of his connection to the Romans, the companions of the Messenger of God were afraid of him. Every day, many companions came to the Messenger of God to report new rumors and news. The hypocrites told many lies and slanders about Akidar among the followers of Prophet Muhammad. They claimed that Akidar had mobilized his men. The hypocrites whispered in the ears of the weak Muslims and asked, "Where are the companions of Muhammad compared to Akidar? They threatened that he would soon attack Medina, kill his men and take his children and women captive." This frightened the believers. They complained to the Messenger of Allah about the deceptions they were being subjected to.

Figure 60: An illustrative depiction of the meeting of the hypocrites who conspired against the Prophet.

The hypocrites did not stop spreading rumors among the Muslims, but even contacted Akider in Dumat al-Jandal so that he could come to Medina and support them against the Messenger of Allah and the Muslims. They hoped that this would put power in their hands. They collaborated with Abu Aamer, a monk, in their plan. They promised him loyalty and made him their leader. Abu Aamer was careful not to be suspected of having schemed on behalf of the hypocrites. He therefore preferred to stay away from Medina.

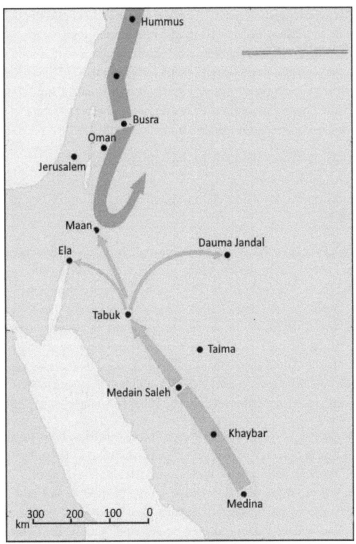

Figure 61: Map of the Battle of Tabuk.

The situation in Medina was very critical due to the growing psychological warfare of the hypocrites and their external support. It was necessary to take measures to manage and alleviate this situation. The Prophet was aware of the danger threatening the Islamic community and realized that it was necessary to take measures to counter this danger. Therefore, he turned to God in prayer and asked for help and victory, saying, "O Allah, if this group perishes, You will

355

no longer be worshipped on earth." The Messenger of God said the same thing in Badr while prostrating because the Battle of Badr was decisive for the fate of Islam and Muslims. His uttering this word this time indicates that there is a real danger threatening the entire group of people of faith, and that there is no doubt that the destruction of this group will be the result of not worshipping God on earth. This is tantamount to eradicating the characteristics of religion and removing every trace of it from the mind and soul.

God revealed to the Prophet Muhammad the secret meetings of the hypocrites and what they were planning. He ordered him to march to Tabuk with an army and surprise them. The city of Tabuk is located exactly 700 kilometers north of Medina.

When the Prophet wanted to lead a campaign, he normally concealed his intentions and plans. But in the campaign to Tabuk, he made his intentions clear and ordered them to prepare for it. The Prophet informed his companions that God had revealed to him and God would grant him victory over Akidar, capture Akidar and force him to reconcile and pay him a thousand ounces of gold and two hundred garments in the month of Safar and another thousand ounces of gold and two hundred garments in the month of Rajab and after eighty days the Prophet and the Muslims would return unharmed and victorious without any war having taken place and without any believer having been captured.

The Messenger of God said to them: "Moses promised his people forty nights, and I promise you eighty nights. Then I will return safe and sound, victorious without war, and none of the believers will be taken captive." A group of hypocrites heard his words, they spoke among themselves and said: "No, by God, it is the last of his breaks, after which he will not heal. Indeed, some of his companions will die in this heat, the desert winds and the foul stagnant waters, and whoever is safe from it will either be a prisoner in the hands of Akidar or will be killed."

In the month of Rajab of the ninth year, the Prophet put his plan into action. He wrote to the Arab tribes who had already converted to Islam and sent them messengers. He encouraged them to jihad and conquer. This happened in the midst of intense heat, while the land was parched. It was the time when the fruits were ripening. People loved to linger in their gardens and under their shade, and they preferred not to go out in the scorching summer heat. When the Messenger of God decided to travel to Tabuk, these hypocrites deliberately built a mosque outside the city. They claimed it was a place for prayer and worship, but in reality they met there and plotted against Islam and the Prophet. This was the idea of their leader Abu Aamer. Abu Aamer said to them before he went out into the Levant: "Build your mosque and seek therein what strength and weapons you can find, for I am going to Emperor the King of the Romans and bring an army of Romans. [1]"

After they finished building the mosque, a group of them came to the Messenger of God and said: "O Messenger of God, our houses are far from your mosque and we would like to pray together, since it is difficult for us to come here, we have built a mosque. If you visit it and pray in it, we will be blessed and we will pray in your place of prayer." The Messenger of God did not know their plan and intention because God did not reveal their conspiracy and hypocrisy to him. He said: "I am on a journey and I am busy. When we come back, God willing, we will pray for you in it." When Prophet Muhammad left for Tabuk, the hypocrites spoke among themselves and said: "Muhammad believes that the war against the Romans is like any other war. No one will ever return from them." Some of them even mocked and said: "I doubt that God will inform Muhammad of what we have done and what is in our hearts and reveal to him a Quran that people can read." But God revealed to his Prophet what they kept secret among themselves. The Prophet said to Ammar ibn Yasir, "Catch up with the people. For they have been burned." Ammar sought them out and asked, "What did you say?" They replied, "We didn't say anything, we were just playing and joking a bit." But God revealed a Quran that exposed them and said: "Tell them, Muhammad, are you making fun of God, His signs and His messengers? God rejected their excuse and rejected them because it was a false excuse. He regarded their mockery as open disbelief after it was hidden." God, in His mercy to them, said: "We will overlook a group of you because they repented and returned to the truth, but We will also punish another group who persisted in their hypocrisy and deviation and continued in their criminality." [452]

When the Islamic army left, some Muslim men stayed behind for various reasons. The Prophet gave permission to eighty-eight men not to participate, citing various reasons. Some of them were suffering from the heat, some were sick, some had to take care of their sick family members, and some came to the Prophet without giving a reason. The Prophet gave them permission not to attend. In this context, Al-Jedd ibn Qais came to the Prophet when he was in the

---

1 Then he moved to the Romans and died there in the ninth or tenth year of the Hijra. [500]

mosque with a group of people and said: "O Messenger of God, allow me to stay because I am poor and sick and this is an excuse not to go." The Messenger of God said: "Get ready, get ready. You are solvent." Al-Jedd said: "Let me stay and do not seduce me, for by God, my people know me well. No one loves women more than I do, and I fear that I would not be patient when I see Roman women." The Messenger of God turned away from him and said: "We have given you permission."

His son Abdullah bin Al-Jedd came to him and said to his father, "Why do you refuse the request of the Messenger of God? By God, there is no one among the Banu Salamah who has more wealth than you. Will you not go out?" He said: "My son, I have nothing to do with going out, going to the Romans in the wind and the great heat. By God, I do not feel safe for fear of the Romans, even when I am in my house. Should I go to them and attack them?! By God, my son, I know the consequences of these actions." Then his son became harsh with him and said: "No, by God, but it is hypocrisy." The father became angry and lifted his shoe and struck his son in the face with it, so that his son turned away and did not speak to him. God said about him that he had tried to escape the temptation of the women of Banu Al-Asfar(Byzantines) by telling a lie. But he fell into a greater temptation, namely the temptation of hypocrisy, retreat from jihad and disobedience to God and His Prophet. Allah said to him and those like him that Hell would be their reward and that it would surround them all. [453]

Ibn Ubay went back to Medina and stayed behind among the hypocrites. He said: "Muhammad attacks the Banu Asfar despite the difficult circumstances, the heat and the long distance which he can not bear. Muhammad thinks that fighting the Banu Al-Asfar is a game. By God, it is as if I see his companions in shackles." The hypocrites were not content with being absent; they also encouraged others to stay. Thus Al-Jedd ibn Qais and other hypocrites discouraged the Muslims from leaving. Al-Jedd said to Jabir ibn Sakhr and those of Banu Salamah who were with him, "Do not leave in the heat", to dissuade them from jihad and to sow doubt about the decisions of the Messenger of Allah to leave at such times.

Allah rebuked the hypocrites for staying in the city and withdrawing from the Messenger and rejoicing that they did not participate in jihad with their own means or money in support of the Muslims. They said to their Muslim brothers, "Do not go to war with the Messenger, for the time is hot, the movement is difficult and jihad is hard." Allah said: "O Muhammad, tell them: Hell is hotter if they would understand things in their truth." These hypocrites may laugh for a while because they have withdrawn from the jihadists, but it is a brief joy and laughter followed by much weeping and regret in the Hereafter as punishment for their bad deeds and continued hypocrisy. [454]

The basic challenge in the war of Tabuk was the fear and terror of Banu Al-Asfar. They expected no booty, no prisoners of war and no victory in this campaign, so they hesitated to move out in the heat. Before they set out, God revealed to the Messenger of God: "O Muhammad, the Most High God sends greetings to you and says to you: Either you go out and Ali stays, or Ali comes out and you stay." The Prophet informed Ali. Ali replied, "I hear and obey the command of Allah and the command of His Messenger, even though I would prefer never to be separated from the Prophet in any situation." The Messenger of God said: "Are you not content to be of me as Aaron was of Moses? but there is no prophet after me. It is not right for me to leave without you being my successor." He said: "I am satisfied, O Messenger of God." The Messenger of God said to him, "O Abu al-Hassan, you have the reward of going out with me even if you stay in Medina. And God has made you alone a nation, just as He made Abraham a nation. Your authority will prevent the group of hypocrites and disbelievers from taking action against Muslims."

The hypocrites in Medina shamed Ali for staying there and not leaving with the Prophet Muhammad, and they said: "The Messenger of God did not keep him in Medina out of respect and affection, but he left him out of burden." Others said: "The Messenger of God bored him and hated his company." When Ali was informed of what the hypocrites were saying, he wanted to deny them and expose their scandal. He followed the Prophet and said: "O Messenger of God, the hypocrites claim that you left me behind out of burden and hatred." The Prophet said: "Go back, my brother, to your place, for Medina is not suitable except by me or you. You are my successor in my household, the place of my emigration and my people."

Then the Messenger of Allah departed with his companions, leaving Ali in the city to manage their affairs during his absence. Some of the hypocrites remained behind in the city instead of joining the Islamic army. The presence of these hypocrites in the city posed a danger, as they were possibly planning an overthrow and wanted to take control of the city and the government. They said among themselves, "This time, Muhammad will not come back." Every time they plotted something to harm the Muslims, Ali prevented their scheming.

The Messenger of Allah was saddened that many of his companions refused to go out with him, disobeyed his orders and stayed in Medina or delayed marching with the Muslims. While they were on their way, the Muslims saw one of the men behind them. The Prophet's companions said: "O Messenger of Allah, this man has stayed behind." The Prophet replied to them, "Leave him, if he has good in him, Allah will bring him to you, and if not, Allah has saved you from him." This situation was repeated with several people who were late, and the Prophet gave them the same answer until the Prophet was asked, "O Messenger of God, Abu Dhar was delayed because of his camel." The Messenger of God said: "Leave him, if he has any good in him, Allah will bring him together with you. If not, Allah has saved you from him."

The Muslims observed Abu Dhar trying to speed up his camel, but it did not obey him due to extreme exhaustion. When the camel became too slow, Abu Dhar took his belongings and carried them on his back. He followed the Messenger of Allah on foot. At noon, Abu Dhar managed to approach the caravan of the Messenger of Allah, although he was completely exhausted and thirsty. An observer among the Muslims noticed him and said: "O Messenger of Allah, this man is walking alone on the road." The Messenger of Allah looked into the distance and said: "Be Abu Dhar." with a slight hope and joy in his voice, as he hoped for confirmation of his suspicion that it was his faithful companion. When the people looked at him, they said: "O Messenger of God, he is - by God - Abu Dhar!" The Messenger of God said: "May God have mercy on Abu Dhar. He walks alone, he dies alone and he will be resurrected alone." When Abu Dhar came to the Messenger of God, he told him his story. The Prophet replied: "God has forgiven you, O Abu Dhar, a sin at every step until you reached me."

Among the believers, there were men like Abu Dhar who were ready to go out with the Messenger of Allah at any cost. They put their provisions on their backs and drew water before setting out into the barren desert, which was particularly dangerous during the heat and drought of summer. They encountered the relentless wind and faced the risks of death from hunger and thirst or attacks by wild animals. The one who comes alone from the heart of the desert, what did he desire but reward and martyrdom in the way of God .

When the Messenger of Allah rode through the region of Al-Hijr (Medain Saleh), he covered his head with his cloak while sitting on the camel, lowered his head and passed through the houses of Thamud. When he arrived there, people rushed to the houses of Al-Hijr and entered them. They drew water from the wells from which Thamud had drunk. They kneaded dough and set up pots of meat. When the Messenger of Allah heard about this, he called out to the people, "Gather for prayer." When they gathered, the Messenger of Allah said: "Do not enter that dwellings of those who have wronged themselves until you weep that the same thing could befall you as it has been befallen them. Do not drink from their water and do not perform ritual ablution with their water before prayer. Instead, feed the camels with the dough you prepared with this water."

Then he traveled with them until he came to the water from which Salih's camel mare had drunk. He said: "Don't ask for signs. The people of Salih had once asked their Prophet for a sign, and God, the Blessed and Exalted, had sent them the camel mare. She used to pass by that place regularly and one day she drank their water while the other day the people drank from her milk. Salih's people, however, disobeyed their master's orders and killed the camel mare. As punishment, God ended their life with a cry from heaven. Only one man was spared the punishment because he was in the sanctuary of the god. But when he left the sanctuary, the same thing happened to him as to his people." A man said: "This is a strange thing." The Messenger of Allah said: "Shall I not tell you something more astonishing. There is a man among you who will tell you about what was before you and what will come after you. So align yourselves and stay on the right path, for Allah is not interested in your punishment (if you disobey His commandments)..." [1].

He continued: "Tonight a strong wind will blow over you. No one should get up, and whoever has a camel should tie his rope, and none of you should go out without his companion." The people did as the Messenger of God commanded them, with the exception of two men from Banu Sa'idah, one of whom went to the latrine and the other looked for his camel. The one who went out for his need was suffocated. The one who went out in search of his camel was caught by the wind and carried up to Mount Tai. The Messenger of God was informed of this, and he said: "Did I not warn you that none of you should go out except with his companion?" Then he prayed for the suffocated man and

_____

1 This prophecy was fulfilled after the death of the Prophet, as the man who tells them what was and what will be, was Imam Ali.

he recovered. The others brought the people of Tai to the Messenger of God when he returned to Medina.

The Muslims moved on and reached another shelter where there was no water. They complained about this to the Messenger of God. The Prophet prayed two rak'ahs, then he offered a prayer to Allah, and God sent a cloud and it rained on them until they drew water from it. A man from the Ansar said to another who was accused of hypocrisy: "Woe to you. You saw the Messenger of God offer a prayer to Allah and then God rained on us." He said: "It rained because of the heavenly bodies, not because of his supplication." The Messenger of Allah said to them, "How can you express your gratitude for the blessing of rain from Allah by denying and rejecting his signs. "[455]

Then the Messenger of Allah continued his journey and came to another place where his camel was lost. His companions set out in search of it. One of the hypocrites, Zaid ibn Al-Lusait, who was in a tent of Amara ibn Hazm with a group of Muslims, said: "Muhammad claims to be a prophet and tells you about the news of heaven, but he does not know where his camel is!" At that time, Amara was with the Prophet and heard the Prophet say, "A hypocrite said: 'Muhammad claims to be a prophet and he tells you about the heavens, and he does not know where his camel is.' By God, I know nothing except what God has taught me, and God has led me to the camel. It is in this valley. It got stuck with its reins in a tree. Go and bring it to me." So they went and brought it. Prophet Muhammad was not present when Zaid said this. However, he was told through revelation what had happened. Amara returned to his tent and said: "By God, it is amazing what the Messenger of God told us just before about what someone said. God, told him about it." And he mentioned what the Messenger of God said. A man from those who were in Amara's tent, Amr bin Hazm, Amara's brother - and he was not present with the Messenger of God - said: "Zaid, by God, is the one who said that before you came to us." Amara approached Zaid, pulled him by the neck and said: "O servant of God, there is a hypocrite in my tent, and I do not know it! Get out of my tent, O enemy of God, and do not accompany me."

The Islamic army moved on until they reached Tabuk. The Messenger of God leaned against a palm tree and addressed the people after praising God, saying, "O people, the truest speech is the Book of God, the most reliable handbook is the word of piety, the best religion is the religion of Abraham." The Prophet went on to exhort them and instruct them about the rules of their faith until he said: "Whoever forgives, Allah will forgive him, whoever restrains his anger, Allah will reward him, and whoever is patient in times of hardship, Allah will grant him compensation..."

When the Messenger of Allah arrived in Tabuk, he laid down a stone to mark the direction of the Kaaba. He then built a mosque on this site and prayed there with the Muslims. The mosque was the starting point for their movements in the area. Then he turned to them and said: "Here is Sham (Levant)," pointing with his hand towards Sham, "and here is Yemen," pointing with his hand towards Medina. So that, above all, they would know their location and the direction from which their enemy might be lurking or from which danger might threaten.

The Muslim army's first task was to protect the surrounding villages from any threat that might reach the Islamic State from the north. Therefore, they took the initiative and signed treaties with the tribes in the southern part of the Levant desert who were seeking protection. They agreed to pay the jizya tax, join the Muslims and leave the polytheists. This gave them security. The inhabitants of Maqna, Ila, Jarba, Athrah and Malik ibn Ahmar came to the Messenger of God to conclude these treaties.

Heraclius was in Homs or Damascus, and the Prophet again sent him a letter inviting him to Islam or asking him to submit and pay the jizya. A man asked, "And what if he refuses?" The Prophet replied, "Even if he refuses." The messenger went and delivered the letter from the Messenger of God to Heraclius. However, the Emperor of Rome again declined the prophet's invitation. When Heraclius learned that the Prophet's army was approaching Roman territory and that treaties had been signed between the Messenger and the villages in the south of the Levantine desert, which had previously been part of the Roman state, he decided to withdraw his army and avoid military confrontations with the Muslims. He left his positions without fighting against the Islamic state. Thus, the Messenger of God achieved victory and secured the Muslim territories in the north and protected them from danger. [456]

During his stay in Tabuk, the Prophet sent a brigade under the leadership of Khaled bin al-Walid to the region of Dumat al-Jandal. Dumat al-Jandal is located about 400 km east of Tabuk and is a green, water-rich region ruled by a Christian man named Akidar ibn Abd al-Malik. The Prophet sent a force to subdue him. Khaled bin al-Walid managed to capture him by surprise during a hunting trip and bring him to the Prophet. Akidar declared his submission, accepted the payment of the jizya and remained true to his faith. He concluded a treaty with the Prophet, who then brought him back to his homeland with a special escort. This ended the military operations in Tabuk. [457]

It is true that the Muslim army led by the Prophet did not meet the Roman army as planned. But the sudden retreat of the Romans and their avoidance of fighting the Muslims made the Muslims the most formidable force in the entire Arabian Peninsula. They ensured the security of this region through these treaties and were able to extend the prestige of the Islamic state to many isolated villages in the north of the Hejaz. The inhabitants of these villages were defenceless and had no choice but to make peace with Islam.

Plot of Al-Aqaba[1]

There were some who were not satisfied with the Muslims' victory over the Romans, as another group in the Islamic army - the hypocrites - had a different opinion and plan. However, these hypocrites saw the victory at Tabuk as a positive development for the future and wanted to be part of it. They were aware that their wishes could not be fulfilled in the presence of the Prophet. Moreover, they feared that the Prophet would still confirm the succession of Ali, which would make their situation with Ali similar to that with the Prophet, since Ali was seen as an exact copy of the Prophet.

The hypocrites had a secret plan to insidiously eliminate the Prophet without being noticed by the other Muslims. They planned to portray his death as an accident on the way by frightening his camel and causing it to fall into a nearby ravine. Another option they considered was to roll stones from the mountain onto him to make him fall into the valley.

God revealed their plot to his messenger. The Messenger of God intended to expose their machinations and enable the identification of the perpetrators. When the Messenger of God was on his way back from Tabuk to Medina, he reached the area of Al-Aqaba. The Al-Aqaba region was divided into a narrow path and a wide valley.

---

1   Al-Aqaba: It is a difficult path on the mountain.

Figure 62: The hypocrites gather to execute their plan on the hill.

The Prophet's caller shouted to the people: "The Messenger of God will take Al-Aqaba. None of you should go with him. Go through the valley, for it is easier and wider for you." Meanwhile, the hypocrites took the opportunity to catch the Prophet Muhammad alone and carry out their plans. They crept up the mountain in front of him and waited for him to pass by on the serpentine road. They said: "If he takes the mountainous path through Al-Aqaba, we will knock him off his camel." The people followed the path through the valley, except for those who were plotting against the Prophet Muhammad. They chose the path over the mountain and hid behind masks. The Prophet ordered Hudhayfah to wait at the foot of the mountain and keep an eye out for anyone passing by. He also ordered him to disguise himself like a stone. Hudhayfah said: "O Messenger of Allah, I recognize evil in the faces of the leaders of your army and I fear that if I sit at the foot of the mountain and someone comes and discovers and recognizes me, they will accuse me and kill me." Hudhayfah did as the Prophet had commanded him. He saw twenty-four men on their camels, some of whom were talking to each other: "If you see anyone who is here, kill him so that he does not tell Muhammad that he saw us here. Muhammad would then retreat and only take this route in daylight, which would thwart our plan." Hudhayfah heard this, but no one could see him. Hudhayfah then returned to the Prophet and told him what he had heard.

The Messenger of God passed through Al-Aqaba with Ammar bin Yasir and Hudhayfah bin Al-Yaman, and he ordered Ammar bin Yasir to take the reins of the camel and lead it. He ordered Hudhayfah bin Al-Yaman to follow him. While the Messenger of Allah was traveling in Al-Aqaba, they heard the sound of people approaching them. They pushed the Messenger's camel so hard that some of his belongings fell off when his camel became frightened. They rolled boulders and stones off the mountain in Al-Dabab[1] to throw the Prophet into the valley. The Prophet became angry and struck the faces of their horses with a stick and said: "Go away, you enemies of Allah!" He also ordered Hudhayfah to drive them away. At that moment, Gabriel spread his wings and lit up the Al-Aqaba region. Their camels and their masked faces became visible, and Hudhayfah could see them. The group realized that the Messenger of Allah was aware of their plan, so they hurried down from Al-Aqaba until they mingled with the people. Hudhayfah came back to the Messenger of God. The Messenger of God said: "Go on, O Hudhayfah, and you go, Ammar!" They hurried until they reached the top.

The Messenger of God came out of Al-Aqaba, waited for the people and said to Hudhayfah, "Did you know anyone from the gang you drove out?" Hudhayfah replied, "O Messenger of Allah, I knew their horses, but the people were masked and because of the darkness of the night I could not see them." The Messenger of Allah asked, "Did you know what they were planning and what they wanted?" They replied, "No, by Allah, O Messenger of Allah." The Prophet said: "They planned to accompany me, and when I was in Al-Aqaba, they pushed me and tried to drive me away. Allah has revealed to me their names and the names of their fathers. I will share them with you, Allah willing." They asked, "Should we not order that when the people come to strike their necks." He replied, "I do not want people to say, 'Muhammad used violence against his companions.'" He told them their names and then said: "Keep it a secret. Go, bring them to me tomorrow." Hudhayfah said: "O Messenger of Allah, these are not companions. " The Messenger of God said: "Have they not testified that there is no god but Allah?" Hudhayfah replied, "Yes." The Messenger of God said: "Have they not testified that I am the Messenger of God?" Hudhayfah replied, "Yes." The Messenger of God said: "I was commanded not to kill them."

The Prophet's passage through Al-Aqaba, despite the dangers involved, was not to facilitate the passage of the army through the valley or to reduce the number of people, as the reduction of one or two people had no effect on the movement of the army of hundreds of people. The real aim of the Prophet's passage through Al-Aqaba was to expose this misguided, hypocritical group

---

1 Al-Dabab refers to a type of leather bag, which is used to transport oil and grain. This bag is filled with stones here.

that was plotting against the Messenger of Allah to get rid of him so that they could take control of the government. This group had a prestigious position in Islamic society, which qualified them for this task in the eyes of the people. Those who wanted to kill the Prophet were greedy for worldly concerns and enjoyed a prestigious position that enabled them to pursue this plan. They were feared and possessed a strength and power that no one could withstand. Hudhayfah hid their names out of fear of them. Among those involved in this conspiracy were Abu Bakr bin Abi Quhafa, Omar bin al-Khattab, Othman bin Affan, Talha bin Ubaidullah, Abu Sufyan bin Harb, Muawiyah bin Abu Sufyan, Mughira bin Shu'bah, Amr bin al-Aas, Saad bin Abi Waqqas, Abd Al-Rahman bin Awf, Abu Ubaidah bin al-Jarrah, Abu Musa al-Ashari and Khaled bin al-Walid. The conspiracy against the Prophet was not planned spontaneously, but was part of a comprehensive and detailed plan. This plan defined the objectives and course of action and expected their attacks to be decisive, influential and protected. Every event was precisely calculated and measures were taken. Allah mentions that a group of those who had set out with the Prophet had conspired in Mecca to plot against the Prophet. They kept this secret among themselves and became disbelievers after their Islam. They made a decision in Al-Aqaba to execute the plan they had agreed upon, which was to assassinate the Prophet. But Allah thwarted their plans and exposed them, so they did not succeed in what they had planned. When they were questioned, they were afraid and swore that they had said nothing. But Allah punished them for lying and confirmed the truth of what was attributed to them. Many of them had suffered from poverty and misery before their conversion to Islam. After their conversion to Islam, the bounty flowed in on them, for the Prophet treated them the same as all other Muslims in terms of booty and paid off some of their debts. Their reward for him was that they said what they said about him and then plotted to assassinate him. Allah rebuked them for their ingratitude and treachery. Despite all this, Allah says to them that his door is wide open to anyone who knocks, and the way to him is simple and easy, even for the disbelievers and hypocrites, if they want to repent. All they have to do is ask forgiveness for the past and be sincere in the future. However, if they persist in their deeds and do not repent, then Allah's punishment in this life and in the Hereafter will be severe, and they will not find anyone to help them against Allah. [458]

After the Messenger of Allah returned victorious and triumphant from Tabuk to Medina, he had to complete the task and expose the leader of the hypocrites, Abu Aamer. As the Messenger of Allah approached Medina, he said to his companions: "There are people in Medina who were present during your journey and who crossed the valley with you. " They said: "O Messenger of Allah, even though they are in Medina?!" He replied, "Although they are in Medina, an excuse is holding them back." He meant that the men who could not participate in jihad due to illness or other excuses and had remained in Medina would receive the same reward as those who had actually participated. This is because their intentions were sincere and they had the desire to participate. The Prophet confirmed this to those who were with him to reassure them and prevent them from boasting or belittling others. As happened when the Prophet supported Asma Bint Umays against Omar Ibn Al-Khattab, who told her that he had a greater claim on the Prophet than she did because of emigration (see page 255).

When the Messenger of Allah came to Medina, the women and children went to the Farewell Mound (Thaniyyat al-wadā) to greet him. They sang with joy at his arrival:"The moon has risenOver the hills of farewell.Gratitude fills our heartsFor Allah's invitation without conditions.You, Prophet chosen from among us,Came with an invitation great and goodHave managed to raise the honor of MedinaBe welcome, be welcome with great courage."

He entered the mosque, then prayed two rak'ahs and sat down to greet the people. He said: "Praise be to God, who has provided us with a reward and goodness on our journey.".

The hypocrites who had withdrawn from the Messenger of Allah spread bad news about him and said: "Muhammad and his companions were exhausted on their journey and perished." However, when they learned that their claims were disproved and that the Messenger and his companions were safe, this angered them. [459] Allah reveals the sick souls of these hypocrites, for when they see the Prophet attaining prosperity, booty and triumph, this angers them and they suffer from it. However, when a calamity in the form of defeat or injury befalls the Prophet, they say that they prepared the causes for it before it happened, because they did not go out with them and did not experience what the Muslims experienced. They turn away from the Messenger and rejoice at what has befallen the Muslims. [460]

Demolition of the hypocrite mosque

When the Messenger of Allah arrived, the angel Gabriel came to him and informed him of the intentions of the hypocrites who were building a mosque to harm the Muslims and forbade him to pray in it.[461] He then summoned a group of his companions and said: "Go to the mosque of the evildoers, tear it down and burn it." They quickly went and took palm branches, lit them and marched to the mosque between sundown and dinner. There they met the followers of the evildoers. They burned the mosque and destroyed it to the ground. Those who were inside were able to escape. The Messenger of God ordered that the place be used as a dumping ground for waste.

The hypocrites intended to build this mosque to conceal their machinations and conspiracies. They wanted to pretend to be people of faith, worship and devotion. Then they asked the Prophet to pray for them in their mosque in order to gain legitimacy and show people that they revere the prophet Muhammad and seek his blessings and prayer in their mosque. They seized the opportunity and chose this sensitive time, namely the time when the Prophet left for Tabuk. The people were busy preparing for the journey and thinking about how they could confront the enemy and ward off the danger. However, the Prophet did not punish anyone involved in this dangerous conspiracy. He was content to destroy the Mosque of Temptation that they had built and where they were meeting and plotting against the Prophet. The demolition of this mosque was the best way to eradicate the germ of corruption and to make it clear to the people that there is no leniency in the matter of hypocrisy and no compromise with the hypocrites. For the existence of the mosque and the mere condemnation could have tempted them to use another misleading method by claiming that what they have been accused of is not true, but only false rumors. Perhaps they could win over many weak minds and faiths. [462]

The proclamation of Surah Bara'a

During the Hajj season in the ninth year, the Messenger of God commanded Abu Bakr to march to Mecca to guide the people on their annual pilgrimage and to convey to them the first verses of the Surah Bara'a as well as other instructions that the people should commit to. Therefore, the Messenger of God sent two books with him.

The first book contained verses from Surah Bara'a: {And an announcement from the side of Allah and His Messenger to the people on the Day of the Great Pilgrimage that Allah is free from (obligation to) the idolaters, and so is His Messenger.}[463] Moreover, he wrote: It is not permissible for them to circumambulate the house naked. Muslims and idolaters are not allowed to pray together. Whoever has a contract with the Messenger of God should honor it. If there is no contract, the period is four months. Allah and His Messenger are free from obligations to the idolaters. Only Muslims will enter Paradise. A polytheist may not approach the Sacred Mosque after this year. And other commandments and instructions. The second: a book containing the sunnahs of the Hajj.

When Abu Bakr was accompanied by Omar bin Al-Khattab on the way, they heard the rumbling of the camel of the Messenger of God, and it was Ali, accompanied by Ammar bin Yasser. Abu Bakr asked Ali and Ammar the reason for their coming. Ali informed him that the Prophet had sent him and that he was carrying a book from the Prophet to Abu Bakr. This book stated that the Prophet had chosen Ali instead of Abu Bakr to proclaim these words during the season and to perform the pilgrimage of the people instead of Abu Bakr. He also informed him that he should give Abu Bakr the choice of either traveling with him or returning to Medina. Abu Bakr and Omar were worried about sending Ali and they wanted the Prophet to send someone older. Ali was 32 years old at the time. Abu Bakr was 59 years old and Omar was 49 years old. Ammar ibn Yasir was the oldest of them and he was 65 years old. Abu Bakr and Omar tried to intimidate Ali and Ammar with the people of Mecca. They were harsh with them and said: "Abu Sufyan and the people of Mecca have gathered for you!" Ali said: "God is sufficient for us, and He is the best protector," and they moved on.

Abu Bakr and Omar returned to Medina and expressed their displeasure: "This boy was sent, if only someone else had been sent to the people of Mecca. After all, the respected people of Quraysh and their men are in Mecca. By God, we prefer unbelief to what we find ourselves in." Abu Bakr returned to the Messenger of God distraught and fearful. When he visited the Messenger of God, he said: "O Messenger of God, you qualified me for a matter that many hoped for, but when I wanted to leave, you sent me back. What is wrong with me? Has Quran been revealed about me?" The Prophet said: "No." Then said Gabriel came to him and said to him that no one should deliver his message except him or a man from him.

Ali recited Surah Bara'a during the pilgrimage and announced in Mecca, Mina, Arafat and all the holy places that the Messenger of God is free from any polytheist who, after that year, performed Hajj naked or circumambulated the house naked. Ali came to Mecca and read his book to them, but they met him with threats and showed him hatred. Kharash bin Abdullah met him and said: "There is nothing between us and your cousin except the sword and the spear, and if you wish, we could start with you." Ali said: "Yes, yes, if you want, come!"

After Ali finished, he set off for Medina, but took his time on his journey, delaying his return to Medina. Likewise, the revelation to the Prophet regarding Ali and his situation was delayed. The Prophet feared that something might have happened to him. It was the Prophet's custom that when he prayed the morning prayer, he would turn towards the Qibla and Ali would turn towards the people behind the Prophet so that he would receive the people and respond to their needs. When Ali was in Mecca, he did not make anyone in Ali's place, but the Prophet himself used to receive people. Abu Dhar sensed the Messenger of God's concern for Ali because of the seriousness of the mission entrusted to him. He wanted to go out and see if he was near the city. Abu Dhar asked the Prophet for permission to go out. The Prophet gave him permission. And he went out to look for Ali and met him on the way. He hugged him, kissed him and then hurried and preceded the Prophet to give him the good news of his arrival. The Prophet was delighted and said to Abu Dhar, "You will go to Paradise because of this!" Then the Prophet went with the people to see Ali. When he met Ali, he embraced him and put his cheek on Ali's shoulder.

The Prophet wept with joy at his arrival. Ali wept with him. Then the Messenger of God asked him what he had done. Ali told him, and the Prophet said: "God, the Exalted and Majestic, knew you better than I did when He commanded me to send you."

When Ali announced in Mecca that no idolater should enter the Sacred Mosque after that year, the Quraysh were greatly disturbed and said: "Our trade is gone, our sons are lost, and our houses are destroyed." [464] God then said: "Tell them, O Muhammad: If your parents who bore you, and your children who are nearest to you, and your brothers from whose wombs you have sprung, and those with whom you live, and wealth which you have labored to acquire, and trade goods which you fear to be abandoned, and houses which you have built and which are dear to you, if these things are dearer to you than God and His Messenger and the struggle in His way, then wait for an immediate and a subsequent punishment which God will bring down upon you to disgrace you in this world and in the Hereafter." [465]

631 - 632 AD

The tenth year after the Hijrah

Farewell pilgrimage

A year later, as the Hajj season approached in the tenth year after the Hijrah, the Prophet decided to perform the Hajj. He announced his intention and informed the Muslims about it. He also ordered the loudest voices to announce that the Messenger of God would perform Hajj that year. Until his call reached the farthest corners of the Islamic lands, and people prepared to go out with him. He also wrote to those who had received his letter and converted to Islam that the Messenger of God wished to perform Hajj and invited all those who were able to do so to come with him.

So people came in abundance to perform Hajj with him. He met countless people on the way, and they were in front of him, behind him, to his right and to his left, as far as the eye could see, between 70,000 and 120,000 people, with the exception of the people in Mecca. He took with him all his wives, all in Howdahs, and his household, the Muhajirun and the Ansar and almost all the Arab tribes, and many people who did not belong to any tribe.

The Messenger of God performed the noon prayer in Medina, then spoke to the people and taught them the rites before them. He then dismounted, took a bath and anointed himself with oil. He wore the two robes of Iḥrām and replaced them with two robes near Mecca. Then he said: "O God, make it an accepted pilgrimage in which there is no hypocrisy or prestige."

He appointed Abu Dujana in charge of Medina, und went out during the day at the end of the month of Dhu'l-Qa'dah until he came to Dhu al-Hulayfah through Wadi al-Aqiq and camped there (see Figure 63). Then his companions gathered to him and he led them in the afternoon prayer with two rak'ahs. He ordered them to pray in this valley in the Al-Shajara Mosque.

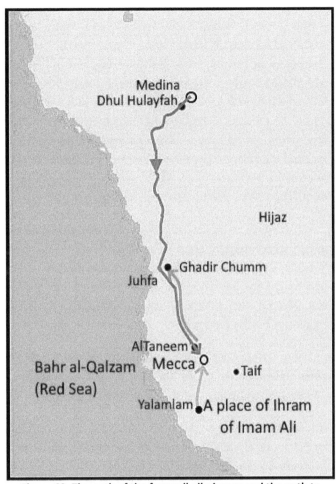

Figure 63: The path of the farewell pilgrimage and the path to
Ghadir Khumm.

The Prophet brought a hundred camels as an offering and entered the Ihrām from Al-Shajara Mosque. He began the pilgrimage of the Qiran[1] and the recitation of the Talbiyah 2 and said: "I am at Your service, O Allah, I am at Your service. Verily. Praise, mercy and dominion are Yours. You have no partner." The Prophet took the albaydā' (desert way) and continued walking between the houses and leading his companions in prayers. His companions built mosques in the places of his prayers to gain blessings and follow him. He recited the surah Al-Ma'arij often. He repeated the Talbiyah whenever he met a horseman, climbed a hill or descended into a valley, at the end of the night and after prayers, until he entered Mecca at Dhul-Hijjah from the upper hill north of Mecca, which overlooks Al-Hajjun. When he ended at the door of the Great Mosque, he reached the Kaaba. He praised God and prayed for his father Abraham. Then he came to the Black Stone. He wiped the stone with his hands and put his face on it. Then he placed his lips on it and wept for a long time.

The Prophet's weeping as he held the stone was not out of fear of punishment for a sin he had committed. He is an infallible prophet, absolved from error. Rather, it is the weeping of longing for God and the joy of fulfilling the covenant. Then he circumambulated the house seven rounds while riding his camel al-Adbaa. He did not circumambulate it on foot because of his weak body and the illness that afflicted him.

He began to touch the pillars with his sticks. When the Messenger of God finished circumambulating the house and the people circumambulated with him, he prayed two rak'ahs behind the shrine of Abraham.

Then the Messenger of God came to the well of Zamzam and drank from it and then said: "O God, I ask You for useful knowledge, abundant provision and a cure for every disease and ailment." He said to the people when he arrived in Mecca and began the rituals: "Take your rituals from me, for I do not know, perhaps after this Hajj, I will not perform Hajj again." He repeated this in Arafat when he stoned the Jamrat and on the Day of Sacrifice. Then the Messenger of God came to al-Safa and ascended it facing the Yemeni corner of the Kaaba, thanking God and praising Him. He said: "This is Gabriel, and he pointed behind him with his hand, commanding me to order those who had

---

1 Hajj of the Qirans: It is one of the three types of Hajj. It is obligatory for those whose family is present in the Holy Mosque or near Mecca. It is prescribed for this Hajj that the person brings an al-Hadī at the time of Ihrām.

not brought al-Hadī that they should exit the Iḥrām. And it is something that God has commanded." The people exited the Iḥrām.

Hajj rituals

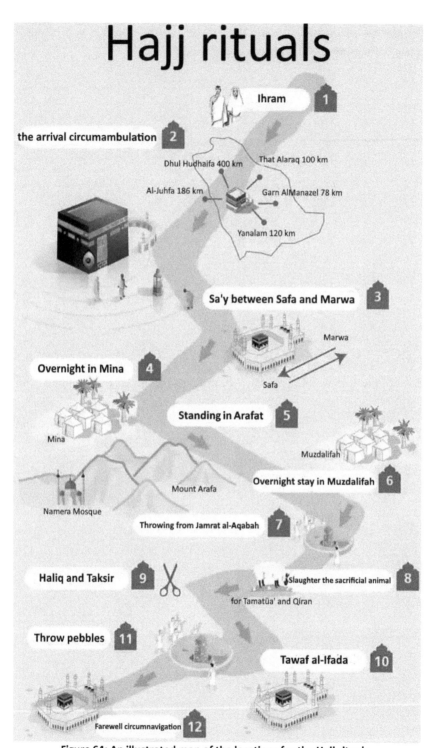

Figure 64: An illustrated map of the locations for the Hajj rituals.

The Messenger of God said: "If I had known earlier what I knew later, I would have done what I commanded you. But I have brought the offering, and who leads the sacrificial animals with him, should not step out of the Ihrām state until the sacrificial animals reach its destination." Suraqa bin Jusham said to him, "O Messenger of God, explain our religion to us as if we were just created. Is this what you have commanded us to do for this year only, or for the future as well?" The Messenger of God said: "No, it is for ever, until the Day of Resurrection." Then he intertwined his fingers and said: "Umrah is included in Hajj until the Day of Resurrection." Omar bin Al-Khattab said to the Messenger of God in a tone of astonishment, "Should we go on pilgrimage while our heads and hair are dripping wet?!" Omar disagreed with the Prophet's order and protested by asking how we could be allowed to have intercourse with women between Umrah and Hajj. Then we would go out for Hajj after Umrah while the water of ritual purification is still dripping from our heads and hair.[466] The Messenger of God said: "You will never believe in this."

The people who came with the Messenger of God and did not bring sacrificial animals had to perform the Hajj of Tamattu'[1]. But Omar ibn al-Khattab did not like this because the Quraysh do not usually perform Umrah during the Hajj season; instead, they postpone it so that the pilgrims have to return after Hajj and then come to Mecca again for Umrah. This keeps them in Mecca longer and Mecca's trade continues to flourish. Omar and the other companions from Quraysh wanted the people of Mecca to benefit from the pilgrims' income.

Hafsa, the Prophet's wife, said to him, "O Messenger of God, what is wrong with the people, why have they left their Umrah. And you have not?" He said: "I have applied oil on my head and brought the sacrificial animals. I will not step out of Ihrām until I have sacrificed." Ali bin Abi Talib came from Yemen at this time when he was in Ihrām. The Prophet asked him, "How was your Ihrām?" He said: "Ihrām like the Prophet's Ihrām." The Messenger of God said to him, "Remain in your Ihrām like me. You are my partner in the sacrificial animal." He then ordered him to return to his brigade and accompany them to Mecca.

---

1 The Hajj of Tamattu': is one of the three types of Hajj in Islam, and this type of Hajj is obligatory for those who are more than 48 miles away from the Great Mosque. Hajj at-Tamatu' consists of two parts: Umrah at-Tamatu' and Hajj at-Tamatu'. The pilgrim must perform the Umrah before the Hajj.

Then the Messenger of God camped in Mecca in al-Bathaa, east of Medina, in a dome that had been built for him, and stayed there for four days. At noon on the day of al-Tarawiyah, he asked the people to take a bath and recite the Talbiyah for Hajj. He went out with his companions to recite the Talbiyah for Hajj. Finally, he reached Mina (see Figure 64) and prayed noon, afternoon, evening, night and morning prayers.

On the ninth day of Dhu al-Hijjah, the Messenger of God and the crowd of Muslims made their way to Arafat. Then he landed in Namira and pitched his tent there. When it was noon, the Messenger of God went out with the Quraysh. He had washed himself and stopped reciting the Talbiyah until he stood in the mosque, preached to the people and prayed. Then he went to the standing area in Arafat. People crowded around to stand next to his camel. The Messenger of God said: "O people, the place of my camel's hooves is not the only place to stand, but all this is a place to stand."

Then Surah Al-Maida was revealed and the Messenger of God recited it to the people. Gabriel came to command him in the name of God to inform him about Imamate[1] of Ali Ibn Abi Talib. The Messenger of God said: "My people are on the verge of the age of Jāhilīya, and there is competition and pride among them. There is no man among them who has not killed Ali, one of his masters. And I fear that if I tell them this about my cousin, someone will say, 'He preferred his cousin to us,' and they will dispute it." God has revealed in his book: {O Messenger, announce that which has been revealed to you from your Lord, and if you do not, then you have not conveyed His message.} [467] This verse was revealed to emphasize the need for the Prophet to be informed about the matter of leadership and the Imamate of Ali over the people. [468]

The Prophet knew that most of the people had declared Islam after the conquest of Mecca and that the Islam of most of them was superficial, rather symbolically imposed by the circumstances that arose in the region after the conquest of Mecca. They did not know much about this religion because they lived in their lands according to their pre-Islamic ways and tribal customs and their leaders did not allow the Muslim messengers to reach them or tell them anything about this religion, its rules, concepts and details. Even those of them who converted to Islam also lived their lives according to the concepts of

---

1 Imamat: From a Shiite perspective, it is the fourth foundation of religion. It describes the fact that the religion after the Prophet can only be preserved by infallible and pure leaders, called Imams. These Imams serve as spiritual and political leaders for Muslims.

Jāhilīya. They did not deviate from its customs and were not yet educated about the importance of faith and Islam. Rather, their leaders were the ones who controlled them, managed their affairs and dominated their movement. On the other hand, there were ambitious people whose ambition was ignited by this rapid and tremendous expansion which the Muslims achieved in a very short period. An expansion that brought them plenty of money, great prestige, influence, power and other things they had not dreamed of.

And from a third aspect: there were people in and around Medina who did not like the idea of merging with Islamic society and dissolving into it and thus starting out in life. Therefore, they secretly plotted against Islam. They took part in everything that harmed Islam, regardless of its size and nature, and they also found support in this direction from many of the new Muslims on the day of the conquest of Mecca. Apart from other groups who did not convert to Islam but surrendered, and once they found the opportunity to show their real face, they would not hesitate to do so. All this would escalate the level of danger that Islam and its sincere people would face after the death of the Messenger of God. The greatest and most important goal was to preserve the teachings of this religion, to protect its beliefs and concepts, and to enable it to overcome these barriers and pass them on to the next generations. This is exactly what the Messenger of God did during the Farewell Pilgrimage and in many situations thereafter.

This explains to us his gathering of these large and enormous crowds that he brought to the holiest place in the holiest time to perform a ritual of worship, which is one of the greatest rituals. The Quran revealed to us that there were groups of people who confronted the Messenger directly and tried to obstruct his movement and prevent him from clarifying the matter of Imamate. The Prophet therefore sought protection from God in order to confront them. Here the question arose: Who are these criminal scoundrels actually trying to prevent the transmission of the message of Allah? Unfortunately, they are the people of the Messenger of God, especially the Quraysh, who fought against Islam at the beginning of its emergence, and fought it when it was weak, and fought it after it became strong and spread, and worked to shake its pillars.

The Prophet preached to the people in Arafat before the sun set, while he was on his camel Al-Qaswa. Ali stood near him in another place, conveying his words to those who were on the other side. After praising and glorifying God, he said: "O people, your Lord is one, and your father is one. You are all of

Adam, and Adam is of dust. The most honorable of you in the eyes of God is the most pious of you. An Arab is superior to a non-Arab only in piety. Have I informed you." They said: "Yes." He said: "Let the witnesses among you inform the absent ones. O people, your blood and your wealth are sacred to you until you meet your Lord, as sacred as this day of yours, in this month of yours, in this land of yours. You will meet your Lord and He will ask you about your deeds. I have informed you. So whoever has a trust, let him return it to the One who entrusted it to him. Indeed, every matter of ignorance will be placed under my feet." The Prophet continued with his sermon. He then commended them to the women, saying, "O people, fear God and treat women well, for they are with you like prisoners who can do nothing for themselves." And when he finished with his instruction about the women, he continued advising them while pointing with his index finger first to the sky and then to the people, saying, "O God, bear witness, O God, bear witness, to your service, O Allah, to your service."

Then he said: "O people, remember my words that I have said to you. Indeed, I have left among you something that you will not go astray from if you hold on to it: the Book of God and my family, the people of my house." Then the Messenger of God began to address the issue of imamate, and he began to pave the way for it by saying that the imams after him will be twelve. He said: "This religion will continue to be powerful, invincible and victorious over those who oppose it as long as twelve men take over this matter who are incomparable. They will all be accepted by the community and all will act in accordance with the guidance and the true faith and all..." And here shouted the crowd, their loud cries drowned out the prophet words. He could not be heard any more. The people chatted and argued and cut off his speech. Some of them got up and down restless. They did not understand what the Messenger of God said after the word "all".

One of the seated people asked his father: "What did the Messenger of God say? What did he say after the word 'all'?" He said to him, "The Messenger of God said: 'They are all from Quraysh, or they are all from Banu Hashem.'" At this point, the Messenger of God ended his sermon without being able to convey the message of his Lord to the people. The Messenger of God feared that his people and the hypocrites would return to Jāhilīya. This was because he knew what was hidden in the souls of enmity and hatred towards his cousin Ali ibn Abi Talib. Therefore, he asked Gabriel to ask his Lord for protection from the people.

The Messenger of God stood in Arafat until sunset of the ninth day, and the people stood with him. Then at night he rode his camel and went back. He ordered the people to move until they reached Muzdalifah. There he prayed and stayed in Muzdalifah.

When dawn broke, he ordered Al-Fadl ibn al-Abbas to pick up seven pebbles for him. Then he set off for Mina and reached it at dawn. On the way there, at Masjid al-Khaif, Gabriel came to him and ordered him to inform the people about the Imamate again. However, he did not bring him immunity. Then he threw the stones of al-Aqaba and went to sacrifice in Mina. He held the sacrificial animals while Ali slaughtered them. Then the Prophet ordered him to donate the meat and skin of the sacrificial animals to the poor. Then he shaved his head.

In Mina, the Messenger of God dispersed the people and separated the Muhajirun and the Ansar and made each one sit individually so that the people would know who would stir up riots against the Prophet when he delivers a sermon in Mina and mentions the Imams after him. He said: "Let the Muhajirun stay here." and pointed to the right side of the Qibla. Then he said: "And the Ansar are here." and pointed to the left of the Qibla. Then he said: "Let the others come down around them." When he wanted to address them, they asked if they should build a roof for him to protect him from the heat. The Messenger of God did not accept this and delivered an eloquent sermon on his camel, saying, "O people, your Lord is one and your Father is one. You are all from Adam and Adam is from dust. The most honorable of you in the eyes of God is the most pious of you. Have I informed you?" They said: "Yes." He said: "Let the witness inform the absent one.".

The Prophet addressed them, and his voice reached everyone who was in Mina, since God opened the ears of the people of Mina so that they could hear him in their homes. And so that no one would dare to make noise and prevent him from conveying what he wanted, as happened in Arafat. He said: "O people, your Lord is one, and your father is one." Verily, there is no superiority for an Arab over a non-Arab, nor for a non-Arab over an Arab, nor for a black over a red[1], nor for a red over a black, except with piety. Have I informed you?" They said: "The Messenger of God has informed." He said: "Let the present inform the absent, for often the informed is more attentive than the listener." Then he said: "What month is this?" They were silent. He said: "A holy

---

1 Red refers to a white or not dark skin color.

month, which land is this?" They were silent. He said: "A holy land. What day is this?" They were silent. He said: "It is a holy day." He continued, "Allah has declared your blood, your property and your honor inviolable, like this month of yours, in this land of yours, on this day of yours, until you meet your Lord. Have I conveyed the message?" They said: "Yes, you have." He said: "O God, be a witness. You will meet your Lord and He will ask you about your deeds. Have I informed you?" The people said: "Yes." He said: "O God, bear witness. Let the one who is present inform the one who is absent. Verily, it is forbidden for any Muslim to wrong another Muslim. Hear from me and you will live, do not commit injustice, do not commit injustice, do not commit injustice. It is not permissible to take a Muslim's money unless he is agreeable to it..."

The Messenger of God continued as he did in Arafat, informing the people of the rules of their religion and advising them until he said: "I have left among you what, if you hold fast to it, you will not stray from the path - the Book of God and my family, the people of my household. Have I informed you?" The people said: "Yes, you have." He said: "O God, bear witness." But what happened in Arafat also happened in Mina, for they challenged God and the Prophet and tried to stop the people from listening to him and to stop him from informing the matter of the Imamate, as they did in Arafat. They shouted and raised their voices, prevented him from completing his words, and met him with malice, insult and aggression. The Messenger of Allah realized that the Quraysh would not allow him to deliver his message. He therefore decided to leave Mecca in haste, without bidding farewell to the House of Allah, to meet the crowds of pilgrims who had already departed. He wanted to delay them and keep them away from the noise and confusion of the Quraysh in order to convey to them the matter of the Imamate apart from everything.

Any delay would mean that a fraction of the people would return to their land and the Prophet would not be able to deliver to them what he wanted to deliver. The Prophet's delay in conveying what was revealed to him in the matter of Imamate was due to the great resistance he found among the Quraysh. They did not hesitate to confront the Prophet not only with noise and shouting but also with accusations against his person and to sting and question his integrity and the sincerity of his work and intention.

On the eleventh day, the Prophet went out of Mina until he reached Al-Abtah. There, Aisha asked to perform Umrah, but he was not satisfied with her Umrah and told her that her circumambulation of the House and Safa and Marwah were sufficient for her Hajj and Umrah. She said: "Your wives go back with Hajj and Umrah. And I will only return with Hajj!" She did not accept it except to do one more Umrah. He finally sent her with her brother Abd al-Rahman, and the Messenger of God waited for her. She performed the Umrah, then came to the Prophet at night. The Messenger of God left Mecca without circumambulating the house at sunset, prayed Maghrib (evening prayer) in Saraf. He and the Muslims hastened their walk and spanned over 150 km from mecca to Al-Juhfa, where Ghadir Khumm lies, in only four days. [469]

In Ghadir Khumm

On Thursday, the eighteenth day of Dhu al-Hijjah, in Ghadir Khumm, the command of Allah descended: "O Messenger, announce to the people the leadership of Ali ibn Abi Talib and inform them of what Allah has revealed to you. If you do not fulfill this great task, it would be as if you have not fulfilled Allah's message and have not conveyed it to the people, and all your deeds will be in vain. Fear no one, for Allah will protect you from rebellion and disobedience in your preaching. Allah does not guide those who deny this and disbelieve in it." [470]

The Messenger of Allah ordered those who had rushed forward to return and called those who had stayed behind and were late. He ordered them not to sit under five large trees that were there. He also ordered the removal of thorns and the smoothing of the place. They followed his instructions and the people sat down in their places. When he noticed that some people were late, he was worried. He ordered Ali to gather them, and when they were assembled, he stood among them and leaned on Ali bin Abi Talib. He thanked and praised God and then said: "O people, I detest it when you stay away from me, until it occurred to me: there is no tree that you detest more than a tree that approaches me.

**Figure 64: The Prophet announces the Imamate of
Ali ibn Abi Talib.**

Then some of his companions asked permission to leave, and the Prophet allowed them. He said with regret, "Why is the branch in the tree that follows the Messenger of Allah more hated by you than the other branch?" When they heard this, most of them burst into tears.

Then the noon prayer was called, and the Prophet stood under one of the trees he had specified and prayed with the people. It was a very hot day, so people put part of their clothes on their heads and another part under their feet to protect themselves from the heat of the sun. The messenger of God was shaded from the sun with a robe on a tree. The people also collected the saddles of the camels and used them to build a raised platform.

When the Prophet had finished his prayer, he stood on the platform and preached among the people. He raised his voice and said: "Praise be to God. We seek His help. We believe in Him, we trust in Him, and we seek refuge in Allah from the evils of our own souls and from evil deeds. There is no guide for the one who goes astray and no one who goes astray for the one whom Allah has guided. And I bear witness that there is no god but Allah and that Muhammad is His servant and His Messenger. O people, the All-Knowing has told me that no prophet has lived more than half the life of the one before him. And I am about to be called and I will have to answer. I will be called to account, and you too will be called to account. So what will you say?" They said: "We testify that you have delivered the message, advised, and strived, So may Allah reward you for it. "

He said: "Do you not bear witness that there is no god but Allah and that Muhammad is His servant and Messenger, that His Paradise is true and His Hell is true, that death is true and that without doubt the Day of Resurrection will come and Allah will raise up those who are in the graves?" They said: "Yes, we bear witness to that." He said: "O God, bear witness." Then he said: "O people, do you listen?" They said: "Yes." He said: "I will go before you to the pond, and you will return to the pond. The pond stretches between Sana'a and Basra and there are cups of silver there in the number of stars. So look, how will you act with regard to the two weights [thaqalain] after me." Someone called out, "What are the two weights, O Messenger of Allah?" He said: "The greatest weight is the Book of God. One part is in the hands of God, the Exalted and Majestic, and one part is in your hands. Hold on to it so that you do not go astray. And the other is the lesser weight, my offspring. And the All-Knowing told me that they would not separate until they come to me by the pond. I asked my Lord for them. Do not overtake them or you will perish, and do not neglect them or you will perish." Then he took Ali by the hand and lifted them until all the people recognized him. Then he said: "O people, who is closer to the believers than they themselves?" They said: "Allah and His Messenger know best.".

He said: "Allah is my Lord, and I am the Lord of the believers, and I have more rights over them than they have over themselves. The one whose master (maula) I am, his master (maula) is also Ali." He says it three times: "O God, be the protector of the one who has him as his protector, and be the adversary of the one who has him as his adversary. Love the one who loves him, hate the one who hates him. Help the one who helps him and disappoint the one who disappoints him. Let the truth be with him wherever he is. Let the witness inform the one who is absent." Then they did not disperse until Gabriel revealed the revelation of God by saying, {Today I have perfected your religion for you, and I have completed My blessing upon you, and I have approved Islam as your religion.} [471] The Messenger of God said: "God is the greatest. (Allahu Akbar) for the perfection of religion, the completion of blessings and the satisfaction of the Lord with my message and the leadership of Ali after me." Then the Messenger of God placed the turban on Ali so that he let one end of it fall over his shoulder, and then he said: "God supported me in the days of Badr and Hunayn with angels who wore this turban. O people, say: 'We give you on it an oath from ourselves, a covenant with our tongues and a handshake with our hands, which we pass on to our children and families without changing it. And you are a witness over us, and Allah is sufficient as a witness.' Say what I have said to you, and greet Ali as the Prince of the Believers, and say: 'Praise belongs to Allah, Who has guided us here. We could not have found guidance if Allah had not guided us.'[472] Indeed, Allah knows every sound and knows the treachery of every soul. So whoever breaks (his word) breaks it only to his own detriment, but whoever keeps what he has pledged to Allah, He will give him a great reward. [473] Say what Allah is pleased with of you, for if you disbelieve, Allah has no need of you." [474]

The people began to congratulate the Prince of the Believers[1]. Among those who congratulated him at the head of the Companions were Abu Bakr, Omar, Talha and Al-Zubair, each of whom said: "Congratulations, bless you, son of Abi Talib. You have become my master and the master of all believing men and women." The people hastened to say, "Yes, we have heard and obeyed what God and His Messenger have commanded us, with our hearts, our souls, our tongues and all our limbs." They prayed Zuhr (noon prayer) and Asr (afternoon prayer) at the same time and Maghrib and Isha at the same time, and they continued to swear allegiance for three days. The Messenger of God said whenever a group pledged allegiance to him, "Praise be to God who has favored us above all worlds."

After that, the Messenger of God sat in a tent that belonged to him and ordered the Prince of the believers to sit in another tent and ordered the people to congratulate Ali in his tent. When the people finished congratulating him, the Messenger of God ordered the Mothers of the Faithful (the Prophet's wives) to come to him and congratulate him, and they did so.

Hasaan bin Thabit said: "Allow me, O Messenger of God, to say a poem about Ali." He said: "Speak, with God's blessings." Hasaan stood up and said on this occasion:"

A call is sounding on this day,

in Khumm, the Prophet speaks the question.

'Who is your Lord and Protector?

Clearly and distinctly, without pomposity.

The answer is given, there is no hiding,

---

1 The title (Amir al-Mu'minin); 'Prince of the Believers' was given to Ali bin Abi Talib by the Prophet Muhammad.

'God is our protector, you are our Lord,'

no one has resisted him so far. Stand up,

O Ali, he then says, You will be imam and leader after me.

And whoever I am his master, you will be his master,

Be his loyal supporters, so be it.

And in the midst of all the believers,

he prays to God, the Most High,

'Be the protector of those who love Ali,

Opponent of those who choose him as their enemy. „

Omar ibn al-Khattab said: "O Messenger of Allah, a young man with a beautiful face and a pleasant fragrance was with me. He said to me, 'O Omar, the Messenger of Allah has made a treaty that only a hypocrite breaks. Then the Messenger of Allah took Omar by the hand and said: "He is not from Adam's descendants, but Gabriel wanted to confirm to you what I said about Ali." The hypocrites were only found as a few individuals, their number did not exceed a few people among the thousands who were there. They left their followers and tribes in Mecca, not daring to utter a single word aloud but only in whispers. Perhaps the reason for this apparent insolence and impudence displayed during the farewell sermon was the feeling of this group of Muhajirun from Quraysh of strength they had in their homeland and among their followers and friends, i.e. in the area of Mecca and its surroundings.

A news about the event of Ghadir Khumm spread. Al-Harith bin Na'man Al-Fihri came to the Messenger of God and said: "O Muhammad, God has commanded us to bear witness that there is no god but Allah and that you are the Messenger of Allah, and that we should pray, fast, make Hajj and give the Zakat. We accepted this from you, but it was not enough for you until you lifted up your cousin Ali ibn Abi Talib and spoke about him, saying, 'Whoever I am his master, Ali is also his master. Is this from you or from God?" The Messenger of Allah said: "By the One who there is no god but He, this is from Allah." Al-Harith wanted to go to his camel and said: "O Allah, if what Muhammad says is true, then rain stones from the sky on us or bring us a painful punishment!" But before he reached his camel, a stone hit him on the neck and killed him. Then Allah revealed: "This questioner has asked for himself the punishment that Allah has prepared for the unbelievers. But he has asked for it prematurely, and it will surely come upon the disbelievers, and nothing can ward it off. It comes down from Allah, the Owner of the high levels and exalted positions. "[475]

The people returned to Medina, and some returned to their homes on the way, bidding farewell to the Messenger of Allah. Everyone who had accompanied the Prophet on this spiritual journey will remember the most accurate memories, for they will be precious memories in his heart that will remain alive in his soul and conscience for days, months, years and decades, as long as this is the last time he sees the Messenger of Allah. [476]

632 - 633 AD

The eleventh year after the Hijrah

Osama's army

After his pilgrimage, the Messenger of Allah spent the rest of Dhul-Hijjah and Muharram in Medina and continued to remember the deaths of Zaid ibn Haritha, Ja'far ibn Abi Talib and their companions in Mu'tah, feeling deep sorrow. In the year 11 after the Hijrah, Prophet Muhammad encouragd and ordered the Muslims to prepare for war against the Romans.

The next day he called Osama ibn Zaid and said: "O Osama, lead a campaign in the name of Allah and his blessings until you reach the place of your father's death. Then attack the people of Banu Abna[1] early in the morning with the horses and set them on fire. Hasten your march before the news, and if Allah grants you victory, do not stay long there and take guides with you and send the spies ahead of you. " The Prophet wanted to protect him from the danger of the roman, since Heraclius might be able to send his huge armies to save the people of Abna and that he might harm Osama and his army.

A few days later, the Messenger of Allah began to suffer from an illness that afflicted him and caused him pain. When Thursday came, he put Osama at the head of an army and said: "Fight in the name of Allah for the cause of Allah against those who do not believe in him. Fight, but do not betray and do not kill a child or a woman and do not wish to meet the enemy, for you do not know whether you will be tested by them. Say instead, 'O Allah, protect us from them as it pleases you, and protect us from their evils.' When they meet you, they will shout loudly, but you should remain calm and quiet and not argue, lest you fail and your resolve falter. Instead, say: 'O Allah, we are your servants and they are your servants. Our destinies and their destinies are in your hands. You alone can defeat them.' And know that paradise lies beneath the swords."

Osama went out with his forces and gave the banner to Buraydah bin al-Hasib al-Aslami, and they encamped in Al-Jurf. There remained no one from the early Muhajirun and Ansar who had not participated in this brigade, including Abu Bakr, Omar ibn al-Khattab, Abu Ubaidah ibn al-Jarrah, Saad ibn Abi

---

1   Abna is a district in Balqa' between Ashkelon and Ramla, which is near Mu'tah.

Waqqas, Saeed ibn Zaid ibn Amr, and other Ansar such as Qatada ibn al-Nu'man and Salama ibn Aslam ibn Hareth. The only important figure who was not ordered by Prophet Muhammad to join Osama's army was Ali bin Abi Talib. This was a strategic move by Prophet Muhammad to smooth the transfer of power to his destined successor, Ali. [501]

When Osama took charge of an army consisting of prominent Muslims, both Muhajirun and Ansar, he was not yet eighteen years old. This caused some resentment and anger among some of them, as they believed they were more suitable for the position than he was. A man from the Muhajirun, Ayyash ibn Abi Rabia al-Makhzumi, asked, "Will he appoint this young man over the Muhajirun?" Much discussion arose about this, and Omar ibn al-Khattab heard something about it and reported it to the Prophet Muhammad, who became very angry. The Prophet went to the pulpit with a headband around his head and a cloth over it and praised and thanked Allah. Then he said: "O people, I have heard that some of you are questioning the leadership of Osama. If you doubt Osama's leadership, then you have already doubted the leadership of his father before him. By Allah, he deserves this position, and his son after him is also suitable for this position, and they are both capable of every good deed. Treat him well, for he is one of your best." Then the Messenger of Allah descended from the pulpit and returned to his house. The Muslims who had left with Osama came to the Prophet and bid him farewell. Among them was Omar ibn al-Khattab. The Prophet urged them to hurry. They then went to the army in al-Jurf.

Umm Ayman entered and said: "O Messenger of Allah, why don't you allow Osama to stay in his camp until you recover. Because if he leaves in this condition, he will have no benefit for himself." The Prophet replied, "Carry out the mission of Osama." The people went to the camp and spent the night there on Sunday. A few days later, Osama came and the Messenger of Allah was lying seriously ill. They had given him medicine. He entered the room, and there were men and women around him. His eyes were tired and he did not speak. Osama bent over him and kissed him, and the Prophet raised his hands to the sky and then placed them on Osama as if he were praying for him. Osama returned then to his camp, and hesitated to carry out the task, and the army hesitated because of his hesitation. The Muslims who had gathered in Al-Jurf returned to Medina again with Osama, and Buraydah bin al-Hasib arrived with his banner and stuck it in front of the Prophet's door.

Osama was delayed, and the army was also delayed and did not carry out their mission. The Prophet's condition worsened at times and improved a little. He again emphasized the necessity of carrying out Osama's mission. Finally, Osama asked him, "By the life of my parents, will you allow me to stay for a few days until God heals you?" He replied, "Go out, and may Allah bless you." Osama said: "O Messenger of Allah, if I leave and you are in this state, I will feel hurt." He replied, "Go your way, may Allah give you victory and protect you." Osama said: "O Messenger of Allah, I hate being worried about you." He said: "Do what I have commanded you." Then the Messenger of Allah lost consciousness.

The elders and leaders in Osama's army played a role in this hesitation. Their interests required them to stay in Medina during these sensitive times. This drove them to reach an understanding regarding this hesitation with Osama, if they were not the ones who had urged him or imposed it on him for a period of about half a month.

Prophet Muhammad still had seven dinars that he had deposited with Aisha. When he was sick, he said: "O Aisha, send the gold to Ali." Then he lost consciousness and Aisha was busy with it. When he woke up, he asked, "O Aisha, what have you done with the gold?" She said: "It is with me." He said: "Spend it. " Then he lost consciousness again. When he woke up again, he asked, "O Aisha, did you spend the gold?" She said: "No, by Allah, O Prophet." She then placed the money in his hand and he counted it. It was seven dinars. He asked himself, "What does Muhammad think about his Lord when he meets God and this is with Him?" Then he gave all the money as alms. [477]

The Tragedy of Thursday

On Thursday, the 25th of the month of Safar, Prophet Muhammad's condition worsened and he lay sick on his bed surrounded by his companions. In this state, he said: "Bring me katif[1] and writing materials. I will write you a book that you will follow so that you will never mislead yourselves." The people started to argue and engage in loud discussions. There was a lot of noise in the house and Omar tried to dissuade the Prophet from his intention. Omar said: "The

---

1   Katif (Shoulder): It is the shoulder blade bone. The Arabs used to write on it, just as they wrote on papyrus.

Prophet is delirious because of the illness, and we have the Book of Allah. The book of Allah is enough for us." The people in the house argued and disagreed about whether the Prophet should write the book or not. Some said: "Let him submit it so that he can write the book," while others said the same thing Omar said. They continued to argue. They said about the Prophet, "What is wrong with him. Is he hallucinating? Ask him about it?" The Prophet said in a weak voice, "Leave me alone. It is not proper to dispute in the presence of the prophet." The people in the house went away and came back to talk to him. The prophet said: "Leave me alone. For I am in better state than what you are calling me to."

A woman who was present said: "Woe to you. The Prophet of God has imposed an obligation on you." Some people said to her, "Keep quiet, you have no Mind!" The Prophet said angrily, "You have no Mind!" Ibn Abbas came out and said: "It is a real calamity what happened when they stopped the Prophet when he wanted to write a book for them."

They defied the command of the Prophet of God by raising their voices, making noise and arguing in his presence, which made him angry. They even said: "We have the Quran, that's enough for us." Thus they excluded the prophetic tradition. But even in this matter, they did not act in accordance with the Quran, which called on them to obey Allah and his Prophet. When the Prophet was on his deathbed and saw the determination and resistance of the leading Companions to disregard the opinion of their Prophet and prevent him from writing this book, he changed his mind. Although he himself had asked to write it for them, their surprising words forced him to do so. After these words, the book could no longer be written, because writing it might cause strife and disagreement. Omar ibn al-Khattab later said: "He wanted to write down the name of Ali ibn Abi Talib during his illness, but I prevented him from doing so out of consideration and caution for Islam. By the Lord of this Kaaba, the Quraysh would never agree on Ali ibn Abi Talib." [478]

The death of the Messenger of God

On the 28th of the month of Safar, the Prophet was exhausted in bed due to his illness. Bilal came in and called for prayer, it was the morning prayer. The Messenger of God said in a weak voice: "O Bilal, you have delivered the message. Whoever wishes, can lead the people in prayer, and whoever wishes, can refrain." Abu Bakr then came forward to lead the prayer. When the Messenger of God heard about this, he wanted to intervene personally.

He felt a little stronger and stood up with his head bandaged between two men who were supporting him. His feet dragged on the floor as he walked into the mosque. Then the rows of people opened for him, and Abu Bakr realized that the people were only doing this for the Prophet of Allah. The Messenger of Allah withdrew Abu Bakr from leading the prayer, and Abu Bakr gave up his place of prayer so that the Prophet could pray as an imam.

After that, Abu Bakr asked the Prophet for permission to visit his house in Al-Sanh[1]. Then the Prophet said: "Call Ali ibn Abi Talib and Osama bin Zaid for me." They came, and the Messenger of Allah put his hand on Ali's shoulder and the other on Osama's and said: "Take me to Fatima." They took him there, and Hassan and Hussein were there.

He greeted her and put her on his side, and she threw herself on him and kissed him. He whispered something to her so that she cried. Then he whispered again and she laughed. Aisha and Umm Salama asked her, "Tell me, what did he whisper to you?" She replied, "I will not reveal the secret of the Messenger of Allah." When he died, Aisha said to her, "I am asking you because of the right I have over you that you tell me what he told you." She replied, "Yes, I can now. He came to me and said: 'Gabriel used to recite the Quran to me once every year, but this year he recited it to me twice. I see that my end is near. And you will be the first of my family to follow me. What a good predecessor I am to you.' I wept at this. Then he said: 'Wouldn't you like to be the mistress of the women of the worlds? I had to laugh at that.".

Some of the companions of the Prophet Muhammad were with him, including Ammar ibn Yasir. Ammar asked him, "May my father and mother be sacrificed for you, O Messenger of Allah, who will wash you from us if it is to be?" He said: "Ali ibn Abi Talib will do that, for he will be assisted by angels." Ammar asked him again, "May my father and mother be sacrificed for you, O Messenger of Allah, who will pray for us when the time comes for you?" He said: "Quiet, may Allah bless you." Then he said to Ali, "O son of Abi Talib, when you see my spirit leave my body, wash me. Put my head in your lap, for Allah's command has come. When my soul leaves my body, take it with your hand,

---

1 Al-Sanh: a place in Medina, which is about a mile from the house of the Prophet. Abu Bakr had a house there, where he lived with his wife Asma bint Kharija.

wipe your face with it, then turn me to the Qibla and cover me and be the first among men to pray for me and do not leave me until you laid me to rest me in my grave."

The Prophet Muhammad lay on his deathbed in the house of his daughter Fatima. He was surrounded by his loved ones from his family who wanted to bid him farewell. In his last moments, his last looks and words were very meaningful to them, always illuminating their lives and guiding their path. As the Prophet's state of health did not allow any visits, his daughter Fatima made sure that no one visited him during his extreme weakness and kept apologizing to those who wanted to come.

But a stranger insisted on asking about the Prophet, and Fatima told him, "The Prophet of Allah is busy right now and has no time for you." The man went away, but then returned and asked for permission again. Then Gabriel told the Prophet, "The angel of death is asking permission from you. No one before or after you has ever been asked for permission." The Prophet informed his daughter Fatima that he was the Angel of Death, and she allowed him to enter. The Prophet asked him, "Would you do that, O Angel of Death?" He replied, "Yes, I have been instructed to obey what you command me to do." Gabriel said: "O Ahmad[1], God has missed you and longs to meet you." The Prophet said: "O angel of death, go and do what you have been commanded." Gabriel said: "This is my last visit to earth. You were my only business in this world."

Ali took his head and placed it in his lap. Then the Prophet took his last breath while the hand of the Prince of the believers was under his chin. Ali raised it to his face and wiped his face with it. Then he aligned him, closed his eyes and spread his cloak over him. Then he placed him in the qibla. Immediately after the transfer of the Messenger of God to the Supreme Companion (Allah), the people of his household wept and wailed. The rest of the Muslims gathered around the Prophet's house in the mosque and on the roads. They were overwhelmed with anticipation, sadness and fear. As soon as they heard the sound of weeping through the closed door, they rushed and gathered in their mosque, bowing their heads, their eyes full of tears, their hearts shaken and their souls torn. Undoubtedly, there is no reason for them to deny the truth. When Omar ibn al-Khattab heard about this, he fell to the ground. Shortly afterwards he woke up, but he refused to accept the Prophet's death

---

1   Ahmad is one of the names of the Prophet Muhammad.

and shouted threateningly: "The Messenger of God has not died and will not die until his religion triumphs over all other religions. He will return and cut off the hands and feet of the men who said so. I don't want to hear a man say: The Messenger of God is dead, or I will slay him with my sword." Omar swore to the people with everything he had that the Prophet was still alive, and his feelings were inflamed. But then Abu Bakr came from Al-Sanh. He revealed the face of the Prophet Muhammad and said to Omar, who was still swearing, "O you who swear by your Prophet, sit down." He ordered him to sit three times, but Omar refused.

Then Abu Bakr gave a speech in another corner, and the people left Omar and turned to Abu Bakr. He said: "Whoever worships Muhammad should know that Muhammad has died. But whoever worships Allah should know that Allah lives and never dies." Then he quoted the word of Allah: {So if he was to die or be killed, would you turn back on your heels [to unbelief]?} [479] Omar calmed down and said: "It was as if I had not heard this verse!" When Abu Bakr saw Ali mourning over the loss of the Prophet of Allah, he scorned him for it and said: "Why do I see you so upset!" Ali said to him, "It has affected me what has not affected you."

The heated emotions were different, for while the community was in grief and sorrow for their prophet, there was a group of opportunistic hypocrites who hid their joy for salvation and hope for change, aiming to gain control and positions that would bring them money and fame. In the meantime, the Ansar quickly gathered in Saqifa Banu Sa'idah[1] to discuss a topic that was on their minds, namely the fate of the community after the death of the Prophet of Allah. When Abu Bakr and Omar learned of this meeting, they left the Prophet of Allah and were accompanied by Abu Ubaidah bin al-Jarrah to join the Ansar. Ali and those in the house of Banu Hashim and the rest of the Muhajirun and Muslims knew nothing of all that had happened, nor of what Abu Bakr and Omar had planned. One of Prophet Muhammad's last wishes was to be buried in his own house where he died. He was to be wrapped in three robes and no one except Ali was to enter his grave. Ali washed the Prophet in his shirt as the Prophet had commanded. He had blindfolded al-Fadl ibn al-Abbas so that he would not see the Prophet's body. He placed the Prophet's cheek on the ground and faced him to the right in the direction of prayer. No one looked at

---

1 Saqifa Banu Sa'idah: was a covered structure belonged to the Banu Sa'idah and is located 200 m west of Masjid-e-Nabwi (the mosque of the Prophet). It is currently a library.

the Prophet's body except Ali. He said with tears in his eyes as he washed the Prophet, "By the life of my parents, you are blessed in life and in death. With your death, something was ended that was ended by the death of none other than you - prophethood and the prophets. Your calamity is specific to the people of your household, so they do not care about the other calamities that will befall them after you, nor what befell them before. This calamity has also spread to the people, so that all people are also equally affected by this calamity. It is a private and public disaster. If you had not commanded us to be patient and forbidden us to complain, we would have drowned ourselves in tears for you. The illness from his death is incurable and the grief accompanies us, and both are but a small tribute to you. But it's something we can't turn away from." Then Ali wept and kissed the Prophet's face.

As the Prince of the believers washed him, he covered him in a robe. Afterwards, the mourners were allowed to enter in groups and said: "Peace be upon you, O Prophet, and God's mercy and blessings." They circled him. Then the Commander of the believers stood among them to pray for him and said: ﴾Allah and His angels pronounce blessings on the Prophet. O you who believe, pronounce blessings on him and greet him with proper salutations﴿ [480] The people said the same as the Commander of the believers until the people of Medina and its surroundings prayed for him.

The Prince of the believers, Al-Abbas ibn Abdul Muttalib, al-Fadl ibn al-Abbas and Osama ibn Zaid entered to take charge of the Prophet's burial. The Ansar shouted from outside the house: "O Ali, we remind you of Allah and of our right today to bury the Prophet. Let one of us go in who is fortunate enough to bury the Prophet." Ali then said: "Let Aws bin Khawli come in." He was a brave and noble man from the Khazraj of Banu Awf who took part in the Battle of Badr. When he entered, Ali said to him, "Come in." The Prince of the believers laid the Prophet on his hands and placed him in his grave. When the Prophet was on the ground, he said to Aws, "Get out." He got out, and Ali opened the grave and placed the face of the Messenger of God on the ground, turning his head to the right and facing the Kaaba. He then placed mud bricks over him and covered him with earth. This took place on a Monday, the 28th of Safar of the eleventh year after the Hijrah of the Messenger of God, when he was sixty-three years old.

People took the opportunity that Ali bin Abi Talib was busy with the burial of the Messenger of God and that Banu Hashem were separated from them due to their pain over the Messenger of God, and rushed to discuss the issue of succession. Most of the people were not present at the funeral of the Messenger of God due to the dispute between the Muhajirun and the Ansar over the succession. Therefore, most of them did not pray for him. When the Prophet was buried, his daughter Fatima said in tears:

"The sky turned dark, and the sun set,

and the afternoon became gloomy.

The Earth became sad after the prophet.

Alas, it's rumbled a lot for him.

Let the east and west of the land weep for him,

and let Medina and all Yemen cry for him.

O the last of the messengers, his light blessed,

prayed for you, the one who revealed the Quran."

When the dust was sprinkled on the grave of the Messenger of God, Fatima came and stood by his grave and took a handful of the grave dust and put it on her eyes and wept and said:

"Ahmad's earth smell,

a fragrance so deep and full of life,

Once you have breathed in this fragrance,

forgets all the scents of this world.

Misfortunes have befallen me,

had they been poured on days,

they would have been nights, an infinite length."

After the death of her father, Fatima remained sad and with her head bowed, her body exhausted, her pillars collapsed, her eyes crying and her heart burning. Every hour she fainted from grief. She said to her children, "Where is your father who always honored you and carried you on his shoulders. Where is your father who had the most compassion for you and did not let you walk on the ground. I will never see him opening this door again and not carrying you on his shoulders as he always did." [481]

The coup

The Ansar believed that they were the ones who provided protection and support, that they converted to Islam and sacrificed their lives and wealth for Islam. Therefore, they were truly "Ansar" i.e. supporters, as the Prophet called them. They believed that they had a right to Islam and played a great role in building the community. Therefore, they hoped for a leadership role in the Muslim community as a reward for their sacrifice for Islam. On the other hand, the Ansar movement and the meeting in Saqifa Banu Sa'idah also arose from the fear that the matter might deviate from their people and that possibly the control of the community would end up to those who killed their sons, fathers and brothers.

The Ansar fought the Quraysh and the Arabs and captured their men until the Arabs surrendered to their swords. The Ansar were afraid of these people if they got rule, that they would take revenge especially because of their killings. In addition, the words of Prophet Muhammad revolved in their minds, "You will experience injustice and oppression in power after me, so be patient until you meet me at the pond." Therefore, the Ansar decided to take the initiative and take control of the situation before it was too late. They wanted the leadership not to control the power and affairs of the community but to protect them. But the Ansar were not as smart and strong as the Quraysh. They were weaker in will and planning and also had limitations in their opinions.

Although the Ansar wanted to swear allegiance to Saad bin Ubadah, it was only the Khazraj, not the Aws. Even though the Aws outwardly rallied with the Khazraj in the Saqifa, it was more of a common fear that brought them together. At the same time, however, they harbored hidden resentments and fears towards the Khazraj due to old wounds.

When Abu Bakr, Omar ibn al-Khattab and Abu Ubaidah bin al-Jarrah came to the gathering in the Saqifa, Saad ibn 'Ubadah encouraged the Ansar to take the initiative without paying attention to people's opinions by saying, "Take this matter into your hands regardless of the people. " They agreed to choose him

and give him leadership, and they agreed that they would respond to the Muhajirun's objection by saying, "A leader from us and a leader from you, and we
will never be satisfied without this point." When Saad ibn 'Ubadah heard this,
he said: "This is the first step towards weakness." An unpleasant exchange of
words ensued, which almost led to violence. Then Abu Bakr spoke and the
people listened to him. He said: "Allah sent Muhammad with guidance and the
religion of truth. The Messenger of Allah called us to Islam, and Allah took our
hearts and minds to what he called us to. So we were the first among the people
to embrace Islam, the community of Muhajirun, his relatives and those who
were close to him. We are the people of prophecy and the people of succession.
Among the Arabs, we are the noblest lineage. Our entire birth was under
Quraysh, and the Arabs will never allow it unless there is a man of Quraysh at
the top. Quraysh have the most beautiful faces among the people. They are the
most eloquent people and are the best in their speech. The people are followers
of Quraysh, and we are the leaders, and you are the ministers. This is a division
between us and you. And you, O Ansar, are our brothers in the Book of Allah,
our partners in faith, and those who are most dear to us. You have welcomed
us and supported us, and you are the most worthy people to accept Allah's
judgment and follow His guidance, which He grants to your brothers from the
Muhajirun. You are also the most worthy people not to envy them for the
blessings Allah has given them. You are able to accomplish this, and the Arabs
will not recognize this except for Quraysh. And I have accepted one of these
two men for you, so pledge allegiance to one of them whom you choose." Then
Omar ibn al-Khattab and Abu Ubaidah bin al-Jarrah took. [482] Omar and Abu
Ubaidah said: "After the Messenger of Allah, no one should be above you, O
Abu Bakr. You are the companion of the cave with the Messenger of Allah, the
second of two[1], and when the Messenger of Allah became ill, he asked you to
pray for the people. So you are the most worthy for this matter."

The Ansar said: "By Allah, we do not envy you for the good that Allah has
brought you. Allah has not created people who are dearer to us than you, more
important to us than you and more accepted to us than you. But we are concerned about the days ahead. If you choose a leader from among you today and
he dies, you take a man from the Ansar and make him your leader. Then when
he dies, we will take a man from the Muhajirun and make him our leader. We
will always be like this as long as this community exists. We have sworn alle-

---

1   He refers to the Surah At-Tauba 9:40: '...him as second of two...'. See 'The
    Prophet in the Cave', page 100.

giance to you and are satisfied with your command. It is better that way so that the Qurayshi does not fear that the Ansari will attack him if he is elected."

Omar said unwaveringly: "This is not appropriate, and it is only suitable for a man from the Quraysh. The Arabs will only be satisfied with him, and they will only be ruled by him. No one will be suitable for it except him, and by Allah, if anyone contradicts us, we will kill him." The talk increased and the voices became loud until they were afraid of disagreement. One of the Ansar said: "Stretch out your hand, O Abu Bakr." He stretched out his hand and they swore allegiance to him, first the Muhajirun, then the Ansar. Omar jumped up and took Abu Bakr's hand, and Asid ibn Hudair al-Ashhali and Bashir ibn Saad rushed ahead of him to swear allegiance to Abu Bakr, then they swore allegiance one by one.

Figure 65: The takeover of power by Abu Bakr.

Saad ibn Ubadah lay there, feeling unwell. The people crowded around Abu Bakr to swear allegiance. A man from the Ansar said: "Be careful with Saad, don't step on him or you will kill him." Omar said angrily, "May Allah kill Saad, for he is the cause of the unrest."

After the Saqifa, Abu Bakr and whoever was with him returned to the mosque. He sat on the pulpit and the people continued to swear allegiance to him. But Ali was not at the Saqifa. He was busy with the burial of the Prophet.[483] After Abu Bakr had received his pledges of allegiance, a man came to the Prince of the believers while he was digging the grave of the Prophet of Allah and said to him, "The people pledged allegiance to Abu Bakr, And the treachery was on the part of the Ansar because of their differences of opinion, and the freedmen (Al-Tulqaa) hastened to pledge allegiance to the man for fear that you would take the matter before them."

403

Then he put the shovel in the ground and put his hand on it and said: {Alif, Lam, Meem Do the people think that they will be left to say, "We believe" and they will not be tried? But We have certainly tried those before them, and Allah will surely make evident those who are truthful, and He will surely make evident the liars. Or do those who do evil deeds think they can outrun Us? Evil is what they judge.} [484].

After the oath of allegiance for Abu Bakr had been taken in the Prophet's Mosque, a group went to the house of Ali ibn Abi Talib to obtain the oath of allegiance for Abu Bakr from him. They knocked hard on the door behind which his wife Fatima was at the Prophet's grave, as the Prophet Muhammad had been buried there. She asked, "Who is knocking at the door?" When they found out that someone was inside, they suddenly stormed the door with force and pushed her between the door and the wall, causing her to scream and suffer a miscarriage. Fatima was also injured. The attackers wanted to take Ali with them to swear allegiance. Ali heard their voices and rushed towards the attackers. They then fled, leaving Fatima alone. This all happened within a few moments. Ali returned to help his wife Fatima and stayed with her until morning. The attackers were at the door of his house.

On the same night that the Prophet was buried, thousands of fighters from the surrounding tribes entered the city, especially the tribe of Aslam, and supported Abu Bakr. Omar was certain of their victory. The few Muslims who had not yet sworn allegiance to Abu Bakr hid in their homes, a very small minority. Omar and his group searched the houses for them, while the people pointed them out to the soldiers, saying, "There are two in this house and three in that" or "one or more". They stormed the houses, pulled the people out by force and took them to the mosque to pledge allegiance.

There was no one in Ali's house who could defend him against the attackers or fight for him. If he had put up even the slightest resistance, no believer in the city would have remained alive. The streets were full of armed men and no one could stick their head out, let alone go to Ali to support him or fight with him. Al-Zubair sneaked into Ali's house during this time to announce to Ali that he was on his side. Omar, Khaled, Asid bin Hudeir, Muadh bin Jabal, Thabit bin Qais bin Shammas, Salama bin Waqsh, Qunfudh bin Umair and Al-Mughirah came again with others in a group to the house of Fatima and Ali and brought wood. They lit the fire at Fatima's door. Al-Zubair came out at that moment and they took his sword and struck the stone with it and broke it.

Then they stormed the house of Ali and Fatima. She tried to steer them away from the house, but they beat her. The gang overpowered Ali, arrested him and took him outside to force him to swear allegiance. They also beat Fatima again when she followed him, and Salman brought her back into the house on Ali's instructions. When Ali reluctantly swore allegiance to Abu Bakr, Ali was released and returned to the house. Eight days later, they took Fatima's land (Fadak[1]) and beat her again. [485]

The painful truth is that the Arabs detested the affair of Muhammad and envied him for what God had given him in grace. They plotted against him, tried to kill him and hurt his family, despite his great kindness to them and his enormous benefits for them. The Arabs agreed since his lifetime to turn affairs away from his family after his death. If the Quraysh had not taken his name as a pretext for leadership and surrendered to fame and rule, they would not have worshipped God for a single day after his death and would have returned to their Jāhilīya.[486]

Conclusion

In conclusion, the Prophet Muhammad, as described by those who lived with him, was the person with the biggest smile. He never refused anyone at his meals. He had a mat on which he slept at night and which he spread out to sit on during the day. But he gave everything he got without fear of poverty, as one Bedouin described him. This does not mean that he loved poverty or was satisfied with it. No, he sought refuge from it, saying, "O Allah, I seek refuge from poverty, deprivation and humiliation..." But as long as he lived in a society in which there were poor people, the best system is the one that places the ruler on the side of the poor and puts him on an equal footing with them in terms of food, housing and clothing.

The Prophet was the first to warn his closest relatives when Allah commanded him: {And warn your closest relatives} [487] He said to them, among other things: "Who among you will support me in this matter so that he will be my brother, my deputy and my successor among you!" All of them hesitated except Ali ibn Abi Talib who said: "It is I, O Prophet of Allah." He took him by the neck and said: "This is my brother, my deputy and my successor among

---

1 See page 253 for more detail about Fadak-Land.

you, so listen to him and obey him!" The people stood up, laughed and said to Abu Talib: "He commands you to listen to your son and obey him." Muhammad first called his fellow Arabs and then all those whom his message reached, to faith. Thus Allah testified: ❨And We have sent you for all people❩ [488]. While other prophets were sent only to their people or the people of their time, Muhammad addressed all people, regardless of their race and language, in every era and country. He wrote to the kings of the earth, including Khosrau and Heraclius, and sent his messengers to them to call them to believe in his message, saying what Allah had commanded him: ❨Say: O people. I am Allah's Messenger to you all❩ [489].

Muhammad was a human being, and whoever describes him with one of the characteristics of the Creator, the Provider, has exaggerated and disbelieved in Allah. But not all people are like Muhammad. His greatness lay in the fact that he took care of everyone's worries and did not burden anyone, near or far, with his own worries. He walked with the widow and the poor and met their needs. No one prevented him from meeting them. Everyone, whether friend or foe, found interest and compassion in him. Thus Allah said about him: ❨And we have sent you only as a mercy for the worlds❩ [490]. This means that his care and interest was not only for his closest relatives or his followers, but was open to all people, enemies and friends.

They hurt his face and wanted to kill him, but he said: "O Allah, guide my people, for they do not know." He not only asked Allah for guidance for them, but also excused them for their ignorance and lack of knowledge. It is not surprising that Muhammad did not get angry for himself and did not keep any of the goods of this world for himself. The surprising thing would have been if he had become angry and kept something for himself. This trait is inevitable and obligatory for someone who was sent to perfect the noblest character traits and call all people to believe in his message. One day a man called him and said: "O our Lord and son of our Lord, our best and son of our best." He replied, "Do not be deceived by the devil. I am Muhammad, the servant of Allah and His Messenger. By Allah, I do not want you to elevate me above my status." His companions did not stand up when they saw him coming, even though he was their favorite, because they knew that he did not like it when they stood up for him. He also didn't like it when his companions walked behind him and took the hand of the one who did to let him walk beside him. These are the character traits of Muhammad, and not all people are like Muhammad, there is no doubt about that, but his character traits reflect the truth of Islam.

The Messenger of Allah may have passed away physically, but spiritually and legally he is still present. He leaves behind a tremendous legacy that has changed the course of humanity forever. It has changed the way people view life and the world and restored what was forgotten from the teachings of the previous prophets. This legacy consists of the Quran and the Sunnah of the Prophet.[491]

Sources

1. The Holy Quran Translation: Saheeh International, Ali Quli Qara'l
2. Biography of the Prophet by Ibn Hashim, died 218 AH
3. Al Tabakat Al Kubra by Ibn Saad, died 230 AH
4. Al-Musnad by Ahmad bin Hanbal, died 241 AH
5. Diwan by Abi Talib bin Abdul Muttalib by Al-Mahzami, died 257 AH
6. Sahih Muslim by Al-Nisaborie, died 261 AH
7. Ansab al-Ashraf by al-Baladhari, died 279 AH
8. Tarikh al-Tabari by Ibn Jarir al-Tabari, died 310 AH
9. Tafsir Al-Qummi by Ali bin Ibrahim al-Qummi, died 329 AH
10. Al-Amali by Sheikh Al-Saduq, died 381 AH
11. Ilal Al-Sharaa by Sheikh Al-Saduq, died 381 AH
12. Al-Bidaya wa Al-Nihaya by Ibn Kathir, died 774 AH
13. Imtaa Alasmaa by Taqi al-Din al-Maqrizi, died 845 AH
14. Tarich Al Khamis by Diyar Bakri, died 968 AH
15. Tafsir Al-Safi by Al-Kashani, died 1091 AH
16. Al-Burhan in Tafsir of the Quran by Al-Bahrani, died 1109 AH
17. Bihar Al Anwar by Al-Majlisi, died 1111 AH
18. Tafsir Noor Al-Thaqalayn by Al-Huwaizi, died 1112 AH
19. Al-Saqifa by Muhammad Rida al-Muzaffar, died 1383 AH
20. Al-Mizan in Tafsir of the Quran by Al-Tabataba'i, died 1402 AH
21. Hadith Al-Iffik by Ja'far Murtada al-Amili, died 1441 AH
22. Al-Sahih Men Sirat Al-Nabi Al-Azam
   (https://books.rafed.net/view.php?type=c_fbook&b_id=1092) by
   Ja'far al-Amili, died 1441 AH
23. The Sealed Nectar by Sheikh Safi-ur-Rahman al-Mubarakfuri, died
   1427 AH
24. Al-Amthal in Tafsir of the Book of God by Nasser Al-Shirazi, born
   1345 AH
25. Al-Siraa Al-Muhammadia by Jafaar Al-Subhanie, born 1347 AH
26. The History of the Seal of the Prophets, Prophet Muhammad by
   Kazem Yassin, born 1369 AH
27. Kaegi, Walter E. (1992). Byzantium and the Early Islamic Conquests.
   Cambridge: Cambridge University Press. ISBN 978-0521411721
28. Muhammad: A Very Short Introduction by Jonathan Brown.
   And many other sources, see footnotes for further references.

Foot notes

0: Ancient Yemen, al-Jawf, statuettes of seated women, 3rd-1st century BCE (https://en.m.wikipedia.org/wiki/File:Antico_yemen,_al-jawf,_statuette_di_donne_sedute,_III-I_sec._ac._03.JPG), by I, Sailko (https://commons.wikimedia.org/wiki/User:Sailko), is licensed under CC BY 4.0 (https://creativecommons.org/licenses/by/4.0/).

1: Sunan at-Tirmidhi, Abu Isa at-Tirmidhi, 3788.

2: Surah An-Nisa, Verse 174.

3: Interpretation by Al-Ayashi, Muhammad bin Masoud Al-Ayashi, Al-Ba'thah Foundation, First edition, Volume 1, Page 457, 311/1153. Interpretation by Al-Qumi, Ali bin Ibrahim Al-Qumi, Imam Al-Mahdi Foundation, First edition, Volume 1, Page 234.

4: Quranic Arabic, Marijn van Putten, ISBN 978-90-04-50624-4, 2022, Chapter 8, Page 217.

5: Surah Al-Hijr, Verse 9.

6: Quranic Arabic, Marijn van Putten, ISBN 978-90-04-50624-4, 2022, Chapter 1, Pages 8,9.

7: Cook, Muhammad, 70.

8: Al-Sahih Men Sirat Al-Nabi Al-Azam, Ja'far Murtada al-'Amili, Dar Al-Hadith for Printing and Publishing, Volume 1, Page 11.

9: Doctrina Iacobi, 208–210, v.16.

10: Fragment on the Arab Conquests, 11. 8-11, 14-16, 17-23.

11: Wright, Catalog, 1.65 (No. 94); Noldeke, "Zur Geschichte der Araber," 76.

12: J. Walker, A Catalog of the Mohammedan Coins in the British Museum, 1941, Volume I - Arab-Sassanian Coins, British Museum: London, p. 97.

13: Watt, Muhammad in Mecca, 103.

14: Al-Sahih Men Sirat Al-Nabi Al-Azam, Ja'far Murtada al-'Amili, Volume 2, Page 201.

15: Crone and Cook, Hagarism, especially 3–34.

16: I. Goldziher, Islamic Studies (Halle, 1990), 2.5.

17: Particularly see H. Lammens, 'Quran et tradition: Comment fut compose la vie de Mahomet', Recherches de science religieuse, 1 (1910): 27–51. The term "packages of historical truth" is found in his 'L'âge de Mahomet et la chronologie de la Sîra', Journal asiatique, 17 (1911): 249.

18: P. Crone, Meccan Trade and the Rise of Islam (Oxford, 1987), 214–15.

19: Surah Quraysh 1-4: 106.

20: Cook, Muhammad, 72.

21: Crone, Meccan Trade, 204–13, 210.

22: Serjeant, R. B.; Crone, Patricia (1990). "Meccan Trade and the Rise of Islam: Misunderstandings and Faulty Polemics". Journal of the American Oriental Society. 110 (3): 472. doi:10.2307/603188. JSTOR 603188.

23: Detailed Interpretation of the Sent Down Book of Allah, Sheikh Naser Makarem Shirazi, Volume 20, Pages 473-480.

24: The Balance in Interpretation, Sayyid Tabatabai, Volume 20, Page 366.

25: See the interpretation of "Ozha Al-Bayan" by Sayyid Abbas Ali al-Mousawi.

26: Writing the Biography of Prophet Muhammad: Problems and Solutions, Robert Hoyland.

27: Watt, Muhammad in Medina, 338; Watt, Muhammad in Mecca, xiii.

28: The Origins of Islamic Jurisprudence, 1950, pp. 171-179.

29: Kurt Bangert: Muhammad: A Historical-Critical Study on the Emergence of Islam and its Prophet. Springer VS, Wiesbaden, 2016. pp. 147–151.

30: Shiites on the Scale - Mohammad Jawad Maghniyyah - Hadith Science among the Imamiyya - Page 317.

31: Faiq al-Maqal fi al-Hadith wa al-Rijal, Sheikh Mahdhib ad-Din Ahmed al-Basri.

32: Shiites on the Scale - Mohammad Jawad Maghniyyah - Hadith Science among the Imamiyya - Pages 320-318.

33: Sepehri, A Glorious Biography, 1384SH, Volume 1, Page 19.

34: Detailed History of the Arabs before Islam: Volume 1, Page 140 ff.

35: Detailed History of the Arabs before Islam: Volume 1, Page 157 ff.

36: See the explanation of the path for the Mu'tazila Volume 13 Page 174.

37: Sahih Al-Bukhari, AH 1309: Volume 3, Page 133.

38: Detailed History of the Arabs before Islam, Jawad Ali, Volume 120, Volume 15, Page 114.

39: Detailed History of the Arabs before Islam, Jawad Ali, Volume 114, Volume 14, Page 231.

40: Goldziher: What Does "Al-Jahiliyya" Mean? In: Goldziher: Islamic Studies. Volume 1. 1889, pp. 219–228.

41: Detailed History of the Arabs before Islam, Jawad Ali, Volume 1, Book 2, Page 40.

42: Detailed History of the Arabs before Islam, Jawad Ali, Volume 1, Book 2, Page 37.

43: Detailed History of the Arabs before Islam, Jawad Ali, Volume 1, Book 2, Page 38.

44: Encyclopaedia Britannica, 9th edition, 1883, Volume 16, p. 546.

45: Diwan of Imru' al-Qais, Imru' al-Qais, Dar Al-Ma'arif.

46: Al-Sahih Men Sirat Al-Nabi Al-Azam, Ja'far Murtada Al-Amili, Volume 2, Pages 34-35.

47: Detailed History of the Arabs before Islam, Jawad Ali, Volume 7, Page 9.

48: Al-Sahih Men Sirat Al-Nabi Al-Azam, Ja'far Murtada Al-Amili, Volume 2, Page 122.

49: Al-Sahih Men Sirat Al-Nabi Al-Azam, Ja'far Murtada Al-Amili, Volume 2, Pages 38-40.

50: Al Kitabat Statues, Jawad Ali, Dar Al-Waraq, First edition 2007, Pages 10-11.

51: Inscription CIH 543.

52: Al Kitabat Statues, Jawad Ali, Dar Al-Waraq, First edition 2007, Pages 39-43.

53: Inscriptions of the Museum of Zafar 5+8+10.

54: Glaser 554, 406-410, Halevy 63, CIH, Pars 4, Volume, I, Capt. I, 1ft. 6. p. 9-15, n, 537 - 543, p. 257 - 300, CIH, 6, 45, 537 - 542, MM, Attsud., 19, Rep. Epig., 3904, 4069, 4109, Stambul, 7608, Asmara, I, Le Museon, Ltl, p. 51.

55: Margoliouth, The Relationship between Arabs and Israelites before the Rise of Islam, p. 67.

56: Detailed History of the Arabs before Islam, Jawad Ali, Volume 11, Pages 37-38.

57: Ford, Clifford (2001). Healey, Derek. Oxford Music Online. Oxford University Press.

58: The Book of Statues, Shams Al-Kalbi, p. 6 and following.

59: Surah Fussilat: 41:37.

60: Surah An-Najm: 53:20-19.

61: Surah Nuh: 71:23.

62: Detailed History of the Arabs before Islam, Jawad Ali, Volume 12, Chapter 75, Page 38.

63: Remnants, S., J.A. Montgomry, Ascetic Currents in Early Judaism, JBL, Vol. LI. 1932, p. 238.

64: Surah Al-Baqarah: 135:2.

65: Bihar al-Anwar - Al-Allama Al-Majlisi - Volume 15 - Page 184.

66: 2 Ibn Hisham "1/244 and thereafter", Irschad Asari "6/190", Asad Al-Ghaba "2/236", Tabaqat Al-Shu'ara "p. 66" "Leyden Edition", Al-Bidaya Wal-Nihaya "2/237", Ibn Khaldun, first part, Volume two "p. 707", Al-Mas'udi, Meadows "1/70" "Muhammad Mohiuddin Abdul Hameed" Al-Aghani "3/113", Al-Bukhari "5/50" Al-Ma'arif "27".

67: Al-Sahih Men Sirat Al-Nabi Al-Azam, Ja'far Murtada Al-Amili, Volume 2, Pages 45-46.

68: See: Al-Ihtijaj, by At-Tabrisi Volume 2, Pages 91-92 and Al-Bihar, published by Al-Wafa Institute Volume 78, Page 8.

69: Al-Sahih Men Sirat Al-Nabi Al-Azam, Ja'far Murtada Al-Amili, Volume 2, Pages 39-40.

70: DASI: Digital Archive for the Study of pre-Islamic Arabian - Ry 506 Murayghān DASI: Digital Archive for the Study of pre-Islamic Arabian - DAI Ja 547+Ja 546+Ja 544+Ja 545 Sadd Ma'rib 6.

71: Ibn Qutaybah, Al-Ma'arif, Page 638.

72: Al-Sahih Men Sirat Al-Nabi Al-Azam, Ja'far Murtada Al-Amili, Volume 2, Page 115.

73: Al-Sahih Men Sirat Al-Nabi Al-Azam, Ja'far Murtada Al-Amili, Volume 2, Page 118.

74: Al-Sahih Men Sirat Al-Nabi Al-Azam, Ja'far Murtada Al-Amili, Volume 2, Page 119.

75: Ibn Hisham, Volume 2:190, also in Ibn Kathir, Volume 1:230.

76: Maghlatay's Biography, p. 6-7, and Al-Khamis History, Volume 1, Page 195.

77: Wasa'il Al-Shi'a (Ahl al-Bait), Al-Hurr Al-Amili, Volume 10, Page 456, Hadith 13834.

78: Al-Sahih Men Sirat Al-Nabi Al-Azam, Ja'far Murtada Al-Amili, Volume 2, Page 173.

79: Al-Sahih Men Sirat Al-Nabi Al-Azam, Ja'far Murtada Al-Amili, Volume 2, Pages 163-164.

80: Al-Sahih Men Sirat Al-Nabi Al-Azam, Ja'far Murtada Al-Amili, Volume 2, Pages 148-149.

81: Al-Tabaqat Al-Kubra, Ibn Saad, Volume 1, Page 92. Al-Nuwayri, Volume 16, Page 86.

82: Al-Ya'qubi's History, Volume 2, Page 10. History of Nations and Kings, Volume 1, Page 573.

83: Al-Sahih Men Sirat Al-Nabi Al-Azam, Ja'far Murtada Al-Amili, Volume 2, Page 174.

84: Al-Sahih Men Sirat Al-Nabi Al-Azam, Ja'far Murtada Al-Amili, Volume 2, Page 175.

85: Muktasar Tarikh Dimashq: 2/161-162.

86: Al-Sahih Men Sirat Al-Nabi Al-Azam, Ja'far Murtada Al-Amili, Volume 2, Page 175.

87: Musannaf Al-Hafiz Abdul Razzaq, Volume 5, Page 318, and Ibn Hisham's Biography, Volume 1, Page 194.

88: The Prophet's Biography - Ibn Kathir, Volume 1, Pages 254-256.

89: Al-Sahih Men Sirat Al-Nabi Al-Azam, Ja'far Murtada Al-Amili, Volume 2, Page 225.

90: Sharh Nahj Al-Balagha by Al-Mu'tazili, Volume 14, Page 129, and the Attribution of Quraysh to Mus'ab, Page 383, Al-Bidaya Wal-Nihaya Volume 2, Page 293.

91: Al-Sahih Men Sirat Al-Nabi Al-Azam, Ja'far Murtada Al-Amili, Volume 2, Pages 228-229.

92: Al-Isti'ab in Distinguishing the Companions, Volume 4, Pages 281-282, Al-Bidaya Wal-Nihaya Volume 2, Page 294, History of Islam by Al-Dhahabi Volume 2, Biography of the Prophet Page 152, and Al-Khamis History Volume 1, Page 264.

93: Al-Bihar Volume 16, Page 22 of Al-Bukhari, Page 3 of Al-Khara'ij and Al-Jara'ih, Pages 186-187.

94: Al-Sahih Men Sirat Al-Nabi Al-Azam, Ja'far Murtada Al-Amili, Volume 2, Page 192.

95: Kashf Al-Ghumma Volume 2, Page 139, Al-Bihar Volume 16, Page 12, Al-Waqidi Page 19.

96: Al-Kafi Volume 5, Pages 374-375, Al-Bihar Volume 16, Page 14, Alman Layahterahu Al-Faqih Page 413, and Al-Sirah Al-Halabiyya Volume 1, Page 139.

97: Al-Sahih Men Sirat Al-Nabi Al-Azam, Ja'far Murtada Al-Amili, Volume 2, Page 200.

98: Al-Sahih Men Sirat Al-Nabi Al-Azam, Ja'far Murtada Al-Amili, Volume 2, Page 192.

99: Al-Sahih Men Sirat Al-Nabi Al-Azam, Ja'far Murtada Al-Amili, Volume 2, Page 209.

100: Al-Sahih Men Sirat Al-Nabi Al-Azam, Ja'far Murtada Al-Amili, Volume 2, Page 107.

101: History of the Arabs in Islam, Jawad Ali, Pages 146-147.

102: Al-Baladhuri 84/1.

103: History of the Arabs in Islam, Jawad Ali, Pages 149-150.

104: Al-Sahih Men Sirat Al-Nabi Al-Azam, Ja'far Murtada Al-Amili, Volume 2, Page 249.

105: Manaqib Al-Al Abi Talib Volume 2, Page 180, The Authentic Biography of Imam Ali, Ja'far Murtada Al-Amili, Volume 1, Pages 127-128.

106: Al-Sahih Men Sirat Al-Nabi Al-Azam, Ja'far Murtada Al-Amili, Volume 2, Pages 259-264.

107: Al-Sahih Men Sirat Al-Nabi Al-Azam, Ja'far Murtada Al-Amili, Volume 2, Pages 299-300.

108: History of the Arabs in Islam, Jawad Ali, Pages 178-179.

109: Al-Sahih Men Sirat Al-Nabi Al-Azam, Ja'far Murtada Al-Amili, Volume 2, Pages 289-290.

110: Surah Al-'Alaq: Verses 1-5.

111: Nöldeke, Volume I, Page 5.

112: Majma' Al-Bayan Volume 10, Page 384, and Al-Tamheed Volume 1, Page 50.

113: Al-Sahih Men Sirat Al-Nabi Al-Azam, Ja'far Murtada Al-Amili, Volume 3, Pages 13-40.

114: Al-Sahih Men Sirat Al-Nabi Al-Azam, Ja'far Murtada Al-Amili, Volume 3, Pages 43-52.

115: Surah Al-Baqarah 119:2.

116: Al-Sahih Men Sirat Al-Nabi Al-Azam, Ja'far Murtada Al-Amili, Volume 3, Pages 66-76.

117: Al-Sahih Men Sirat Al-Nabi Al-Azam, Ja'far Murtada Al-Amili, Volume 3, Pages 79-85.

118: Al-Sahih Men Sirat Al-Nabi Al-Azam, Ja'far Murtada Al-Amili, Volume 3, Pages 75-78.

119: Surah Ash-Shu'ara (The Poets): 26:214.

120: Ibn Al-Athir, Fiqh Al-Sirah, Pages 77, 78.

121: Al-Sahih Men Sirat Al-Nabi Al-Azam, Ja'far Murtada Al-Amili, Volume 3, Pages 152-196.

122: Surah Al-Hijr: 15:94-95.

123: Al-Sahih Men Sirat Al-Nabi Al-Azam, Ja'far Murtada Al-Amili, Volume 3, Pages 73-74.

124: See: Tafsir Nur Al-Thaqalayn Volume 3, Page 34, according to Tafsir Al-Qummi.

125: The Prophet's Biography, Ibn Hisham, Volume 1, Page 191.

126: Surah Al-Isra (The Night Journey): Verses 90-95.

127: Al-Kafi: Volume 1, Page 449, published by Maktabat Al-Saduq, and Munyat Al-Raghib: Page 75. See also Al-Ghadir: Volume 7, Pages 359 and 388, Volume 8.

128: Imta' Al-Asma' Volume 14, Pages 331-332, Ansab Al-Ashraf Volume 1, Page 31.

129: Majma' Al-Bayan, Al-Tabrisi, Volume 7, Page 211.

130: Surah Al-Furqan: Verse 27.

131: The Biography of the Prophet, Ibn Hisham, Volume 1, Page 195.

132: Ansab Al-Ashraf, Al-Baladhuri, Volume 1, Page 140.

133: Surah Al-A'raf: Verse 185.

134: Surah Al-Masad: Verses 111:1-5.

135: Al-Sahih Men Sirat Al-Nabi Al-Azam, Ja'far Murtada Al-Amili, Volume 3, Pages 200-201.

136: Al-Sahih Men Sirat Al-Nabi Al-Azam, Ja'far Murtada Al-Amili, Volume 3, Page 92.

137: Tafsir Al-Qummi, Ali Ibn Ibrahim Al-Qummi, Volume 2, Page 3.

138: Hidayat Al-Riwayah, Ibn Hajar Al-Asqalani, Number: 5863, Bihar Al-Anwar, Al-Allama Al-Majlisi, Volume 81, Page 151, Sahifah Al-Ridha, Institution of Imam Al-Mahdi, Page 227, Number 115.

139: Al-Amali, Al-Saduq, Page 534, 720/2.

140: Tafsir Firat Al-Kufi, Firat Ibn Ibrahim, Volume 1, Page 208.

141: Al-Tawhid, Al-Saduq, Page 263.

142: Tafsir Al-Qummi, Ali Ibn Ibrahim Al-Qummi, Volume 2, Page 243.

143: Bihar Al-Anwar, Volume 18, Page 286.

144: Bihar Al-Anwar, Al-Allama Al-Majlisi, Volume 18, Page 373.

145: Bihar Al-Anwar, Al-Allama Al-Majlisi, Volume 18, Page 374.

146: Surah Al-Baqarah: Verses 2:285-286.

147: Al-Burhan Fi Tafsir Al-Quran, Al-Bahrani, Volume 4, Pages 641, 9068/[3].

148: 'Ilal Al-Shara'i: 14.

149: Wasa'il Al-Shi'a, Al-Hurr Al-Amili, Volume 5, Page 369.

150: 'Ilal Al-Shara'i: 55.

151: Tafsir Al-'Ayyashi, Muhammad Ibn Masoud Al-'Ayyashi, Volume 2, Page 279, Al-Burhan Volume 2:401, Bihar Al-Anwar Volume 6:392.

152: Al-Amali, Al-Saduq, Page 533.

153: Tafsir Nur Al-Thaqalayn, Sheikh Abd Ali, Volume 5, Page 155.

154: Surah An-Najm: Verses 53:1-18.

155: Al-Sahih Men Sirat Al-Nabi Al-Azam, Ja'far Murtada Al-Amili, Volume 3, Pages 124-125.

156: Al-Sahih Men Sirat Al-Nabi Al-Azam, Ja'far Murtada Al-Amili, Volume 3, Pages 106-107.

157: Subul Al-Huda Wal-Rashad, Al-Salhi Al-Shami, Volume 5, Page 244.

158: Al-Sahih Men Sirat Al-Nabi Al-Azam, Ja'far Murtada Al-Amili, Volume 3, Pages 201-202.

159: Bihar Al-Anwar, Al-Allama Al-Majlisi, Volume 35, Page 87, Dalail Al-Nubuwwah by Al-Bayhaqi, Volume 2, Page 188.

160: The Biography of the Prophet, Ibn Hisham, Volume 1, Pages 282-286, Al-Bidayah Wal-Nihayah Volume 4, Pages 147-149, and Tafsir Al-Tabari Volume 2, Pages 65-68.

161: Al-Sahih Men Sirat Al-Nabi Al-Azam, Ja'far Murtada Al-Amili, Volume 3, Pages 204-206.

162: Surah An-Nahl: Verses 16:101-103.

163: Al-Sahih Men Sirat Al-Nabi Al-Azam, Ja'far Murtada Al-Amili, Volume 3, Pages 207-208.

164: Al-Sahih Men Sirat Al-Nabi Al-Azam, Ja'far Murtada Al-Amili, Volume 3, Page 209.

165: Al-Isabah Fi Tamyiz Al-Sahabah, Ibn Hajar Al-Asqalani, 3/648.

166: Asad Al-Ghabah - Ibn Al-Athir - Volume 4 - Page 44.

167: Tafsir Al-Mizan An Al-Dur Al-Mansur - Sayyid Tabatabai - Volume 12 - Page 357.

168: Al-Baghawi: Ma'alim Al-Tanzil 5/316, Ibn Al-Jawzi: Zad Al-Masir Fi 'Ilm Al-Tafsir 4/498, Al-Razi: Mafatih Al-Ghayb 32/320, Ibn Kathir: Tafsir Al-Quran Al-'Azim 8/504.

169: Sahih Al-Bukhari - Volume 4 - Page 21, A'lām Al-Warā: Page 150, Al-Bihar: Volume 43, Page 40.

170: Al-Sahih Men Sirat Al-Nabi Al-Azam, Ja'far Murtada Al-Amili, Volume 3, Pages 241-246.

171: Al-Bidayah Wal-Nihayah Volume 3 Page 83, Al-Bihar Volume 18 Page 418, A'lām Al-Warā Page 46-45 regarding the stories of the prophets.

172: Surah Maryam: Verses 19:16-21.

173: Al-Sahih Men Sirat Al-Nabi Al-Azam, Ja'far Murtada Al-Amili, Volume 3, Pages 242-256.

174: Al-Sahih Men Sirat Al-Nabi Al-Azam, Ja'far Murtada Al-Amili, Volume 3, Page 258.

175: Al-Sahih Men Sirat Al-Nabi Al-Azam, Ja'far Murtada Al-Amili, Volume 3, Pages 277-280.

176: A'lām Al-Warā: 49 and 50, and his student Al-Rawandi in Qasas Al-Anbiya: 329.

177: Al-Sahih Men Sirat Al-Nabi Al-Azam, Ja'far Murtada Al-Amili, Volume 3, Pages 327-330.

178: Diwan Abu Talib 41, quoted by Ibn Abi Al-Hadid from Al-Amali 3:310.

179: Surah Ar-Rum: Verses 30:1-5.

180: Al-Sahih Men Sirat Al-Nabi Al-Azam, Ja'far Murtada Al-Amili, Volume 3, Pages 335-346.

181: Surah Al-Qamar: Verses 54:1-2.

182: Al-Sahih Men Sirat Al-Nabi Al-Azam, Ja'far Murtada Al-Amili, Volume 3, Pages 346-348.

183: Al-Sahih Men Sirat Al-Nabi Al-Azam, Ja'far Murtada Al-Amili, Volume 3, Pages 351-352.

184: Al-Sahih Men Sirat Al-Nabi Al-Azam, Ja'far Murtada Al-Amili, Volume 3, Pages 358-359.

185: The Biography of the Prophet Ibn Hisham Volume 1 Page 245, Ghayat Al-Maram Page 100, Dalail Al-I'jaz Pages 40 and 41, Al-Jawharah Fi Nasb Al-Nabi Volume 1 Page 252, A'yan Al-Shi'a Volume 8 Page 121.

186: Al-Sahih Men Sirat Al-Nabi Al-Azam, Ja'far Murtada Al-Amili, Volume 4, Pages 73-81.

187: Al-Sahih Men Sirat Al-Nabi Al-Azam, Ja'far Murtada Al-Amili, Volume 4, Page 85.

188: Al-Tabarani, Ad-Du'a Page 315, and the expression is attributed to him by some scholars to cite it in "Al-Mu'jam Al-Kabir" by At-Tabarani, Al-Diya Al-Maqdisi, Al-Mukhtār 9/179, Ibn 'Adi, Al-Kamil 6/111, Ibn 'Asakir 49/152, Lakhītib Al-Baghdadi, Lujam Li Akhlaq Al-Rawi (2/275).

189: Al-Sahih Men Sirat Al-Nabi Al-Azam, Ja'far Murtada Al-Amili, Volume 4, Pages 87-90.

190: Al-Sahih Men Sirat Al-Nabi Al-Azam, Ja'far Murtada Al-Amili, Volume 4, Pages 91-93.

191: Surah Al-An'am: Verses 6:151-152.

192: Al-Sahih Men Sirat Al-Nabi Al-Azam, Ja'far Murtada Al-Amili, Volume 4, Pages 121-122.

193: Al-Sahih Men Sirat Al-Nabi Al-Azam, Ja'far Murtada Al-Amili, Volume 4, Pages 127-132.

194: Al-Sahih Men Sirat Al-Nabi Al-Azam, Ja'far Murtada Al-Amili, Volume 4, Pages 133-147.

195: Tarikh Al-Umam Wal-Muluk Volume 2 Page 68, Al-Bidayah Wal-Nihayah Volume 3 Page 175, Tarikh Al-Khamees Volume 1 Pages 321-322.

196: Surah Al-Anfal: Verse 8:30.

197: Al-Sahih Men Sirat Al-Nabi Al-Azam, Ja'far Murtada Al-Amili, Volume 4, Pages 179-180.

198: Surah Ya-Sin: Verse 36:9.

199: Al-Sahih Men Sirat Al-Nabi Al-Azam, Ja'far Murtada Al-Amili, Volume 4, Pages 213-215.

200: Surah Al-Baqarah: Verse 2:207.

201: Al-Sahih Men Sirat Al-Nabi Al-Azam, Ja'far Murtada Al-Amili, Volume 4, Pages 181-186.

202: Tafsir Al-Qummi - Ali Ibn Ibrahim Al-Qummi - Volume 1 - Page 276.

203: Al-Sahih Men Sirat Al-Nabi Al-Azam, Ja'far Murtada Al-Amili, Volume 4, Pages 187-188.

204: Al-Sahih Men Sirat Al-Nabi Al-Azam, Ja'far Murtada Al-Amili, Volume 4, Pages 194-196.

205: Surah At-Tawbah: Verse 9:40.

206: Al-Sahih Men Sirat Al-Nabi Al-Azam, Ja'far Murtada Al-Amili, Volume 4, Pages 201-213.

207: Al-Sahih Men Sirat Al-Nabi Al-Azam, Ja'far Murtada Al-Amili, Volume 4, Pages 273-276.

208: Surah Al-Imran: Verses 2:191-195.

209: Al-Sahih Men Sirat Al-Nabi Al-Azam, Ja'far Murtada Al-Amili, Volume 4, Pages 276-279.

210: Surah Al-Ankabut: Verse 29:10.

211: Check Tafsir Al-Amthal by Sheikh Nasser Al-Shirazi, Tafsir Al-Mizan by Sayyid Tabatabai.

212: Al-Sahih Men Sirat Al-Nabi Al-Azam, Ja'far Murtada Al-Amili, Volume 4, Pages 286-293.

213: Majma' Al-Bayan, Sheikh Tabarsi, Volume 10, Page 10.

214: Al-Sahih Men Sirat Al-Nabi Al-Azam, Ja'far Murtada Al-Amili, Volume 4, Pages 335-336.

215: Al-Sahih Men Sirat Al-Nabi Al-Azam, Ja'far Murtada Al-Amili, Volume 5, Pages 77-95.

216: Al-Sahih Men Sirat Al-Nabi Al-Azam, Ja'far Murtada Al-Amili, Volume 5, Pages 9-11.

217: Al-Isabah, Ibn Hajar, Volume 3, Page 119.

218: Salman Al-Farsi, Ja'far Murtada Al-Amili, Page 19, quoted from Tarikh Al-Khamees, Volume 1, Page 351.

219: Salman Al-Farsi, Ja'far Murtada Al-Amili, Page 20, quoted from Al-Isabah, Volume 2, Page 62, and other sources.

220: Al-Sahih Men Sirat Al-Nabi Al-Azam, Ja'far Murtada Al-Amili, Volume 5, Pages 99-123.

221: Al-Sahih Men Sirat Al-Nabi Al-Azam, Ja'far Murtada Al-Amili, Volume 5, Pages 127-144.

222: The Israeli Democracy Index 2013, Tamar Hermann, Ella Heller, Nir Atmor, Yuval Lebel, https://en.idi.org.il/media/3958/democracy-index-english-2013.pdf, Pages 72-74, from the Encyclopedia of Judaism, Zionism by Dr. Abdul Wahhab Al-Masiri, Volume 5, Part 2, Chapter 2.

223: The Barbarity of Zionist Teachings, Paulus Hanna Mas'ad, Pages 54-88, quoted from August Rohling, Der Talmudjude, 1871.

224: A'lām Al-Warā Page 69, Al-Bihar Volume 19 Pages 110-111, from the biography of the Prophet by Dahlan Volume 1 Page 175.

225: Al-Sahih Men Sirat Al-Nabi Al-Azam, Ja'far Murtada Al-Amili, Volume 5, Pages 210-220.

226: The Biography of the Prophet by Ibn Hisham, Al-Matba'ah Al-Khayriyah, First Edition, Volume 2, Page 190.

227: Sahih Al-Bukhari - Hadith: 3703.

228: Al-Sahih Men Sirat Al-Nabi Al-Azam, Ja'far Murtada Al-Amili, Volume 5, Pages 223-238.

229: Al-Sahih Men Sirat Al-Nabi Al-Azam, Ja'far Murtada Al-Amili, Volume 5, Pages 227-228.

230: Surah Al-Baqarah: Verse 2:217.

231: Al-Sahih Men Sirat Al-Nabi Al-Azam, Ja'far Murtada Al-Amili, Volume 5, Page 269.

232: Al-Sahih Men Sirat Al-Nabi Al-Azam, Ja'far Murtada Al-Amili, Volume 8, Pages 12-32.

233: Surah Al-Baqarah: Verse 2:144.

234: Al-Sahih Men Sirat Al-Nabi Al-Azam, Ja'far Murtada Al-Amili, Volume 6, Pages 285-288.

235: Tafsir Majma' al-Bayan - Sheikh Tabarsi - Volume 7 - Page 156.

236: Surah Al-Hajj: Verses 22:39-40.

237: Al-Sahih Men Sirat Al-Nabi Al-Azam, Ja'far Murtada Al-Amili, Volume 5, Pages 270-271.

238: Surah Al-Anfal: Verses 8:5-6.

239: Al-Sahih Men Sirat Al-Nabi Al-Azam, Ja'far Murtada Al-Amili, Volume 5, Pages 275-278.

240: Sirat Ibn Hisham, Volume 1, Page 619.

241: Al-Sahih Men Sirat Al-Nabi Al-Azam, Ja'far Murtada Al-Amili, Volume 5, Pages 280-281.

242: Al-Sahih Men Sirat Al-Nabi Al-Azam, Ja'far Murtada Al-Amili, Volume 5, Pages 296-297.

243: Sirat Al-Nabiyya - Ibn Kathir - Volume 2 - Page 398.

244: Surah Al-Ma'idah: Verse 5:24.

245: Surah Al-Anfal: Verse 8:7.

246: Al-Sahih Men Sirat Al-Nabi Al-Azam, Ja'far Murtada Al-Amili, Volume 5, Pages 282-293.

247: Al-Sahih Men Sirat Al-Nabi Al-Azam, Ja'far Murtada Al-Amili, Volume 5, Pages 294-297.

248: Surah Al-Anfal: Verse 8:11.

249: Surah Al-Anfal: Verse 8:9.

250: Sirat Ibn Hisham, Volume 2, Page 266; Ma'rifat Al-Sahaba, (Page 303/1); Ibn Al-Athir in Asad Al-Ghaba (2/332).

251: Al-Sahih Men Sirat Al-Nabi Al-Azam, Ja'far Murtada Al-Amili, Volume 5, Pages 302-303.

252: Al-Sahih Men Sirat Al-Nabi Al-Azam, Ja'far Murtada Al-Amili, Volume 5, Pages 310-313.

253: Al-Isti'ab fi Tamyiz Al-Sahaba, 5391.

254: Surah Al-Ahzab: Verse 33:23; Shawaahid Al-Tanzil - Al-Hakim Al-Haskani - Volume 2 - Page 5; Tafsir Majma' al-Bayan - Sheikh Tabarsi - Volume 8 - Page 145.

255: Al-Sahih Men Sirat Al-Nabi Al-Azam, Ja'far Murtada Al-Amili, Volume 5, Page 317.

256: Surah Al-Anfal: 8:17; See Tafsir Al-Amthal, Surah Al-Anfal.

257: Al-Sahih Men Sirat Al-Nabi Al-Azam, Ja'far Murtada Al-Amili, Volume 5, Page 340.

258: Surah Al-Anfal: 8:43-44.

259: Surah Al-Anfal: 8:48; Al-Sahih Men Sirat Al-Nabi Al-Azam, Ja'far Murtada Al-Amili, Volume 5, Page 320.

260: Al-Sahih Men Sirat Al-Nabi Al-Azam, Ja'far Murtada Al-Amili, Volume 5, Pages 323-329.

261: Al-Sahih Men Sirat Al-Nabi Al-Azam, Ja'far Murtada Al-Amili, Volume 5, Page 330 and onwards.

262: Al-Sahih Men Sirat Al-Nabi Al-Azam, Ja'far Murtada Al-Amili, Volume 6, Pages 22-26.

263: Surah Al-Anfal: 8:67.

264: Al-Sahih Men Sirat Al-Nabi Al-Azam, Ja'far Murtada Al-Amili, Volume 6, Pages 28-42.

265: Al-Sahih Men Sirat Al-Nabi Al-Azam, Ja'far Murtada Al-Amili, Volume 6, Pages 67-68.

266: Al-Sahih Men Sirat Al-Nabi Al-Azam, Ja'far Murtada Al-Amili, Volume 6, Pages 49-50.

267: Al-Sahih Men Sirat Al-Nabi Al-Azam, Ja'far Murtada Al-Amili, Volume 6, Page 78.

268: Al-Mustadrak - Al-Hakim - Volume 3 - Page 24, Hadith 4305.

269: Al-Sahih Men Sirat Al-Nabi Al-Azam, Ja'far Murtada Al-Amili, Volume 6, Pages 42-48.

270: Surah Al-Anfal: 8:70.

271: Al-Sahih Men Sirat Al-Nabi Al-Azam, Ja'far Murtada Al-Amili, Volume 6, Pages 55-56.

272: Al-Sahih Men Sirat Al-Nabi Al-Azam, Ja'far Murtada Al-Amili, Volume 6, Pages 66-67.

273: Al-Sahih Men Sirat Al-Nabi Al-Azam, Ja'far Murtada Al-Amili, Volume 6, Pages 291-292.

274: Al-Sahih Men Sirat Al-Nabi Al-Azam, Ja'far Murtada Al-Amili, Volume 6, Pages 68-70.

275: Al-Sahih Men Sirat Al-Nabi Al-Azam, Ja'far Murtada Al-Amili, Volume 6, Pages 188-195.

276: Surah Al-Ahzab: 33:33.

277: Al-Sahih Men Sirat Al-Nabi Al-Azam, Ja'far Murtada Al-Amili, Volume 6, Pages 292-293.

278: Al-Sahih Men Sirat Al-Nabi Al-Azam, Ja'far Murtada Al-Amili, Volume 7, Pages 7-19.

279: Surah Al-Ma'idah: 5:52.

280: Surah Al-Imran: 3:12-13.

281: Surah Al-Anfal: 8:58.

282: Al-Sahih Men Sirat Al-Nabi Al-Azam, Ja'far Murtada Al-Amili, Volume 7, Pages 39-32.

283: Al-Sahih Men Sirat Al-Nabi Al-Azam, Ja'far Murtada Al-Amili, Volume 7, Pages 51-52.

284: Sunan an-Nasa'i, Book of Marriage, Chapter on Permission for Seclusion, Hadith Number: 3375.

285: Al-Hakim in Al-Mustadrak 2/167, Al-Haythami in Majma' al-Zawa'id 9/204.

286: 'Uyun Akhbar al-Ridha - Sheikh Saduq - Volume 2 - Page 203.

287: Sheikh al-Tusi, Al-Amali, previous source, Pages 40-41.

288: Al-Jahiz - Al-'Uthmaniyya - Page: 289/299.

289: Surah An-Nisa: 4:153; At-Tabari in Tafsir, Volume 3, Page 375.

290: Al-Sahih Men Sirat Al-Nabi Al-Azam, Ja'far Murtada Al-Amili, Volume 6, Pages 342, 347, 350.

291: Al-Sahih Men Sirat Al-Nabi Al-Azam, Ja'far Murtada Al-Amili, Volume 7, Pages 7, 10, 11 and Volume 8, Pages 289, 290, 294, Volume 9, Pages 38, 71, 81, 86, 115.

292: Surah Al-Hijr: 15:2-4.

293: Al-Sahih Men Sirat Al-Nabi Al-Azam, Ja'far Murtada Al-Amili, Volume 9, Pages 53, 54; At-Tabaqat al-Kubra, Volume 2, Page 57; Dalail al-Nubuwwah by Abu Nu'aim, Page 425; As-Seerah an-Nabawiyyah by Dahlan, Volume 1, Page 260; Zad al-Ma'ad, Volume 2, Page 71; As-Seerah al-Halabiyyah, Volume 2, Page 263; 'Umddat al-Qari, Volume 17, Page 125.

294: Al-Sahih Men Sirat Al-Nabi Al-Azam, Ja'far Murtada Al-Amili, Volume 9, Pages 83, 120, 121, 126, 128, 140, 159, 160.

295: Al-Sahih Men Sirat Al-Nabi Al-Azam, Ja'far Murtada Al-Amili, Volume 9, Pages 40, 163, 161.

296: Surah Al-Hashr: 59:5.

297: Surah Al-Hashr: 59:9.

298: Al-Sahih Men Sirat Al-Nabi Al-Azam, Ja'far Murtada Al-Amili, Volume 9, Pages 235, 217, 211, 212, 213, 248-252.

299: Al-Sahih Men Sirat Al-Nabi Al-Azam, Ja'far Murtada Al-Amili, Volume 6, Pages 195-198.

300: Al-Kafi - Sheikh Kulayni - Volume 5 - Page 339.

301: Al-Sahih Men Sirat Al-Nabi Al-Azam, Ja'far Murtada Al-Amili, Volume 6, Pages 297-305.

302: Al-Sahih Men Sirat Al-Nabi Al-Azam, Ja'far Murtada Al-Amili, Volume 6, Pages 209-211.

303: Al-Sahih Men Sirat Al-Nabi Al-Azam, Ja'far Murtada Al-Amili, Volume 6, Pages 329-330.

304: Al-Sahih Men Sirat Al-Nabi Al-Azam, Ja'far Murtada Al-Amili, Volume 7, Pages 52, 53, 55.

305: Al-Fayeq in Ghareeb Al-Hadith by Al-Zamakhshari, Volume 177: 1.

306: Al-Sahih Men Sirat Al-Nabi Al-Azam, Ja'far Murtada Al-Amili, Volume 7, Pages 63, 64, 65, 66, 75, 90, 106, 107.

307: Surah Al-Imran: 2:166-167.

308: Al-Sahih Men Sirat Al-Nabi Al-Azam, Ja'far Murtada Al-Amili, Volume 7, Page 107.

309: Surah Al-Imran: 2:122.

310: Al-Sahih Men Sirat Al-Nabi Al-Azam, Ja'far Murtada Al-Amili, Volume 7, Pages 123, 132-130, 151, 146-145.

311: Surah Al-Imran: 2:152.

312: Al-Sahih Men Sirat Al-Nabi Al-Azam, Ja'far Murtada Al-Amili, Volume 7, Pages 153-151, 148.

313: Surah Al-Imran: 2:153.

314: Al-Sahih Men Sirat Al-Nabi Al-Azam, Ja'far Murtada Al-Amili, Volume 7, Pages 149-147, 198-197, 204-202, 200, 224-223, 229, 255, 227-226, 262.

315: The Biography of the Prophet by Ibn Hisham, Volume 3, Page 94.

316: Narrated by Imam Ahmad: 15492, Al-Bukhari in Al-Adab Al-Mufrad: 699, confirmed by Al-Hakim: 4308, and Al-Albani.

317: Al-Sahih Men Sirat Al-Nabi Al-Azam, Ja'far Murtada Al-Amili, Volume 7, Pages 300-299, 259.

318: Surah Al-Imran: 2:159-160.

319: Surah Al-Imran: 2:168.

320: Al-Sahih Men Sirat Al-Nabi Al-Azam, Ja'far Murtada Al-Amili, Volume 7, Pages 302-303.

321: Surah Al-Imran: 2:140.

322: Surah Al-Imran: 2:166-167.

323: Al-Sahih Men Sirat Al-Nabi Al-Azam, Ja'far Murtada Al-Amili, Volume 7, Pages 318-320.

324: Surah Al-Imran: 2:139, see also: Majma' Al-Bayan Volume 2 Page 509 and Al-Bihar Volume 20 Page 22.

325: Al-Sahih Men Sirat Al-Nabi Al-Azam, Ja'far Murtada Al-Amili, Volume 7, Pages 314, 319, 320, 325, 317, 318.

326: Surah Al-Imran: 2:172,173,175.

327: Surah Al-Imran: 2:174.

328: Al-Sahih Men Sirat Al-Nabi Al-Azam, Ja'far Murtada Al-Amili, Volume 7, Page 323.

329: Al-Sahih Men Sirat Al-Nabi Al-Azam, Ja'far Murtada Al-Amili, Volume 7, Pages 35-60.

330: Wasail Al-Shi'a: 10/313, Hadith Number: 13494, by Sheikh Al-Hurr Al-Amili.

331: Al-Sahih Men Sirat Al-Nabi Al-Azam, Ja'far Murtada Al-Amili, Volume 8, Pages 69-78.

332: Al-Sahih Men Sirat Al-Nabi Al-Azam, Ja'far Murtada Al-Amili, Volume 10, Pages 77-104.

333: Al-Sahih Men Sirat Al-Nabi Al-Azam, Ja'far Murtada Al-Amili, Volume 10, Pages 139, 140, 143, 192, 193, 219, 222, 258.

334: Surah Al-Ahzab: 33:12.

335: Surah Al-Hujurat: 49:17.

336: Al-Sahih Men Sirat Al-Nabi Al-Azam, Ja'far Murtada Al-Amili, Volume 10, Pages 247-246, 270-267, 209-208, 236, 319-311, 308-307, Volume 11, Pages 70-69, 81-80, 11.

337: Surah Al-Ahzab: 33:10-11.

338: Surah Al-Ahzab: 33:22.

339: Surah Al-Ahzab: 33:12-19.

340: Al-Sahih Men Sirat Al-Nabi Al-Azam, Ja'far Murtada Al-Amili, Volume 11, Pages 113, 19, 15.

341: Al-Sahih Men Sirat Al-Nabi Al-Azam, Ja'far Murtada Al-Amili, Volume 11, Pages 114, 120, 125, 123, 132, 144, 149-148, 202, 210, 215, Surah Al-Ahzab: 33:9.

342: Al-Sahih Men Sirat Al-Nabi Al-Azam, Ja'far Murtada Al-Amili, Volume 11, Pages 217, 231, 232, 233, 20.

343: Surah Al-Ahzab: 33:20.

344: Al-Sahih Men Sirat Al-Nabi Al-Azam, Ja'far Murtada Al-Amili, Volume 11, Pages 243-245.

345: Ibn Sayyid al-Nas: 'Ayun al-Athar 1/261 and Ibn Kathir: Al-Sirah Al-Nabawiyyah 2/322, Ibn Hisham: Al-Sirah Al-Nabawiyyah 1/503.

346: See the commentary of Al-Razi on Surah Al-Anfal, Verses 55-56, by Ibn Abbas.

347: Al-Sahih Men Sirat Al-Nabi Al-Azam, Ja'far Murtada Al-Amili, Volume 11, Page 259.

348: Surah Al-Anfal: 8:55-58.

349: Al-Sahih Men Sirat Al-Nabi Al-Azam, Ja'far Murtada Al-Amili, Volume 11, Pages 312, 302-278, 157, 260, 71-50.

350: Al-Sahih Men Sirat Al-Nabi Al-Azam, Ja'far Murtada Al-Amili, Volume 12, Pages 30, 66, 85-82.

351: Kitab al-Amwal, Ibn Zanjawayh, Page 299, Hadith 461.

352: Surah Al-Ahzab: 33:26-27.

353: [Link to Anti-Slavery International](https://www.antislavery.org/slavery-today/modern-slavery/)

and [Wikipedia article on Slavery in the 21st century](https://en.wikipedia.org/wiki/Slavery_in_the_21st_century).

354: The Civilization of the Arabs, Gustave Le Bon, Pages 387-386.

355: Sahih - Al-Bukhari, Book of Faith, Number 30, Muslim, Book of Faith and Vows, Chapter: Feeding a slave with what he eats, Number: 1661.

356: Sahih - Abu Dawud, Chapter on the Right of the Slave, Hadith: (4492).

357: Sahih - Abu Dawud, Hadith: 5156, Ahmed: 585.

358: Surah An-Nisa: 92:4, Surah Al-Maidah: 89:5, Surah Al-Mujadila: 3:58.

359: Surah Al-Baqarah: 177:2, Surah At-Tawbah: 60:9.

360: Surah Al-Balad: 13:90.

361: Al-Sahih Men Sirat Al-Nabi Al-Azam, Ja'far Murtada Al-Amili, Volume 12, Pages 207-228.

362: Al-Sahih Men Sirat Al-Nabi Al-Azam, Ja'far Murtada Al-Amili, Volume 8, Pages 143-145.

363: Al-Sahih Men Sirat Al-Nabi Al-Azam, Ja'far Murtada Al-Amili, Volume 8, Pages 145 and following.

364: Al-Sahih Men Sirat Al-Nabi Al-Azam, Ja'far Murtada Al-Amili, Volume 12, Pages 233-257.

365: Al-Sahih Men Sirat Al-Nabi Al-Azam, Ja'far Murtada Al-Amili, Volume 12, Pages 280-279.

366: Surah Al-Munafiqun: 63:7-8.

367: Al-Sahih Men Sirat Al-Nabi Al-Azam, Ja'far Murtada Al-Amili, Volume 12, Pages 284-288.

368: Surah Al-Munafiqun: 63:5.

369: Al-Sahih Men Sirat Al-Nabi Al-Azam, Ja'far Murtada Al-Amili, Volume 12, Pages 261-275.

370: Surah Al-Ahzab: 33:36.

371: Surah Al-Ahzab: 33:37.

372: Al-Sahih Men Sirat Al-Nabi Al-Azam, Ja'far Murtada Al-Amili, Volume 14, Pages 41-79.

373: Al-Sahih Men Sirat Al-Nabi Al-Azam, Ja'far Murtada Al-Amili, Volume 15, Pages 33-38.

374: Al-Sahih Men Sirat Al-Nabi Al-Azam, Ja'far Murtada Al-Amili, Volume 15, Pages 59, 60.

375: Al-Sahih Men Sirat Al-Nabi Al-Azam, Ja'far Murtada Al-Amili, Volume 15, Page 71.

376: Surah Al-Fath: 48:11.

377: Al-Sahih Men Sirat Al-Nabi Al-Azam, Ja'far Murtada Al-Amili, Volume 15, Pages 75, 79-81.

378: Al-Sahih Men Sirat Al-Nabi Al-Azam, Ja'far Murtada Al-Amili, Volume 15, Pages 85-86, 114.

379: Surah Al-Ma'idah: 5:24.

380: Al-Sahih Men Sirat Al-Nabi Al-Azam, Ja'far Murtada Al-Amili, Volume 15, Pages 115, 116.

381: Al-Sahih Men Sirat Al-Nabi Al-Azam, Ja'far Murtada Al-Amili, Volume 15, Pages 225, 116, 115-230, Surah At-Tawbah: 9:80.

382: Al-Sahih Men Sirat Al-Nabi Al-Azam, Ja'far Murtada Al-Amili, Volume 15, Pages 256-260.

383: Surah Al-Hujurat: 49:1.

384: Al-Sahih Men Sirat Al-Nabi Al-Azam, Ja'far Murtada Al-Amili, Volume 15, Pages 260-262.

385: Surah Al-Fath: 48:26.

386: Surah Al-Fath: 28:24.

387: Al-Sahih Men Sirat Al-Nabi Al-Azam, Ja'far Murtada Al-Amili, Volume 15, Pages 289-295, 322-324.

388: Al-Sahih Men Sirat Al-Nabi Al-Azam, Ja'far Murtada Al-Amili, Volume 16, Pages 11-9, 19-17.

389: Surah Al-Fath: 48:18-19.

390: Al-Sahih Men Sirat Al-Nabi Al-Azam, Ja'far Murtada Al-Amili, Volume 16, Pages 53-50, 74-57, 56-54.

391: Surah Al-Fath: 48:25.

392: Surah Al-Fath: 48:1-3.

393: Surah Al-Fath: 48:5.

394: Surah Al-Fath: 48:1-3.

395: Surah Al-Ahzab: 33:10.

396: Surah Al-Fath: 48:27.

397: Surah Al-Mumtahanah: 60:10.

398: Al-Sahih Men Sirat Al-Nabi Al-Azam, Ja'far Murtada Al-Amili, Volume 16, Pages 171-173, 135, 145-144, 154-151, 158-156, 83-88.

399: Surah Al-Mujadila: 58:1-2.

400: Al-Sahih Men Sirat Al-Nabi Al-Azam, Ja'far Murtada Al-Amili, Volume 16, Pages 208-215, 158-156, 83-88.

401: Al-Sahih Men Sirat Al-Nabi Al-Azam, Ja'far Murtada Al-Amili, Volume 17, Pages 78-75, 85-89, 109-101, 119-117, 126, 142-134, 146, 155-150.

402: Al-Sahih Men Sirat Al-Nabi Al-Azam, Ja'far Murtada Al-Amili, Volume 17, Pages 198, 151-152, 176-171, 193, 233-234, 217-218, 230-227, 317-315, 294-291, 240.

403: Surah Al-Ahzab: 33:29.

404: Al-Sahih Men Sirat Al-Nabi Al-Azam, Ja'far Murtada Al-Amili, Volume 18, Pages 62-61, 90-80, 225-219.

405: Al-Sahih Men Sirat Al-Nabi Al-Azam, Ja'far Murtada Al-Amili, Volume 18, Pages 307-291.

406: Surah An-Nisa: 4:94.
407: Al-Sahih Men Sirat Al-Nabi Al-Azam, Ja'far Murtada Al-Amili, Volume 19, Pages 55-52, 78-64, 113-109.
408: Surah Al-Imran: 2:64.
409: Surah Al-Imran: 2:64.
410: Al-Sahih Men Sirat Al-Nabi Al-Azam, Ja'far Murtada Al-Amili, Volume 16, Page 235 and beyond.
411: Al-Sahih Men Sirat Al-Nabi Al-Azam, Ja'far Murtada Al-Amili, Volume 9, Pages 316-348, Volume 10, Pages 54-53, 53-39.
412: Surah Al-Ahzab: 33:33.
413: Al-Sa'di in "Ahadith al-Zuhri" p. 462, no. 403. Ahmad ibn Hanbal in "Al-Musnad" (6/292). Al-Tahawi in "Mushkil al-Athar" (1/228), no. 775. Al-Tabarani in "Al-Mu'jam al-Kabir" (3/54), no. 2668. Ibn Asakir in "Tarikh" (13/205), no. 3186. Ibn Jarir in "Jami 'al-Bayan" (22/217). Abu Ya'la al-Mawsili in "Al-Musnad" (6/73), no. 6852. Ibn Abi Shaybah in "Al-Musannaf" (6/373), no. 32093. Muslim in "Al-Jami 'al-Sahih" (2/283), no. 2424. Ibn Abi Hatim in "Tafsir al-Quran" (9/3131), no. 17674. Ibn Jarir in "Jami 'al-Bayan" (22/5). Al-Hakim in "Al-Mustadrak" (3/147). Ibn Asakir in "Tarikh" (13/202), no. 3179 (42/260). Also see "Alam al-Ulum wal-Ma'arif wal-Ahwal", Sheikh Abdullah Al-Bahraini, about Jabir ibn Abdullah al-Ansari.
414: Al-Sahih Men Sirat Al-Nabi Al-Azam, Ja'far Murtada Al-Amili, Volume 19, Pages 157-152, 164, 196-190, 203-201, 260-252.
415: Al-Sahih Men Sirat Al-Nabi Al-Azam, Ja'far Murtada Al-Amili, Volume 19, Pages 275-314.
416: Surah Maryam: 19:71.
417: Sunan Al-Tirmidhi, No. 3159. Ahmad, No. 4128. Al-Darami, No. 2810. Al-Hakim, No. 8741.
418: Kaegi, Walter E. (1992). Byzantium and the Early Islamic Conquests. Cambridge: Cambridge University Press. ISBN 978-0521411721, p. 72.
419: p. 36, The Chronicle of Theophanes, translated by Harry Turtledove, University of Pennsylvania, 1982, ISBN 978-0-8122-1128-3.
420: Surah Al-Anfal: 8:15-16.
421: Al-Sahih Men Sirat Al-Nabi Al-Azam, Ja'far Murtada Al-Amili, Volume 19, Pages 329-322, Volume 20, Pages 21-12, 147-121, 101-103, 334.
422: Surah Al-Ahzab: 33:6.
423: Surah Al-Ahzab: 33:53.
424: Surah Al-Ahzab: 33:53.
425: Surah An-Nur: 24:11-13.
426: Surah At-Tahrim: 66:1.
427: Surah At-Tahrim: 66:3-5.

428: See Al-Sahih Men Sirat Al-Nabi Al-Azam by Ja'far Al-Amili, Volume 13 or the history of the lie by the same author.

429: Surah Al-Adiyat: 100:1-11.

430: Al-Sahih Men Sirat Al-Nabi Al-Azam, Ja'far Murtada Al-Amili, Volume 20, Pages 237-241, 246-247.

431: The Biography of the Prophet, Ibn Hisham, Volume 2, Page 394.

432: Al-Sahih Men Sirat Al-Nabi Al-Azam, Ja'far Murtada Al-Amili, Volume 21, Pages 22, 32-30, 37, 86-75, 48-47.

433: Surah Al-Mumtahanah: 60:1-4.

434: Al-Sahih Men Sirat Al-Nabi Al-Azam, Ja'far Murtada Al-Amili, Volume 21, Pages 131, 173-168, 217-216, 223, 234-233, 306-294.

435: Surah Al-Fath: 48:1-3.

436: Surah Al-Isra: 17:81.

437: Surah Yusuf: 12:92.

438: Surah Al-Hujurat: 49:13.

439: Al-Sahih Men Sirat Al-Nabi Al-Azam, Ja'far Murtada Al-Amili, Volume 22, Pages 88-58, 122, 127-141, 183-181, 278, 249-248, 291-292, 320-319-233, 306-294.

440: Al-Sahih Men Sirat Al-Nabi Al-Azam, Ja'far Murtada Al-Amili, Volume 23, Pages 9, 58, 100-12.

441: Al-Sahih Men Sirat Al-Nabi Al-Azam, Ja'far Murtada Al-Amili, Volume 23, Pages 201, 261-246, 291, 322.

442: Surah At-Tawbah: 9:25-26.

443: Al-Sahih Men Sirat Al-Nabi Al-Azam, Ja'far Murtada Al-Amili, Volume 24, Pages 11-17, 26-20, 35, 66, 84, 104, 126, 197-191, 308, 274-273, Volume 25, Pages 218-220.

444: Surah Al-Fath: 48:27.

445: Al-Sahih Men Sirat Al-Nabi Al-Azam, Ja'far Murtada Al-Amili, Volume 25, Pages 18-17, 54-48, 109-112, 166-165.

446: Al-Sahih Men Sirat Al-Nabi Al-Azam, Ja'far Murtada Al-Amili, Volume 25, Pages 188-181, 134, 239-237, 268-263, 286.

447: Al-Sahih Men Sirat Al-Nabi Al-Azam, Ja'far Murtada Al-Amili, Volume 26, Page 205, 222-221, 259, 246-245, Volume 27, Pages 13-11.

448: Al-Sahih Men Sirat Al-Nabi Al-Azam, Ja'far Murtada Al-Amili, Volume 27, Pages 282-281, 316-309.

449: Surah Al-Imran: 3:59-60.

450: Surah Al-Imran: 3:61-63.

451: Al-Sahih Men Sirat Al-Nabi Al-Azam, Ja'far Murtada Al-Amili, Volume 28, Pages 309-300, 157-156.

452: Surah At-Tawbah: 9:64-66. See the comments of Ali ibn Ibrahim and "A'udhu al-Bayan" by Abbas al-Mousawi.

453: Surah At-Tawbah: 9:49.

454: Surah At-Tawbah: 9:81-82.

455: Surah Al-Waqi'ah: 56:82.

456: Al-Sahih Men Sirat Al-Nabi Al-Azam, Ja'far Murtada Al-Amili, Volume 30, Pages 156-153, 165, 205-204, 19, 51, Volume 29, Pages 196-195, 111, 275-274, 149-148, 166, 291-290, 305-304.

457: The Muhammadan Biography - Sheikh Ja'far Al-Sobhani in Bihar Al-Anwar 246/21, Ibn Saad's Categories 166/2.

458: Surah At-Tawbah: 9:74.

459: Al-Sahih Men Sirat Al-Nabi Al-Azam, Ja'far Murtada Al-Amili, Volume 30, Pages 162-123, 179, 201.

460: Surah At-Tawbah: 9:50.

461: Surah At-Tawbah: 9:107.

462: Al-Sahih Men Sirat Al-Nabi Al-Azam, Ja'far Murtada Al-Amili, Volume 30, Pages 208-217.

463: Surah At-Tawbah: 9:3.

464: Al-Sahih Men Sirat Al-Nabi Al-Azam, Ja'far Murtada Al-Amili, Volume 30, Pages 242-237, 269, 281-280.

465: Surah At-Tawbah: 9:24.

466: Investigations into the Explanation of the Hajj Rituals by the Authors Sheikh Amjad Riad and Sheikh Nizar Youssef, Volume 9, Page 484.

467: Surah Al-Ma'idah: 5:67.

468: Al-Sahih Men Sirat Al-Nabi Al-Azam, Ja'far Murtada Al-Amili, Volume 30, Pages 304-288, Volume 31, Pages 47-46, 16-11, 87, 30, 172.

469: Al-Sahih Men Sirat Al-Nabi Al-Azam, Ja'far Murtada Al-Amili, Volume 31, Pages 204-200, 134, 75-71, 169-163, 18-16, 90-85, 95-93.

470: Surah Al-Ma'idah: 5:67.

471: Surah Al-Ma'idah: 5:3.

472: Surah Al-A'raf: 7:43.

473: Surah Al-Fath: 48:10.

474: Surah Az-Zumar: 39:7.

475: Surah Al-Ma'arij: 70:1.

476: Al-Sahih Men Sirat Al-Nabi Al-Azam, Ja'far Murtada Al-Amili, Volume 31, Pages 229-226, 172, 238-233, 201, 325, 209.

477: Al-Sahih Men Sirat Al-Nabi Al-Azam, Ja'far Murtada Al-Amili, Volume 32, Pages 165, 173, 184-183, 170-166, 142.

478: Al-Sahih Men Sirat Al-Nabi Al-Azam, Ja'far Murtada Al-Amili, Volume 32, Pages 219-215, 225, 246.

479: Surah Al-Imran: 3:144.

480: Surah Al-Ahzab: 33:56.

481: Al-Sahih Men Sirat Al-Nabi Al-Azam, Ja'far Murtada Al-Amili, Volume 32, Pages 336-335, 260, 268, 70-69, 24, 94-90, 53-52.

482: The Sakeefa - Sheikh Mohammad Reza Al-Mozaffar - Pages 96-100.

483: The Authentic Biography of Imam Ali, Volume 9, Pages 125-143.

484: Surah Al-Ankabut: 29:1-4, Bihar Al-Anwar - Al-Allama Al-Majlisi - Volume 22 - Page 519.

485: Al-Sahih Men Sirat Al-Nabi Al-Azam, Ja'far Murtada Al-Amili, Volume 33, Pages 287-286, 317, 324.

486: Ibn Abi al-Hadid in Sharh Nahj al-Balaghah: 20/298.

487: Surah Ash-Shu'ara: 26:215.

488: Surah Saba: 34:28.

489: Surah Al-A'raf: 7:158.

490: Surah Al-Anbiya: 21:107.

491: Tafsir Al-Kashif, Mohammad Jawad Mughniyah, Surah Al-Imran, 3:159.

492: Amraalkais, ed. Slane, No. 10, p. 33; ed. Ahlwardt, No. 5.

493: Paul B. Henze: Layers of Time. A History of Ethiopia, Palgrave, New York 2000, p. 41

494: Al-Baladhuri, 1/292; Compare: Abu al-Faraj, 4/173-174, Al-Waqidi, 1/33.

495: Al-Sahih Men Sirat Al-Nabi Al-Azam, Ja'far Murtada al-Amili, Volume 7, Pages 34, 42.

496: Surah Ya-Sin: 36:70.

497: Surah 3: Al-i-Ilmran (The Family of Imran) Verse 64.

498: Al-Sahih Men Sirat Al-Nabi Al-Azam, Ja'far Murtada Al-Amili, Volume 19, Pages 150-214.

499: Al-Sahih Men Sirat Al-Nabi Al-Azam, Ja'far Murtada Al-Amili, Volume 19, Pages 252-254.

500: See Al-Muntazam in the History of Kings and Nations, Volume 4, Page 13.

501: Bihar Al-Anwar - The Scholar Al-Majlisi - Volume 38 - Page 301, Musnad Ahmad 6:300, Al-Mustadrak ala Al-Sahihain (Hadith Collections) 3:149, authenticated by Al-Hakim and agreed upon by Al-Dhahabi, as in the appendix of Al-Mustadrak, Majma' az-Zawa'id 3:149.

502: Al-Sahih Men Sirat Al-Nabi Al-Azam, Ja'far Murtada Al-Amili, Volume 22, Pages 22-44.

Index of Persons

Milton Keynes UK
Ingram Content Group UK Ltd.
UKHW010104030424
440481UK00005B/291